BROADWAY
LIBRARY
of
LARCENY

D1403518

Do You Sincerely Want to Be Rich?

●

THE FULL STORY
OF BERNARD CORNFELD
AND I.O.S.

●

Charles Raw, Bruce Page, and Godfrey Hodgson

LIBRARY OF LARCENY
BROADWAY BOOKS
NEW YORK

First published in 1971 by the Viking Press, Inc.
625 Madison Avenue, New York, NY 10022.

PRINTED IN THE UNITED STATES OF AMERICA

BROADWAY BOOKS and B colophon and Library of Larceny and colophon are trademarks of Random House, Inc.

Visit our website at www.broadwaybooks.com

First Broadway Books trade paperback edition published 2005

Book design by Elizabeth Rendfleisch

Cataloging-in-Publication data is on file with the Library of Congress

ISBN 0-7679-2006-6

10 9 8 7 6 5 4 3 2 1

Table of Contents

Services. Eminent international citizens are brought into the company. They are carefully excluded from real power.

Preface to the 2005 Edition

On first looking into this book, people who have followed the events at Enron, WorldCom, Fannie Mae, and so on, may see its principal characters, Bernard Cornfeld and Edward Cowett, as small-change operators. After all, the funds they pillaged so dashingly at Investors Overseas Services (IOS) didn't contain much more than two billion dollars, and they left behind nearly three-quarters of a billion to be stolen by others.

Of course, you should multiply about sixfold for a current comparison. Even so, it doesn't match Enron, whose directing geniuses wiped out a good $60 billion in shareholder value.

But this overlooks the pioneer status Bernie and Ed deserve. John Moses Browning and Hiram Maxim aren't considered negligible figures because their original machine guns are outdone in lethality by those you find mounted nowadays on a helicopter gunship.

The great thing about the IOS people is that they went where others did not dare to go—more exactly, had not dared in many years—on a scale so expansive and systematic. Notoriously, IOS itself didn't survive that expeditionary voyage. But you will observe, reading on, that it took along some institutional allies which survived to be conspicuous quite recently in brave catastrophes. Note, particularly, Arthur Andersen, auditors to IOS, who applied their moniker to Bernie and Ed's last set of accounts, containing a remarkable—indeed desperate—and altogether ridiculous tenfold "revaluation" of certain Arctic oilfields which had no significant existence. It took thirty-odd years to work up from certifying IOS fantasies to doing so for Enron's grander ones, but the world's largest single auditing partnership finally got there.

Of course, "finally" is the operative word now, in Andersen's case. But this evidences a great IOS achievement: to have revived, in the financial community, readiness to act on that principle William Blake put so neatly in *The Marriage of Heaven and Hell:* "You never know what is enough, until you know what is more than enough." The IOS story contains many other proud vessels since scuttled or beached: Drexel, Harriman, Ripley, for instance, and Guinness Mahon. But you will also find famous ones which sail on and have yet (at the time of writing) to discover what is more than enough. Try as they will.

Bernie and Ed were pioneers because they helped financial practitioners regain faith in recklessness as likely to provide superior rewards and surprisingly tolerable costs (from their own viewpoint, anyway).

After the Great Crash of 1929 and subsequent Great Depression, the U.S. Government imposed many restrictions on the financial services industry, which was held to have displayed lunatic greed and done much to cause the Depression. Simultaneously the Securities and Exchange Commission (SEC) was created, with extensive powers to supervise and regulate. The Roosevelt Administration called this a program of "reform."

Bankers and their associates disliked such a usage bitterly: the measures struck them as more like vicious, totalitarian assaults upon men (now and then women) who had sought no more than to make ordinary Americans prosperous. They said so with a certain caution in the 1930s, as ordinary Americans, feeling distinctly unprosperous, might have turned obstreperous. But the moral core of capitalism seemed in peril from prohibitions like the Glass-Steagall Act, seeking in principle to part investment bankers from retail bankers, thus to separate the business of accumulating people's money from that of devising ways to spend it. This, surely, institutionalized the notion that financial executives might yield to conflicts of interest. It was a low view of human nature—found also in the federal arrangements to guarantee bank deposits, as well as to supervise them instead of trusting to decent bankerly instinct.

As matters turned out, the Administration's program didn't trigger social ruin. Quite shortly American prosperity began an upswing not matched in any other national history. We cannot say that sedating Wall Street was the sole cause (there was, for instance, war, which galvanized American industry while zapping every principal competitor). But even within the securities business itself, the effects were hardly inimical. And ordinary Americans enjoyed gains in quality of life also outside experience, for there occurred at the same time another phenomenon long advertised as fatal to liberty and civilization: a great equalizing of incomes and life-chances. America became admired throughout the world for its egalitarian praxis.

Consequently it grew easier in the 1950s to tell people they were living alongside a mighty engine of wealth—the stock market—which might grow more productive should it lean somewhat more toward . . . exuberance. Societies and individuals seem to cool their skepticism whenever they feel prosperous. It is an important rule of doorstep salesmanship—a culture from which IOS drew much of its operational lore—that the likeliest place to sell an encyclopedia is a household which somehow has got hold of one already.

Quite clearly an efficient financial sector brings important benefits to a modern economy. It's not at all clear that "exuberant," "speculative"—or "unregulated"—are terms synonymous with "efficient." Nor that a financial sector to which they can be applied benefits anyone much except its own denizens. But such distinctions aren't always drawn, and certainly weren't by the IOS team. They proposed that the best way for people to turn a modest amount of money into a large one—to show sincerity about getting to be rich—was turning it over to one of their unregulated investment funds.

IOS was not purely original. Efforts were made from the first to defeat counter-speculative measures inspired by the Crash. But Cornfeld and Cowett were original in devising the first really big financial machine which operated as if those measures didn't really exist. By way of a period feature, their innovation was labeled "People's Capitalism": no such egalitarian camouflage would be thought necessary today.

As the book says, they worked "offshore": that is, the innovators inhabited a meta-world cobbled up from jurisdictional oddments left over from the Holy Roman Empire, from Europe's early-modern religious conflicts, and from the decayed oceanic empires of Britain, the Netherlands, France, Spain, and Portugal. It turned round an axis set in Protestant Switzerland, rich with mechanisms of independence and secrecy generated while holding out against the Counter-Reformation: in the 1960s these nicely protected Ed and Bernie's altogether unspiritual purposes from the SEC. Their meta-world contained no restriction on financial machinations except their own honesty, good sense, and judgment—present only in homeopathic quantity. (Homeopathy, it will be recalled, treats the human condition by keeping doses very tiny, hoping to produce effects just opposite to those of a large intake.)

One can see *"Do You Sincerely Want to Be Rich?"* as the story of Cornfeld reversing time's arrow to create his own personal Roaring Twenties, followed by his own personal Great Crash. Readers will find that his last inspirational speech actually threatened America: Wall Street had always been the chief speculative destination of the funds he and Ed controlled from Geneva, but the SEC was interfering more and more because of conflicts of interest perceived in the IOS system. If this went on, said Bernie, IOS—about to become "the greatest single economic force in the free world"—might eschew America and send its dollars elsewhere. Just where we never heard, for even as he spoke, the great "economic force" was already hollowed out fatally—if not yet visibly—by internal misappropriations and kickbacks prohibited under the U.S. regulations it had been set up to avoid.

We supposed the IOS debacle might warn people off the malign nostalgia from which it derived—might convince them that the financial culture of the 1920s, instead of being revived, should be returned to the graveyard with a stake through its chest. This is not quite how things have turned out. Since then the essentials of the IOS system have been remade in several louche editions—and firmly installed on present-day U.S. soil. Within a retrospect which now includes Michael Milken's junk-bond saturnalia in the 1980s (at Drexel) and the 1990s era of Enron, WorldCom, and the dot-bubblers, the uniqueness of Bernie and Ed is that they actually had to do their thing offshore—in deference to legal and moral inhibitions since dissolved. Offshore remains useful for tax-avoidance schemes, but it now provides few facilities for speculation and corruption not available to mainland operators. When Glass-Steagall was repealed in 1999, not even regulation's remaining champions cared. Diluted, amended, modified, and qualified, it had become no more than an aggregation of loopholes.

The IOS experiment of course failed by every publicly defensible test of financial efficacy. But where it succeeded, historically, was in showing what, after all, it was possible to get away with for extended periods of time, and how modest any terminal penalties might be. Cornfeld and Cowett lavishly stole other people's property: it afforded them kingly lifestyles for more than a decade, and made them multimillionaires. Certain disagreeable consequences applied when the grotesque enterprise collapsed, but nothing comparable to the affliction among their victims. Cornfeld revisited Switzerland injudiciously soon after the crash, and landed in jail, but he was quite soon bailed out and the charges dropped. Very likely the worst pain—for men of certain vanity—was that people stopped inviting them to pontificate about the world economy.

As pioneers, they were less sophisticated than present-day successors. By various shrouded devices, they certainly held on to some comfortable remnant of their speculative gains. But ten directors of Enron between them collected $250 million of real money—behind a veil of phoney accounts—while that $60 billion of shareholder value was going blooey. And they have open legal rights to keep 90 per cent, provided 10 per cent is dropped into the oceanic bucket of loss. (As Lucian Bebchuk of the Harvard Law School sardonically asked: "What's a few million between friends?")

To be sure, there must be some criminal prosecutions when larceny has become so egregious, but the record current at this writing doesn't suggest that any perps who actually get nailed should dread any very fearful fate. As Professor Frank Partnoy has shown, the twentieth century closed with a very manifest decline in the rule of law—the law, that is, insofar as financial transactions are concerned. According to the professor, individuals whose activities "in most other industries would lead to a sting operation" routinely avoid jail.

Imagine if the U.S. Attorney's Office found out about a kick-back scheme of the magnitude of the IPO scheme in any other industry. Imagine if . . . this scheme were related to a bunch of garbage collectors paying kickbacks. Well, these people would already have been put in jail and the full force of the U.S. Department of Justice would have been brought to bear.

And here, doubtless, is the chief outcome of the experiment Cornfeld and Cowett set going. Disintegration of their essentially lawless enterprise occurred within a context of large-scale U.S. stock-market collapse: due correction for wild, lengthy speculation in which IOS itself took prominent part (when investment-fund managers began to preen themselves if the financial press identified them as "gunslingers"). But the aftermath didn't include any such social dislocation as struck America and the world of the 1930s. Then, real fears arose of a new Crash wrecking capitalism—perhaps opening the way to revolution, either of Left or Right.

Certainly the 1970s saw much economic tribulation—disillusion after the optimistic 1960s. But there were a decent number of suspects to share the blame with stock-market folly: notably, the Vietnam War and the "oil-shock" combined to destabilize an international currency system which had seemed like the postwar settlement's unshakable core. Speculation's aftermath created, of course, a good deal of poverty, but most institutions—if not their customers—survived quite nicely, and often profitably. Society, it turned out, had somehow become less sensitive to share-price volatility, a discovery which has been remade and adventurously reinforced several times since then.

A good deal has been said in financial circles about the enhanced craft of central bankers, especially, in recent years, that of Alan Greenspan, the Federal Reserve's philosopher-king. But there still exists a bequest from the Roosevelt Administration which financiers rarely discuss in any systematic way: namely, it created the social-security structure around which American middle-class and working-class families subsequently developed capacities for dealing with economic misfortune quite absent prior to the Second World War. America, like every other industrial nation, acquired impressive new levels of social resilience in the second half of the twentieth century. And perhaps this, as much as bankerly cunning, is what has enabled it to survive powerful, successive bouts of speculative fever.

Peak temperatures since the latter 1960s have several times dwarfed their predecessors. Each time—and doubtless next time—turning the heat up further is the financial community's response. As Blake indeed suggests, you can't know you have gone far enough until you have gone collectively too far. Notably, the poet provides no advice on how to get back from there, but the present U.S. authorities seem happy to let that problem arise before considering it. Meanwhile, they eschew Professor Partnoy's belief that market abuse should attract deterrent penalties.

For speculators, supposedly, are benefactors. The "irrational exuberance" to which IOS showed the way back is glowingly defended as the proper, inescapable price of innovation: lacking it, there would be no vivid entrepreneurship to enhance the world's material condition.

It is not, however, obvious that entrepreneurship of the type Wall Street values is close-coupled to technical progress in society.

This is not to say that the Internet and the World Wide Web are less than genuine advances because they fueled the dot-com craze. But neither in the first place had speculative roots. The Net and its packet-switching infrastructure came from academic technologists employed by the U.S. Government, and the World Wide Web—making it usable to consumers—we owe to Tim Berners-Lee and state-funded European science. Stock-market investment was of course needed to bring Net and Web products to the public, but as they had to pass through a wildly hyped process, much corruption and degradation attached, and still persists. The bubble was not blown because the requirements of technical change made it necessary. Rather, its distension occurred because by the 1990s America's economy needed share-price advance—however speculative—to keep on growing, and dot-com fantasies came opportunely to hand as a gaseous medium.

For many years now, bankerly craft, confronted by the need to sustain the stock market's upward momentum, has chiefly consisted in keeping credit cheap, producing thereby a U.S. economy massively in debt to the rest of the world, with an effective domestic savings rate of zero. And the imposing financial apparatus which has been fed upon several waves of—fairly—painless speculation now accounts for some 40 per cent of U.S. corporate profits. Doubtless this contributes to the present Administration's belief that it should be given the bulk of Social Security revenues to manage—though doing so would subordinate the most stable component in America's socioeconomic anatomy to the one which has been most consistently inconsistent.

Many financial and economic adepts see in this a system certain to voyage permanently onward and upward. To others, it looks like a general agreement to defer sensible behavior until its absence becomes truly catastrophic; we have no space here to examine or predict. Let us allow that the speculative cycle would doubtless have been re-energized somehow even if Bernie and Ed had never got together and launched IOS. But we can nonetheless say that as history did turn out, the honor of first pointing the way—if "honor" turns out to be the appropriate word—is one to which they have a matchless claim.

Orders of magnitude aside, you will not find much in this book which is altogether obsolete.

—The Authors
January 2005

Acknowledgments

No book worth reading is easy to write, and this one was harder than most. It could not have been done if there had not been a large number of people who were prepared to help us discover the truth about Investors Overseas Services—even when it was embarrassing or painful for them to do so.

We lost count of how many people we talked to, after the number passed five hundred. Apart from IOS salesmen, secretaries, and executives, there were bankers, brokers, accountants, oilmen, policemen, government officials, and lawyers. There were IOS's competitors, and IOS's customers. The particular difficulty was that, in the nature of the case, these people were scattered all over the world. The three authors conducted interviews in Geneva, Zurich, London, New York, Munich, Berlin, Paris, Rome, Luxembourg, Denver, Amsterdam, Los Angeles, Washington, Miami, Toronto, the Bahamas, and some other places; even then that did not cover all the places where IOS did business. Researchers and correspondents made inquiries for us in Philadelphia, Seoul, Tokyo, Bangkok, La Paz, São Paulo, Beirut, Montreal, Athens, Málaga, Manila, Taipeh, Tel Aviv, Tehran, Madrid, Düsseldorf, Hamburg, Stockholm, Sydney, Guatemala City, Hong Kong, Bonn, and some other spots beside. It would be impractical to list all the people who helped us during the process. But we would like to thank at least some people by name.

Chief among these are Bernard Cornfeld and Edward M. Cowett. This may seem odd in a book which is so critical of their activities: however, we can only say that our relations with them both remained courteous and personally agreeable even after it was apparent that our attitude to the IOS phenomenon was not one of admiration. We were also greatly helped by Allen Cantor, Harvey Felberbaum, C. Henry Buhl, George Landau, Kenneth Beaugrand, Martin Seligson, James Roosevelt, Pasquale Chiomenti, Eli Wallitt, Harold Kaplan, and Sir Eric Wyndham White.

We received much patient help from fellow reporters in the United States: in particular Morton Margolin of the *Rocky Mountain News* of Denver, Colorado; Paul Steiger of the *Los Angeles Times*; Philip Greer of the *Washington Post*; and also César Tácito Lopes Costa, editor of O *Estado* of São Paulo, Brazil.

We owe a great deal to the reporters and foreign correspondents of our own paper, *The Sunday Times* of London, and its stablemate, *The Times*. We especially think of Anthony Terry, Richard Hughes, Christopher Reed, Eric Marsden, Geoffrey Sumner, Mark Ottaway, Paul Martin, Stephen Holmes, Tim Brown, Philip Jacobson, Desmond O'Grady, and Stacy Waddy. Stephen Fay, *The Sunday Times*'s New York correspondent, and Robert Ducas, New York advertising manager of Times Newspapers, were especially patient with our demands. Our thanks also go to Sheila Robinette, Laurie Zimmerman, and Joe Petta of the New York staff, and to Wendy Hughes, who reinforced them in summer 1970. Sue Dakin undertook, with unfailing patience and dispatch, the typing and retyping of our manuscript.

Any book like this, drawing on the resources of a newspaper group, benefits from the help of an enormous number of people, but there were certain talented reporters who made indispensable contributions to our project: Alexander Mitchell, now of Granada Television; Andrew Hale, our Italian economic correspondent; William Shawcross, who trekked back and forth across Germany and Southeast Asia on our behalf; and Phillip Knightley, who conducted some critical interviews for us in Switzerland and Spain. Another indispensable contribution was that of Nelson Mews, our chief researcher, who must now know more about IOS than any other one person.

Elisabeth Sifton, our editor at The Viking Press, also exhibited great patience, and clarified our language on the many occasions that it was necessary.

In a special category is Murray Sayle, who might well have written a book about IOS himself, but was too busy winning awards as a foreign correspondent. Had he done so, Murray's conclusions would probably have been different from ours. All the same, it was he who introduced us to some of the people in this book, and to the title.

This book could not have been published at all but for the shrewd and patient counsel of our legal advisers—or without the conviction of Harold Evans, the editor of *The Sunday Times*, that it is important to do the big stories really thoroughly, and to go on until you sort out what really happened.

And our thanks, with great feeling, go to those people who did our jobs while we were doing this one.

Charles Raw
Bruce Page
Godfrey Hodgson
London, February 1971

Do You Sincerely Want to Be Rich?

A Warning to Investors from Mr. Bernard Cornfeld

In which we introduce Bernard Cornfeld in the role of international economic statesman and give a preliminary statement of the real nature of Investors Overseas Services.

I t was Bernard Cornfeld's declared ambition to make Investors Overseas Services the most important economic force in the Free World.

The game was mutual funds. Thousands of salesmen, calling themselves "financial counselors," combed the earth for people's savings, and put them into the funds which IOS managed, creaming off enough in the process to make the most successful of them wealthy men.

Mutual funds in themselves are an old and well-tried form of investment. A special variant was that IOS was the biggest and best-known of the "offshore" funds. That meant that these funds, and the companies that managed them, were carefully registered and domiciled wherever in the world they would most avoid taxation and regulation. There was nothing new about that either.

What was phenomenal about IOS was its success. On the foundation of its offshore mutual funds it built up a complex of banks, insurance companies, real-estate promotions, and every other kind of financial institution you can think of. "Total Financial Service" was the slogan. By the end of the 1960s, Cornfeld's men had a shade under two and a half billion dollars of other people's money to manage, and Cornfeld was publicly announcing plans to push that to $15 billion by the mid-1970s.

By the end of the 1960s, IOS had also made a fortune valued at over $100 million for Bernard Cornfeld personally. It had made around a hundred of his associates millionaires as well. Cornfeld was the most talked about financier in Europe since the Great Depression, and IOS was insistently—and on the whole successfully—asserting the right to sit at the golden table of the world's most respectable financial institutions.

The only trouble was that IOS was not a respectable financial institution. It was an international swindle.

That is not a word which should be lightly used about any organization, let alone one which acquired control over more than two and a half billion dollars of other people's money. We must, therefore, explain precisely what we mean by it.

IOS was the creation of Bernard Cornfeld and Edward M. Cowett. Together these two men built up an organization so steeped in financial and intellectual dishonesty and directed so recklessly that it was absurd that it should have been entrusted with so much of other people's money, let alone praised for the brilliance with which it was managed.

The organization which they built up has not, of course, disappeared without a trace, although the two men no longer have any say in it. At the time this is being written, men sit on the board of IOS Ltd. in Geneva who are responsible for safeguarding well over a billion dollars—which is what remains of the money that hundreds of thousands of investors were induced to part with. And of course IOS did a great deal of business which was perfectly honest in itself, and continues to do so. We have talked to many of the people who work for IOS, and there were a lot of decent, even idealistic, people among them. Few were aware of the essential dishonesty of the thing they worked for.

Most people have a good deal of difficulty in accepting the idea that a large and well-publicized international business could have been run in such a manner. "It can't be true," is the natural reaction, "because if it was true, how did they get away with it?" There are many answers to that question.

Charles Dickens suggested one, looking back on the career of the financier in *Little Dorrit*. "The next man," he wrote, "who has as large a capacity for swindling will succeed as well. Pardon me, but I think you have really no idea how the human bees will swarm to the beating of any old tin kettle; in that fact lies the whole manual of governing them. When they can be got to believe that the kettle is made of precious metals, in that power lies the whole power of men like our late lamented." The one thing IOS always did best was to beat the old tin kettle.

But there is another answer to the question why Cornfeld and Cowett were able to create the edifice they did. It can be summed up in the single word "offshore." By working in the interstices, so to speak, between the world's legal jurisdictions and administrative systems, they were able to do with impunity things that would have been illegal had their enterprise been located in any one place. Below are just some of the kinds of misbehavior that IOS committed under Cornfeld and Cowett:

1. Money which they said was held on trust for the customers was used to finance maneuvers for the benefit of IOS itself, its directors and employees, and their friends.

2. At many times, and in many parts of the world, the IOS sales force engaged in illegal currency transactions on a massive

scale. Attempts have been made to pretend that this was somehow peripheral to the company's main activities—but as late as 1970 the IOS Board still acknowledged in their meetings that important sections of the IOS sales operations were illegal.

3. IOS consistently misrepresented the investment performance of its largest fund, and used the misrepresentation to sell hundreds of millions of dollars' worth of fund shares.

4. The basic nature of the best-known IOS fund, the Fund of Funds, was systematically disguised. It was supposed to offer the investors a diversity of investment advice. For most of the time, it did nothing of the kind—it merely charged its investors a double fee on the pretense of doing so.

5. The customers' money, in the funds, was frequently invested in unmarketable shares, and often in securities which IOS was floating for its own profit. There was a series of reckless speculations that culminated in a catastrophic venture into oil and gas exploration rights in the Canadian Arctic.

6. IOS paid itself a fee of nearly $10 million for having "revalued" those Arctic rights. Not only were the grounds for revaluation dubious, but in some cases the rights had not even been earned at the time they were "revalued."

7. As well as selling shares in the funds it managed, IOS eventually sold $100 million worth of its own shares to the public. These shares were sold on the basis of prospectuses which were misleading by reason of omission and misrepresentation.

8. Cash raised in this manner (see 7) from the public was used for the personal benefit of directors of IOS—and in the end the controllers of the company lent to themselves so large a proportion of the company's liquid cash that they brought it to the brink of collapse, and damaged the interests of thousands of their customers.

9. Ed Cowett, who had already left the IOS Board after an episode involving financial impropriety, was restored to power and given, by Cornfeld, complete day-to-day control of IOS and its system of banks and investment funds.

Bad as the particular items in this short summary of IOS's misdeeds are, they are only individual instances of a general proposition: IOS pretended to be creating wealth for the many when it was really making money for the few. That proposition will be demonstrated again and again in this book. But now it is time to take leave of generalities and to take a closer look at the remarkable figure of Bernard Cornfeld. There can be no better moment to savor the full absurdity of the contrast between the façade that IOS presented to the world, and the reality back-stage, than the zenith of Cornfeld's power and reputation.

. . .

In the first week of February 1970, Cornfeld flew to New York to be the principal speaker at a conference organized by a periodical called the *Institutional Investor*. The invitation was a re-markable enough accolade in itself: the use Cornfeld chose to put it to was a breath-taking illustration of his nerve.

It is important to understand the setting, the occasion, and the time.

The setting was New York, the true test and only stage for success in Bernard Cornfeld's world. He had first come to the city as a child from Turkey in 1931. He was nearly thirty when he left to seek his fortune in Europe. It had been one of the proudest moments of his life when he came back to New York in 1960, as a rich man, and the New York papers interviewed him as the latest verification of the American dream. Making it in New York, he told the reporters then, was what counted. But in 1967 he had been banished from New York. Or rather, while he himself could go there as often as he liked and could cut a flamboyant figure in the East Side discotheques, his firm was banned from doing business there by order of the Securities and Exchange Commission, because of certain irregularities and deceptions. Now he was back in New York again, and with the financial community literally at his feet.

The *Institutional Investor* is a plump journal, whose elegant pages are not available to the general public. You may subscribe to it if you belong to a firm that is a member of the New York Stock Exchange or if you are otherwise engaged full time in the investment business. Its editor, George J. W. Goodman, is a friend of Cornfeld's and has written for the IOS magazine. But his chief claim to fame is the authorship, under the pseudonym Adam Smith, of the best seller, *The Money Game*, in which he described the antics of the new generation of Wall Street money managers. He called them "the gunslingers" and it was a good name, because they brought to the responsibility of managing other people's money roughly the degree of prudence which cowboys brought to town on a Saturday night in the Old West. (It should be said that Goodman was not especially wide-eyed about the atmosphere he described, but the market was still buoyant when the book came out, and the customers were more amused than alarmed.)

Naturally, there were "gunslingers" among the "institutional investors" who gathered to hear Cornfeld on February 4. Not that it was in any sense a disreputable audience. Far from it; all who were there were citizens of the highest probity and reputation—as Wall Street measures those values. It was a gathering of men, and some women, who were collectively responsible for managing tens of billions of dollars of other people's money entrusted to the insurance companies, pension funds, and mutual funds which they advised on investment. But where the word "institution" in New York, in a financial sense, had once carried connotations of staid conservatism, by 1970 many "institutional" investment professionals were committed to "aggressivity," "performance," and the other slogans and catchwords of the peak market years. Risks which had seemed daunting ten years or even five years earlier now seemed commonplace. For twenty years, share prices on Wall Street and indeed on most other exchanges in the world had risen with only brief interruptions, and there was a growing confidence that they would go on rising forever. "These guys," reflected one old Wall Street reporter, "really thought they had repealed the law of gravity."

By the time Bernard Cornfeld appeared before them, it is true, this professional optimism had been considerably shaken. The market had passed its peak, with the Dow-Jones index a fraction above the magic 1000 mark, just over a year before; and since then it had fallen by an uncomfortable 15 per cent.

That was not, in itself, a disastrous decline. What was more worrisome was that the particular category of stocks on which the institutional professionals had put their main hope of getting the all-important "performance" had begun to slither down faster than the index or the market as a whole. There were the jerry-built "conglomerates," piled up through takeovers mainly paid for with inflated paper. Many of them were collapsing like so many card houses.

Among the more intelligent of Cornfeld's listeners, therefore, there was a sense of unease about the market. But prices had only slipped. They had not yet crashed, and the fashionable attitude was to see what had happened as a minor setback. Few of them seemed to have any serious forebodings about the market; fewer still saw anything fundamentally wrong in the feverish atmosphere and gunslinging techniques of the Great Bull Market which—though a very few were willing to acknowledge it—had now come to an end at last. It was easier to look for scapegoats and, for this mood, Bernie Cornfeld was their man.

With a salesman's flair for divining what an audience wants to hear, Cornfeld plaited his speech out of two themes. One was Messianic confidence about the potential glories of the market. And the other was denunciation of the agency which he blamed for the market's immediate difficulties: none other than his old antagonist, the Securities and Exchange Commission.

Short, plump, with a wide mouth, Bernie Cornfeld speaks in private for the most part in an intense whisper. On the platform, his manner is evangelical and his language grandiloquent. "I am convinced," he told the *Institutional Investor*'s conference, "that the American securities business is at the heart of what makes this country vital and dynamic." The years of the bull market, he said, had seen "an extraordinary creative development of new ways of marshaling the money which is the lifeblood of enterprise." He did not stop to say whether he was thinking of the conglomerate, the offshore mutual fund, or the hedge fund, or which of the other new ways of marshaling money looked rather less creative today. He swept on into a passage of prophetic eloquence.

"This is the promise," he declaimed, "that everyone who is willing to work and to save can participate in economic development. . . . That the dream of a more equitable distribution of wealth can be realized within the structure of the free-enterprise system. It is also the promise that the dynamism of our economy will result in the knitting together of the shattered bits and pieces of our society. . . . This is why I am convinced that what is good for the American securities industry is good for the country."

But then he turned to his second, less optimistic theme. His own company, he predicted, would have $15 billion to invest by 1975. In the past, it had invested overwhelmingly in Wall Street. But now he could give no guarantee that this would continue. "From our vantage point in Europe, we sense a malaise within the investment community here. . . ."

What was the cause of that malaise? Fear that the market might continue to fall, as it had been falling for about a year? An uneasy recognition that much of the rise in the market in the last years of the boom had been due to reckless speculation in largely worthless paper? Nothing could have been further from Cornfeld's mind. He spoke of the Vietnam war, of the decay of great American cities, of the alienation of the blacks, and of atmospheric pollution. It was not too much to say, Cornfeld thought, that America was in a state of crisis. And it was at this moment that the Securities and Exchange Commission had chosen to make its spring. The SEC, he said, had "adopted the simple device of attacking virtually every sector of earnings in the securities business. And a weak, unprofitable securities business means a weak, unprofitable market." The point had been reached, he said, when "the public interest seems to be the least of all considerations when the Commission moves into action."

Insofar as he chose to support this sweeping allegation with specific charges, he accused the SEC staff of misusing its power—by blocking the prospectus of any firm that continued to do business with IOS. He attacked the Commission for not regulating the trade in unregistered securities, and for impoverishing brokers by suggesting that commissions might be cut for the benefit of the customers. And he deplored its attitude to the enormous flood of brokerage commissions generated by the market. The SEC wanted these diverted back to the customers: that, said Cornfeld, would impoverish Wall Street.

It was an inspirational performance, and the audience acclaimed it rapturously. A few years earlier, most of them would have examined the entrails of a goat for economic pointers as readily as they would have listened seriously to Bernard Cornfeld. Some of them remained a little dubious about some of the things they had heard about his early days, a little shocked by some of the things the SEC had found out about him. Others were amused by his personal flamboyance—the tufty beard and the nippy-waisted French-tailored suit. But after all, they liked to think of themselves as a bit piratical too. "Conservative" had become a bad word in their vocabulary, and many of them, while not going so far as to sport beards, had been carefully growing their side whiskers for several months in search of a more emancipated image. The main point was that Bernie Cornfeld was playing their tune: happy days are here again, and to hell with the spoilsports from the SEC.

Cornfeld had shown that his heart was sound by paying tribute to the social importance and wisdom of his hearers. And had he not proved his worth—while incidentally demonstrating the superiority of American get-up-and-go to the effete European establishment—by accumulating more than $2 billion in assets under his management?

There seems often to be a moment, just before the climax of a great folly, when even the sturdiest skepticism surrenders. Wall Street is not mainly populated by fools, and there were plenty of clever men present to hear Cornfeld's speech who knew what nonsense he was talking. Many of them knew, for example, that while he was denouncing the SEC for not having regulated unregistered securities, his own funds were stuffed with them. Some of them, come to that, had sold them to him. Again, when he talked piously about brokerage commissions, there were plenty who knew that the SEC had caught IOS diverting brokerage on a massive scale—not to the customers, but to themselves, via, on one occasion, a lady named Gloria Martica Clapp, who lived in the Bahamas. In more general terms, few who stopped to think for a second could have seriously accepted the thesis that the SEC was out to destroy the securities business. But when the old tin kettle is drummed hard enough, disbelief is often silent.

It was not only Wall Street that acclaimed Bernie Cornfeld that week. The night before his speech, he attended the annual cocktail party which the *Washington Post* gives in New York. The guest list reflects that well-informed newspaper's judgment of who really matters in the city. It includes writers, bankers, politicians, political hostesses, and artists. In 1970 the unofficial but undisputed guest of honor in this company was the legendary Bernard Cornfeld, prophet of People's Capitalism. He was, from all accounts, the success of the evening: warm, modest, amiable, and statesman-like—drinking, as always, nothing stronger than Coca-Cola, speaking softly, and retiring early.

A short while later, *New York* magazine published an article which rounds out this picture of Cornfeld at the height of his glory. It described an extraordinary meeting, a sort of Field of the Bed of Mink, between Cornfeld and that other merchant of fantasy, Hugh Hefner. Shortly after the *Institutional Investor* meeting, the two of them had retired, with their respective retinues of counselors, hangers-on, girl friends, and servants, to Acapulco, where they wished to discuss possible joint ventures in the real-estate business. (Cornfeld, apparently, was not much taken with the layout in Hefner's private aircraft, known as the Black Bunny.) Altogether, the article portrayed Cornfeld as frivolous in a way which would have been lethal, a few short years before, to a man who depended as he did on the approval of the financial community. No damage seems to have been done: the late Roman private life was taken as completing the enviable splendor of his image.

In February 1970 Bernie Cornfeld seemed to stand on a high mountain. He owned more chateaux, town houses, villas, and apartments in the world's capitals than any Rothschild or Estérhazy in their high times: a few days before he flew to New York he had just bought his second castle. He owned horses, wild animals, boats, airplanes, cars, fashion houses, and model agencies. He moved incessantly between these luxurious possessions, surrounded by as numerous and pleasure-loving an entourage as a prince of the Holy Roman Empire. And there was something more flattering, and more interesting, about his famous "life-style" than the ordinary spending power of great wealth. He had contrived to recruit, in the envious and egalitarian twentieth century, what amounted to a private army of vassals: his sales force. Many of them were fanatically loyal; and he knew how to keep them that way with a complicated system of lavish gifts, grants of profitable territory, and elaborately structured financial rewards. It was even rumored—and Cornfeld himself did little to scotch such rumors—that he lived in the middle of an adolescent's fantasy of a harem.

But what impressed the hostesses and journalists of New York was not so much the picturesque surface of Cornfeld's life; it was that it seemed to be solidly built on a golden foundation of money. On one single day the previous summer, investors had poured $30 million into the IOS funds. "The most important economic force in the Free World"? The shrewd thing to say in February 1970, was that, by God, Cornfeld might just make it.

· · ·

AS it turned out, that was almost the last moment when it would have been shrewd or even sensible to have said any such thing.

And nobody would have been saying it then, if they had realized the extent of the financial shambles the statesman of People's Capitalism had left behind him in Geneva.

On February 11, just seven days after Cornfeld's speech to the institutional investors, the financial controller of IOS, a young accountant named Melvin Lechner, finished the consolidation of the 1969 accounts for IOS's many subsidiaries and arrived at a tentative total for the company's profits.

We shall see that the profit of IOS, as such, was by no means the all-important figure that it would be in more orthodox concerns. Profit or no profit, the operations of IOS enriched the men who ran it in various ways. Nevertheless, even the least skeptical of Cornfeld's hearers in New York might have been less willing to take him seriously as a prophet and teacher if they had realized the truth about his own business.

The figure that emerged from Lechner's calculations was $17.9 million. That might sound like a lot of money. But Lechner knew that in terms of IOS's expectations, and of the way those expectations had been capitalized in the price of its shares, it was a catastrophe.

Cornfeld had airily predicted profits as high as $30 million. In the end, as we shall see, even Lechner's first figure proved to be a mighty overestimate.

When Lechner had reached and checked his alarming figure, he did not call Cornfeld. For more than a year, Cornfeld had delegated most of the day-to-day management of the business to Ed Cowett. Slim, cool, a trifle saturnine in appearance, Ed Cowett was now master of detail. He was even farther away than Mexico: he was in Tokyo. As soon as Lechner confided the profit figure to him, Cowett's assistant, Hal Vaughan, called Tokyo and gave Cowett the figure over the phone. Cowett canceled his plans and was back in Geneva by the following weekend.

Cowett knew perfectly well how serious the situation was. Already, in January, Lechner had been sufficiently worried by the financial trend to have written Cowett a confidential memorandum, describing in detail the alarm bells he could hear ringing. So Cowett reacted to the bad news with his habitual coolness. For some time, he continued to insist that the profits were not the $17.9 million his own controller had told him, but $25 million.

But the truth could not be hidden forever. That telephone call to Tokyo was the beginning of the end. Bit by bit, the real state of affairs began to leak out. The sales operation was running into a loss. . . . The profits from managing the funds had been propped up by the Arctic deal. . . . The money raised from the public issue of IOS Ltd. shares, little more than six months before, had all been spent.

At the very moment when Cornfeld, parading himself to the world as a major prophet, was achieving his greatest public acceptance, the train of events was under way which was to expose the absurdity of his pretensions.

Less than a year later, he was back in Acapulco. His shares in IOS had been sold, and he had cut his last links with the business he had created. Hardly anyone wanted to hear his views on the future of society any more. No one in their senses could believe any longer that Investors Overseas Services would ever have $15 billion under management, still less that it would be the most important economic force in the Free World.

Within weeks of Cornfeld's tirade against the SEC, the stock market cracked and fell even more steeply. "This decline, the largest and most protracted since World War II," one of the best-respected investment men on Wall Street wrote, "was a severe reaction to a period of excessive speculation." Cornfeld blamed the SEC for what had happened. We shall see that his own organization was not merely a victim of the market break; by a combination of sheer size and reckless commitment to "excessive speculation," it was one of its causes.

It is only fair to say that *Institutional Investor* remained loyal to the prophet it had sponsored. At its annual conference for 1971, Mr. Bernard Cornfeld was again asked to speak. This time, however, his appointed topic was: "What went wrong?"

It is time to take a detailed look at what did go wrong. When we have done so, it will become plain that the really interesting question is not so much why Cornfeld and his friends failed. It is how they managed to succeed as long as they did.

For this is not only a story about Bernard Cornfeld and Edward Cowett. They could never have flourished as they did without the acquiescence and, sometimes, the active help of others. Victory, they say, has many fathers, but defeat is always an orphan. It was the same at IOS. After the crash, it was surprising how many people gave us the same excuse, "We never knew!" It is hard to believe that they could not have found out if they had wanted to. This is a story largely populated by people who didn't want to know, and grew rich in ignorance.

Not all of them were inside IOS. Outside the company and its associates, there were concentric rings of others, less responsible for what happened, but still willing to profit in some degree from what was done. IOS worked with accountants, lawyers, bankers, brokers, advertising men, and publicists of every kind. No doubt they didn't know quite how dishonest IOS was capable of being. But again, in too many cases, they didn't want to know.

For the real importance of this story is not that a particular group of men managed to get away with certain maneuvers which are not allowed by most developed legal systems. It is not even that a very large number of people lost a great deal of money as a result. The real lesson of the IOS story is an old one: it is that human communication is so fragile that a man can put out whatever propaganda he likes in his own interests and be sure that enough of it will be believed to make his fortune.

The dwindling but still huge pile of money in the IOS funds is a monument not only to the energy of the legendary sales force, but also to the proposition which Dickens expressed in his phrase about the human bee, and how they will swarm when the old tin kettle is beaten.

Or as that skeptical Scottish philosopher David Hume put it, "No man need despair of gaining proselytes to the most extravagant hypothesis, who has art enough to represent it in any favourable colour. The victory is not gained by the men at arms, who manage the pike and the sword, but by the trumpeters, drummers and musicians of the army." Let us go back to the apprenticeship of a master drummer.

• 2 •

The Making of a Conceptual Salesman

In which we examine the political and psychological background of Bernard Cornfeld and the early growth of his talents.

The most durable of all the legends about Bernard Cornfeld concerns his original financial motivations, and the impulse which started him along the road to Geneva and People's Capitalism. The story is usually told like this:

Bernard Cornfeld, an idealistic young socialist, is the son of a widowed immigrant in New York. Fresh from Columbia University's School of Social Work, he takes up a post as a social worker in Philadelphia. The exact nature of his duties is not stated, but "slums" are mentioned. His income as a social worker is slender, and in order to have enough money to take girls out, he begins selling mutual-fund shares in his spare time. Now, the young socialist experiences a conversion; he perceives that the open-end investment fund can be made to resolve the cruel contradictions of capitalism.

Why is it that only the rich can invest in the wealth created by capitalism and thus increase their wealth? It is because the poor have few dollars left over from purchasing the necessities of life. They cannot afford to tie up this slender surplus in investment. To sell shares successfully, you need expert brokers. And there is the eggs-in-one-basket problem: what about the widow who has invested her $50 in the shares of a company which collapses?

But now the mutual-fund salesman goes among the people. Through him, they are enabled to turn their savings into shares in a Fund. Many mites are thus assembled into a great whole. Wise men invest this ample Fund in the shares of many industrial concerns. And if, as should normally be the case, most of these investments rise in value, then the rise increases the value of each of the shares of the Fund. Thus the savings of the poor are multiplied, without risk. And the Fund undertakes that it will always redeem a customer's shares, immediately, for cash. The advantages of investment are combined with the blessings of its great opposite, liquidity.

In the legend, at least, Bernard Cornfeld accepted with religious fervor the excellence of this vision. He has himself recalled the birth of a conviction that "money possesses a strange kind of purity," and the further conviction that capitalism could now be employed to bring about that equitable distribution of wealth which was the aim of socialism.

This idealized portrait of the open-end fund mechanism is not totally at odds with reality. But there are some important variations possible, such as the size of the cut that the salesman takes for himself, and the manner of insuring that the little people's savings are deployed with suitable wisdom. The picture of Cornfeld's youth similarly differs in some significant ways from what actually occurred.

Cornfeld did spend the better part of one year as a social worker, but it was nowhere near the slums. He worked among the middle class as a youth leader, and he had already made his acquaintance with mutual funds before he reached Philadelphia.

• • •

Cornfeld's father, Leon, was a Romanian: he was an actor, impresario, and film producer. He must, in the 1920s, have been one of the pioneers of the movie business in Central Europe; he had offices in Vienna and in Istanbul, where Bernard was born on August 17, 1927. Leon Cornfeld had been married once before when he met Sophie, Bernard's mother, in Vienna, and he already had four sons by his first wife. In Istanbul, the family suffered an appalling setback when Leon fell through a defective pavement grille into a basement. His injuries ended his acting career at once.

The family removed to America—first to Providence, Rhode Island, and then to New York. Leon began teaching German literature, but died three years later, aged over seventy. Bernard can just remember his father taking him to the Yiddish theater. Sophie Cornfeld, who was clearly a woman of great character, went to work as a nurse, which in those days required "working for twenty hours a day and sleeping four." It was a role that she apparently bore with considerable fortitude, although it was not one for which she was prepared by her family background. Her own family were Russian Jews, who had enjoyed a moderate prosperity until disturbed by the Revolution.

Bernard Cornfeld thus belonged by birth to the displaced intelligentsia of Central Europe, not to the wave of immigrants who came to America from a background of real poverty. There is little doubt that Sophie Cornfeld consistently expressed a belief that the Cornfelds were entitled to something better than the shabby gentility which they endured in Brooklyn. It is tempting, too, to guess that Cornfeld inherited important traits of character from his actor father: a flair for taking on whatever role would best enable him to manipulate a situation to his advantage. He can talk like a broker among brokers, a film producer among film producers, a banker among bankers.

All of the four earlier sons of Leon Cornfeld are now dead, one having been killed while serving in the U.S. Navy in the Second World War. Eugene became sales director of a paint firm in Boston, but both Sam and Albert (who spelled the name *Cornfield*) were in movies like their father. Quite clearly it was from his family that Bernard Cornfeld acquired his lifelong fascination with show business. Albert Cornfield became a fairly successful movie executive and an intense conservative in all business affairs, who consistently maintained for many years that the financial theories of his young relative Bernard were not to be taken seriously. Albert was horrified by Bernard's famous advertisement in the Paris *Herald Tribune* which asked for salesmen with "a sense of humor." But in the end, the old gentleman's skepticism was eroded, and according to his son, Hubert, he put some money into IOS not long before his death in the summer of 1970. "The crash came as a blow to my father," Hubert recalls. "He could have said to Bernie, 'I told you so.' But he didn't."

Bernard Cornfeld grew up as a plumpish boy of rather less than middle height. Probably Sophie Cornfeld's most important influence on her son was her powerful devotion that accustomed him early in life to occupying the center of the emotional stage. Her political sympathies, which Cornfeld once described as "tsarist," clearly made little overt impression. As a small boy in the 1930s, he claims to have been an avid collector of nickels and dimes to support volunteers of the Abraham Lincoln Brigade, who were fighting against General Franco in the Spanish Civil War.

Cornfeld derived his early political coloration from influences outside his home. He grew up in an energetic and attractive Jewish community in which a liberal, frequently socialist cast of thought was accepted as part of the norm.

The Cornfelds lived in several apartments in Brooklyn, winding up with the ground floor of a house at the corner of Farragut Road and Avenue H. The environment was seedy and depressing, rather than poverty-stricken. Cornfeld recalls taking night-work in a fruit store to earn money for a bicycle, and spending his weekends selling lollipops at Coney Island. He went first to Public School 153, and then to P.S. 225, and then to Abraham Lincoln High School. Archie Roth, an almost exact contemporary, first met Bernie at a Boy Scout camp in upper New York State, during the early 1940s.

Roth recalls that Cornfeld the boy scout "wasn't the outdoor physical type. . . . He was a very independent cuss. He knew what he was after, and could be very single-minded. He wasn't a robust guy as I remember it. In fact, I seem to remember he had some trouble getting his life-saving certificate. He wasn't studious either. To sum up Bernie, I'd say he liked crowds, and he liked organizing people."

In Cornfeld's own recollections of youth and childhood, he sees himself as a dominant, organizing personality. In 1970, he told James Fox, a colleague of ours, "I was always the neighborhood leader. I was the leader of my neighborhood club, then I became leader of my boy scout troop. . . . You know, a lot of these things are elected kind of roles. Kids choose their leaders, and I was chosen as their leader. Every now and then you had to make your point in a fist fight. . . . But in almost every situation, there is a kind of group protectiveness. You always operate in groups, and in any group there are some big guys and some little guys."

There is an anecdote, from scouting days, of Cornfeld the organizer, aged fourteen or fifteen. Each summer the scoutmasters and scouts used to choose the scout who had most notably "given cheerful service" during the period of the camp. This award was regarded as a considerable honor. One year, Cornfeld decided to win it and began to organize support. He had not understood that an award given to recognize uncalculating generosity becomes pointless if people calculate to win it.

This youthful maneuver is said to have failed because the canvassing became too blatant. (Cornfeld did acquire an authentic distinction in his scouting career: in October 1944 he became an eagle scout, having reached a suitable level in map-making, knot-tying, and tests of initiative.)

Brooklyn College, where Bernie went after Abraham Lincoln High School, was naturally important in the formation of his early political attitudes. But even before that, he came under the influence of the Three Arrows Camp.

This had its origins in the Jewish community of Parkchester, in the Bronx. Its members were wealthier people than the Cornfelds of Brooklyn. They were successful doctors, lawyers, and businessmen, with a sprinkling of teachers and social workers. During the 1930s, the Jewish people of Parkchester lived in an atmosphere of continuous political debate. The aftermath of the Depression, and the rise of anti-Semitism in Europe combined to engender a powerful left-wing mood.

Just before the outbreak of the war, some seventy-five families from Parkchester got together and bought some cheap land in the north of New York State, where they established the Camp of the Three Arrows to combine holiday making with a practical experience in communal socialism. The tradition was for the men to take strenuous walks, to fell trees, and to till the soil, while the women sunbathed and prepared meals over open fires. The evenings, naturally, were devoted to animated and wide-ranging political debate.

The Three Arrows became one of the more important social centers of American left-wing politics. Norman Thomas was a frequent guest. Naturally, the relatively well-to-do people who founded the Three Arrows were determined that its benefits should be available to all, and so a tradition was rapidly established in which members of the Young People's Socialist League (who were known as "Yipsels") were invited to the camp from all parts of New York. Cornfeld enjoyed at least one such holiday in the late 1940s, sleeping on the floor of a barn.

The aspirations expressed at the Three Arrows were more vehemently expressed at Brooklyn College, where Cornfeld arrived in 1948 after serving two years as an assistant purser in the merchant marine. (He made several trips in tankers down to the Maracaibo oil fields in Venezuela. From this experience would seem to date Cornfeld's interest in foreign currency and his seminal observation that "no matter what it looks like, it's all money.") Brooklyn College was then in a state of fierce political ferment. The students were united in a desire to avoid the classroom at all costs. Julius Jacobson, who was a student at that time, says, "We were all engaged in one basic course. We wanted to major in cafeteria."

Majoring in cafeteria—where one table carried the slogan, "Peasants' and Workers' Soviet of Brooklyn College"—meant strenuous mental exercise. It was a matter of hours of merciless political debate, of producing leaflets, setting up meetings, writing tracts. As one veteran of the period put it, "All you needed in those days was a nut and a mimeograph machine, and you were in business as a party on the American left."

Cornfeld's time at Brooklyn straddled the presidential year of 1948, which sharply intensified the political ferment. To the Brooklyn radicals, naturally, the Democrat Harry S Truman was only slightly, if at all, less contemptible than the Republican Thomas E. Dewey. But there was little agreement on which tactics would most suitably expose the hollowness of Establishment pretensions. The Communists on campus came out without hesitation for Henry A. Wallace of the Progressive Party. But for most other people, Wallace's approval of Stalinist Russia was too much. The American Socialist Party decided to try to draft Norman Thomas, and the enterprise is now remembered with affection as one of the great lost causes of the Left.

Cornfeld had arrived on campus as a member of the Yipsels, which decided his loyalties, and he threw himself enthusiastically into the task of organizing for the Thomas campaign. It appears that Cornfeld and a young man named Shim Levy were the effective leaders of the Brooklyn College socialists.

Already the nucleus of the IOS high command was beginning to assemble. Two prominent members of the group that Cornfeld and Shim Levy led were Richard Gangel and Eli Wallitt, both of whom became IOS sales chieftains of the first rank. These young people had a political mentor a few years older than themselves. In 1970, he remembered them with some clarity. "The first time I met them half a dozen of them came to the house where I was living in a basement apartment, and we had a huge discussion about Thomas as opposed to the capitalist candidates. The leader of the group was a guy called Shim Levy. The only time I came across him later he was selling mutual funds, oddly enough, but for some outfit that was nothing to do with Cornfeld, as far as I knew.

"Anyway, these young kids were clawing and searching for some kind of role for their idealism in a confusing world. They were just young enough that I felt I could help them, being a little bit detached from their problems and so on. What I am coming to is that Cornfeld struck me—and I saw quite a lot of him for about a year—as one of the most egocentric people I had ever met and I found him very irritating. It was inconceivable for him ever to admit that he was wrong about anything.

"He was always bringing girls around, to show them off I felt. They were the sort of girls you would expect, highly intellectual Jewish girls, not fashionably dressed, some rather nice. But you felt he just wanted to show them off."

The prime aim of the Norman Thomas campaign was to obtain enough voters' signatures to have their man placed on the ballot for President. Brooklyn produced more signatures for Thomas than any other part of the United States. But not all campus radicals accepted the aims of the Thomas campaign. The Trotskyite Socialist Youth League (SYL), in particular, was bitterly anti-Thomas. In the infighting that ensued, Cornfeld showed few inhibitions. He went to the Faculty Committee on Student Affairs, and tried to have the Socialist Youth League bounced off the campus. The charges were damaging ones: that the SYL's founder, Julius Jacobson, an ex-GI, was not a genuine student, but a specially imported agitator, and that the SYL was a revolutionary group aimed at overthrowing society.

An afternoon was set aside to hear the case. Cornfeld made a speech in which he damned the SYL as subversives. Jacobson followed with an eloquent address on intellectual liberty—and pointed out shrewdly that the Debs Society which formed the basis of SYL had been on campus long before Cornfeld and the Yipsels showed up. The committee threw the charge out.

It seems fair to ascribe Cornfeld's denunciation of the SYL to tactical necessity rather than any profound ideological principle. For when the Thomas band wagon limped to a halt a few months later, Cornfeld and most of the Yipsels joined up with the SYL, and remained dedicated members for something like a year. "Yes," says Jacobson, "it is true. At one point in his life, Bernie really was a socialist revolutionary."

Bernard Cornfeld, like most of his contemporaries, was casting about intellectually and emotionally—"looking for something," in the usual formulation. As he appears in the recollection of his contemporaries, it seems that he was not looking for political belief as such, but for some means of making an impact in the world.

• • •

Cornfeld started at Brooklyn College under a considerable disadvantage. He had a stammer that was bad enough for him to ask teachers not to put questions to him in public. This speech impediment, and the successful treatment which he received for it, may well have affected the whole course of Cornfeld's life.

By the time he came back from the sea in 1947, his stammer was proving enough of a liability to make him seek treatment. He consulted a lay therapist, named Willard Beecher, and told him that he wanted to cure his stammer in order to become a salesman like his elder half-brother, Eugene. He had made an interesting choice. For Beecher and his wife, Marguerite, were followers of Freud's great rival Alfred Adler, whose theories of "Individual Psychology" were undergoing something of a renaissance at that time. Adler's disciples often seem to be able to read as many meanings as they care to into his writings. But virtually all of them follow the master in being particularly interested in stammering, and Willard Beecher was no exception. The treatment he offered for stammering was a quintessentially Adlerian blend of elaborate theorizing and blunt common sense.

Beecher declares that stammering is a "plea for mercy." He

then divides stammering into two basic groups: there are those who open their mouths and their eyes, and then splutter incoherently, and there are those who silently purse their lips. He placed Cornfeld in the group of mouth-pursers, who are supposed to be demanding "exemption." In Beecher's words, "they want time to think while the other guys open their mouths and make idiots of themselves." It is also part of his theory that the pursed "rosebud" mouth is a signal meaning "kiss me" or "admire me."

At a practical level, Beecher told Cornfeld that he must cease asking his teachers to exempt him from questions. On the contrary, he must seek out every opportunity for public speech and performance. Cornfeld acted upon this advice, and, within a very few months, his stammer came under control and virtually disappeared. The experience was the starting point in Cornfeld's love affair with applied psychology.

The relationship with Willard Beecher swiftly widened. Cornfeld persuaded Beecher to give a lecture to the Brooklyn College Psychology Club early in 1948, taking some pride in presenting Beecher to fellow students as "my psychologist." Within a few weeks, a custom was firmly established in which Cornfeld and a dozen or so friends would go for long evening sessions to Willard and Marguerite Beechers'. They became an informal study circle, endlessly discussing Adlerian theories of human motivations, and anatomizing their own personalities and actions. Richard Gangel was an early participant. Eli Wallitt, for some reason, long resisted joining the group, but joined up eventually. Off and on, the weekly Adlerian sessions at the Beechers' continued for more than a decade.

Attempts by non-Adlerians to analyze the master's views are apt to incur the wrath of the faithful. But to a layman it sometimes appears that Adlerianism is as much as anything a style of language: there is much talk of "goals" and "strivings," of "positive outcomes," "negative outcomes," and "interpersonal factors." Nevertheless, some general propositions can be picked out.

Adler rejected the Freudian notion that human personality is assembled from the id, ego, and superego. He claimed that the personality is unitary, that is, individual in the sense of "undividable." He also rejected the Freudian idea of motivation by irrational "drives," libidinous or other. Human motivation, for Adler, was a process of "goal-seeking," and the most important goal for which people strive is "superiority." Adler does not make the nature of this "superiority" very plain: it could mean some kind of ethical nobility, but more frequently it seems to be little more than success, wealth, or dominion.

Adlerians believe that people who have suffered from "organ inferiority," such as a stammer, are apt to "overcompensate" by striving especially hard to achieve superiority. In the Adlerian world, you might expect an ex-stammerer to become a great orator.

The striving for superiority is supposed to be moderated by another principle, which Adler called *Gemeinschaftsgefühl*, best translated as "social interest." By this he meant some kind of general desire on the part of the striving individual to order his actions for the benefit of the community. It was, by all accounts, extremely strong in Adler himself, who was a kindly doctor and a hard-working teacher. But it might well be absent in a person whose training had been unsuitable—in which case "negative actions" might be expected.

Whatever may be said about the clinical or moral validity of the Adlerian system, it obviously made an important impact on Cornfeld. It had helped him to overcome his most important personal disability. Now, the Beecher study group provided a framework for the real interest of his life, which, consciously or otherwise, had been developing for some years. This was the engineering of emotional relationships.

From his high-school days, for example, to the admiration of his friends, Bernie always pursued the most desirable and inaccessible of girls. Eventually he captured the affection of one particular, extremely pretty, girl. Having done so, however, Bernie became capricious.

"She would be left waiting on her doorstep for hours when Bernie didn't show up," recalls a contemporary. "He broke dates without telling her, and then wouldn't call to her house for weeks. Then, out of the blue, he would arrive one night and get terribly upset that she was out with someone else."

There were to be many, many, other instances of the same phenomenon. No one who ever came into his orbit ever quite knew how Bernie would receive them. You might be weighted down with charm and hospitality; or screamed at in merciless tirades; or put down, in such ways as being made to wait for six hours. "He is certainly lovable when he wants to be," says his cousin Hubert Cornfield, "and incredible when he doesn't."

Willard Beecher—who was himself rather fascinated by the young acolyte he had acquired—described Cornfeld tolerantly, but bluntly, as "a manipulator."

Cornfeld graduated in 1950 with a BA in psychology, but without any clear purpose as to where to deploy his growing ability to command and control. One might take him for the material of which politicians are made: but, for all the radical coloration he had absorbed from his background, there is no evidence that he possessed even that spark of obsession with political ideas which is usually to be found in the most mechanical of party professionals. He did toy briefly with a vision of himself in the slightly similar role of a union leader.

After graduating from Brooklyn, Cornfeld made several more trips as a purser, chiefly on the European run. It is hard to believe that Cornfeld saw himself spending a lifetime as an ocean-going bookkeeper. But the idea of organizing his fellow pursers into a union was more in his line, and he got as far as obtaining an introduction to Paul Hall, boss of the Maritime Union, and discussing tactics.

Cornfeld's union of pursers was never organized. He was, however, right to think that he was cut out for some considerable career. Inheritance had provided him with an actor's ear and sensitivity to mood. His upbringing had accustomed him to predominance. One might wish to be skeptical about some of Alfred Adler's claims, but his thesis of organ inferiority and compensation does seem suggestive in the case of his student Bernard Cornfeld.

Cornfeld's education and environment had provided him with the jargon, and some of the mechanism, of psychological analysis, and with the exciting rhetoric of equality and social reform. His capacity to use such tools had been refined by vigorous experiences in dialectic and maneuver. Many years later, John M. King—himself no mean persuader—called Cornfeld the world's greatest "conceptual salesman." He meant, presumably, one who sells ideas, or "concepts," rather than things. Cornfeld's early years did much to equip him for the role.

And at least one "goal" was beginning to come into focus even before the end of Cornfeld's Brooklyn period. Bill Kolins studied English literature at Brooklyn at the time that Cornfeld studied psychology, and they shared some classes. "Bernie's ambition," he says, "was always to make a very great deal of money." Kolins is quite sure of this, because it was a most unusual ambition for a Brooklyn student to have—or at least to admit to—in those days.

Cornfeld would not have to wait long for an opportunity to match his talents to his ambitions. Financial revolution was brewing, and he was an early recruit to the cadres.

The Financial Revolutionaries

The rise of the mutual-fund idea, and Bernard Cornfeld's early days as social worker and fund salesman. In which a young lawyer named Edward Cowett also learns about mutual funds.

Walter and Ruth Benedick were active members of the Three Arrows community. Walter Benedick arrived in America in 1932 from a tiny town in southern Germany, and worked for the First Investors Corporation throughout the Depression.

Toward the end of 1952, Benedick was approached by a member of the New York Stock Exchange named John Kalk with the suggestion that they might start a mutual-fund business together. In June of the following year, they established the Investors Planning Corporation with a capital of $320,000. "I feel sick whenever I think about the shoestring we started on," says Benedick in recollection. And, indeed, the organization was to experience an awkward infancy. But IPC could not easily have been a total failure, for it had behind it the power of an idea whose time had very definitely come.

Over the next decade and a half, open-end investment companies were to alter the financial landscape even in countries so un-American as not to call them mutual funds. But at first the mutual-fund revolution was confined to the United States, and IPC was launched remarkably near to the actual moment of take-off. At the start of 1953, six months before IPC began operations, there were about $4 billion in mutual funds throughout America. Within five years that figure more than trebled, passing $13 billion at the end of 1958—and everything that happened in the 1950s was, it turned out, mere curtain-raising for the 1960s. It was thought remarkable in 1955 when, for the first time, the public put $1 billion into mutual funds in a single year. But in a single year ten years after that, the mutual funds received $5 billion to be channeled into investments. As this was more than twice the value of the new stock which American corporations made available for investment that year, some people became uneasy about the progress of the revolution. The majority of professionals in the investment business, however, merely admired the very large increases in stock-exchange prices.

In the latter years of the 1960s some hard questions were asked about the mutual-fund concept. But at the start of the boom the mood of the business was evangelical. Everybody involved was convinced that the benefits of capitalism were at last being brought to ordinary folk. It had always seemed the most convincing claim against capitalism that the ownership of industrial wealth should be concentrated in the hands of the few. Who could deny that spreading ownership more widely must be a noble as well as a rewarding task? Again, it had always seemed inexcusable that the money of the rich, deployed with skill and security, should multiply rapidly while the small surpluses of the unrich should gather slow increments in savings banks, or dwindle in mattresses. The mechanism of the open-ended fund appears at first glance to abolish these inequities. It was entirely possible in the early 1950s to regard the mutual fund as a promising engine of social justice. It was for this reason that stalwarts of the Three Arrows community, like Walter and Ruth Benedick, found the idea an acceptable and exciting one, and also found that many of their salesmen—and customers—should be drawn from the socialist and liberal connections of the Three Arrows. "If we couldn't sell them a program, we recruited them," said Richard Roberts, an early IPC salesman and a veteran of the Yipsels and the Three Arrows. And it also meant that the concept was ideally suited to the talents and interests of Bernard Cornfeld.

Every Sunday, IPC placed a "Help Wanted" advertisement in *The New York Times*, and this usually brought sixty or more aspirant salesmen around to the office on Monday morning. Benedick would pack them into a lecture room and give them an introductory dissertation on mutual funds that carried an invitation to come back for a two-week training course. Usually, something like half of them would return for the course—and soon the intake began to speed up. Nine months after starting operations IPC had a sales force of nearly 1500 people, with Walter looking after the recruitment and training and Ruth handling the administration.

One of the first stars of the sales force was Gabriel ("Gabe") Gladstone, who was equally celebrated for the volume of his sales and the flamboyance of his character. "Gabe was a real scatterbrain," said Walter Benedick. Richard Roberts recalled that Gabe used to visit a psychiatrist—which seemed very impressive to young men like Roberts in the 1950s. Toward the end of 1953, Gladstone introduced a friend of his from Brooklyn College and Three Arrow days, a quiet-spoken young man named Bernard Cornfeld. The Benedicks had not met him before, although Walter seemed to remember the name as having belonged to someone in a group from the Socialist League for Industrial Democracy which spent time at the camp. Benedick agreed to see Gabe's recruit in a private session rather than the regular Monday lecture.

"Bernie had never had anything to do with mutual funds before," recalls Benedick. "He seemed reluctant to have anything to do with the company at first. But he went to a course in the company and my impression is that he was a very good student. He was handicapped because he didn't have any money. . . . On one occasion, he asked me to lend him $80. I still have the receipt. He paid me back—he was the sort of boy you could trust."

• • •

The idea to which Benedick introduced Cornfeld was older than most mutual-fund salesmen of the time realized. The device of forming a company whose business would consist in collecting money from the public and investing it in other companies— light-bulb companies, steel companies, or what have you—can be traced back to Britain in the late 1860s. The most dexterous early exponent was a Scottish textile executive named Robert Fleming, grandfather of the man who invented James Bond.

Since its inception, the idea has been shuttled back and forth across the Atlantic. Its most consistent attraction has always been the claim that by putting up a relatively small sum, an investor can participate in the advantages of a large, diversified, and professionally managed block of investments. This has usually diverted attention from a number of important subtleties and problems.

The basic investment-company idea has proliferated into a confusing variety of different types, but the vital distinction is that between the *closed-end* type and the *open-end* type.

Examples of both existed in the 1920s, but in those days the closed ends were much the more fashionable. In the more recent boom, the fashion was reversed. The difference owes something to the historical effect of the first boom upon the second, and something to the social changes that took place between the two eras.

It is a question of attitudes to liquidity. The essence of a closed-end investment company is that it operates with a finite quantity of capital: therefore, when you put your money into it you receive in exchange securities not essentially different from those you would get if you put your money directly into a company making light bulbs. Your money has been locked up as part of the capital of the company, and can be turned back into cash only by selling your securities to someone else. It requires, in fact, a considerable degree of financial sophistication: the investor needs to be able to cope with some of the complexities of operating on the stock exchange.

In 1924, the first American investment concern was started that did not use a finite sum of capital raised in a finite operation, but, instead, proposed to create and sell new shares in itself on a continuous basis. This was the Massachusetts Investment Trust, which was able to offer, as a result of its originality, the classic open-end advantage that the company itself would always buy back its own shares from investors, for cash, on demand.

At the time, it did not occur to the people who put their money into closed-end investment companies that they would ever have any difficulty in selling their shares on the stock exchange. Many of them, probably, could not imagine that they would ever *want* to sell—so the idea of a company which "redeemed" its own shares had no particular appeal. Before 1929, people did not anticipate that stock-exchange conditions might be such as to reduce their closed-end shares to unsalable pieces of paper. Such horrors as the decline of the Goldman, Sachs Trading Corporation lay in the future.

The securities of this classic closed-end investment corporation were first sold on the New York Stock Exchange at $104 per share, which was reduced by the crash to $1¼ per share. "After 1929," a subsequent report of the Securities and Exchange Commission* noted drily, "closed ends lost much of their former favor with investors."

Falls like that of the Goldman, Sachs Trading Corporation were not isolated events, and by the end of 1929, "professional expertise" was thoroughly discredited. Stock-exchange prices which had been allowed to climb far too high now fell, as a consequence, much too far. At the end of the year, the total salable value on the stock exchange of *all* shares in closed-end investment companies was 35 per cent below the actual value of the assets that the companies owned. Therefore, anyone who had to sell would lose more than a third of the value of the investments made with his money.

• • •

There are without doubt more pure intellectuals in finance than in any other occupation—if it is fair to call an intellectual one who conceives of large, abstract principles and whose delight is then to observe the working out of those principles in actual experiments. Nothing has excited the attention of financial intellectuals more consistently than the principle of leverage. Variations upon the theme of leverage, and associated mechanisms for putting other people's money to work on one's own behalf, run through the whole of our story.

Nonexpert heads are inclined to swim when considering the applications of leverage, but the process can be grasped by any-

---

*"Public Policy Implications of Investment Company Growth," December 2, 1966, p. 43.

one who understands the operations of A. J. Liebling's Telephone Booth Indians. According to Liebling, a destitute Telephone Booth Indian could always restore his situation with the aid of a telephone, a phone book, and a list of horses in tomorrow's race. The Indian would telephone a number, say Joe Brown's, at random. The Indian, before Mr. Brown can speak, thanks "good old Joe" effusively for the great favor Joe did him last time they met. It was so great a favor that he is calling now to pass on a hot tip. . . . The Indian gives the name of the first horse on tomorrow's list; it is, he says, a certainty. No thanks are required, but if Joe does want to do anything—well, just put on five bucks extra and send the winnings to the following address. The Indian rings off, leaving a puzzled but hopefully acquisitive citizen at the other end.

He then goes through the whole field in the same way, and having done so starts again. He may tip each horse to five, even ten "old friends." Some of them will assume that it is the *Indian* who is making a mistake, and will follow up tips with bets. A diligent Indian should thus be able to get enough money—none of it his own—working to cover the whole field. In that case, one "investor" at least must win, and will thus be delighted with his good fortune. He will then send the winnings or five dollars to the address given by the Indian: not out of gratitude, but on the theory that this will make another such "error" more likely, with profitable results to himself.

Neither the crusty and respectable firms of Wall Street and the City of London, nor IOS itself, would ever behave in so gross a manner as the Telephone Booth Indians. But all investment concerns, in greater or lesser degree, rely upon a similar basic idea: getting other people to do something with their money that, hopefully, will benefit them—and if it does, and there are enough of them, will benefit you even more.

What the smarter citizens realized in the 1920s was the potential for leverage arising out of the fact that most companies have two classes of capital. One class—fixed-interest securities, such as bonds or debentures—assures the investor of a fixed return on his money. The other class—equity capital—offers him a share of what profit is left over after fixed interest has been paid. In hard times, there can be little or nothing left over for the equity owners, while the holders of fixed-interest securities continue to get their returns. But in good times, the venturesome equity investors do very much better.

The ratio between a company's fixed-interest and equity capital can be adjusted as finely as the gearbox on a Maserati. The higher the proportion of fixed-interest capital, the more dramatically the profits accumulate for each equity share. The ratios used by the closed-end investment companies of the 1920s were high in themselves. But a refinement was introduced which multiplied even more dramatically the concentration of the underlying profits for the benefits of a knowing minority of the investors.

This was the idea of superimposing company upon company in a pyramid of tiers or layers, with a tiny proportion of equity creaming off the richest share of the profits at each tier. The classic example is the Goldman, Sachs Trading Corporation. This was an investment company. It controlled the Shenandoah Investment Corporation, which in turn controlled the Blue Ridge Corporation. Both Shenandoah and Blue Ridge were "highly geared," with ratios between fixed-interest and equity capital of around 20:1. Shenandoah owned almost all the equity of Blue Ridge; and Goldman, Sachs owned 40 per cent of the equity of Shenandoah. The effect of this double process of concentration was magical from the point of view of Goldman, Sachs. If the market went up by 50 per cent, it had the effect of making

Goldman, Sachs's original stake go up by no less than 1220 per cent.

This daring structure had only just been finished when the boom broke. No one, therefore, could find out how long it would have been possible to go on persuading large numbers of people to go on investing money for small returns so that a few people could invest small sums for large returns. What was discovered, as John Kenneth Galbraith put it in *The Great Crash*, was that the magic of leverage "was equally dramatic in reverse."

When the crash stripped the closed-end investment companies of their liquidity, the advantages of the open-end mutual-fund idea came sharply into focus. Even during the Depression, the mutual funds found it possible to attract some new investors, while the closed-end companies lost popularity.

In 1944, the total of assets in mutual funds became, for the first time, larger than those in closed end—and the mutual-fund business was poised to take advantage of the surge in American industrial earnings over the next years. And there was something besides the folk memory of 1929 to focus attention upon their virtues. During the 1950s, the disposable incomes of Americans rose by 40 per cent and this increase was sufficient to create investable surpluses among whole new classes of people. A portrait of the new investor was drawn a little later by the Securities Research Unit of the Wharton School of Finance at the University of Pennsylvania:

He is a man in his middle to late forties who is married and has about three dependents. His formal education probably stopped after highschool graduation; but there is a fair chance that he has done a small amount of college work. Moreover, he is employed most likely in a capacity involving specialized skills—but somewhat short of professional training. His annual income falls in the $5000 to $10,000 range.*

Such people wanted to put their money to use, but they could not handle or afford stock-market transactions. They therefore required the simple liquidity of mutual funds.

With history reinforcing its natural advantages over its main rival, the mutual-fund concept made astonishing inroads upon the new wealth of the postwar world. Its general impact is expressed in the growth figures quoted earlier in this chapter. The impact upon Bernard Cornfeld was also considerable, and best expressed in a delighted *aperçu* which is ascribed to his early days as a fund salesman. "If you want to make money, don't horse around with steel and light bulbs. Work directly with money." To young men like Gladstone and Cornfeld, it seemed that a field of boundless opportunity was opening up before them.

And so it was. But the open-end mechanism, though capable of collecting enormous amounts of money, has uniquely treacherous potentialities. A clue to their nature was given by a mutual-fund executive, Richard Cutler of the Putnam Management Corporation, in *Barrons* magazine on January 10, 1966. He said, "The inexorable law of this business is that when assets rise, redemptions rise proportionately, so the more you succeed, the harder you have to sell, just to keep your place on the treadmill."

It is a little-known paradox that when mutual-fund organizations are biggest, it may be hardest to extract honest profits from them, and "Cutler's Law" is part of the reason for this. The

---

*Report of the Special Study of Securities Markets, Securities and Exchange Commission, 1964, part 4, p. 273.

problem derives, naturally, from the intrinsic liquidity of the fund. When the value of investments rises, there is, to some extent, a desire for customers to benefit from their good fortune by asking the fund to "redeem" (buy back) their shares, now of increased value. Although "Cutler's Law" may not be entirely inexorable, it is clear that profit taking—which cannot so directly affect a closed-end company—can diminish the size of an open-end fund and undermine its capital strength. And the people who organize a mutual fund take their fees according to the size of the fund.

This problem had been taken into account in the grand ancestor of all modern open-end investment companies, the Foreign and Colonial Government Trust, formed in London in 1868 with notables like Lord Eustace Cecil in charge. The trust had a degree of "openness," in that it undertook to redeem all of its own shares, but the problem of overspeedy liquidation was prevented by holding a drawing each year to decide which shares should be bought back. This system was eventually prohibited, on the grounds that it was a lottery—although whether it was any more chancy than some of the supposedly open-ended devices which succeeded it a century later is open to question.

Lacking recourse to Lord Eustace's sporting expedient, modern mutual funds must simply sell harder and harder to maintain their size. There is only one sure way to sell more, and that is to pay more to the salesmen. And in order to pay the salesmen more, it is necessary to take more money off the customers.

It is because of the need to sustain large and active forces of salesmen that, when a customer spends $1000 to take part in an American mutual fund, no more than $915 is usually invested for him. The remaining 8½ per cent goes in charges. In such a case, the customer cannot get back $1100—his own outlay plus *ten* per cent—until the investments made by the fund have risen by at least the *twenty* per cent which turns $915 into $1100.

There are many arguments about the fairness of such arrangements, and about the extent to which the ordinary customer understands them. For the moment, it is enough to say that while none of these proves that the mutual-fund concept is unworkable, it does prove that it requires constant regulation and examination.

• • •

Young Cornfeld hesitated, briefly, before becoming an investment professional. Having made a few sales for the Investors Planning Corporation, he left New York for Philadelphia around the end of 1953, and he worked there for nine months for the B'nai B'rith cultural and philanthropic organization before returning to IPC as a salesman. This was his period as a social worker, and the evidence does not make it clear whether he distinguished himself or not.

What is clear is that his work had nothing to do with the usual impression that the words "social worker" convey, especially in Europe: that is, of a public employee of some sort, spending most of his or her time caring for aged tramps or abandoned families. What Cornfeld was entering was a profession of service to the middle class less glamorous than the law, but conferring reasonable status. Seymour Cohen, who was then his boss and is now head of B'nai B'rith, says, "Bernie worked with us as a group counselor among middle-class children." Cornfeld's job was to lead a program of religious, social, cultural, athletic, and philanthropic activities. Another thing which is clear is that Cornfeld was already feeling the fascination with mutual funds which was moving bright young men all over America. Sol Kaslow, who was then a lay officer in B'nai B'rith, recalls, "I had just moved from an insurance business into a brokerage office when Bernie arrived. He asked a lot of questions about mutual funds, about how they should be presented, how the investments worked, and so on."

Cornfeld had acquired considerable qualifications before he arrived in Philadelphia. After his brief return to seafaring, he had decided to push ahead with his psychological studies and, in February 1952, he had signed up at the Columbia University School of Social Work to take a master's degree in a new field which was then called "group study." This was a natural development of his completed, formal studies at Brooklyn, and of his continuing informal studies with the Adlerian circle he had brought together around the Beechers.

The essential feature of the group-study system is the communal analytic session in which the psychiatrist goes into a room with several patients at the same time and prods them into expounding their own, and each other's, problems, motivations, weaknesses, shortcomings, and the like. The Columbia group-study students did some practical work with groups of patients at the Yale Psychiatric Institute, where Cornfeld acquired a reputation for great sensitivity, and for interest in his patients. While working at the Yale Institute, he used to bring patients and fellow students back to Brooklyn on occasion and introduce them to the Beechers. "He thought it was his duty to bring us as much business as possible," recalls Willard Beecher, who was a little startled by the gesture.

Cornfeld cut a considerable figure as a postgraduate student, driving around town in a yellow Chevrolet, with a much-prized Siamese cat perched on his shoulder. Ever since his youth, when his early operations as a lollipop seller at Coney Island developed into a part interest in a guess-your-weight stand, Bernie's friends had been impressed by his ability to get cash together.

The first car, however, seems to have been a product of his discovery of the credit system. Hubert Cornfield remembers Bernie bursting in with the news that he had just bought a car by an ideal system which required no capital outlay. "For some reason," said Hubert, "he just would never put oil in that car. Sometimes he just could not get round to doing the smallest material things." However, the yellow Chevvy did get as far as Philadelphia, where it was eventually abandoned in a snowdrift.

With the Chevrolet and subsequent cars, Cornfeld habitually acquired extraordinary numbers of parking tickets. In Philadelphia he carried a cigar box crammed with tickets. Seymour Blau, a B'nai B'rith executive, used to puzzle over Cornfeld's attitude. "I couldn't see who he was fighting."

Cornfeld was not elegant in those days. "Today, you'd probably call Bernie a hippie," says Steve Adelman, who knew him then. "To us he was a Bohemian. I can see him now—always in a red-checked shirt and a black suit. He had some kind of black string tie hanging around his neck, but he never did it up properly." And the first function he organized, the Purim Festival in March 1954, was quite a break with the staid existence of the B'nai B'rith in Philadelphia. "In past years," says Seymour Cohen, "the carnival had been modestly organized—dancing, that sort of thing. Well I asked Bernie to look after it that year. It was the biggest thing that ever happened at Purim. At the end of the festival we had several thousand dollars collected, instead of a few hundred. When I saw the amount, I called Bernie in and said, 'Hey, Bernie, you've got something there. You can really turn a dollar.'"

Perhaps Seymour Cohen was the man who really started Bernard Cornfeld off on the road to Geneva. In any case, Cohen declares stoutly that Cornfeld was a "great social worker . . . because of his ability to relate to people." Others seem less sure.

Dr. Florence Kaslow, now an assistant professor of social work at Pennsylvania, says Cornfeld had a "creative spark" and "operated with youth groups in a way which was out of the traditional realm," but rates him "just fair" as a social worker.

Cornfeld's salary was only about $400 a month, but at this time his interest in money seems to have been an intellectual fascination rather than a desire for consumption. Steve Adelman says, "He didn't buy clothes. Food, he didn't buy. A snack to Bernie was a meal. He didn't smoke. There was always a bottle of whisky or wine in his flat, but it wasn't for himself. The only expense he had was gas."

Whatever the problem—some people suggest that the B'nai B'rith matrons thought the AZA Sweethearts' Dance rather too swinging in Bernie's year—something brought the appointment to an end rather prematurely. Seymour Cohen says he cannot recall how Cornfeld came to leave B'nai B'rith. Edward B. Schifreen says, "Bernie wasn't fired. We made some arrangement." There was, naturally, a collection before Bernie took off for New York. Suitably enough, they presented him with a wallet.

• • •

Cornfeld returned as a serious recruit to the IPC sales force, at a time when sales of mutual-fund shares were about to touch the billion-dollar-a-year mark. By this time, at the end of 1954, Walter Benedick had four full-time coaches training salesmen at day and night classes.

Several versions have given the impression that the eighteen months or so Cornfeld spent with IPC were somewhat undistinguished, but this can be misleading. The impression is based on Walter Benedick's remark that Cornfeld did not personally bring in a large volume of shares for IPC, although he made some "nice sales." But his capacity for making sales was never especially important. While at IPC, he began to demonstrate a more valuable capacity for impressing his own personality upon groups of people whose trade in turn consists in impressing their personalities upon others. Bernie, as Richard Roberts recalls, was always the center of events.

"Whenever you rang Bernie and said, 'Hey, what's doing?'— there was *always* something doing. He was trying to make some time with an actress, he was driving up to Montreal for the weekend, he was dating some girl from Manhattan. It was just like when he had IOS: if you wanted some action, you rang Bernie."

It was impressive; when other IPC salesmen were riding subways, Bernie always had a car. "He used to keep it parked outside his house in Brooklyn. The keys were kept under the mat in the front seat. Anybody could use it. If you asked Bernie for it, so you could take out a date, Bernie would say, 'You don't have to ask me. It's yours. Take it, take it.'"

Cornfeld's prominence is the more remarkable in that it quite transcended the formal hierarchy which the Benedicks had worked out with some care. There were four grades in the IPC sales force. Each recruit started as a Basic Salesman, rose to Advanced Salesman, then Senior Salesman, and then Career Senior. With each promotion, which depended upon the volume of sales made, the salesman received a larger share of the sales charge extracted from the customer. Above these four ranks were three more: Supervisor, Group Manager, and Branch Manager.

In order to break into these upper levels, it was necessary to recruit other salesmen, and promotion depended partly upon further recruitment, partly upon volume of sales made by the Supervisor or Manager and his team.

Gladstone had reached the level of Supervisor, and one of the recruits who enabled him to do so was Bernard Cornfeld. But, within a fairly short time, Gladstone found himself in the intolerable position of having a mere Basic Salesman as a rival for the informal dominance of his group. It was very shortly after having recruited Cornfeld that Gladstone came storming into Benedick's office with a demand. "I'm the greatest group salesman you've got," declared Gladstone, "and I'm asking you to get that Cornfeld out of my group." It was probably a mistake on Gladstone's part to see Bernie as a rival; almost certainly, Cornfeld's ambitions already went beyond competing for a position as a supervising salesman in the IPC sales force. But the Benedicks, somewhat alarmed by the outburst, agreed and moved Cornfeld into another group.

What impressed Cornfeld's colleagues was his life-style more than his sales. His most remarkable achievement, perhaps, was the apartment known jocularly, but incorrectly, as "Bernie's Whorehouse"—which was also a considerable piece of financing, as far as it went. One day, he saw advertised in *The New York Times* a huge apartment in the West Sixties. It had ten rooms, a triplex living room of cathedral proportions, a room with an organ whose pipes ran up all three floors, and other splendors.

"Bernie," said Richard Roberts, "you must be mad. You can't live there." But Cornfeld took the apartment, canvassed eight friends, and formed a syndicate to cover the rent: the result must have been the Ultimate Pad of the 1950s. The rooms were hung with tapestries, and in a corner of the master bedroom stood an object of the most *outré* fashion, an orgone box, crackling and flashing with electrical energy. It would appear that Cornfeld, the follower of Adler, had some consideration for the rival guru Wilhelm Reich, and his amazing theories about the relationships among "orgone energy," orgasm, and electricity. Of such feats is personal charisma made.

• • •

At the precise mid-point of the 1950s, financial charisma was accumulating at great speed around the person of a forty-year-old member of the New York Stock Exchange named Jack J. Dreyfus, Jr., who had bought a mediocre, open-end concern named the Nesbett Fund and relabeled it with his own name. On January 1, 1955, there was $2.3 million in the Dreyfus Fund. By December 31, that sum had risen by 143 per cent to $5.6 million, and the fund was firmly established in its explosive pattern of doubling, or more than doubling, roughly every year over the next half-dozen years.

Nearly all of the daring, eventually frantic, "go-go" funds which proliferated over the next few years represented some kind of attempt to emulate the brilliant assault that carried the Dreyfus Fund from obscurity to eminence within a decade. And Dreyfus was also, quite clearly, the exemplar of the "offshore" funds, and of the IOS funds in particular.

To people making their own discovery of mutual funds, there was a magic aura around Dreyfus. Especially the legend attached to his famous hunch about the Polaroid camera, and to the fund's purchase, at 31⅞ each, of 400 Polaroid shares which were not even listed at that time on the New York Stock Exchange, but which eventually rose to a value of $6372 apiece. Hopes of encountering his own Polaroid glowed somewhere in the bosom of every money manager in New York, Geneva, or San Francisco who purchased an unregistered curiosity during the ten years after Dreyfus's coup. But the Polaroid legend misrepresented what Dreyfus was about.

Dreyfus capitalized on two propositions. One was that there

was a new class of people available to become investors, willing to respond to the Dreyfus Lion in the television commercials for the fund, and to the efforts of newly raised armies of salesmen using a prospectus in which Dreyfus made a serious effort to translate financial terms into language that ordinary people could understand. And Jack Dreyfus's other proposition was that such people, exactly like wealthier investors, were eager to make money with their money.

Previously, the managers of mutual funds had tended to assume that it was their job to employ the clients' money to buy a mixture of good-class shares and bonds, and leave it there regardless of peaks and troughs in the graph of stock-exchange prices. Dreyfus and his colleagues took the view that the investors wanted a mutual-fund manager to be constantly looking for new growth shares, and to move their money into them.

It was inevitable that a well-managed fund, growing rapidly in a period of generally rising stock-exchange prices, would acquire some meteoric stocks. But it was an optical illusion, indeed a kind of wish fulfillment, that caused the spectators to imagine that it was the acquisition of meteoric stocks that caused the rise of the fund rather than the other way round. The illusion, on the subsequent record, seems to have been imparted especially powerfully to two young men who sat, so to speak, at Jack Dreyfus's feet during those vibrant years in New York.

One was Bernard Cornfeld, who was growing rapidly dissatisfied with his role as a Basic Salesman at Investors Planning Corporation. And the other was Edward Morton Cowett, a distinguished graduate of the Harvard Law School, employed in the Wall Street law firm of Stroock & Stroock & Lavan, counsel to the Dreyfus Fund. From the moment that he joined Stroock & Stroock, it was notorious that Ed Cowett had little time to spare for more routine tasks of the law. He was always around the Dreyfus office, trying to learn about mutual funds from Jack Dreyfus.

In physique and in manner, there has never been much in common between the creator and the assistant creator of IOS. Cowett, with his slim build, black hair slicked-down, dark-rimmed spectacles, and sharp, precise lawyer's manner, is the antithesis of Cornfeld, with his soft, slow voice, his tendency to plumpness, his slightly unkempt hair. Even today, when Cowett wears a Pierre Cardin suit, it is likely to be cut along much the same lines as any other business suit.

Cowett was born on April 10, 1930, in Springfield, Massachusetts, where his father had a law practice. Edward was sent to Deerfield Academy, and then to Harvard. Having completed his undergraduate degree, Cowett hesitated for some time about postgraduate studies. He could not decide until enrollment day whether he was more attracted by the Harvard Business School or the Harvard Law School; but he was never in much doubt, it seems, that he would eventually turn his legal training to business use. "Ed was brilliant academically," recalls Lewis Kaplan, who was a couple of years behind him. "He has a very challenging personality, and he didn't accept the orthodox answers." Cowett graduated from the Law School within the top forty students, a ranking which made him automatically a member of the American elite. His educational record and his upbringing were incomparably more advantageous than Cornfeld's: he could have taken his pick of politics, law, the State Department, or business. It would have seemed most obvious for him to follow the path of his brilliant elder brother, Wilbur, already a partner in the investment banking firm Wertheim & Co.

However, Cowett wanted to marry a fellow student who was one year behind him in Law School, and so he needed to stay around Harvard for a year. Fortunately, a suitable opportunity arose: an eminent Harvard professor, Louis Loss, was preparing the definitive work on Blue Sky Law, the picturesquely named body of regulations which are supposed to prevent American investors being deceived by unscrupulous company promoters. (The name is derived from a judge's remark that a certain security seemed to have "about the same value as a patch of blue sky.") Loss and Cowett's book was addressed to the problem that Blue Sky Laws exhibit many complicated differences in different parts of America, so that activities legal in one state may be illegal in the one next door. So, while Carla Cowett concluded her studies at the Law School, her husband and Professor Loss combed through the security statutes of every state in the union, analyzing the differences between them and drafting a model statute which could unify practice throughout the country. Loss and Cowett's *Blue Sky Law* became the standard textbook on the subject.

With all this behind him, Ed Cowett must have seemed exactly the kind of young man that Stroock & Stroock & Lavan were looking for, but he clearly flourished better in the more freewheeling mutual-fund world. "Jack Dreyfus liked him a lot," said one friend, "and I think there was even some suggestion that Ed might join Dreyfus and become a partner in the stock-brokerage firm, but it didn't come to anything." Indeed, Cowett's direct connection with Dreyfus broke off after a couple of years, when he left Stroock & Stroock. But he was there long enough to negotiate on Dreyfus's behalf with Bernard Cornfeld, who was making considerable impact as a Dreyfus Fund dealer in Paris.

One might have expected the two of them to have run into each other while Cornfeld was selling in New York, but Cornfeld's impatience with IPC had boiled over too soon. By Richard Roberts's account, he was planning an expedition to Paris almost as soon as he started work at IPC, and originally, indeed, a group removal was proposed. "The idea was that we would land in Paris and contact Bernie's half-brother, Albert Cornfield, who was vice president of Twentieth-Century Fox in Europe by then," says Roberts. Cornfeld, Roberts, and a friend booked passage for Paris. "But Bernie missed the boat. He missed it by several months."

It was not until 1955 (while Ed Cowett was still researching at Harvard) that Cornfeld finally did get on the boat. By that time, Roberts and his companion had given up and sailed back to New York.

Bert Cantor's account is that Bernie left New York because, at long last, his backlog of parking tickets was catching up with him,* and he wanted to avoid being caught and fined. This is not so; Cornfeld was caught and fined rather heavily for an impressive log of unpaid tickets. And there is no need to assume any such motivation on his part.

The likeliest thing is that he left New York because he was still looking for the environment which would let his talents flower to their fullest. A short acquaintance with mutual funds seems to have left him in no doubt about the nature of those talents. But New York was a difficult environment, where the competition between rival fund-selling organizations was already intense. It was a highly developed and regulated market, in which the fund organizers and sellers had to contend with each other, and with the skeptical officials of the Securities and Exchange Commission. It was the home of the brave—but no country ruled by the Securities Act (1933) could ever be the land of the free to a man with Bernie's ambitions.

Before he left New York, Cornfeld sought and obtained an

---

*Bert Cantor, *The Bernie Cornfeld Story*.

interview with Jack Dreyfus himself. "At that time, you could walk in off the street and get to see Jack," recalled a Dreyfus executive of that period. "We were still, relatively, a small fund; we were still hungry for dealers." If Cornfeld angled for a dealership at this meeting, he did not do so very hard. He complimented Dreyfus effectively upon the simplicity and excellence of the Dreyfus prospectus, and made enough of an impression for the great man to remember him. In the fall of 1955, with a few hundred dollars in his wallet, Bernard Cornfeld arrived, alone, in Paris.

• 4 •

The First Missionary Journeys

Paris, Geneva—and many other places, from Caracas to Cox's Bazar.
How a sales force was mustered, a technique was refined, and young
men learned how to "put their egos in their pockets." Some observa-
tions on Swiss banks.

One evening in 1958 the door-
bell rang in an apartment in
one of the drab housing areas
attached to the big U.S. Air Force base at Orléans, fifty miles
south of Paris. The sergeant who lived there opened the door to
be confronted by a slim, pleasant young American who proceeded to do a very odd thing.

"Good evening," he said. "My name is Allen Cantor, and I
would like to introduce you"—he made an assured gesture—"to
my colleague, Mr. W. Thad Lovett."

The odd thing about Cantor's introduction was that he was
at that moment quite alone outside the door. The reason for this
was that Mr. W. Thad Lovett, who was by no means a figment
of Cantor's imagination, had gone down to sit in the car again,
shivering with sheer horror at the idea of ringing the doorbells
of perfect strangers and intruding upon them for the purpose of
selling mutual-fund shares.

Thad Lovett was neither designed by nature nor prepared by

upbringing for door-to-door selling, least of all to enlisted men in the U.S. Air Force. He is a shy, plumpish man with exquisite manners and a dry sense of humor, who loves music and lives with nine living cats and innumerable china ones. Having inherited what he calls "an Income," he had knocked about Europe until the age of forty-five without having needed to earn a living. Then the Income came dramatically to an end, in the way Incomes sometimes do, and there was nothing for it, short of going back to America and working in an office, but to sell mutual funds for Bernie Cornfeld.

Allen Cantor's background was very different. His family ran a store in Brooklyn, and after a successful academic career, Allen traveled to Europe and put in a spell as a rare-book dealer: it was not an orthodox background for a mutual-fund salesman. While outwardly very different, they were both representative of the superficially unlikely material from which Bernie Cornfeld recruited the IOS Old Guard.

Within weeks of arriving in Paris, Cornfeld had made an interesting discovery. He had found that there were at least two types of Americans in Europe. One was the serviceman, who had reasonable quantities of money in his pocket, but who more and more frequently was accompanied by a wife and children—which made him increasingly unanxious to blow all his pay on living it up.

And then there was the exile. Today, large herds of gentle, conformist rebels against American culture graze anywhere in Europe they can find grass. In 1955, in Paris, Cornfeld was among the vanguard of the invasion. The exiles he met were on the whole well educated. Many of them had come to Europe as students, on the GI Bill or on Fulbright grants. Theirs was a tolerant society: a mildly Bohemian life-style was expected, and some vague stirring of political radicalism was almost demanded. It was a world of frustrated intellectuals, mild neu-rotics, political nonconformists, and cultural misfits—with the occasional drunk or homosexual. Most American businessmen would have written them off as being hopelessly deficient in ac-quisitive instincts.

It was the inspiration of Bernie Cornfeld, the psychologist and social worker, to see that these exiles could be remotivated and put to work selling mutual funds to the servicemen. His suc-cess in doing this was so enormous that the originality of his per-ception has been forgotten. It is hard to imagine any ordinary mutual-fund sales boss perceiving commercial talent in Thad Lovett, as Mr. Lovett himself admits.

The fact that his recruits were people who had found that their careers were crumbling, or that they had overestimated their talents, did not dismay him, as it might have dismayed some IBM-trained personnel manager. Indeed, it may well have served some deep need of his own: for it carried the promise that his recruits would become devoted followers of the man who could perform an act of liberation for them. In the beginning, In-vestors Overseas Services sometimes seemed more like a thera-peutic community than a money-making device.

Bernard Cornfeld told *Time* magazine in 1962 that he had started IOS with a capital of $300. It sounds like a rags-to-riches beginning, but in fact he began in Europe with most of the things that his new acquaintances were struggling to get: a flat, a girl friend (two, by his own account), a sporty little Simca, a type-writer, and a promising source of income in good, green dollars. In Paris, no less than New York, Bernie was the boy who always knew how to get hold of wheels, a girl, a pad, and a few bucks.

Cornfeld had brought with him to Paris a rather tenuous re-lationship with Investors Planning Corporation, and on the ba-sis of this he started, experimentally, selling a few mutual-fund shares. He wrote off to the Benedicks for supplies of literature and prospectuses, and for a while they kept him supplied. But Cornfeld, now that he had seen the large possibilities of the American expatriate market, decided to become an independent dealer—which would, of course, entitle him to a larger slice of the commission on any sales he could procure. Quite early in 1956, Jack Dreyfus in New York received a letter which reminded him of the young man who had dropped in and complimented him upon the readability of the Dreyfus prospectus. Cornfeld wrote that he had been expecting to sell for IPC in Europe, but that the arrangement was not working out as he had hoped. What about the prospects of selling for the Dreyfus Fund?

The result was that Cornfeld exchanged his links with IPC for a dealership selling the hottest fund in New York. From Jack Dreyfus's viewpoint, his decision to accredit Cornfeld was nearly as good a buy as Polaroid: within three years Cornfeld's European-based sales crew were selling almost 16 per cent of the fastest-growing section of the Dreyfus Fund's new business. This was the category "contractual programs," under which investors agreed to pay a certain amount into the Fund every month, instead of putting up a single lump sum. Cornfeld was an early enthusiast for "contractuals": from a salesman's viewpoint, the great feature was that commission could be calculated upon the total volume of money that the customer would eventually pay during the life of the program. By 1962, IOS was bringing in close to 40 per cent of all the Dreyfus program business and 31.1 per cent of all the Dreyfus Fund's new money.

The salesmen Bernie recruited did not at all resemble the salesmen of legend or Arthur Miller's imagining. Robert Marx was reasonably representative. Like Cornfeld, he had joined the merchant marine around the end of the war. On discharge, he became a reporter, which he saw as an interim period on the way to becoming a novelist. By 1955, he was working for Reuters in Paris, on very slender wages indeed, which he eked out by contributions to an international veterans' journal. In March 1956 he was introduced to a girl friend of Cornfeld's who suggested that Bernie might be able to provide some supplementary income. Marx trudged up to 22 Boulevard Flandrin, a small white house behind a big block of flats, to meet Bernie.

"Physically, he was completely unprepossessing," Marx remembers. "His clothes were baggy—there was never a suit off the rack which could fit Bernie. But then he started to speak. His voice is very soft and reassuring. His smile is very engaging.

"I didn't at all like the idea of selling mutual funds. And he didn't seem to sell the idea very hard. But by the time I left the flat, I had agreed to give it a try."

There was nothing elaborate about the operation Marx joined. The firm's chief and almost only asset, a Chrysler Imperial convertible, has become firmly established as part of the IOS legend. "It was the headquarters of the firm, really," says Marx. "Each weekend Bernie would load it up with salesmen and sales material, and drive out to Orléans. Sometimes, we would sleep over Saturday night in the car before starting in again on Sunday." But by the time Marx joined, the firm was on its way to fame. Bernie's advertisement in the Paris *Herald Tribune*, offering "American men and women" over $10,000 a year for "sales ability, a willingness to work hard in a fast-growing industry, and a sense of humor," was running regularly, and striking a very effective chord in the exile community, which prided itself, above all, on its sense of humor.

Marx's close friend, John Curran, a quiet, bookish, unsalesman-like figure, quit rewriting cables for the *Herald*

Tribune and joined up. Lester Hayes was a professional ball-room dancer, who had been working the cruise ships with his wife. Jack Himes had been in the merchant marine, too. Alvin Ostroff had known Bernie in Brooklyn College, and trekked to Europe to join him. Berton Cantor (not to be confused with Allen Cantor) had been studying at the London School of Economics on a Fulbright grant: before that he had been a newspaperman in Chicago. Gladis Solomon was the first woman aboard, the den mother of the crowd. Her previous occupation had been reading your character from the way you drew a horse.

Victor Herbert joined in characteristic circumstances. He had been bouncing around Europe since 1949, making a living by purchasing rare music and musical manuscripts for an antiquarian bookshop in New York. By 1956, Herbert had reluctantly acknowledged that there was no real future in what he was doing. The prospect of going back to Chicago appalled him, but although Herbert had met Cornfeld, he did not care for the idea of selling mutual funds. By way of a reprieve before the trek home, Herbert decided to take a holiday, with a friend who knew Errol Flynn, on a yacht moored off the Algerian coast, and spent a memorable fortnight of Mediterranean pleasures in this company.

Under the influence of sea and sun, Herbert decided that *anything* was better than going back to Chicago. He went back to Paris, and looked up Cornfeld. Bernie asked him only one question: "Do you want to start selling tonight or tomorrow?"

Despite his lack of initial pleasure at the idea of selling mutual funds, Herbert found Cornfeld as impressive as Marx did. Especially, he was impressed by Bernie's account of "dollar-cost averaging." The use of this piece of arithmetical patter reveals a great deal about the essential techniques of mutual-fund selling. The standard sales pitch is predicated upon the idea that stock markets everywhere are set upon an upward course. Get your money in now, the customer is exhorted, before prices rise even higher.

From time to time, however, stock markets actually do fall. What to say then? Well, when stocks are going *down*, then it's an even better time to buy. Suppose shares are worth buying at 100. If the market drops, they must still be worth buying—but for the same amount of money, you can buy even more of them. You get better value for your money! The flaw, of course, is that some shares may fall and never rise again. But in 1956, Herbert was hardly alone in being impressed by this magical calculus.

Still, Herbert wanted to know a little more about what was involved in selling for IOS. Cornfeld brushed this aside. "Let me tell you about the opposition," he said. "There's one guy who smokes big cigars, and another guy who wears big cuff links." What he meant was that the other enterprising fellows who had seen the potential of the military market were out to make themselves rich fast. He, Cornfeld, had a more enlightened self-interest in view. He proposed to make the salesmen rich along with himself. "He said he would make us all millionaires," says Herbert, a by no means uncritical admirer in later years, "and he did."

• • •

Bernie might never have been able to implement that promise without the intervention of Charles de Gaulle. Any American organization as brash as Bernie's was an automatic victim of the change of mood after his return to power in May 1958. Almost inevitably, the infant IOS did things which were sinful in the eyes of Gaullist officials. American mutual funds were a new and puzzling phenomenon: the French authorities entertained dark suspicions that IOS was selling fund shares to French citizens, and suddenly raided the mail at one of the post offices IOS was using.

Although they found no evidence, this was a lethal attack, because a mutual fund must have reliable postal communication with its clients. And this applies especially to one which is developing "contractual" plans. The French said that their regulations made it illegal to send negotiable instruments through the mail. Cornfeld claimed this was irrelevant, because IOS was not selling to French citizens. The French bureaucracy deployed its full capacity for non-cooperation. They agreed to give clearance for one post office to pass IOS mail, but they refused to say they would not raid IOS mail at other offices. It was very clear that the time had come to move on. A police visit to Boulevard Flandrin drove the message home.

Casting around for an alternative haven, Cornfeld hit upon the idea of Geneva. It seems to have been a genuinely casual decision, based upon little more than the fact that it was a city outside French regulation where they spoke French, a language in which Cornfeld was now reasonably fluent. Chuck Kleinmann, an ex-mate in the merchant marine, went ahead to set things up. He acquired a pleasant apartment at the top of 119 Rue de Lausanne with a splendid view, across the trees of a small park, of the lake and beyond it the long limestone ridge of the Salève. About one day in five, the occupants of the apartment could see the shining triangle of Mont Blanc, fifty miles away on the frontier between France and Italy. The apartment became Bernie's headquarters when, in the autumn of 1958, he shifted the headquarters of his growing sales force from Paris to Geneva. The HQ all fitted into the one apartment; it consisted of Cornfeld, Kleinmann, Bert Cantor, and two secretaries.

By 1958, Calvin's and Voltaire's city of refuge had turned into the last best hope for the world's unloved rich and their money. Ever since the Reformation, Geneva, a Protestant island hemmed by Catholic seas, had maintained a tradition of sanctuary. In the 1930s and 1940s Geneva, like Switzerland as a whole, helped to save many thousands of people from the Nazis and the Fascists. But after 1945, the new refugees tended more and more to come from outside Europe: from the Middle East, North Africa, Latin America. Not all of them were innocent victims of persecution.

For all those who went to Geneva in person, thousands more sent their money. It had always been possible to rely upon the personal integrity of bankers in the original homeland of the Protestant ethic and the individual—but strictly individual—conscience. And by the time that Bernie arrived, the advantages of Swiss bank accounts were being discovered by spies, gamblers, and dictators, as well as by Middle Western dentists, New York stockbrokers, and other honest folk with no love for the taxman. Money, the chairman of Crédit Suisse (the Swiss Credit Bank) has noted, "tends to flow to those places where its owner believes it finds maximum security." Like all good Swiss bankers, he maintains that most people who send their money to Switzerland have paid their taxes first, but it is a proposition which cannot be put to the test because of the Swiss bank secrecy laws.

In most countries, banks are expected to protect the secrecy of their clients' affairs and may be sued in the civil courts for damages if they fail to do so. The first remarkable thing about Switzerland is that the additional sanction of the criminal law is invoked to reinforce the civil obligation to secrecy. Article 47(b) of the Banking Act of 1934 provides that any officer of a bank, or of the government's own Banking Commission, shall be liable to a fine of 20,000 francs, or six months' jail, or both, if he betrays a bank customer's secrecy deliberately. This applies to all

Swiss bank accounts, not merely numbered or coded ones. Only the Bahamas and Indonesia have followed Switzerland in applying the criminal law to bank secrecy.

In every legal system the banker's duty of secrecy must give way at some point to the concept of general public interest. There does not seem to be a country anywhere that does not make bankers break secrecy to testify in criminal proceedings. In the vast majority of countries, the tax authorities have the right to demand information from the banks. But in Switzerland, the taxmen have no such rights. The Swiss do not think it worth breaking bank secrecy to catch their own tax avoiders; still less do they think it worth pursuing the tax avoiders of other countries.

The remarkable point about the Swiss banking system is that it combines this rigor of secrecy with great freedom in other directions. "Compared with [that of] other countries," wrote Dr. M. Magdalena Schoch,* "the Swiss system has been characterized as one of the most liberal laws. . . . No charter or license is required for establishing a bank. The Commission does not decide whether the founders of a new bank have expert knowledge of banking, or whether the basic capital is adequate."

Provided the legal organization of a bank is in the correct form, it can be entered in the Commercial Register and start banking at once. Allied with Switzerland's native tradition of independence and security, this law has produced a rich growth of banks. By 1958, Geneva, a city of 175,000 people, had 76 banking institutions. And while this total included respectable Protestant houses of two hundred years' pedigree, there were some odd specimens as well. In some of them the doctrine of individ-

*Advice to the Committee on Banking and Currency, House of Representatives, Hearings on Foreign Bank Secrecy, March 9, 1970.

ual conscience was being turned to account in ways that would have astonished John Calvin.

Bluntly, Geneva was the center of the international flight-capital business. Bernie Cornfeld arrived with a set of commercial techniques that were admirably suited to that business.

. . .

According to early IOS company reports, the regular sales force was seventy-seven strong at the time Bernie moved into the top floor at 119 Rue de Lausanne. According to Bert Cantor's recollection, it was much less—but it would have been hard to be quite sure, because all the salesmen were self-employed and self-financing. It was Cornfeld's view that whenever a man was paid a salary, then someone was being exploited—either the employee or the employer. This meant, inevitably, that IOS was a personal syndicate, with only such control over individual salesmen as might derive from the sanction of syndicate membership.

In their recollections, the veterans of the period make much of the point that Bernie himself showed energetic form as a doorstep salesman—but no overwhelming brilliance. In the early days, Cornfeld used to go out with groups of salesmen on training expeditions. They would go to houses in threes and fours, or as many as eight at a time. In Cornfeld's own words, "We would knock on the door and say 'We are going to take over the place.' That is how we sold." If they made a sale, Cornfeld would split the commission with the whole team. "He wasn't a great salesman," says Robert Marx. "He held to a fairly standard line of patter." Yet on Marx's own account, Cornfeld had sold him, with some speed, an originally distasteful idea about how to make a living.

Cornfeld's interest in his own selling performance was probably about the same as Napoleon's interest in his own prowess with a musket. When the general joins in practice on the range, his purpose is to inspire the soldiery by showing them that he does not despise the duties he orders them to perform. If Cornfeld had devoted himself to selling mutual funds in person, he could no doubt have built up an impressive commission income. Instead, what he sold was the idea—the concept, if you like—that others should sell mutual funds for him.

Cornfeld was endlessly patient in overcoming the hesitations, errors, and reluctances of his recruits. Each salesman began his career by walking into Cornfeld's office and trying to sell to Cornfeld. After each such exercise, they would sit down together and go through the flaws in the new salesman's "presentation." There were lengthy group sessions in which Bernie and his men picked over the techniques of their craft. They practiced "sincere smiles" in front of mirrors—in later, more opulent days, training films were made on the finer points of smiling—and they practiced "firm handshakes" on each other. Cornfeld impressed upon them that they should always try to sit next to a prospect, rather than across the table from him, where it would be harder to "win his confidence." He was assiduous in explaining the delicacy required when talking about a man leaving investments to his family. They should always say "if something happens to you," not "when you die."

He was even more assiduous in remedying personal, psychological hesitations. Such "blocks" would be discussed at great length, with much Adlerian speculation about the inner weaknesses and difficulties of the subject. Thad Lovett, for instance, especially dreaded "cold calls," which have to be done when the salesman runs out of introductions to follow up and has to go pressing doorbells unannounced. When Thad's block overcame him, Bernie swept down to Orléans in person and spent an evening with Lovett, fixing up appointments on the phone for the next day.

With the move to Geneva, the training became more formalized. The advertisement was still running in the Paris *Herald Tribune* and it brought aspirant salesmen and women to Geneva in surprising quantities, considering that they had to pay their own fares, support themselves during training sessions, and then finance their first selling trips. Customers were naturally recruited with some frequency as salesmen. There was no more natural question for the prospect to ask than "Is it difficult to sell these things?"

At ten in the morning on the third Monday of every month, a dozen or more hopefuls would assemble at 119 Rue de Lausanne to start their course. Bert Cantor had the job of teaching them how to sell. Bernie Cornfeld's job was to make them *want* to sell. They were asked numerous rhetorical questions. "Are you Wellington Winner or are you Louie the Loser? Do you want to be used by the capitalist system or do you want to use it?" It was a catechism in which the right answers were obvious.

The most important question was asked implicitly in many forms, and explicitly in the form we have used as the title of this book. It was:

"Do you sincerely want to be rich?"

This was a brilliant reading by Cornfeld from Adler and the theory of goals. For most people, the answer is no—they would like to be rich, or would not mind being rich, but they *sincerely want* something else. Cornfeld's question was calculated to sort out the attitudes of his recruits. For those who said yes, they did sincerely want to be rich, there was a logical follow-through. If that was what they wanted, they must do what Bernie wanted them to do. And then he would make them millionaires.

The classes bore the aspect of a sales pitch, to the salesmen.

Cornfeld would start by asking them all to write down the names of their nearest relatives. "Now write down your doctor's name. And your dentist's." And so on. "Now tear up the list!"

Then he would tell them that after one week's training they would have to be able to go out and sell mutual funds to complete strangers, anywhere in the world.* To do that, he would explain, they had to master one fundamental secret: always to control the conversation with the prospect. Here, as in several respects, he owed an organizational debt to his early mentors, Walter and Ruth Benedick. The basic tool with which the IOS salesmen were first equipped was a text, cast in the form of a dialogue between salesman and prospect, which was largely taken over from Investors Planning Corporation. The salesman was supposed to learn his text by heart, and delivery-time was reckoned at twenty minutes. There were six sections:

1. (Create Interest) Introduction and short explanation of mutual fund.
2. (Explanation) Fund Quarterly Report and $250-month sheet.
3. (Explanation) Four ways to get your money out.
4. (Explanation) Dollar-cost averaging.
5. (Personalization) "Captain Geldt, what is your age?"
6. (Close) Name wife as first beneficiary.

More usually, a mutual-fund salesman would address himself to "Mister Prospect": "Captain Geldt" was an IOS invention. The rank was a tribute to the military market with which Cornfeld's operation began, and "geldt," being the Yiddish for money, was a humorous label.

---

*Bert Cantor, *The Bernie Cornfeld Story*.

But Cornfeld did not merely copy a pitch and remain content with it. He and his acolytes ceaselessly polished and remodeled the presentations their salesmen used. They added wise saws, modern instances, jokes, and touches of sentiment. ("There are only two financial problems, Captain Geldt. One is that life is too short—too short to earn all the money you need. The other is that life is too long—you may live too long for the money you can earn.")

Cornfeld was tirelessly fertile in small psychological insights, designed, of course, not to search the secrets of the human psyche, but directed to the master goal of turning prospects into customers. Some of these devices have been so thoroughly assimilated into the collective culture of IOS that it would be hard to say now whether it was Bernie or someone else who first used them. What one can say—and what Cornfeld's pupils are the first to acknowledge—is that if the words are the words of Cantor or of George Landau, the spirit is the spirit of Cornfeld.

By April 1960, a new-model presentation was on offer which was reckoned to concentrate its whole "interesting, even exciting" message into five minutes. IOS was beginning to move into civilian markets, and "Captain Geldt" dropped his military rank. " 'Mister Geldt,' it began, '. . . let's presume that you had $1 million. You don't mind presuming you have $1 million do you?' " (He doesn't.)

It was then explained to Mister Geldt that if he really did happen to be a millionaire, he certainly wouldn't be keeping his money in the bank. He would hire professional investment managers, who would, through the advice of economists and statisticians, select numerous investment positions and spread the money out among them.

"Now then, Mister Geldt," said the salesman coyly, "unless you have been keeping something from me, you don't have $1 million." However, some of the benefits of millionairehood could be available to even the smallest of investors. Have the advantages, Mr. Geldt was counseled, of "a millionaire's method of investing." This was, said the salesman importantly, "a mutual fund." (The news, perhaps, would have surprised the average millionaire.)

Computations were then produced, suggesting that a mutual-fund investor could expect to see $10,000 turn into $54,000 within ten years. "If this had happened to you, Mr. Geldt, would you have been pleased?" asked the salesman. And it was not even necessary to have $10,000 to put up at once. Just putting up $100 a month for ten years would result in a payout of $34,000. Optimism, it was explained to the salesman, was the essence of the business. Don Juan, said the IOS salesmen's *Bulletin*, was not a handsome man. He was even unattractive. But he was an *optimist*. Good salesmen, it was implied, should emulate the great seducer.

And of course, they should always sell whatever the client wanted to have. George Tregea, who rose to be a director of IOS, was thought to be an admirable practitioner by the *Bulletin*. "George's approach is based on the notion that everyone should have a plan. . . . Whatever it is that the client is concerned with—whether it's taxes, inheritance, insurance, savings, or just plain getting rich, that's what George sells."

It was a vital principle to anticipate every objection a prospect might make. But if an objection broke through, it must be disarmed—by the trick of restating it in terms more extreme than any the prospect was likely to use. Thus, Eli Wallitt has explained the correct counter for a salesman to use when the prospect says he has no money. The salesman says, "Oh gosh, I'm sorry, I didn't realize. Listen, I could lend you a few bucks to eat for a few days." Whereupon the prospect hastily explains that things aren't as bad as all that . . . and the salesman is back in the game with a chance.

Even now, a dozen years later, pupils of Cornfeld's who rose to be sales bosses and executives of IOS still fall back on the same device in conversation. A reporter dealing with the IOS high command in the weeks after the crash would often find himself confronted by an immaculately preserved figure of un-flappable presence. The reporter gently frames a question which suggests that this immaculate figure and some of his colleagues might have been concerned in unorthodox financial operations. The IOS man's face lights with grave understanding. "What you mean," he says, "is that I was hopelessly greedy. That's ab-solutely right." The reporter can scarcely do other than mutter shocked disavowal of any such intention. Gradually, we our-selves learned to recognize in such self-flagellation the survival of a dialectical device—learned in those early training courses and sharpened in a thousand "presentations."

The vital discipline that the salesman had to acquire was that he must be prepared to humiliate himself. Whatever happened, he was the winner only if he came out with the prospect's signa-ture on a contract in his pocket. That is not quite how the veter-ans put it, but that is what the words mean. "When you go out selling," said George Landau, one of the great masters, "you have to put your ego in your pocket." He did not mean "ego" in the technical, Freudian sense. He meant that when you go out selling, you must school yourself to put your pride in your pocket. Landau's meaning is reinforced by his further dictum that "if I am selling something to you, you cannot say anything to me that will make me take offense."

The gambits an IOS salesman had to learn only began with his "sincere smile." The lore of "closes" was elaborated espe-cially—the "close" being the move in which the customer is brought to sign. Its ultimate development seems to have been the "sign-or-tear-up" close, a piece of dramatics in which a contract and a fountain pen are placed before the prospect, and he is given the challenge to use the pen or tear up the paper. This was regarded as a dangerous technique, only to be used by a master salesman confronted with a prospect stubbornly refusing to see what was good for him.

The art of supplementary dialogue was probably raised to its highest point by Philip Bell, a flaxen-haired Australian with a visionary and innocent eye, who specialized in selling IOS programs linked to life insurance. He recommended goosing the prospects with this kind of phrase. "Let's lean over your executor's shoulder for a moment. How long is it before your widow is working?" Or, "Have you ever seen a bankrupt family?" Or, he suggested, a salesman could tell the prospect "about the letter you once saw which said, 'I don't want you to think my husband didn't love his family. It's just that he didn't plan to die at this time.' "

It was on the basis of learning and elaborating such devices that the IOS salesmen convinced themselves that selling was a "profession." But, in the end, it came down to "putting your ego in your pocket"—a process of unrelenting emotional control in which every nuance of human intercourse was directed toward persuading a prospect to give his money into IOS's care.

The salesmen often compared themselves to missionaries, and certainly they shared the missionary's belief that he has the duty to impose his will upon others. But there the resemblance to missionaries ended. Converts without commissions would not have interested them.

Perhaps the best way to illustrate what sincerely wanting to be rich meant, in practice, is to look at four young men from one particular Geneva training session. Three made good, in IOS terms, and the reasons why the fourth man failed to make the final grade tells us a good deal about the IOS system.

Some fifteen recruits turned up for the class of July 1959. One was George Landau, a tall dark man with a surprising resemblance to Boris Pasternak. He had been born in Poland, brought up in Russia, and reached America after many hardships. He first returned to Europe as an optical engineer with Westinghouse, working on the atomic-powered lighting for the 1958 Brussels Expo. Returning the next year for a vacation, he saw Bernie's advertisement and moved in with some relatives near Geneva.

Landau was the star of the course—he is said to have floored Cornfeld once or twice with questions about the applied science of selling. He served his apprenticeship in the military market at Orléans, where he teamed up with Don Q. Shaprow. Landau and Shaprow formed a partnership, which lasted ten years, in which they agreed to split all their commissions and all their expenses.

By the end of 1959, the Landau-Shaprow team had earned enough to finance an expedition into new territory. Together with Gladis Solomon, they set off for West Africa. In time they raised enough money for them to follow some Dutch prospects back to Holland. There they set up their own independent IOS territory, setting up headquarters and branch offices with their own money, and—most important—advancing money to new salesmen to get them on the road. Landau went on to become No. 4 in the unofficial IOS hierarchy, after Cornfeld, Ed Cowett, and Allen Cantor.

Ben Heirs and Howie Dressman did almost as well. Heirs was an ex-USAF officer, who went off after the course to sell to American servicemen in Spain. After a spell in Japan he rose to be Executive Vice President of IOS Financial Holdings, which controlled the IOS banks.

Dressman had been a teacher in New York City. He went to sell in the Far East, where he ran the Philippines operation before coming back to Geneva and a sales-executive's job.

Oddly enough, there was only one man on the course who had sold mutual funds before. This was a cheerful, shortish, broad-shouldered New Yorker named Lou Ellenport. At nineteen, Ellenport was already selling securities for a "boiler-room operation," which is a roomful of men with telephones, extolling shares to farmers and other moneyed but unsophisticated persons some distance from Wall Street. The key to boiler-room cost-control is to keep down the phone bills; true experts work with a three-minute egg timer beside each phone. If the prospect isn't hot in three minutes, down goes the receiver, in mid-sentence if necessary.

In 1958, Ellenport had come over to Europe to sell for one of Cornfeld's rivals in the military market. It was hard work scratching out $50 a month, however. The end came in the small French town of Chaumont; Ellenport simply walked into the local IOS salesman's hotel room and surrendered with the memorable line, "I'm your competition, and I haven't eaten for two days." The IOS man—"a very gentlemanly type"—obliged with a five-spot, and sent his defeated rival back to Geneva to be reindoctrinated.

Ellenport's first sales assignment was the U.S. base at Glyfada in Greece. But after only a few months there, earning some $400 a month "by lamming away at those Goddamned sergeants with granite-like persistence," it suddenly struck Lou, not by any means for the last time, that the grass might be greener elsewhere. He had read in the monthly *Bulletin*, which Bert Cantor and later Thad Lovett got out for the homesick salesmen, that George Landau had struck a gusher to the tune of $150,000 sales a month in, of all places, Liberia.

Eager to prove himself as good a salesman as Landau, Ellenport belted off a cable to Bernie, pleading to be turned loose on some civilians. And Bernie cabled back, "Go to Libya!"

Oil had been struck, the first in what is now the major Libyan field, in June 1959. Traveling by ship to Alexandria, and then in an ancient Opel Kadett, with a German girl friend, through El Alamein and Tobruk and all the battlefields of the Western Desert, staying in hotels so primitive that "the fleas were walking away with the sheets," Lou reached Tripoli on October 9.

It was easy enough selling to the oilmen. The snag was that the Libyan government refused to give you a visa for more than three months. Early in 1960, Ellenport had to move on, to be replaced by two more itinerant IOS men.

And so began his extraordinary odyssey. For the next five and a half years, sometimes alone, sometimes with another IOS salesman as a companion, sometimes with the faithful German girl, Ellenport roamed the earth, always searching (as Captain Ahab sought the great white whale, Moby Dick) for the lush territory that would enable him to settle down and never quite finding it.

From Tripoli, he went to Tunis, then to Madrid, where Ben Heirs warned Lou sharply off his beat, then to Lisbon. (We will mention only the places where he actually sold mutual funds, or tried to.) Then to digs with a vicar and his unmarried daughter in the Norfolk village of Sculthorpe, near a U.S. Strategic Air Command bomber base. It was a top-security base, and Lou was eventually thrown off it. He drove the Opel all the way across Europe to Ankara. Then Izmir, Adana, Iskenderon, Beirut, Latakia, Amman, Jerusalem, Tel Aviv, and, by boat via Marseilles, to Algiers.

In Beirut he waited for days to board the flagship of the U.S.

Sixth Fleet, only to find himself barred by the executive officer, who had the dealership to sell to another mutual fund himself.

In Algiers, somebody tossed a grenade into a *café* where he was sitting, and a few days later someone started firing rifle rounds a few feet above the car. "I didn't want a commemorative plaque at 119 Rue de Lausanne, it wasn't worth getting killed for!" So back to Geneva, to Holland, to Belgium, and then, by way of Manila, to Singapore.

On September 21, 1961, at ten-thirty at night, Ellenport landed in Indonesia, and there, for the first and last time while he was with IOS, he really struck it rich. A man from the American embassy lent Lou his house, complete with servants; from the very first evening, everything went well. As for selling, it was like shaking fruit off the trees. "Plop, plop!" Ellenport remembers wistfully, "down they fell, nice and ripe."

In nine weeks, working the embassies, the foreign business community, and the oil camps in the jungle, Lou and another salesman sold $1.5 million worth of the Dreyfus Fund.

He flew straight up to Tokyo, and met Bernie Cornfeld there on New Year's Eve 1961. Bernie was full of congratulations, and presented him with a Patek Philippe gold watch.

Then Bernie asked what Ellenport was going to do with the money his sales breakthrough had earned him, and Ellenport said he was thinking of putting it into Fidelity, one of the big, established American mutual-fund groups. Cornfeld exploded. "With Bernie, you're either the greatest guy in the world, or you're nowhere," says Ellenport in wry recollection.

Cornfeld's fury sprang from the fact that he had turned IOS into a formally organized company—and he had plans for it which went very much further than continuing to sell other people's mutual funds. Look, said Cornfeld, couldn't Lou see that he ought to invest in IOS itself?

Cornfeld gave Ellenport, along with the gold watch, options on a thousand shares in Bernie's new company, IOS. The cost $21,000. Ellenport agreed. But now he must earn enough money in commissions, over and above his expenses, to pay for his options. It took him four years, and until he had finished paying for them, he was hooked.

(Those who have never worked as salesmen might suppose that a salesman's income comes only from what he sells himself. This is not so: he may also share in the commissions of those under him in the hierarchy through what are known as "overrides." At the bottom of the IOS scale, a salesman shared part of the commission on each sale with those who had recruited and trained him. As he rose through the grades, he became entitled to a growing share of the commission on his own personal sales. Eventually, he was allowed to recruit other salesmen and exact a share of their commission in turn.) Allen Cantor, now head of the sales force, offered Ellenport an exclusive territory of his own, covering Burma, Indonesia, and Malaysia. But Ellenport turned it down, for what seemed like good reasons at the time.

Without a territory and overrides, Ellenport must earn all the money himself. He set off again, in pursuit of his grail. He had worked out that in any capital where there was an American embassy, he could sell enough programs to live for one month by going through the diplomats, and the people with AID and the ancillary agencies. (Every time you sent a contract off to Geneva, you got an advance equal to the commission on your last sale.)

Once, briefly, Geneva gave him a territory. But it was the Indian subcontinent, stony ground for a salesman seeking money. He tried Australia, but found that Harvey Felberbaum had been through it before him.

He heard there were American scientists to burn at Mc-

Murdo Sound in the Antarctic. But when he tried to get on the supply ship at Christchurch, New Zealand, the U.S. Navy turned him brutally away. He went to Fiji and to American Samoa. He made a small strike among the storekeepers in Pago Pago. He went to Honolulu, San Francisco, and back to New York, where he found Bernie and Ed Cowett.

Presumably, thoughts of American operations were beginning to stir in their minds, because when Bernie said, "Why don't you go down to Jamaica?" Cowett added, "Why don't you try Huntsville, Alabama?" So Lou went to Jamaica, and to Huntsville, and to Washington, and back to New York.

And then he went round again. Tripoli. Cairo. Khartoum. Addis Ababa. Alexandria. Back to Geneva.

He remembers asking himself what he was doing in a potato field outside Kabul, Afghanistan, at ten o'clock at night. The answer—trying to sell mutual funds—sounded improbable, even to himself.

Dacca. Chittagong. Cox's Bazar. Karachi. Lahore. He was thrown out of a construction camp at a big dam site. He moved on to Rawalpindi, Peshawar, Kabul, and Kandahar.

In Zanzibar, he found five Americans building "something secret," and they asked him to come back after they had thought over his proposition. "Who do you think I am?" Ellenport asked them. "The Good Humor ice-cream man?"

He went up to Chisimaio, in Somalia, on the back of an old truck. Cries of "Simba! Simba!" wakened him as an old lioness walked across the road. He left the African mainland for a detour to Mahé, in the Seychelles Islands. Thence to Mombasa and Nairobi, and again briefly back to Geneva.

From Geneva to Monterrey, Mexico City, and Acapulco, then back to Africa. In Bangui, when he explained his purpose, the American consul said, "Mutual funds? You must be crazy.

You'll have to sell them to the gorillas around here." But Lou sold one program to the consul himself, and one to each of his assistants.

More place names, more prospects, more spiels, more hotels, more airports. Kinshasa and Brazzaville in the Congo, Douala and Yaoundé in the Cameroons. Then north to Düsseldorf, Nuremberg, and Berlin. East again to Delhi, Bombay, Cochin. In Karachi the big black birds on the lawn outside the hotel window seemed to be croaking, "Schmuck! Schmuck! Schmuck!"

That August, he reached the end of the road. It happened in Kuwait on the Persian Gulf, a place where only "mad dogs and mutual-fund salesmen go out in the midday sun." At last, it looked as though Lou had hit it rich again. Business was beautiful, there were oilmen everywhere, and he had almost paid off his share options. Then, suddenly, a cable came from Geneva. "Get out within twenty-four hours," it said, "or you're terminated."

"Termination" is IOS-ese for the removal of membership in IOS, and this was the only real sanction there was in the organization. What lay behind this was that by selling in Kuwait, Ellenport was trespassing on the territory of the General Manager in Beirut. Nobody who had set up his own territory wanted itinerants trespassing. And by now, most of the world had been fenced up into IOS territories.

Ellenport had no alternative but to go back to Geneva and take an office job with IOS. "By this time," he said, "I realized I had missed the gold ring." His contemporaries—the Landaus and Shaprows, Ben Heirs, and Howie Dressmans—had come home earlier from the road, and handled their baronial relations with Bernie more fortunately. They had built up sales organizations that guaranteed them income from the efforts of other men, and they were halfway through the process of turning themselves from salesmen into financiers.

Rightly or wrongly, Ellenport feels that it was whim or accident that decided whether you got the "override" rights that made you into a master financier, or whether you were left whirling around the world like the Flying Dutchman.

The curious thing is that even though Ellenport had missed the "golden ring," IOS was reluctant to release him. With the lightning growth of the company, his original investment had now grown to be worth something more than $200,000. A friend lent him the money to pay off the last of what he owed, and Ellenport announced that he wanted to sell out his shares and retire.

There was a short, unpleasant row in which the company said that his shares in IOS were going to be frozen, at the price they had reached by the end of the previous year, unless Ellenport agreed to build up a sales group with a certain annual sales volume in the United States or Canada. He refused, and resigned. In the end, he was given his money—and was terminated the same day.

• • •

It is safe to say that in the early years very few of Cornfeld's salesmen realized that they were taking part in the foundation of a financial empire. Robert Marx, who hunted through Venezuela and Brazil for four years—often trekking deep into the jungle—said, "We were all very happy with the commissions we were earning, and we lived it up. But Bernie was always off making bigger deals."

It was the essence of Cornfeld's achievement that he took confused young men and liberated in them the conviction that, after all, what they sincerely wanted was to be rich. Having done that, he sent them out to comb the world for money. Many years later, an IOS "workshop session" decided that "motivation" means "getting people to want what you want them to do." It is a manipulator's definition.

One day, when IOS was riding high, Lou Ellenport met an acquaintance, still with IOS, who asked solicitously after his financial well-being. Ellenport was able to say that, thanks to some successful investments, he was worth over a quarter of a million dollars. "But is that enough?" the IOS man asked sympathetically.

"I tell you," says Ellenport, "they were selling a dream, and to the salesmen most of all."

Early Travels in the Offshore World

In which we explain the capital structure of a dream, and how Bernie and Ed kept the salesmen loyal to IOS. The birth of the first IOS fund, and the Trust that was not a trust.

Salesmen of any sort are creatures of fickle ambition. They are always apt to be seduced by offers from rival outfits, especially if those offers come baited with another half-per-cent commission. And the team Bernie Cornfeld had assembled was a particularly fractious one. Yet Lou Ellenport and many others plowed their lonely and competitive furrow with an enduring loyalty. To insulate such men, for nearly a decade, against most of the wiles of the competition was a considerable feat of business.

It was done, naturally, with the lure of wealth—more precisely, a system of lures designed with all the legal, financial, and personal subtlety of Ed Cowett and Bernie Cornfeld.

Many details played their part in this system: the salesmen, for instance, were always called Associates, which conferred a sense of membership in a professional elite. Then there was Cornfeld's custom of decorating every salesman who did $1 million of business with a gold wrist watch from Patek Philippe. And Bernie's own life-style with its display of chateaux, limousines, and women was intended to be a goal for the ambitions of his Associates, as well as a pleasure for himself. As he once said, in his own splendidly arrogant whisper, "I suppose a salesman might find it easier to identify with me, as a symbol of success, than with mousy Jacob Rothschild, fiddling with his pencil."

But there were motivations built into the system which amounted to more than glamour and gold watches. The essence of it was the quasi-feudal transaction in which each Associate personally became a part of the capital of Investors Overseas Services and then agreed, as it were, to buy himself back. This was the IOS Stock-Option Plan, which arranged the distribution of shares in IOS itself, as distinct from shares in the mutual funds that IOS was selling. The scheme was dressed up as a kind of capitalist socialism, and Cornfeld orated a good deal about IOS being a company which was owned by the people who worked for it. Analysis of the corporate structure shows that the truth was rather the other way about.

Cornfeld and Cowett drew up the first outlines of the stock-option plan as early as February 1960, together with a bonus plan to accommodate executives who were not salesmen. The earliest recorded financial document produced by IOS was a prospectus, dated February 20, in which Cornfeld first offered certain of his colleagues shares in his company. He sold them some 12,000 of his original 56,700: each manager could subscribe for 200 shares at $7.5 each and three directors, Gladis Solomon, Lester Hayes, and Victor Herbert, could each buy 2,500 additional shares at $10. The bashful Lovett was awarded 100 shares as a bonus.

This early prospectus was remarkably sketchy. For one thing, it did not offer any explanation of how the money raised was to be used. For another, nowhere did it tell these first subscribers where the company in which they were buying shares had its legal home. It was indeed not until over a month later, on April 9, that IOS Ltd. (SA) was formed in Panama: it was on this foundation that Cornfeld and Cowett erected the most imposing offshore edifice yet seen.

Cowett and Cornfeld were masters in this field some years before newspapers began using the word "offshore" to denote financial institutions which escape governmental control through geographical selectivity.

Occasionally, offshore operators have found some useful feature in the corporation law of a major nation, such as the provisions for nonresident corporations in the Canadian Province of Ontario. But in the offshore world we are dealing, for the most part, in a mixture of picturesque European principalities and sun-bleached tropical outposts: the Bahamas, Bermuda, the Netherlands Antilles (Curaçao), Panama, Liberia, the Grand Duchy of Luxembourg, the Principality of Liechtenstein, Monaco, and occasionally Andorra, San Marino, or the Virgin Islands, British and American. IOS and its rivals set much store by their modernism. But the environment in which they operated was lashed up out of the juridical anomalies left over by the Holy Roman Empire and the colonial systems of Spain, the Netherlands, and Great Britain.

"Offshoreness" is not quite the same thing as corporate internationalism. Companies like General Motors, Shell, or Phillips conduct relations, for better or worse, *with* national governments. They may well take advantage, when they can, of oddities in the international legal system. But when they do so, it is an incidental activity.

The essence of offshoreness lies in turning an enormous number of loopholes into a viable, but unregulated, corporate structure. For instance, most countries with a developed life-insurance market place tiresome restrictions on people who want to set up life-insurance companies. But Luxembourg is very liberal in this matter and a Luxembourg life-insurance company sounds respectable. Unfortunately, Luxembourg companies do have to publish accounts: if you don't care for that, collect the revenues through a Liechtenstein *Anstalt*, an easily organized entity which has no obligation to keep books or publish names of directors. If you are an American and dislike American taxes, secrete your money in a Bahamas trust. Nassau is only twenty-five flying minutes from Miami, and it is one remnant of the British Empire where they don't allow Uncle Sam to get above himself. In 1969, they tossed out a couple of federal revenue investigators for having the sauce to operate in the colony without work permits.

Discussion of the offshore world usually revolves around matters of tax avoidance or evasion. But taxation is only one of the many kinds of regulation which modern governments impose upon the acquisitive spirit. The popularity of offshore institutions has grown with the growth of "onshore" regulations of all kinds. There were many spurs to the growth of offshore business in the 1960s. There was a tightening of exchange controls, due to balance-of-payments crises in America, France, and Britain. The outflow of dollars created pools of effectively free currency. Capital-gains taxes, and the threat of wealth taxes drove money to seek refuge in out-of-the-way places.

The offshore status of IOS was not an accident, an additional refinement grafted onto a viable structure. It was of the essence of Cornfeld's and Cowett's conceptions that their operation should be as far as possible untaxed, unregulated, and uncontrolled.

The regulations upon investment corporations do not exist simply because of kindly governmental concern for investors. They are there because every Western government believes that uncontrolled financial speculation is a danger to the stability of the State. Ultimately, what IOS did was to get around virtually every control designed to prevent speculation getting out of hand.

· · ·

Originally, Investors Overseas Services was just a label for Cornfeld's highly successful syndicate selling the Dreyfus Fund out of Paris. With the acquisition of Ed Cowett's advice, and two years after the move to Geneva, the business was simply transferred into the hands of the Panama corporation, IOS Ltd. (SA). Panama, which charges almost no company tax on nonresident corporations and requires very little financial information from them, was then a popular "brass-plate" address for American companies.

At the outset, Cornfeld owned all the shares of the Panama company. This was the key to the next nine years of development.

The outline of the IOS Stock-Option Plan was simple enough. All Associates were graded according to the quantities of mutual-fund shares they had managed to sell. The system was similar to that used by Cornfeld's first mentors, Walter and Ruth Benedick, although the IOS grades eventually became a good deal more complicated.

Promotion carried, at each level, an option to buy a certain number of new shares in IOS Ltd. (SA). The price at which you could buy shares in the company was determined by a formula based on the growth of IOS, and of its sales force and its sales. Naturally, the formula price was expected to rise and it mostly did. So it would appeal to a salesman to take up his full option, contracting in effect to pay for shares in the future at the price reigning *now*. Consider the case of a man reaching the grade of

Regional Manager in early 1964. He becomes entitled to an option for 1000 shares. At the formula price of $21.43 of early 1964, he would be contracting to pay $21,430. Even saving all his commission, he would have to sell $300,000 worth of mutual-fund shares to pay it off. Taking realistic account of expenses, he would have to sell another $1 million of mutual-fund shares. At that point, he could step up to being a General Manager and contract for another 1300 shares.

So long as the sales force expanded—and the system goaded each "managerial" salesman to recruit more Associates—then the formula price of shares bought under the stock-option plan would continue to rise. But their owners could not take their gains and get out; because the only shares in IOS Ltd. (SA) that could, in practice, be sold on the open market were those owned by Bernard Cornfeld himself. The shares his salesmen and executives bought could only be sold back to the company at the formula price. Their loyalty was bound; and it was further inspired by a great vision.

This was Cornfeld's promise that the company would eventually be reorganized so that its shares could be sold off on the open market. "We can all cash in," the salesmen used to say, "when Bernie cashes in." Or, as Roy Kirkdorffer, boss of the British sales force put it, "When you sign on with Bernie, it's for keepsville."

Loyalty and diligence were assured by the stock-option plan. But there was more than this. Indeed, there had to be more, because a company that merely deals in mutual funds, as IOS did when it began, is not an especially profitable animal. In 1959, IOS sold nearly $58 million of the shares of the Dreyfus Fund and other funds, but it made a profit of only $75,187. A company which sells shares in funds run by other people profits only on the margin between the fee it gets from the fund organizers and the large commissions it has to pay out to its salesmen. To make more sales requires more salesmen, and squeezes the margin further.

Real profits come not from selling funds, but from managing them. If a fund expands, the managers' fees increase, but not their expenses: it costs little more to make investment decisions about a billion dollars than a million dollars. So Jack Dreyfus and his colleagues were sitting pretty when Cornfeld and other dealers sold for them. In 1961, Dreyfus's management costs were only 39 per cent of the $1.2 million fees they took on the fund, *and* their stockbroking firm was getting brokerage on the fund's investments, *and* as the fund expanded, the costs of running it dropped to about a quarter of the fees.*

The solution for Cornfeld was to start his own fund, but starting a fund organization needs capital. He persuaded the Dreyfus Corporation to lend him $26,000 in 1961. He could hardly expect them to go further. The beauty of the stock-option plan was that it generated the necessary capital. It got the salesmen to put a big slice of their commission back into the company. That money was then available to help start up operations which would really make profits: fund-management companies, investment banks, insurance companies, real-estate concerns.

In the accounting of IOS Ltd. (SA) the salesmen were listed as part of the assets of the company. Indeed, at the start, they were half of all the assets of the company. In early 1961, each salesman was reckoned to be worth about $2000. Each salesman, when he bought shares under the stock-option plan, was then agreeing to buy back the part of himself that he had given to Cornfeld. They were sufficiently in love with the dream of "cashing in" that they didn't, on the whole, see it that way—un-

---

*Dreyfus Corporation: Prospectus 1965.

til, with the collapse of 1970, shares in IOS became virtually worthless.

The ultimate expression of this system was reached in Germany, after the crash. Numerous salesmen had bought their shares with borrowed money. Many of them found that their shares were actually worth less than the amounts they had borrowed. Such men were thus ruined. In a number of cases, men were "terminated" specifically on the grounds that persons in such poor financial condition could hardly expect to impress the customers.

• • •

With supplies of capital thus assured, Cornfeld and Cowett were ready to turn themselves into financiers. In December 1960, eight months after its own formation in Panama City, the IOS parent company sponsored its first mutual fund. This was given the resounding title of "IIT, an International Investment Trust," and eventually it became the largest of all the IOS investment vehicles, controlling $700 million. The corporate existence of IIT, which was rather fuzzily defined, resided in the Grand Duchy of Luxembourg.

The launch of IIT had its haphazard aspects, especially when it came to finding a bank to perform the important-sounding role of Custodian of Securities. Obviously, IIT needed to be able to assure prospective customers that stocks and shares bought with their money would be kept in respectable and independent hands, and it was with this in mind that Victor Herbert, one-time dealer in rare musical manuscripts, journeyed from Geneva to Brussels late in 1960. Herbert had been taken off the IOS sales force for executive duty, and he had with him the draft prospectus of IIT, an International Investment Trust, which he was to show to Banque Lambert of Brussels (a firm of great respectability founded by a section of the Rothschild family). The draft said that Banque Lambert had agreed to be Custodian of Securities for IIT.

This caused amazement at the Banque Lambert's headquarters. No one there had heard of IIT or IOS. Neither did they seem eager to repair the omission. (Later, it emerged that someone from IOS had vaguely mentioned the idea to Banque Lambert's New York office.) Politely and firmly, Herbert was told that Banque Lambert declined the honor, and this created an awkward gap in the organization. In fact, the sales force had been unleashed and money was pouring into IIT before a proper Custodian of Securities was found.

IOS was helped out of this predicament by Crédit Suisse of Zurich. Bernard Cornfeld had been introduced to Crédit Suisse, one of the "Big Three" Swiss banks, by Dr. Bruno A. Hugi, whom he had hired to be investment adviser for the new fund.

Dr. Hugi himself was an ex-Manager for the Union Bank, another of the Big Three. When IIT needed a bank to act as Depository of Cash, Hugi at first took his new colleague along to the Union Bank. But Union already had some funds of their own and felt that they could not take the business. So Hugi took Cornfeld to Crédit Suisse—which first agreed to be Depository of Cash and then, when IOS could not find a Custodian of Securities, helped again. They persuaded a respectable affiliate of theirs, Bank H. Albert de Bary, of Amsterdam, to accept the job. But until that could be done, IIT had to make temporary expedients.

The story suggests a rather lighthearted attitude to the organizing of a new international investment trust. More importantly, it illustrates the attitudes of European banks toward IOS. Cornfeld successfully persuaded almost every journalist who wrote about him that IOS was locked in combat with something called "the European financial establishment." This enabled him to represent legitimate criticism of his methods as mere Old World resentment of brisk American competition and to claim in the end that his downfall was caused by a bankers' plot. The fact is that large sections of the European financial establishment were delighted to work with Cornfeld and to take his money, while other sections were not. It would be hard to say which section was the larger, but it is quite certain that IOS depended, from the start, upon the co-operation of established, old-line European finance houses. In this instance, Banque Lambert of Brussels declined to help IOS, but Crédit Suisse and Bank H. Albert de Bary were ready to do so. Neither of them had any lack of successors.

Even when decked out with a Custodian of Securities and a Depository of Cash, Bernie Cornfeld's creation was a curious animal. It would have been a stillborn one in the harsh legal climate of the United States or Britain.

In the English-speaking world there are two general approaches to the problem of protecting investors and inhibiting speculation. The British law tends to assume that the majority of investors are idiots, and in effect tries to take some ultimate decisions about their money out of their hands. The American law tends to assume that investors are reasonably sensible, provided that they are told exactly what is going on.

But both approaches depend upon there being two clearly separate legal entities in an investment operation: the *fund*, into which the customers put their money to be invested, and the *management company*, through which the organizers of the operation are entitled to earn fees for putting the fund to work. Much hard experience has shown that the crux of investment-company regulation consists in keeping this division hard and fast. As the Senate Committee on Banking and Currency put it:

> Basically the problems flow from the very nature of the assets of investment companies. The assets of such companies invariably consist of cash and securities, assets which are completely liquid, mobile, and readily negotiable. Because of these characteristics, control of such funds offers manifold opportunities for exploitation by the unscrupulous managements of some companies. These assets can and have been easily misappropriated and diverted by such types of managements, and have been employed to foster their personal interests rather than the interests of public security holders.*

In Britain, the law requires that the assets of a unit trust (mutual fund) must be placed under the control of a separate trustee, whose powers are defined by a trust deed drawn up under the strict legal provisions of the Prevention of Fraud (Investments) Act, 1958. The trustee is empowered to dismiss the managers in the last resort, and the aims of investment policy cannot be altered without his approval. In the United States, it is not required that mutual-fund assets must actually be placed in the hands of a trustee, but they are usually placed with custodian banks. The whole process is closely supervised by the Securities and Exchange Commission, which requires full public disclosure of all transactions.

Possibly the fact that Cornfeld called IIT "an International Investment Trust" led people to think it actually *was* a trust. There was, however, no trust deed and no trustee, nor has there

---

*Senate Report 1775, 76th Congress, third session, 1940.

ever been. In smaller print, the prospectus called IIT "a unit trust organized under the laws of Luxembourg," but what that amounts to is not easy to say. The Grand Duchy, an eighty-by-forty-mile piece of well-timbered hill country between France and Germany, is rich in iron ore, deer, and wild boar, but not in securities law. An open-end investment fund has no legally defined qualities in Luxembourg. Insofar as any law applies, it would be ancient common law relating to co-ownership of property. The Luxembourg Banking Commission merely requires mutual-fund organizations to register a management company and a set of rules.

All that IOS set up in Luxembourg was a company called "IIT Management Company," whose purpose was defined as the managing of something called "IIT, an International Investment Trust." This must be one of the most diaphanous structures ever employed to hold $700 million of other people's money. In theory at least, the rules of IIT would give a shareholder some recourse against misbehavior by IIT Management, but the fact that they were not filed until February 14, 1961, a couple of months after the fund began operating, is not encouraging. And, after the original filing, IIT does not seem to have bothered keeping them up to date. For instance, in 1970 it still gave the Bank H. Albert de Bary as Custodian, although that arrangement had ceased in 1964.

The skeletal nature of IIT was not easily apparent to the customers. Another impressive name was added to the mechanism with the selection of the Banque Internationale à Luxembourg, the Duchy's largest bank, as Transfer Agent and Registrar. Money was inserted into IIT by the customers, and it was then placed on account with the Crédit Suisse, the Depository of Cash. Shares of the fund, to correspond with the inflow, were registered and sent out by the Banque Internationale. The cash of the fund was employed to purchase securities in a number of countries and these were placed on account with the Bank H. Albert de Bary in Amsterdam. Investment policy was decided by the Bruno A. Hugi Banque Privée of Zurich.

Few people realized that none of the eminent international concerns whose names appeared on the sales literature bore any responsibility to check up on the nature of investments made by IIT, and that the Bruno A. Hugi Banque Privée was Dr. Hugi operating out of his suburban house in Zurich.

It was virtually inevitable that some of the money going into IIT would be applied unhappily—and so indeed it was.

• 6 •

Ed Cowett's Problem

In which the learned co-author of Blue Sky Law tries his hand at promoting speculative companies, gets into deep financial trouble, and is helped out by Bernie Cornfeld.

The IOS salesmen reacted with vigor to the challenge of having their own fund to sell. Customers in many countries were readily attracted by the idea of a mutual fund that would invest their money on stock exchanges around the world, with a big slice of it going into Wall Street. The first year of operations, 1961, was a buoyant time for share prices in a great many countries, and in America particularly. On the New York Stock Exchange, the Dow-Jones average touched 741, comfortably above the previous record of 688 in 1959.

Few of the salesmen, and probably even fewer of the prospects, appreciated the peculiarities of IIT's legal make-up. On the contrary, it seemed a specially appealing package of American expertise, with respectable Swiss and Dutch connections. If you had dollars, or could find dollars, it might have looked like a very fine investment. Certainly, a lot of people thought so, because in the first twelve months the fund grew to $3.4 million.

But at the end of 1961, Dr. Bruno Hugi reported to the fund's investors in these less-than-ebullient terms:

> The New York market has been consistently good throughout the year. However, the rise was confined to blue-chip stocks of a rather defensive nature. Many of the glamour stocks declined sharply, and frankly, your Fund suffered from such investments. The stocks of the category which we continue to hold have a very fine growth potential and we are not disturbed by their drop in price.

One of the stocks which presumably had a "very fine growth potential" was a little company called Minitone Electronics. The "International Investment Trust" had invested several thousand dollars in this manufacturer of battery-operated pencil sharpeners, shavers, and carving knives. Minitone had first offered its shares for sale in New York in early 1961, when its directors had complied with those strict provisions of American law which require full disclosure of the nature of the investments being offered. "The Common Stock," they wrote in the Minitone prospectus, "is speculative. On the basis of the past and present operations of the company, no representation can be made that the company will be able to conduct future operations profitably."

Edward M. Cowett was one of the Minitone directors who put his name to that statement. He was also New York legal counsel to Investors Overseas Services, the promoters and controllers of IIT, and had been since 1958. He was, in 1961, a director of IOS, and a frequent traveler from New York to Geneva.

Minitone and seven more of the most glamorous of the glamour stocks in which IIT had invested, were listed separately in the report which Dr. Hugi sent out for 1961. They were headed "U.S. Special Situations"; and they were very special indeed, because within a very few months the value of the investment in them was virtually obliterated. Minitone, most of the other "special situations," and a number of other items in the portfolio bought for the customers of IIT, had been "promoted" by Ed Cowett or by associates of his in New York.

Bernard Cornfeld once gave this accurate definition of the nature of the investment-company business. "We are involved," he said, "in getting hundreds of thousands of people to relinquish the decisions of what to invest in, and put these decisions into the hands of experts who can manage this money effectively." The theory is that it is in the expert's interest to do well by the customers, for he will benefit himself thereby. In practice, things are more complicated. Surveying the wreckage of the 1930s, the U.S. government's investigators concluded that there was an intrinsic danger, once people had relinquished effective power over their own money, that the experts might start managing it with their own interests more crudely in view. "Insiders often viewed investment companies as sources of capital for business ventures of their own and as captive markets for unsaleable securities that they, as insiders, wished to convert into cash."[*]

It is for this reason that the U.S. law goes to enormous lengths to limit the opportunities for a mutual-fund company to put the customers' money into concerns owned or influenced by officials of the mutual-fund company itself. The story of IIT and

---

[*]SEC Study of Investment Trusts and Investment Companies (1938–1940) part III, p. 2541.

its "U.S. Special Situations" indicates that this was a piece of legislation which Cowett and Cornfeld regarded as superfluous.

● ● ●

One of the most important, and mysterious, incidents in the history of Investors Overseas Services has always been that disaster which afflicted its first fund, IIT, in 1962. That was, admittedly, a bad year on Wall Street, anyway. In a kind of dress rehearsal for the crash at the end of the decade, there was a sharp break in the early part of 1961. The Dow Jones, which had reached 741 the year before, plunged to 524.6, and, when at last it rose again on its way to still greater heights, many of the brilliant speculations of the previous year failed to rise with it.

The value of a share in IIT slumped by an awful 22 per cent in that year. Since then, the company has gone to considerable lengths to divert attention away from that period: most notoriously, by publishing incomplete performance records for IIT that give the impression that the fund only started at the end of 1962.

Discussion of the period with IOS veterans usually produces little more than a disposition to shift all the responsibility to Dr. Hugi, who resigned at the end of 1961. Sometimes, however, it also produces veiled references to an associated phenomenon called "Ed's problem." Dr. Hugi, like a good Swiss banker, is reluctant to do more than defend his own abilities as an investment adviser, and to say that he resigned his post because Cornfeld and Cowett were disregarding his investment decisions.

It is quite clear that something happened because of the lengths to which IOS went to conceal Cowett's early association with the company. Early *IOS Bulletins* and annual reports clearly record that Cowett was first appointed a director in early 1960 and became Secretary of IOS in the spring of 1962. Yet later IOS publicity material says that Cowett joined IOS in 1963 as General Counsel and a director, thus implying he had no earlier association with IOS.

It is not easy to discover exactly what happened—and it is not especially pleasant, because Ed Cowett, at least on acquaintance, is an agreeable enough citizen, with a touch of lawyer's wit and a passion for backgammon. Further, the truth is plainly distressing to other people besides Cowett, to past colleagues and to relatives. But its relevance to the story of IOS and the offshore world is too obvious to be denied, because Bernard Cornfeld acknowledges that he placed Ed Cowett in virtually sole charge of IOS, when it had control of more than $2000 million.

When Cowett joined Stroock & Stroock & Lavan, people took him for a young man in a hurry. He admits that he was mainly interested in the law as a tool of business promotion. His elder brother, Wilbur Cowett, was already regarded as one of the most brilliant younger men in Wall Street. Edward Cowett's friends thought that his chief ambition was to achieve a success in financial affairs to rival or outshine his brother's. Not that it was easy to divine what was going on in Cowett's mind. He was amiable, but remarkably self-contained.

It was an uncle, Malcolm Kingsberg, who launched Cowett in New York by introducing him to the senior partner of Stroock & Stroock. At that time Kingsberg, more or less the head of the family, was looking after the financial side of Mike Todd's Todd-AO wide-screen business, but he was a business veteran, who had seen at first hand the speculative excesses and market manipulation of the late 1920s. As a partner of Goldman, Sachs he had been specially delegated to look after that firm's business with Mike Meehan, one of the most famous stock manipulators of the era. (Later in the 1930s, Kingsberg went on to be President of the RKO Theater Division.)

Kingsberg had been in a prime position to observe the dangers of speculation on market operations, but if he passed on any advice to his promising nephew, it had no noticeable effect. Ed Cowett left Stroock & Stroock in 1958, having learned his way around New York and the securities business.

Shortly afterward, he embarked upon a series of speculative company promotions which was reckless even by the heady standards of Wall Street in the early 1960s. In his own words he was "caught up in the insanity of the times." This brief but spectacular episode led Cowett into financial difficulty, and in an attempt to stave it off, he plunged into debt to the tune of $800,000—and even drew a check on the bank account of his law partnership to pay some of it off.

• • •

It is through the mechanism of company promotion that capitalism claims to be able to develop new products and techniques with rapidity and economy. Serious investment banks spend their time looking for new companies with good ideas, which can be brought to prosperity by injections of money and advice. When such a company succeeds, arrangements are made to sell off its shares to the public: normally, the investment bankers "underwrite" the issue of shares by guaranteeing to buy the shares themselves if nobody else does.

This useful activity is very unlike what can happen at the other end of the company-promotion business when a group of bright young men decides to "take a company in hand." They buy up the shares of the company, which is usually moribund or embryonic, at a very cheap price. They then ginger it up with some energetic publicity, a well-chosen name, and possibly a little money—but above all, a new "concept." If there is an optimistic atmosphere on the stock market, and people are looking for shares to buy, the rejuvenated company may generate considerable interest. The promoters can now sell off the shares of the company at a handsomely increased price, in an offer which is not usually underwritten.

Ed Cowett's operations as a promoter had more in common with the second model than the first. As co-author of *Blue Sky Law*, Cowett was expert in the legal side of company promotion. Some time after leaving Stroock & Stroock, he formed a partnership with another Harvard man, Bill McGowan, who had had a brilliant record at the Business School, and who had worked for Malcolm Kingsberg at Todd-AO.

Stock-market booms have their fashions in "hot stocks." In 1929, almost anything to do with radio could be sold. In 1958–1962 it was anything to do with computers or electronics.

Early in 1959, McGowan put together a company called Powertron Ultrasonics. The business of Powertron was to develop the commercial potential of inaudible, high-frequency sound waves. It was a small concern and its principal product was a cleaning system consisting of tanks and a generator that produced ultrasonic waves. To quote the company's own description: "When the object to be cleaned is placed in a tank containing an appropriate liquid solvent, the activity attributable to the constant and intense sound waves traveling through the liquid causes a rapid and thorough cleaning."

Cowett played a relatively limited part in this company. When Powertron was formed, McGowan and his associates took up 150,000 shares for a total payment of $900, or 0.6¢ each. Cowett received 3000 of these shares, acting as nominee for Powertron's attorneys. The company spent its first year developing its products and building up debts, losing about $100,000 in the process. By the summer of 1960, Powertron was ready to start raising capital from the public, and the prospectus contained all the caveats legally necessary. It said:

> Although ultrasonic cleaning has been extremely successful in a wide variety of industrial and commercial applications, and some objects can be cleaned more thoroughly and more economically with ultrasonic cleaning than with other recognized cleaning techniques, many attempted applications of ultrasound in cleaning have proved wholly unsuccessful.

Nevertheless, Powertron shares put on quite a performance. They were issued to the public at $2 each, when Cowett received another 3100 shares. The investing public was impressed with thoughts of ultrasonic cleaning, and the shares took off smartly. From Geneva, IIT bought 2500 shares, and Powertron sailed on to a top of $13 per share in March 1961. After that, the glamour began to wear off and vanished altogether in 1962. Powertron Ultrasonics was eventually bought up by a larger firm, at a price per share which would have shown a profit over the issuing price, but little more. It should be said that Powertron had some real qualities, apart from the unreal ones attributed to it by a feverish market. It continues in business today, as a useful subsidiary. The companies in which Cowett assumed a larger role did not always show such qualities.

Cowett started his own promotion activities seriously in the autumn of 1960, and he must have been a busy man in those days. For a little while after he left Stroock & Stroock, Cowett was an adviser to the wealthy Farkas family, owners of Alexander's department store, but after a very short stint there he went back to the law. In May 1961, after brief associations with a couple of firms, he became a partner in a new firm called Feldman,

Kramer, Bam, Nessen and Cowett. The moving spirit was Al Feldman, a real-estate lawyer, rather older than Ed Cowett.

The junior partner brought a fast-growing client with him: Investors Overseas Services of Geneva. Cowett had met Cornfeld while working on the Dreyfus Fund account for Stroock & Stroock. The fund's hottest foreign dealer was a frequent visitor to the Dreyfus office, and he was usually requesting something that required extended negotiation. It did not take the lawyer and the salesman long to see that their abilities were complementary. Cowett brought other clients also, including the little network of companies he was building up. (Bill McGowan also had offices in the same building as the law firm.) Cowett kept rather to himself in a room at the back of the office, and the other partners knew very little about what he was doing.

$$\bullet \ \bullet \ \bullet$$

When Cowett took over Minitone Electronics in the autumn of 1960 its liabilities were substantially in excess of its assets. Through his partnership with McGowan Cowett took up a large block of shares—41,333—paying only a nominal 1¢ a share, or a total of $413. That sum did little to ease Minitone's debt problem, which included $75,000 owed to the Irving Trust (Cowett guaranteed the loan). Nevertheless, Cowett and his fellow promoters had great hopes for their battery-operated gadgets and had plans to add a pot-scourer, also powered by a battery in the handle, to the range. So they turned to the public, and in early 1961 they succeeded in selling 205,003 shares at $3 each, a price which was quite arbitrarily decided.

The prospectus of Minitone conformed with the best principles of Blue Sky Law. It disclosed that if the public took up Minitone's shares at the issuing price, the "present shareholders will benefit from an increase in the book value of their shares amounting to $1.98 per share, such benefit being at the expense of those who purchase at the offering price." But when share prices are soaring, nobody cares about book values. The point is that there are more buyers than sellers, and the hunger of the market is for securities to trade.

The shares of the companies that Cowett promoted were not sold on official exchanges, such as the New York Stock Exchange. They were sold through friends, including, for instance, a former officer of the Netherlands Navy turned stockbroker named John Zeeman, and then traded "over-the-counter." Despite the public's subscription of $600,000 to Minitone, the company never solved its financial problems. Its products were too expensive and did not catch on: the pot-scourer, according to Cowett, was the main cause of the fiasco. In the end, the assets were sold for what they would fetch.

Cowett had one really original company, which was called Geriatric Services. It was based in Boston, and it operated thirty-five nursing homes for old people. The promotional theory was that Geriatrics would be admirably situated to profit from the Kennedy administration's Medicare program for medical subsidy for the aged. This was almost prophetic: seven or eight years later, nursing-home companies were highly fashionable hot stocks in the last 1960s boom.

Cowett, with Zeeman and McGowan, started to take an active interest in the affairs of Geriatrics in February 1961, and in August all three were appointed to the board. Cowett had bought 12,500 common shares at $1.64 each and some preferred shares. The common shares of Geriatrics were offered to the public later that year at $4 each. IIT bought 3000 shares of Geriatrics.

The Medicare program made only slow progress through Congress, and by the time it got through, Geriatrics, after a brief attempt at revival by the Roman Catholic Church, had gone into liquidation. Years later, Four Seasons Nursing Homes became a great investment favorite with IOS fund managers. It, too, went bust.

Cowett's other promotions were nearer to the mainstream of market fashion. There was a color-printing firm in Boston called Color Lithography; there was one which produced a device you affixed to your car and it would warn you automatically when it was time to change the oil. Perhaps the most important of them, as far as IIT was concerned, was a firm called Associated Engineers, which operated in Springfield, Cowett's home town, and which became one of his first clients. Although Associated assembled components for Powertron, McGowan never became closely involved in the project. The company never even got as far as a public issue. But the faithful IIT bought 5000 shares of Associated, which were valued at $15,000 at December 31, 1961. They remained forlornly in IIT's list, valued at zero, until 1965, after which they disappeared.

These were not on the whole the kind of companies to make or break the U.S. economy. But in the markets of the early 1960s, they could make or break a company promoter. From the autumn of 1960 to the end of 1961, the Dow-Jones average rose by more than 30 per cent. But, as Dr. Hugi's report noted at the end of 1961, the glamour stocks had already begun to slide.

In the first few months of 1962 the slide continued, and after a little while prices of blue-chip securities began to slip as well. In April the descent accelerated. Then, almost overnight at the end of May, the bottom fell out of the market, and the game—for the time being anyway—was up. In May and June the Dow fell 25 per cent, and the value of most of Ed Cowett's promotions was obliterated.

Cowett had enjoyed considerable prestige in his circle, a captain of finance only just past thirty. Friends were often sufficiently impressed to invest in the shares of Cowett concerns. Ruefully, one such investor recalled the abruptness of the disaster in these terms. "One moment, my portfolio was up ten times. A couple of weeks later Ed and I were playing darts for them."

Possibly, it had once seemed a brilliant idea for IIT to invest its customers' money in Minitone Electronics, Associated Engineers, Geriatric Services, and the other promotions of IOS's brilliant young lawyer—even if the SEC would not have approved. Cowett told us that Dr. Hugi was under no compulsion to include his promotions in the IIT portfolio, and he claimed that there were promotions of his that the fund did not buy. He acknowledged that Dr. Hugi might have thought himself under pressure to buy them.

Hugi told us that he had played no part in the decision to acquire Cowett's "babies," as he called them, for the IIT portfolio, and that he even resisted their inclusion—for it started a trend toward speculation which he opposed. It was indeed one of the reasons that led to his resignation as President of IIT, he said.

But Cowett's trouble only began with the break. Nobody could be blamed for getting caught up in the gorgeous optimism of 1959–1961. Plenty of investors and operators—such as McGowan and Zeeman—came through somewhat sadder and wiser, but without damaging their integrity. Cowett's real problem appears to have been a refusal to acknowledge that the end had come.

Each of the partners in Cowett's law firm had his own specialty, and they did not work closely together. Cowett, especially, was a "free spirit," as he described himself, and did not always see eye to eye with his partners. Cowett's lone promotion activities began to concern them. The resulting tensions came to a head in the early summer of 1962.

The first thing that worried the partners, however, was not so much Cowett's promotion activities but the state of the firm's business with IOS. A certain amount of work was being done on the account within the firm, but the fees were not making a particularly generous contribution to the firm's expenses. Cowett was a director of IOS and was traveling frequently to Geneva. He had also recently taken a big apartment at Seventy-second Street and Madison Avenue. Cowett's partners, knowing how much he was getting out of the firm, wondered how a young lawyer could afford this style of living.

The partners asked Cowett to meet with them, and they questioned him closely about the IOS account. Coolly and sensibly—the only sign of nervousness was a slight tremor in the hand holding his cigarette—he calmed their worries, and persuaded them again that IOS was an investment for the future.

The worries were not altogether eliminated: the partners wondered uneasily whether Cowett might be getting paid separately by IOS.

Today, Cowett admits that he was spending a lot of money in those days. "I was living at the rate of $60,000 a year—and $60,000 was worth a lot more then—and I was taking $40,000 out of the law firm." Cowett says, however, that all legal fees from IOS and his other clients went into the law firm; he reckons he was contributing more than 20 per cent, *i.e.*, more than his share, to the income of the firm. Everything went to the firm, he says, except for his stock interests. It was these interests that enabled him to live beyond his income: he used them as collateral for bank loans.

At much the same time Bill McGowan also became worried. He discovered that Cowett had borrowed large sums from their business partnership. McGowan began to get calls from stockbrokers, asking him veiled questions about what Cowett was doing. McGowan and Feldman got together, and asked Cowett what was going on. Once again, Ed was cool and assured. "No problem," he told them—it was one of his favorite phrases.

Cowett then disappeared again to Geneva. It was at this point that Cowett's law partners made the discovery that shook them most of all. They found that Cowett had drawn a check on the firm's bank account without telling them. The amount was not particularly large—some $30,000 or so—but it came close to cleaning out the account. Cowett, as a partner of the firm, had access to the account; but his partners were particularly upset because Cowett had not told them he was going to take the money. It was only by chance that one of the other partners had not subsequently and unwittingly bounced a check. One of them now called Cowett in Geneva and said that as far as they were concerned he could stay in Switzerland.

But Cowett was not to stay in Geneva. While he was still away, it became increasingly clear to Cowett's close associates that he had piled up debts in buying up the shares of his company promotions.

In an attempt to assess the seriousness of the financial trouble that was brewing, McGowan and Feldman, acting independently of the other law partners, again got together at Cowett's office. McGowan examined his desk and finally opened a deep bottom drawer that was heaped full of brokers' slips confirming share-purchase orders, many of which were unopened. He immediately telephoned Cowett in Geneva and told him to come back home at once.

McGowan and Feldman met Cowett at the airport and drove him straight to his new apartment, still barely furnished. Cowett coolly tried to rationalize his position and said he was getting some help from Cornfeld. But there was really no alternative except to face the fact that his financial affairs were in chaos. He owed substantial sums to the International Credit Bank in Geneva, to the Irving Trust, and to stockbrokers. He had also guaranteed many of the loans of his companies. (Cowett asked us ruefully if we knew the definition of a guarantor: "A fool with a fountain pen.") Cowett also owed a small sum—$15,000 to $20,000—to IOS itself. Then there was the question of the money he had used from the law firm and from his partnership with McGowan.

Cowett's debts totaled at least $800,000. "That was the low point," he told us. Some idea of the amount of money he had run through in just a few months is given by the fact that Cowett estimated his net worth at the end of 1961 at more than one million dollars.

McGowan had now brought in John Zeeman and they decided that they could not handle the situation on their own; they determined to call in Wilbur Cowett. Cowett, too, felt he had to turn to his brother. Wilbur, although naturally anxious to save the family name, was not sympathetic to his brother's difficulties. Ed had expected more willing co-operation, and relations between the two were not happy. Other close associates take the view that much of the trouble was due to the fact that Ed found it almost impossible to admit that he needed help, and that it was especially difficult for him to admit that he needed help from the elder brother whose achievements he had tried to rival.

Cowett's real savior was Cornfeld. He did not put up much money—only $20,000 or so according to Cowett—but he helped Cowett gain the breathing space he needed to sort out his affairs. Cowett himself raised some $10,000 by selling IOS shares he had bought earlier from Cornfeld. The main buyer was John Templeton, a New York investment adviser close to IOS.

Further bitterness was aroused in the sorting out of Cowett's tangled affairs with his associates like Bill McGowan and John Zeeman. They felt additionally injured when Cowett appointed a lawyer to handle the matter so that they had to deal with him at one remove. (The lawyer was Robert J. Haft of Stamer and Haft, who became important legal advisers to IOS.) At the end of the day there were still some disputed sums outstanding, and both McGowan and Zeeman came out of the episode substantially worse off.

Cowett effectively ceased to be a working partner of the law firm from the moment the other partners called him up in Geneva. But it took some months to wind up the association formally, as Cowett's participation in the firm's financial position had to be ascertained. As for the $30,000 check, Cowett says he drew this money because he realized that his partners wanted to break up the partnership and that he felt this was his share. Nevertheless, the money was paid back, and Cornfeld says it was he who paid it back. Cowett, however, still maintains he was owed money by the firm.

Cowett more or less disappeared from the New York scene in the summer of 1962 and did not finally make Geneva his base until late 1963. In between he traveled a great deal between the two cities and also spent some time in the Bahamas. He also took two long trips to South America.

• • •

The salesmen in their scattered corners of the world never knew the full story, but they were bitter at the slump in IIT's value. (The shares dropped from $4.87 to $3.65 in the first six months of 1962.) Gradually, however, rumors filtered through: it was considered that the most discreet thing for Cowett to do was to resign. This did not happen until the middle of 1963. Cowett did not rejoin the board until 1965, so the publicity material we referred to at the beginning of the chapter was inaccurate in stating that Cowett joined IOS as a director in 1963.

On May 29, 1962, Dr. Hugi was replaced as President of IIT by a youthful and socially eminent stockbroker named Christian Henry Buhl III, who had been working for the brokers McDonnell and Co. in New York, but felt he had grown out of it.

(Buhl's family owns a large piece of General Motors.) The first thing he did was to appoint John Templeton as IIT's principal investment adviser. (Dr. Hugi continued to be associated with IIT until later that year.)

Reporting to the IIT shareholders at the end of 1962, Buhl was at rather a loss to explain the depressing condition of Wall Street. "One fact seems certain," he said, ". . . the companies behind these shares did not suffer special declines; profits were generally as high in 1962 as anticipated." Minitone Electronics had not made any profits and there was no firm reason, when IIT bought Minitone shares, to think that it would. So perhaps that company was not included in Buhl's reflection.

At the end of 1961, IIT had about $3.4 million worth of investments of which about $100,000 was in Cowett's "babies." A not inconsiderable 2.9 per cent of the fund was thus invested in concerns associated with a director of IOS. Just how much IIT lost on Cowett's companies could only be determined by a detailed analysis of IIT's transactions in 1961 and 1962. Cowett himself says the loss was of the order of $70,000 to $100,000.

The disaster that struck Cowett's companies, and glamour stocks generally, sparked off panic measures at IOS: a reaction which was to be duplicated eight years later.

The newly appointed Buhl decided that the best thing to do was to liquidate large parts of the IIT investments. The portfolio that Dr. Hugi had assembled contained a great number of small parcels of different securities—too many, by modern American standards, for efficient handling of the investments. Nevertheless, the wholesale selling on which Buhl embarked meant that a number of better-quality stocks were sold at almost rock-bottom prices. By the end of 1962, the new IIT management had lost $1,133,000 on sales of shares, a staggering ratio of 33 per cent of the value of securities held at the start of the year.

The shrinkage of value was covered only by the gallant efforts of the far-flung salesmen who brought in enough new cash for the fund to increase slightly in size during the year.

The price of IIT shares continued to fall until October 1962, when it had sunk to $3.53. This coincided with the launching of the Fund of Funds and the IOS Investment Program, under which IIT was sold from then on. Later, IOS concealed the early disaster of IIT by calculating all growth records from its nadir in October 1962; this made its performance look reasonably respectable. In reality IIT did not regain its December 1960 launching price of $5 until early 1965. IOS justified this deception by saying that IIT came under IOS's management only in the autumn of 1962. This can now be seen to be untrue. IOS had full control of the management company of IIT from its inception and it played a crucial and fateful role in the selection of some of its investments. Even the replacement of the "outside investment adviser," Dr. Hugi, took place in May and not October. Cowett, at least, is frank about it now. When we asked him why IOS always used October 1962 as the starting point of IIT he answered, "It looked better; that's why."

Cornfeld's behavior toward Cowett in 1962 was in many respects admirable. He rescued an undoubtedly able friend and colleague from the consequences of folly, and at considerable cost to himself. It was, if you like, Cornfeld the social worker, always ready to help a man who has tumbled in his career.

Still, it cannot be left just like that. Cornfeld knew the essential details of Cowett's activities, and was clearly in a position to have known everything had he so desired. Yet Cowett was retained as chief legal adviser of IOS. After a relatively brief absence, he was readmitted to the Board of IOS—and within five years, Cornfeld was ready to entrust him with control over the investments of a million clients around the world.

• 7 •

The Birth of a Superfund

In which we examine the Fund of Funds, which is really a Gimmick of Gimmicks. How it worked to the advantage of its inventors, Ed and Bernie, and to the disadvantage of its investors.

Bernard Cornfeld's niche in financial history is secured, if by nothing else, by his promotion of the Fund of Funds, the classic investment vehicle of the offshore decade. There has been much dispute about who first conceived the idea of a mutual fund whose business would consist of investing in other mutual funds. Nobody has disputed that it was the most potent idea that came out of IOS.

The Fund of Funds was launched in the autumn of 1962, and, according to Ed Cowett, the idea was born when he and Cornfeld were riding on a sleigh together on a winter night in Canada. They were tossing new investment devices to and fro—but Cowett insists that the basic inspiration was Bernie's. Certainly it was Cornfeld who breathed life into it by adding that simple Biblical name. Robert Nagler, a Dreyfus Vice President who had been hired by IOS, arrived in Geneva when the idea was still being worked out, but remained as yet unnamed. One day, Cornfeld walked into Nagler's office at 119 Rue de Lausanne (IOS had by now taken over the whole building). "How about 'Fund of Funds'?" Cornfeld asked. Nagler could only say "Great."

Even by IOS standards, the salesman's rationale for the Fund of Funds was an unusually owlish piece of nonsense—one of those things that sounds impressive until you really think it through. Mutual funds, and all investment concerns, are sold on the proposition that the ordinary man needs investment advisers to make his choices for him. The Fund of Funds went further and suggested that the ordinary man now needed professionals to choose the professionals who would make the choices. The Fund of Funds would take your money and invest it in other mutual funds—but only in those whose values were rising most rapidly. Or, if one mutual fund was good, a mutual fund which contained twenty other mutual funds must be twenty times better.

An SEC lawyer exploded the Fund of Funds argument succinctly. "If funds on funds are permitted to proliferate," he wrote, "how would an investor decide among the many companies seeking his investment dollar? Would he not need a *fund on funds on funds* to make this decision?"

There was another rationale to the Fund of Funds, which was not trumpeted so loudly. Mutual-fund companies, of course, take their profits by charging the customers a management fee. Out of this fee, they have to pay for investment analysts and for the organization necessary to buy and sell large quantities of securities. The FOF charged a management fee; but the only "management" involved was channeling money into one mutual fund rather than another.

This neat charge upon the customers would not have been possible "onshore." Indeed, the Fund of Funds was an animal so curiously made that it could only survive in the kindly offshore waters. It was registered in the Province of Ontario, in Canada.

The Fund of Funds was set up with two classes of shares, something which American investment companies are specifically prohibited from doing. There were Class A Preference Shares, which were the ones that were sold in thousands to the public. These carried no voting powers. There were also common shares, which were not common at all. There were originally only 350 of them, and they were all controlled by IOS. These were the only voting shares, and the result was that Cornfeld and Cowett could do virtually anything they wished with the Fund of Funds.

Originally, its main purpose in life was to invest in mutual funds in the United States, where the mutual funds were most exciting.

American official hostility to the idea of investment companies investing in other investment companies dates from the part played in the 1929 insanity by investment companies which owned securities in other investment companies, in the kind of "tiers" described in Chapter 3. Until the debut of the Fund of Funds, many Americans thought that the 1940 Investment Company Act had made it illegal in America for one investment company to buy another's shares. But for complex technical reasons, the Act does not do that. It merely says in Section 12 (*d*) 1, that no American-registered investment company can own more than 3 per cent of the shares of any other investment company. The Fund of Funds escaped this limitation simply by residing in Ontario.

When the SEC became aware of this arrangement, they pointed out that it could have an effect on stock markets which might be similar to the investment-company speculation of 1929. The SEC's reservations were not widely shared, certainly not by Bernie's sales force. The Fund of Funds, like IIT, was decorated with good names: Crédit Suisse was again Depository of

Cash, and Bank H. Albert de Bary of Amsterdam was Custodian of Securities. Montreal Trust, a subsidiary of the Royal Bank of Canada, came in as Transfer Agent and Registrar. IOS artwork had improved no end since the early days of IIT, and the Fund of Funds literature acquired a coat of arms; a symbolic bull and bear prancing amid oak leaves.

The Fund of Funds really did take off like a rocket. It was under $1 million in October 1962: by September the next year it hit $16.65 million. At the end of 1964, after a little over two years' operation, it hit $100 million. Nothing like it had been seen before—after all, the Dreyfus Fund had taken nearly six years to go from $500,000 to $100 million. The development of the Fund of Funds "has made it the phenomenon of phenomena," observed an awestruck correspondent of the London *Times*, from Geneva.

From the moment the sales force first pushed it out, the proposition looked so bewitching that the customers did not seem to be impressed by the financial disadvantages they suffered from the "layering" of costs. There were two management fees on the customers' money, one taken by IOS and the other taken by the mutual funds in which the Fund of Funds invested. The layering effect also applied to sales loads. As we noted in Chapter 3, an expansion-minded mutual-fund seller has to chop out a chunk of each customer's money in order to pay off his sales force. Competition for salesmen pushed this up in the mid-1960s to a top rate of about $8.50 in every $100 for the U.S. trade,* and it was only to be expected that IOS, with so many salesmen sincerely wanting to be rich, would charge the top rate.

The customers suffered from the fact that there was another sales load when the Fund of Funds bought U.S. mutual-fund

*About 9 per cent of the actual sum invested.

shares. True, IOS was able to make bulk-purchase arrangements which cut this down to under 1 per cent. But it still came out of the customers' money. This was bad enough, one might think, but it was only the beginning. After operating on this model for about two and a half years, IOS had a brilliant idea. Why not re-organize things so that they could appropriate *all* the layers for themselves? This inspiration produced the first period of radical change in the Fund of Funds (in mid-1965, when IOS was still combing the world for money and had not yet run into any serious trouble over the currency-busting activities of its salesmen).

Contrary to the general belief, it was not a prohibition by the Securities and Exchange Commission that prompted Bernie and Ed to modify their original idea. What happened was that the creative minds in Geneva realized IOS could do even better for itself than taking a fee for channeling the customers' money into funds run by other people. Suppose IOS *itself* controlled the funds into which the money went. IOS could then benefit from two levels of management fees. This turned the original idea upside down, but it opened up great possibilities. There was no intention, or possibility, that IOS could set up orthodox mutual funds in America. But what they could, and did do, was set up *proprietary* funds, each one of which would have only one investor—the Fund of Funds. Such funds would not have to be registered with the SEC.

IOS was not only able to benefit from two sets of management fees; a second sales charge, now dressed up as "brokerage" commission, was appropriated by IOS for the onerous duty of transferring the customers' money from the Fund of Funds to the individual proprietary funds!

The great wonder of the Fund of Funds was its plasticity. It transmogrified itself several times, and, eventually, the only characteristic it retained of the original fund-on-funds idea was a layering of charges. To show just how changeable, and how misleading, the form of FOF was eventually capable of being, it is necessary to leap forward for a moment in time and consider some technicalities.

Individuals who trade their own investments on stock markets may wish to make money by wagering on short-term movements of prices. To "sell short" is to bet on a fall: a short seller undertakes, receiving payment at today's price, to deliver at an established future date some set number of shares, which he does not yet possess. Assuming that the price of such shares drops before he has to deliver, he can supply himself with enough of them to honor his commitment, while leaving him a profit on the payment he received earlier. If the price rises, he loses his bet.

To buy "on margin" is essentially to bet on a rise. Brokers at certain times are prepared to give possession of shares on a receipt of cash payment covering only a part of the price. If the value of shares bought goes up, the buyer reaps the same advantage as if he had paid in full. But if they fall, the broker will quickly demand payment of all the original purchase price, and the buyer can easily lose more than he put up in the first place.

Clearly, these activities go beyond the ordinary buying and selling of shares, and are more suitably undertaken with one's own money than with other people's. With this in mind, the law in America, Britain, and most other financially sophisticated places says that open-end funds may not sell short or buy on margin. There are also restrictions on the kind of things that an open-end fund can put money into, and the most important restriction is against investment in real estate. This is designed to preserve the liquidity that persuades many people to buy fund shares. Assuming a fund's assets are all listed on the stock exchange, their value can be checked independently every day, and they can be sold rapidly if people wish to make redemptions. Real estate obviously has no formal market. It may take a long time to sell, and until sold its value is a matter of opinion. Mutual funds and unit trusts are, therefore, effectively prohibited from making real-estate investments. On May 2, 1968, the prospectus of the Fund of Funds made this reassuring declaration:

Investment Restrictions

While professional management, by definition, implies the prudent management of other people's money, *Fund of Funds* management, as a matter of policy, has adopted the following restrictions for the protection of its investors. Among these are that the Fund may not borrow money, purchase any securities on margin, sell securities short, lend any of its assets (except for the purchase of government bonds), or purchase, lease, or acquire real estate. (Funds in *The Fund of Funds* portfolio may, depending upon their respective charters, sell short, borrow money, or purchase securities on margin, and buy, sell, or hold real estate.)

This would appear to suggest that the IOS fund managers would not indulge in such activities—with the proviso that they cannot guarantee that the fellows in whose companies they invest may not do so from time to time. The truth was exactly the other way around. The actual fact was that the managers who controlled the bulk of the Fund of Funds' assets were all appointed by IOS and IOS itself devised a method whereby their customers' assets could be used in 1968, 1969, and 1970 to borrow money, buy on margin, sell short, lend fund assets out, and handle real estate. And the customers' assets were indeed employed in short trading, were lent out to market operators, and were used to buy real estate. Finally, large segments were used, disastrously, in the most esoteric development of the basic real-estate idea, the natural-resources business.

The only funds in the Fund of Funds which could *not* undertake any of these uncertain activities were the ones that IOS did not control. This was because FOF still had some investments in perfectly ordinary U.S. mutual funds, such as it had started out with.

The key to the versatility of the Fund of Funds lay in its original constitution. IIT was not a substantial legal entity, but it did have rules that could not be changed without the permission of the Luxembourg Banking Commission. Fund of Funds was altogether less cramped.

Onshore, mutual funds and unit trusts are only allowed to change their structure and objectives slowly, if at all. Certainly, they cannot do so simply at the will of the management. As a last resort the investors, apathetic though they may be, hold voting rights over the fund's actions. Through its controlling share-holding IOS could, and did, alter the fund's financial policy at will, often without giving its investors any clear idea what was going on. In the end, the Fund of Funds turned in catastrophic directions; it is hard, at any point, to see where its freedom operated to the benefit of IOS's customers rather than to that of IOS itself.

* * *

When Cornfeld adopted the "proprietary" system, he needed to hire money managers in America to run his new funds. A consultant named Conrad Taff introduced Bernie to his first team. This was made up of two young men called Dean Milosis and Carlyle Jones, who had been working for a well-known "hedge-fund" manager named Arthur Jones. The essence of a hedge fund is to operate in short sales, so it was not surprising that when Milosis, Jones, and IOS got together to form the York Fund—sole investor, the Fund of Funds—it set out to engage in short sales. Nobody seemed to think it important that the FOF prospectus assured the clients that it was not allowed to make short sales.

The next manager they hired was Fred Alger, who came, like C. Henry Buhl, from a well-to-do Detroit background, and who managed a fund in New York called the Security Equity Fund, which increased in value per share fastest of all U.S. funds in 1965. With IOS he set up the Alger Fund, and soon there was a whole battery of special IOS funds, while the Fund of Funds' holdings in publicly offered mutual funds began to run down.

Wall Street was in full cry again: the brief distress of 1962 was fading rapidly in memory, conglomerate stocks were sizzling, and Adam Smith's "gunslingers" were beginning to twirl the pearl-handled .45s around their fingers. . . . Rather sadly for the customers, IOS was beautifully positioned to take a leading role in the speculative shoot-out.

This gets ahead of our story—but before returning to the narrative, it is worth anticipating the greatest flexibility of the Fund of Funds. When, in 1967, IOS was forced, under threat of prosecution, to cease making investments in *any* U.S.-registered investment company, this was not mentioned in the annual report of the Fund of Funds to its shareholders. However, a new company called FOF Proprietary Funds Ltd. appeared in the Fund of Funds' list of investments (with remarkably little explanation).

This was another Canadian-registered concern. Now, the SEC ban was avoided by turning all of the separate "funds" into "subaccounts" of the Canadian company. Ostensibly, the *new* Canadian company, and its subaccounts, made investments in

America, while in fact the investments were still run by the same bright young managers in New York. Later, we must describe the system devised to make the continued operation legally defensible. The important point for the moment is that IOS now channeled most of the new Fund of Funds money through this new company, called FOF Proprietary Funds.

All these Canadian operations, of course, were simply legal devices: the money continued to be handled in Geneva and New York. But IOS apparently saw no reason not to do itself a bit of good through their existence. Originally, the IOS parent company had put up $1 million to create a capital structure for FOF Prop. At the end of 1967, IOS took to itself cash dividends of $2,453,696 on this modest investment. Somehow, large profits were being made when the customers' money passed through FOF Prop.

After this rather fine performance, in 1968 FOF Prop. became a wholly owned subsidiary of Fund of Funds Ltd. Now, the whole thing had assumed the shape of an ordinary investment company. It employed managers, and it invested not in investment funds but directly in securities—and, as it turned out, in almost anything else that came to hand. It was not a Fund of Funds at all. Yet the continued legal existence of the "shell" company FOF Prop. not only allowed Bernie and Ed to maintain the appearance that they still had a fund on funds, but also enabled them to continue to lift another 1 per cent of the customers' money, as it passed (only in the books in Switzerland) from the Fund of Funds to its subsidiary.

These rapid evolutions never caused Bernie and Ed to lose the air of gravity and high purpose that is conveyed by the best of their printed work. They liked to decorate their prospectuses with elevated quotations, and the 1968 one, which also contained the assurances about short sales, contained the famous statement of the Prudent Man Rule made by Justice Samuel Putnam of the Supreme Judicial Court of Massachusetts in 1830:

> All that can be required of a Trustee to invest is that he conduct himself faithfully and exercise a sound discretion. He is to observe how men of prudence, discretion, and intelligence manage their own affairs, not in regard to speculation, but in regard to the permanent disposition of their funds, considering the probable income, as well as the probable safety of the capital to be invested.

If there was a light, dry hum to be heard somewhere in Massachusetts in May 1968, it was presumably Mr. Justice Putnam revolving in his grave like a high-speed gas turbine.

• • •

Recalling his first meeting with Jack Dreyfus in New York, Cornfeld gives this account of the exchange. "I told Dreyfus, 'Yours is the only readable prospectus in the industry. I sell more funds using it than I sell using our own.'

" 'Why don't you sell my funds?' Dreyfus asked. I told him, 'Because you have no program.' "*

Taken on its own, the Fund of Funds was a device that provided its operators with unusual opportunities for profit and, having created FOF, Cornfeld and Cowett fitted it into an operating framework called The IOS Investment Program—with breathtaking results. It was this combined machinery which produced, from the resources of the customers, the rich and ample fodder on which Bernie's sales force grazed.

It is one of the features of the open-end fund business, on

---

*Dreyfus officials had actually drawn up a contractual program at about this time.

both sides of the Atlantic, that although it is supposed to exist for the benefit of smaller investors, its operators make more money the larger the average holding of the clients. This is because it costs just as much to administer a small account as a large one. Several methods have been devised to persuade small investors to make larger deposits, and the most potent—which dates from 1930—is the "investment program" or "contractual plan." The investor is persuaded not just to make a single investment, but to pay a regular monthly sum for ten or fifteen years. Mutual-fund organizers say that this makes the benefits of stock-market investment available to even the most limited incomes, because it makes a smaller initial payment possible. That may be so, but the program arrangements are often so complex that the customers do not understand just how much of what they pay is taken in charges. When they were introduced in the 1930s, "programs" involved some horrendous abuses. Not only did companies compute inflated charges for themselves, they extracted, in the small print, rights to take these charges out at the beginning of the program. Sometimes they took the *whole* of the first twelve monthly payments in charges, so that an investor trying to "redeem" after making his first-year payments would get *nothing* back. Thus was created the notorious "front-end load."

Congress then fixed a maximum charge, something never done for any other kind of shares. It was laid down that no more than 9 per cent of the total money paid over to complete a program could be extracted in charges. Further, mutual-fund companies were prevented from taking more than half of the total charge out of the first year's payments. Even so, when the Wharton School of Finance made a survey for the SEC in 1962, they found that about 40 per cent of U.S. mutual-fund buyers had not understood the effect of the "front-end load" on their investment.* The thing people find hardest to grasp is that mutual-fund sales' loads are not a percentage of the sum invested—as are stockbrokers' commissions—but are charges removed before any money is invested. Therefore, in the early stages of his program the customer is putting up nearly as much money to pay off the salesman as he is to invest for his own benefit—and if he has to redeem, he will get back less money than he has paid over.

The effect of this is to add greatly to the risks of investment for the small investor, because he can easily lose money even when the market is going up. It is hard to assess the workings of these risks, even within the regulated U.S. industry, because the relationship of purchase-time to market-movement is so complex. Still, in a set of ten-year programs which ran from 1951 to 1961—a period in which the market went up 175 per cent—nearly as many investors came out with losses (24.1 per cent) as came out with profits (27.4 per cent).† The majority of investors continued payments, so their fortunes could not be pronounced upon. Of course, anyone taking out a new program in 1961 would have been ideally placed to be hit by the front-end load *and* the market break of 1962 during his first year's payments. And the remainder of the decade afforded numerous opportunities for redeeming at a loss. (The SEC has proposed the abolition of the front-end load but so far without result.)

Bernie Cornfeld clearly grasped at a very early stage the dramatic effects of a front-end load in generating commissions out of the money available for investment at any given moment. It worked in the following manner:

An IOS salesman, ego tucked firmly into his pocket, enters a

---

*Special Study of Securities Markets, SEC 1964. Vol. 4, p. 107.
†*Ibid.*

"prospect's" home and persuades him that if he pays over $3000 today for an investment in the Fund of Funds, he will get back $9000 in ten years' time. If the prospect pays up, a sales charge of $255 is cropped off his money, of which $195 goes to the salesman (less any overrides to which he may be subject) and $60 to IOS.

The prospect may be deeply moved by the "presentation," by the wonders of the Fund of Funds concept, and by the bounding Wall Street market. (Between the end of 1962 and the beginning of 1965, the great years of the Fund of Funds, the Dow Jones climbed almost without faltering from 650 to the magic 1000, and the IOS men were all equipped with charts which showed FOF ascending yet more speedily.) But he still might say, "I don't have three thousand bucks, I've only got a hundred." If the salesman takes the $100 as a straight-out payment, he will earn only $6.50 for his evening's persuasion. So the conversation will develop like this:

SALESMAN: "How much could you save each month?"

PROSPECT: "Well, I might manage $25 a month."

SALESMAN: "Fine. Invest $50 now, and $25 every month for the next ten years, and you will have *six thousand dollars* at the end."

What this amounts to is a total investment of $3000. Of the total "program" payments, $325 will be made in the first year. Of that $325, the customer loses half straightaway, with the salesman getting $120 and IOS keeping $40 or so.

It may not amaze anyone to learn that the charges levied on the IOS programs were higher than the maxima permitted in the Investment Company Act. They took half of the first *thirteen* payments, not of the first twelve. And IOS added on an "administrative service fee," which increased the total charges on the life of the program to 12 per cent, instead of 9. Nor was this all.

The investor might then be persuaded to insure himself at the same time with IOS's own insurance company, International Life Insurance of Luxembourg. The standard policy guaranteed to complete the investor's program in the event of death or disablement. For this, ILI would charge $158.12 on a $3000 program, bringing the total cost to 17.2 per cent of the money paid over.

Then there was the 1-per-cent brokerage fee that IOS charged for moving Fund of Funds money into our old friend FOF Prop. That would take another $24.80 out, bringing the charge to *18 per cent*.

All this money is taken before the customer's money actually gets to work in those booming stock markets. In other words, a customer paying $3000 would actually have about $2460 invested.

But even when the money was invested, IOS would take further large bites at it. First, there was the management fee, levied monthly in installments of 1/24th of 1 per cent of the net assets of the fund. Then, at the end of each quarter or of each year, IOS itself shared with its advisers 10 per cent of all gains made in the value of investments, whether those gains were on actual sales or increases in book value.

Then IOS and the advisers collected 10 per cent of all the income produced from fund investments, after deduction of certain running expenses.

These performance fees are prohibited on publicly offered mutual funds in the United States. In rising markets they are highly remunerative to managers of large funds, but they are also a temptation to speculate. It was natural for IOS to start levying such performance charges when it instituted the proprietary system. In 1967, Fred Alger made $500,000 out of his share.

The effect of this terrific battery of charges—which could

only be mounted in an offshore operation—is that wonders have to be performed with the remaining cash before the customers can get any worthwhile return on the risks of investment. Suppose the advisers achieved a steady 1-per-cent-per-month gain through the ten years of a program: this would mean the investor's money they were handling would grow by nearly 100 per cent—if there were no charges. An investor paying in $3000 and subject to all the charges would get back roughly $4750 at the end of ten years, an increase of only 58 per cent. He would do better to leave his money in the safety of a savings account at 6 per cent interest compounded.

On this assumption the customer would have to wait until almost halfway through the sixth year before he could even get his money out without loss. And of course, even to turn in this performance, the actual shares bought by the IOS "professionals" would have to more than double in value to cover the cost of stockbroking commissions on purchasing them. With all this, as we shall see, IOS was still busy devising ways to divert the stockbrokers' commissions back to itself.

Bernie Cornfeld was fond of expounding the superiority of the deal IOS gave its clients over the service given by European banks. "Their idea of money management," he said once, "is to hire a $200-a-month clerk who shifts Nestlé's from one account to the other so that the bank can make two commissions." His own ideas were more elaborate—but even more ungenerous.

We have now described in outline the machine that Cornfeld and Cowett built for marshaling money. It is time to look at the way money was drawn into the machine, and then at the way the money was put to use. But first, an emphasis must be made.

In September 1969, at the height of its powers, IOS listed no less than fifty-five principal subsidiaries. It had formed hundreds of companies around the world—there were sixty listed outside the Nassau offices alone. Cornfeld and Cowett were operating nine banks, with deposits of nearly $100 million. They had started another nine open-end funds, they had a real-estate company with properties valued at $100 million, and they were proposing to finance several major corporations in America and elsewhere.

Somehow, people acquired the idea that all this represented the unintended latter-day proliferation of a successful sales company. On the contrary, as George Landau has pointed out, the growth of the financial empire was implicit from the beginning. Indeed, in the first company report of IOS Ltd. (SA) covering its first year, there was a section boldly headed *"underwriter and investment banker"* expressing Cornfeld's intention to develop strongly in this direction. The only actual investment-banking activity reported there was a deal in which the IOS underwrote an offering of interests in the film *Snobs*, directed by Jean-Pierre Mocky with Bernard Cornfeld as executive producer. The IOS sales force had no trouble selling 35 $1000 participations in the film to their clients. *Snobs* was Mocky's adaptation of William Makepeace Thackeray's book, and although it was one of the first things on which his now considerable cinematic reputation was made, it lost money at the time, and IOS had to reimburse the outside investors.

Probably, Wilbur Cowett of Wertheim would scarcely have regarded it as investment banking at all. But it showed where Bernie and Ed were aiming their sights.

The Jungle Jangle Jingle

The real sources of IOS's wealth. In which we crack some codes, uncover some clandestine financial arrangements, and make some calculations about hot money.

The climactic consecration of the international mutual-fund salesman as a hero of our time was solemnized in the first week of August 1969, thirteen years after Bernard Cornfeld arrived in Paris. First, eighty-three "General Managers" of IOS gathered in the prodigiously expensive Intercontinental Hotel in Geneva. Three days later, they were joined by nearly three hundred divisional and regional managers. More than one hundred of them, Bernie Cornfeld was able to remind them proudly, were on the verge of becoming millionaires.

In inspirational addresses—"address" was always the word used—by Cornfeld himself, by Cowett, and by Allen Cantor, now the captain of the sales force, the managers were exhorted to think of themselves not as salesmen or even as successful business executives, but as missionaries, philanthropists, even statesmen. No flattery was too gross, no hyperbole too pompous for the occasion.

"Today," Cornfeld told his men, "each of us stands in the

forefront of one of the most important developments of our time."

"There are very few companies in the world that will make the kind of money we expect to make this year, next year, and in the years to come," said Cowett.

It would be cruel to dwell too long on the bombast and the boasting of that week. Cowett's friend John McCandish King predicted, for example, that IOS would provide "a major part" of the astronomical—if somewhat arbitrarily precise—figure of $43 billion which, he quoted unspecified economists as saying, must be invested in natural resources over the coming twelve years.

Dr. Erich Mende, the politician whom IOS had hired to put a high finish on the corporate image in Germany, thought the next decade would see "a deepening of this sense of unity among the IOS family." And Gladis Solomon, the first lady of IOS, forecast that the IOS foundation would "easily become the largest agency for international social work in the world." To listen to the speakers, one might have been forgiven for supposing that IOS itself was already the largest agency for social work in the world.

Cornfeld's own claims on behalf of what he was doing had been growing steadily more grandiose. His tone became first Napoleonic, then positively Messianic. He had for some time proclaimed "World-Wide People's Capitalism" as the IOS goal. Now, in 1969, Cornfeld went even further. "The service we perform," he said, "is vital not only to our economic system, but in a real sense it contributes to the survival of the democratic process."

More and more IOS propaganda concentrated on an idea that was perhaps most succinctly put by Wilson W. Wyatt, formerly Lieutenant-Governor of Kentucky, who became a director of IOS. "You are making it possible," Wyatt told the assembled managers, "for the average man to share in the greatest economic development in history. You make it possible for the smallest investor, anywhere in the world, to profit from all the professional expertise that $2 billion can buy."

This was the myth that Cornfeld wanted to put across. His greatest feat, *Newsweek* once noncommittally observed, was to persuade his employees that IOS was "saving capitalism and improving *la condition humaine*." This was the conceptual salesman's greatest sale. For the truth was very different. The engine that drive IOS was not altruism. It was not even some broadbrowed perception of enlightened self-interest that encompassed the potential of a new world-wide class of small investors. It is doubtful whether any such class exists. And, if it did, it is far from certain that the IOS sales force would have been interested in selling to it. One of the most revealing episodes in the history of IOS suggests why.

• • •

One way that Cornfeld convinced a good many people that what IOS was really trying to do was to help underdeveloped countries was that in mid-1966 he hired Ambassador James Roosevelt, son of FDR and regarded as something of an expert on the "Third World." Roosevelt was put in charge of something called the IOS Development Company, and he hired some well-qualified and idealistic advisers. Early in 1968, fired by Cornfeld's rhetoric, a group in the Development Company worked out detailed plans for a "low-income investment plan," which came to be known in the company as the "People's Fund."

"IOS has generally concentrated its activities," they wrote accurately in a paper proposing this project, "on a spectrum of wealth located at or near the top of the income structure of most countries. This has resulted in impressive and profitable business."

"There remains in the world" they went on, "a broad band of smaller levels of income and lesser amounts of savings which IOS has not approached in any way." They proposed, in the most careful detail, a savings plan for "the lower economic elements in the major urban areas of the underdeveloped world . . . office clerks, hotel attendants, taxi drivers, vendors, and thousands of other low-income wage earners who can afford to save only in small amounts."

The plan was to sell savings stamps, in denominations as low as a dollar a week or its equivalent in local currency, which buyers would paste into a cardboard folder. Lotteries would be held to attract interest, and a highly original grass-roots sales structure was proposed.

That, it turned out, was precisely the trouble. It is impossible to say now whether the People's Fund would have worked or not. Perhaps it was predicated on an overoptimistic estimate of the surplus income of the urban poor in developing countries. But that is not the point. The point is that if Cornfeld had meant even a tenth of what he said about People's Capitalism and about helping developing countries, the plan would at least have been given a serious trial. It was not. It was killed at birth by the IOS sales force, because it offered no fat commissions to the salesmen and therefore no "overrides" to their bosses, the real masters of the company.

That is the fact to set against Cornfeld's myth-making. IOS was first, last, and always a sales organization, run by salesmen for salesmen. It was administered, insofar as it *was* administered, so that the boss salesmen—not the investors in the funds, not the outside shareholders, and not even the lesser salesmen—

should profit most from the vast flow of money that IOS handled.

The logic of IOS's expansion was that it would go anywhere that the salesmen could bring in money. And so the first crucial question to ask about IOS is really a very simple one. Where did the money come from?

In the two or three years before the crash, IOS developed new and relatively broadly based markets in prosperous parts of the world, most notably in West Germany. But IOS did not in the first place grow by selling to the middle and lower-middle classes of Europe, or anywhere else. The salesmen turned to those markets only after more profitable fields had been closed to them and after the first half billion dollars, which projected Bernie Cornfeld into the big time, had been collected.

The history of the IOS sales organization passes through five fairly distinct phases. In the beginning, and for some four years after Cornfeld first arrived in Paris, IOS consisted simply of Bernie Cornfeld and a syndicate of salesmen he had assembled selling the Dreyfus Fund from a European base. They had discovered that a small but important section of the American market for the mutual-fund revolution lay outside the continental United States: the 800,000 or so American servicemen who had been removed overseas by the Cold War. It was a fruitful discovery because the military market was not yet subject to the competitive pressures which affected mutual-fund sales organizations in America itself. This was Phase One, and it was still the chief business of IOS when Cornfeld moved from Paris to Geneva.

Phase One overlapped in the early 1960s with Phase Two, in which the salesmen journeying around American military bases made the discovery that U.S. servicemen were not the only, and certainly not the richest, Americans abroad. They began to sell

Dreyfus and certain other funds to the 2.5 million American civilian expatriates: technicians and administrators in the oil fields of Latin America and the Middle East; engineers and hard-hats in construction camps; teachers, government officials, and doctors in schools, embassies, and AID missions from Chile to Pakistan. All of these people had been isolated from the mutual-fund boom.

In Phase Three, the unresting sales force began to discover other kinds of expatriates: British traders in Hong Kong and settlers in Kenya, French rubber planters in Laos and Vietnam, Belgian mining engineers in the Congo, Lebanese shopkeepers in West Africa, overseas Chinese throughout the Far East, Sikh traders in East Africa, German exporters in Mexico, Italian civil engineers in Iran, and merchant seamen of all nationalities almost everywhere. Many of these people had access to dollars, or to funds which they were legally entitled to turn into dollars. And anyway, they did not bother too much about the niceties of exchange regulations when an energetic young salesman was explaining to them that if their money went to buy shares on Wall Street, it would grow with the magic rise of the Wall Street market.

This phase led the logic of the IOS sales operation in two directions. Obviously, many of the expatriates went home to their own countries. Thus IOS followed Dutch oilmen back from Africa, and so went into business in Holland: thus the contacts with the overseas British led IOS back to Britain, and thus into the life-insurance business in London. It was a tortuous, existential kind of growth.

In the same way Phase Three led naturally into another direction. It was a short step from dealing with prosperous European or American expatriates in Rio, Manila, or Mexico City to dealing with the local elite. There was, of course, never any question of being able to sell to any local citizens other than the elite. In most of Latin America and Black Africa, and in all of Asia outside Japan, anyone who can think of investing even $50 a month in a mutual fund is by definition a member of a very small and privileged stratum of society. The *average* income in Brazil, for instance, in the years when IOS was growing with such dazzling speed, was under $250 a year. In no part of Black Africa or Southeast Asia was it above $100 a year between 1960 and 1965.

This was Phase Four, in which IOS found its customers mainly in the "Third World." During the 1960s there were rich and frightened people in many parts of the world who mistrusted, or had reason to fear, the political and economic aspirations of their fellow countrymen. Such people wanted to get their money out. It mattered little to them that in getting it out they might be impoverishing the national economy. This was the basic source of the money that made IOS rich. And this is why the IOS sales operation lived for years on the brink of trouble.

• • •

February 10, 1966, was Ed Coughlin's birthday. Coughlin, a large, calm lawyer who had known Ed Cowett slightly at the Harvard Law School, had joined IOS four or five months before. That particular day he had flown into Geneva from Munich at the end of the afternoon, with his leg still in plaster from a skiing accident. He stopped by his office, intending to stay only a few moments before going out for a quiet celebration dinner.

The dinner had to be postponed. Coughlin had no sooner levered himself behind the desk in his tiny office when Allen Cantor's head appeared round the door, asking him to come down the corridor to Cornfeld's office. As he hobbled in, Cornfeld, Cowett, and Cantor struck up: "Happy Birthday to you, Happy Birthday to you. You're off to *Caracas*, Happy Birthday to you!"

An hour later Coughlin was in a plane, and the next morning he arrived in Caracas, to find the IOS office there in a panic. The Venezuelan authorities had passed a law which seemed to say flatly, "Thou shalt not sell foreign securities." Already the police had raided the offices of another mutual-fund organization in the same building. Coughlin decided to take no chances, and closed down the office.

IOS's legal status in Venezuela was obscure. Other foreign groups continued selling there for some time. What was not in doubt was that the IOS operation was deeply unpopular with the Venezuelan authorities because it was helping itself to ladlefuls of flight capital.

Because of the large hard-currency revenue it earns from oil, Venezuela—unlike almost all other Latin American countries—permits the export of capital. But after the fall of the dictator M. Pérez Jiménez in 1958, and as a result of a series of economic crises under his two relatively left-wing successors, the moneyed class in Venezuela began to fear for its capital.

More and more IOS salesmen turned to selling to Venezuelans. And more and more, correspondingly, the Venezuelan government began to complain about the way mutual-fund salesmen were encouraging capital flight. It was the Venezuelans' turn to learn a lesson which government after government in the developing countries was learning in these years: that it was one thing to turn a blind eye to the traditional habits of a few very rich families, who had been shipping a proportion of their assets abroad for many years; and quite another to tolerate the activity of whole organizations preaching the necessity of sending your money abroad to anyone affluent enough to listen.

In November 1965, the Superintendents of Banks and Insurance in Venezuela announced that they would take joint action to curb the outflow of money into foreign mutual funds. A few days later, the National Economic Council formally attacked the sale of such funds on the grounds that they drained away both national savings and national foreign exchange. Even the *Revista Económica Venezolana*, a publication generally friendly to American business in Venezuela, noted at this time that "capital flight is being encouraged by high-pressure salesmanship of foreign mutual funds. . . . A legitimate complaint exists against certain unethical practices carried out by some sellers." There is no reason to think that the *Revista* was thinking specifically of IOS in this context, but IOS was certainly the biggest mutual-fund operation in Venezuela. By the end of 1964 there were already forty-five IOS salesmen at work in Caracas and another couple of dozen in and around the Maracaibo oil fields. By the time Coughlin closed the office down in February 1966, IOS had brought the best part of $32 million out of Venezuela in cash into its funds; and the face value of clients' commitments to invest in the future was five or six times higher.

Coughlin's trip to Caracas was a picnic compared to some of the expeditions he was to make in the course of the next couple of years. Nevertheless, it passed into IOS legend and became a sort of code. Whenever a manager, anywhere in the world, thought that trouble was coming, off would go a cable to Geneva, "Happy Birthday." Poor Coughlin got birthday cables from Bogotá, Rio, Buenos Aires, Manila, Athens, and Tehran before the joke wore thin. Somewhere in the world, in those years, there was always an IOS operation in trouble with the authorities.

Sometimes, as in Korea, where an IOS manager spent some time in jail in 1965 on currency-smuggling charges, but managed to get bail and then flee the country, the trouble could not be directly attributed to IOS itself. There was, for example, the salesman who was caught smuggling gold bars and gold watches into Turkey: that, obviously, was done completely without IOS's knowledge. The strangest claim made upon IOS, perhaps, came from a German-Croatian businessman in Central America in relation to a block of stamps issued by the Nazi puppet state of Croatia in 1944; the resulting advertisements, conspicuously placed by the businessman in the newspapers, were an embarrassment to headquarters in Geneva.

But it is fair to point out that if IOS as such had no desire to get involved in these deals, it could hardly be surprised if from time to time it did. The whole commission structure was calculated to attract the most aggressive salesmen. Managers in the field were encouraged to drive them on to higher and higher sales volume. It was inevitable that the legal and security departments of IOS should have their hands full of scrapes into which the salesmen had been led by the very acquisitiveness that IOS valued so highly.

Such episodes can be dismissed as peripheral to the IOS story. But they do suggest that the spirit in which the sales force went about its missionary task was not always as high-minded as one would have gathered by listening to the addresses at a managers' conference.

It is not quite so easy to disassociate IOS from the occasions when sales groups got into trouble for illegal selling and for currency offences. As a general rule, IOS has naturally taken the public position that wherever either clients or salesmen changed money illegally or committed any other monetary offense, they did so contrary to IOS policy, and IOS knew nothing about it. All one can say is that after a few years of "Happy-Birthday" cables, any sales executive who did not realize how heavily IOS depended on illegal currency operations must have been singularly naïve. When Bernie Cornfeld bought his first airplane, the joke at IOS was that now he was going to start "Capital Flight Airlines."

The first serious problem Ed Coughlin was sent off to deal with, even before his birthday trip to Caracas, was in Portugal. Late in 1965 the Portuguese Ministry of Finance opened a big investigation, alleging that several IOS managers and salesmen had been involved in illegal money-changing. There were no arrests and no indictments against individuals, though some of the IOS men had their passports taken from them. Finally, some four years later, IOS had to pay a fine of about $175,000.

Then, after Venezuela, came Colombia, in July 1966. That was a much less good-natured affair. IOS had been running a thriving operation there which, as in Venezuela, gradually expanded after 1962 from selling to expatriates to selling to Colombians. Sales increased sharply in 1965, which was a bad year for the Colombian economy. The authorities later said they knew of cases where IOS salesmen went to potential clients and told them that the companies they had their money in were in danger of liquidation, in order to persuade them to switch their money into the Fund of Funds.

In November 1965 the government passed Decreto 2970, setting certain restrictions on mutual-fund selling. The press began an excited campaign, almost certainly with official encouragement, denouncing the harm mutual-fund salesmen were doing to the economy. On July 11, 1966, the IOS managers took space in four Bogotá newspapers to say that they would go on selling.

The Colombian press estimated that IOS had taken $217 million out of Colombia. That may well have been an accurate figure for the face value of programs sold: an IOS official in Geneva told us that the peak total actually taken out of Colombia by IOS salesmen was close to $40 million.

It was only at this point that four IOS men, three foreigners and one Colombian, were thrown into jail. Ed Coughlin arrived to find the IOS men being kept in appalling conditions: one of them had been thrown down a flight of stairs in jail; another had to be taken to the hospital, from which he escaped only after three months under armed guard. It was the end for IOS in Colombia: in November the government passed a law formally forbidding all export of capital.

But Colombia was only a dress rehearsal for what was to come in Brazil. At six-thirty in the morning on November 10, 1966, Mario Venturini, the top IOS salesman in Brazil, was awakened by a knocking on the door of his luxurious apartment in the Rua Bela Cintra in São Paulo. As he sleepily made his way to the door, he assumed it was yet another salesman with yet another problem. It was the police. They gave him time to dress, and to talk to his wife (who then hastily called up as many of the other salesmen as she could find), and took him in for four days' interrogation.

At precisely the same moment, the same thing was happening in some of the more expensive apartments in every major city in the country. In Rio, the police pulled in an Austrian, Baron von Buchenrode; an Englishman, Jack Hunter; and a Swede, Erik Sigrist—respectively the front-office man, office manager, and insurance manager of IOS there. In Belo Horizonte, they arrested Peter Kosovitz and Jacob Tzur, who, they said, had been an Israeli intelligence officer before he joined IOS. More than a thousand miles to the northeast, in Pernambuco, the wife of Norman Gershon, an American ex-paratrooper, who was the IOS manager there, pulled a gun on the police when they came for her husband. And in Bahia, the police reports say, the wife of the local IOS man, Marc Siegel, went one further: she marched down to the police barracks and forced her way at gunpoint into the room where her husband was being questioned. (Those who know Brazil say that it is typical of that chivalrous if excitable country, that when one of these ladies eventually appeared in court she was eloquently commended by the judge for her courage and marital loyalty.)

This IOS sweep had been carefully planned for months by the police, the army, and the secret police—and it was a total success. The night before the two top IOS men in Brazil had been picked up at the airport in Recife. They were John Jessen, originally Danish, and Fred Börlin, German/Swiss. They were held in a steamy lockup in Recife for forty-eight hours, and then flown down to Rio. By that time the police had arrested several dozen salesmen and impounded masses of papers to add to the detailed dossier they had built up by intercepting IOS's communications.

Ed Coughlin, inevitably, flew in a few hours after the catastrophe, summoned by a "happy-birthday" cable. He was more than disconcerted, when he bought his first newspaper in Rio, to see his own arrival reported under a large headline. He was even more surprised, later, when he saw a mug shot of IOS's recently departed General Manager George Tregea, under the headline, "O Cerebro"—"The Brain."

Subsequently, Coughlin had some difficulty persuading Cornfeld that it would *not* be a good idea to send Tregea back to "work things out." It was a recurrent IOS belief that there was a deal for every situation, and that if a government was closing IOS down, it must be because some competitor had fixed them. There was one great telephone conversation on this theme.

"Listen," asked Cowett, "who's the opposition down there?"

"The Department of War," said Coughlin.

"We seem to have trouble on the line, Ed," said Cowett. "For a minute I thought you said the Department of War."

"That's right," said Coughlin. But it was still a little while before the boys in Geneva accepted that the government's determination to run IOS out of Brazil was not negotiable.

George Tregea had in fact been quietly picked up by the police and grilled earlier in the year. And it was after this interrogation that the police had begun to open IOS mail, with the result that they had accumulated all the details they needed: names, code numbers, and addresses of salesmen and managers; names, code numbers, and the size of the accounts of some two thousand clients. Some managers succeeded in hiding their records from the police, and it is probable that the total number of clients was considerably higher. Also, the police made some slightly comic mistakes. They got excited over an old photograph of an IOS party which showed a placard saying "One Hundred Million Dollars," which referred to the total amount in the Fund of Funds at the time, not to the amount that had been spirited out of Brazil. Nevertheless, the Brazilian police had enough detail to give a sharp-focus picture of how the whole massive clandestine operation actually worked in Brazil.

Before we look closer at this picture, it is worth understanding why the Brazilian government was so passionately hostile to what IOS was doing. Under the presidencies of Juscelino Kubitschek, Jánio Quadros, and João Goulart, rich Brazilians sent as much of their money abroad as they could—for fear of the twin peril of communism and inflation. In the last years of the Goulart administration, inflation reached the annual rate of 75–80 per cent, not only threatening to dislocate the entire economy in the future, but already wiping away great slices of everyone's cruzeiros.

The military government which overthrew Goulart in a coup in 1964 was ferociously anti-communist, but it was also puritan, nationalist, and unsympathetic to those in the wealthier classes who were suspected of being "bad Brazilians"—which specifically included those who were dodging their share of taxes or sending their money abroad.

And for all its noisy anti-communism, there was also—there still is—a strong streak of anti-American feeling in the Brazilian officer corps.

One could not expect these middle-class officers and officials, struggling to live off their modest salaries, to have much sympathy for foreigners who seemed to be getting rich out of Brazil's difficulties. "He pays more in rent every month than I earn in salary," said a colonel in the army secret service when he heard about Fred Börlin's apartment, his yacht, his Jaguar, and his Chevrolet; "and he pays less income tax than I do." No wonder, too, that the officers' nationalism was offended when they came upon a passage like the one in the IOS training manual which explains what you must say if the sales prospect says that as a Brazilian he would prefer to invest his money in his own country. "There's no doubt about it," the salesmen were trained to answer, "as a Brazilian you should naturally prefer to invest your money here. But you must see that the political situation is unstable, and the cruzeiro is constantly being devalued. Think first of your children and your wife. Invest your dollars in protection for the future."

Early in its life, in 1964, the military government moved against capital flight and tax evasion by passing a whole series of new laws. The most important of those that IOS was accused of breaking were an exchange-control law of June 14, 1965 and a tax-fraud law passed one month later. The first prohibited changing cruzeiros into foreign currency without informing the Central Bank. The second dealt with those who failed to declare income arising from investments abroad for tax purposes. (In each case the maximum penalty was two years' imprisonment.) It has been suggested that these laws were introduced specifically to give the government the power to act against IOS. But the laws only amplified earlier legislation introduced as soon as the new government came into power. And it was precisely at the time when the government did begin to toughen up its exchange controls and tax law—in 1964—that IOS began to do a big volume of business with Brazilians.

It looks as though the sequence of cause and effect was the same in Brazil as elsewhere—in the Philippines, for example. As long as restrictions on capital flight were ineffective, people sent their money abroad in traditional ways. It was only when the old holes were stopped that they needed an organization like IOS to show them how to beat the controls. And the IOS sales force (some two hundred strong in Brazil at the peak) could preach the gospel of capital flight to people who would never have thought of sending their money abroad through the existing network of money-changers and banks.

Long before the Brazilian operation got under way, IOS had contracted an extremely important relationship with one particular bank in Geneva. It was Gladis Solomon who, in 1960 in Monrovia, Liberia, happened to try to sell a Dreyfus program to a Dr. Tibor Rosenbaum, who had recently started the International Credit Bank in Geneva.

Rosenbaum had immediately grasped the potential for mutual advantage. When they both got back to Geneva, Gladis introduced Rosenbaum to Cornfeld, and within a couple of months a formal contract had been signed: for the next three years, IOS salesmen were able to offer clients the opportunity of becoming depositors in a Swiss bank as well as mutual funds. Clients could even open an account with the ICB in gold bars or coins.

Veteran IOS salesmen have explained to us how useful this was in practice. The commission on bringing customers to the ICB was only 0.5 per cent—"hardly worth having," in one salesman's view. What *was* worth having was the possibility of calling up a prospect and saying, "I'd like to talk to you about Swiss banks and American mutual funds." For the insecure owners of money in Latin America and the Middle East in those years, the thought of Swiss banks was a talisman of great power, a promise of safety, and even a social-status symbol.

In effect, therefore, the link with ICB enabled the salesman to use what is known in the trade as a switch-sale. He would get in the door by mentioning the Swiss bank; then, when he had hooked his prospect's interest, he would have a better chance of selling him mutual funds. In one article of the contract, the ICB bound itself not to go into the mutual-fund management business, and in another IOS promised neither to go into the banking business itself nor to solicit for any other bank. In 1964, however, IOS did buy its own Swiss bank, the Overseas Development Bank (ODB),* whereupon the ICB waived its rights under the 1961 agreement in return for 20 per cent of the equity of ODB (which, however, was subsequently bought by ODB).

• • •

HOW, exactly, did IOS take money out of Brazil? Of course, a good deal of money did not have to be physically taken out of

---

*Technically only a "finance company of a banking character" for the first few years.

the country or even changed. It had already left Brazil and gone into dollar accounts in Switzerland or, for example, in Miami. It was still illegal for the Brazilian holder of such accounts to buy IOS funds unless he registered the transaction with the Brazilian authorities, which he was loath to do. But it was far easier for the IOS salesman if the money was in Switzerland already, as the following letter published by the Brazilian police illustrates. It was written by Fred Börlin to Richard Gangel, now back from being sales manager in Tokyo and learning to be a Swiss banker.

Dear Dick,

One of Norman Gershon's salesmen, Angelo Januzzi, 4158, has made an agreement for U.S. $500,000 in Fortaleza with Sr. J. Macedo. The client has already sent instructions to his bank in Zurich to comply with this agreement. It seems he would like it guaranteed in a safe-keeping account, apparently with the ODB. Would you please, as soon as this account has been opened, or when the money is remitted to ODB or IOS, let us know, by cable, that the operation has been carried out. . . .

The IOS salesmen did not limit themselves to clients who already had bank accounts abroad. As the Brazilian authorities summed it up, "IOS converts money into dollars, in Brazil, through *bureaux de change*. From time to time one of its agents sets off for Switzerland with these dollars hidden in his baggage as an authentic currency-smuggling operation." Sometimes the money was in cash, more often it was in dollar travelers' checks.

IOS headquarters in Geneva, both at the time and since, have taken the line that IOS could not be expected to ask where the clients got their dollars, and that as far as IOS was concerned, its associates only accepted money in foreign exchange. There is good reason to think that this attitude is disingenuous. John

Jessen, the senior man in Brazil after Tregea left, had a written opinion from a lawyer warning him that IOS was breaking the law unless all remittances of money abroad were reported. "The omission of this formality," wrote the lawyer, Luis Claudio Albuquerque Campos, "constitutes a transgression of the law. Such a procedure must be considered by IOS as a calculated risk."

In December 1966, a few weeks after the IOS arrests, the Brazilian detectives found what they said was one of the routes used for getting money converted and taken out of the country. The police uncovered two clandestine banking offices, one in a Copacabana apartment in Rio, the other in a private home in São Paulo. According to the police the "bankers" took money in cruzeiros from IOS clients and remitted it, converted into dollars, to the Foreign Trade Bank of Montevideo in Uruguay. The Foreign Trade Bank is the Uruguay correspondent of the Swiss-Israel Trade Bank; from Montevideo the money was sent to Switzerland, where it was transferred to the ODB. From there it was invested in IOS funds. The "bankers" in Rio and São Paulo falsely represented themselves as agents of the Swiss-Israel Bank.

• • •

The first IOS clients in Brazil had been American and other foreign businessmen. Expansion began soon after George Tregea arrived from Venezuela at the end of 1962. By the end of 1964, Brazil had become IOS's biggest single market in the whole world. Shortly after that, business had settled down to a steady face-value volume of $5–6 million a month, with about 30–40 per cent of that in cash.

At the end, though 5 per cent of sales were still to Americans and some salesmen were still doing well with the foreign communities in São Paulo, the overwhelming majority of the clients, whose names were eventually published in lists of hundreds in the newspapers, were Brazilians. They included landowners, lawyers, industrialists, civil servants, and doctors. They also included a "fiscal judge" whose duties presumably included trying cases like his own; and Gilberto Freyre, the well-known left-wing sociologist. According to one of the managers, they also included more than one police official. (Fred Börlin told us a story about an IOS salesman who left his briefcase at Börlin's flat, saying, "If I don't come back in three hours, inquire at the police station." The associate had a date with a local police chief, and had just succeeded in selling him a $100-a-month plan, when a neighboring police chief stopped in for coffee— whereupon the IOS man sold him, too. The first cop was about to pay when he suddenly stuffed his checkbook away, refusing to sign till his friend departed. Afterward, the IOS man asked the cop what was troubling him. "You crazy?" responded the police chief. "You think I want him to see my account number?")

The list of customers included a stevedore, Alberto Nascimento, with a modest monthly investment program totaling $12,000; and a big cattle baron named Luis Esteves Pinheiro de Lacerda, from the wilds of the Mato Grosso, who put in $200,000 in cash. The biggest single client in Brazil that the police found was Byron C. Photios Tambaoglou, from São Paulo, who was in for $560,000. The average investment of one hundred fifty-seven clients whose holdings were published came to $31,761.

The enormously complicated operation of keeping track of all these clients was unmistakably clandestine. At first salesmen used their own ingenuity to set up mail circuits to communicate securely with Geneva. One São Paulo manager sent and presumably also received mail via an address in Tel Aviv. Later, according to Venturini, Tregea set up a regular secret "mail run." An IOS agent toured the managers in São Paulo, for example, and then handed the "mailbag" of new business, reports, and so on to a pilot for an internal Brazilian airline who flew it to Rio. There it was picked up from a hiding place in a staff lavatory at the airport and taken to an apartment arranged as a "safe house." Then it was taken back out to the airport and handed to another Brazilian pilot who took it to Geneva on a scheduled flight.

These precautions, elaborate as they were, did not save IOS in Brazil and the debacle was total. The official position was unyielding: essentially, any Brazilian who had made surreptitious investments in IOS funds must liquidate the investment and bring the money back to Brazil or face prosecution under the currency laws. At the end of 1966, the redemption figures for IOS programs world-wide doubled from $6 to $12 million a month, largely because of what happened in Brazil.

The Brazilian customers had mainly been buying the Fund of Funds. Those of them who did not quite understand the mechanism of the front-end load must have understood it very clearly when they hurriedly had to cash in programs which they had only bought within the last year.

Cornfeld refused for a long time to give up his ambition to return to Brazil, and this was hardly surprising, for in essence it was Brazil that had made him and his company rich. But all of IOS's efforts were icily refused. On May 30, 1968, the President of Brazil issued a statement that he had communicated to Mr. James Roosevelt that the memorandum by Robert J. Haft, once Ed Cowett's attorney and now retained for IOS, was rejected, and that discussions could continue only if, within ten days from the receipt of the President's letter, IOS put forward new proposals, starting by handing over a complete list of IOS clients in Brazil.

He went on to state Brazil's terms for what amounted to unconditional surrender. IOS clients would be amnestied from further charges on condition they paid any fines due to the revenue department, and then repatriate all the dollars they had invested in IOS and reinvest in Brazilian state bonds.

Before that the great sales force had melted away, although the police tried to block the obvious exits. Venturini managed to find a Pole who had flown for the RAF in World War II and was willing to fly Venturini and Jessen down the coast to the Aeroclub at Punta del Este, near Montevideo, where there is a big casino. Fortunately for them the immigration officials assumed they were big gamblers and didn't ask for their papers.

Börlin also had to smuggle himself out. Luckily one of his wife's relations was the agent for Piper Aircraft. Börlin persuaded him to arrange for two planes, one in a Brazilian city and one in a town just over the frontier in Paraguay. After "fifteen" changes of cars, he took off in the first Piper, but when they were air-borne there was a terrific electrical storm, and they were forced to land inside Brazil at an airstrip in Rio Grande do Sul. As they circled in to land, Börlin—to his horror—saw soldiers with trucks, tanks, and even artillery. He had visions of being dragged back to jail, perhaps to the dreaded Island of Flowers. But it turned out to be routine Brazilian army maneuvers. The Piper managed to get off the ground and landed Börlin in safety in a Paraguayan potato field.

By 1970, virtually nothing was left of the mighty treasure Venturini, Börlin, and the rest had heaped up. Funds under management for all IOS clients in Brazil had dwindled to just over $1 million, less than one-hundredth of the face volume on which the sales force had drawn commission.

• • •

The Brazilian debacle created fall-out all over the southern half of Latin America. Börlin soon found himself down in Argentina, where it took him three weeks to find the first IOS man. The whole operation had gone underground, and half a dozen salesmen and clients had been arrested. "They were in panic: they had split for the high pampas," Börlin recalls. In Chile, things were even worse.

Gradually, IOS was able to rebuild some of its operations in Latin America. They were eventually allowed to start an insurance company in Argentina, for example. But the southern market never recovered from the shock of Brazil. And the official climate was turning chilly.

Bolivia is a good enough example. A sales group had been at work there at least since 1964, under Mario Granado, a man of sufficient substance in that country to be subsequently appointed its Consul General in Buenos Aires. In 1967, presumably with what had happened in Brazil in mind, Granado applied for official permission for IOS activities. On January 3, 1968, he was given permission (by the President of the Republic no less) to set up an IOS branch, but only for "promotional work of consultation, propaganda, and information." "Transactions" were specifically forbidden.

The IOS representative in Bolivia admitted that selling did continue, however. When in October 1969 the new revolutionary-nationalist Ovando government took power, the IOS representative got a nasty letter from the Superintendent of Banks, which ended, ". . . As a consequence of your participation in these operations, which have clearly not been in *ad honorem* form, you must present a concrete declaration of your income from them for consequent taxation." A few days later the Superintendent wrote another letter to the Minister of Finance, which gives a good idea of how the IOS operation looked to the government of a very poor country.*

> . . . allow me to draw to your attention and authority the draft of a Supreme Decree, whose objective is to put an end to the increasing amount of the public's funds that is being obtained for deposit and investment abroad, particularly in those known as "mutual funds."
>
> These savings, which in no way benefit the country, . . . not only mean an outflow of money abroad, but are also in practice not subject to taxation. . . .
>
> We are assured that the considerable sum of tens of thousands of dollars is sent out of the country monthly by methods which have been indicated and denounced by the Association of Private Banks. . . .
>
> Evidently those known as "Fund of Funds," "mutual funds" . . . obtain savings from members of the general public through real promotion and pressure, carried out by agents, brokers, and pseudo-representatives, working clandestinely and avoiding all payment of tax.
>
> . . . The investments make no contribution to the national economy . . . primarily they feed the North American economy.

Once one has grasped how important flight capital was in Phase Four of IOS's development, it comes as no surprise to

---

*Average annual per-capita income in Bolivia in 1969: $147.

learn that in those years Latin America's only rival as a market was the Middle East. The difference was that there were no large clandestine operations. In countries like Egypt and Iraq it would have taken a foolhardy man indeed to try to get around exchange controls; in other territories, such as Lebanon, Kuwait, and the Trucial States in the Persian Gulf, selling mutual funds to nationals was not illegal.

The first ambassadors of IOS to the region were itinerant American individualists like Jack Himes, Bret Davidson, and Lou Ellenport. One of the few veterans of this early period who was shrewd and resourceful enough to carve a sales fief for himself in the Middle East was a tall Coloradan, Sam Welker. (Welker had known George Tregea when they both worked for the same oil-field equipment-supply company in Venezuela.) He got around the difficulty his IOS predecessors had experienced in establishing themselves for more than three months in Libya by boldly registering himself as an investment and insurance broker. He built up a profitable business there selling to British, German, and Italian businessmen. Then he opened up Malta. Later, he became manager of three branches in Saudi Arabia— in Dhahran, Riyadh, and Jidda—and finally he found himself responsible for sales in twelve countries in North Africa and the Middle East.

But the hub of the IOS operation in the Middle East in its most profitable years was Beirut. In 1959, IOS recruited a man named Ray Tabet. A Lebanese who had formerly owned a small bank, Tabet is said to have made the first $1-million sale to one of his rich Lebanese contacts. But Beirut did not begin to reach its full potential as a sales center until around 1962, when Tabet began to open up the Persian Gulf, where Arab sheiks, Indian merchants, and European expatriates all rushed to invest their money. In that same year Tabet recruited Sameera Abou-

Haidar, the attractive wife of a fashionable Beirut doctor, who proved to be one of IOS's most dynamic sales organizers. Within two years, she had sold over $2 million of face value. "When I decide to sell him, I sell him," was her motto.

Toward the end of 1964 one of Tabet's star salesmen, an Egyptian called Adel Gennaoui, pulled off a coup that is talked about in Beirut to this day. In the closing days of the 1964 IOS sales contest, he flew down to Jidda and came back after nine days with enough sales to take second place in the whole world-wide contest. Legend insists that he made £72,000 ($173,000) for his week's work.

• • •

There was never any serious obstacle to the IOS sales operation on capital-flight grounds in those nations of the Middle East where it was operating. Iran was an exception, which we discuss elsewhere. What did close it down, in 1968, was an Arab boycott. The reason for this seems to have been partly that Cornfeld and several of the senior executives of IOS were Jewish, and partly that IOS had been operating in Israel.

The Israeli authorities, in fact, showed themselves far more watchful in their surveillance of IOS than any Arab government.

Bernie Cornfeld had spent some time in Israel, or Palestine as it was then called, as a child. (When he visited Jerusalem in 1970, he insisted on taking General Haim Herzog, one of the directors of the IOS insurance subsidiary in Israel, to see a particular old building in the old Russian compound in Jerusalem. Before World War II it had been an American school run by a Miss Deborah Kalen, and the young Bernie had spent about a year there. He pointed out to the General a tree he remembered climbing as a child.) It was natural, therefore, that once he had created IOS, he should want it to be established in Israel too.

In December 1965, Joseph Melamed, a former Israeli Treasury official, set up a small office in Tel Aviv and recruited a small sales group. Both have been in operation ever since, with the exception of one brief period during which sales were suspended in 1968.

In 1969 a Commission of Inquiry was set up by the Israeli government, partly as a result of concern over IOS operations, as many Israelis had lost money by redeeming shares at well below the value of their original investments.

That was not the Finance Ministry's only worry. "What we didn't like," an official told us, "was their door-to-door canvassing. We felt it would lead to a great outflow of capital." So IOS was asked to give an undertaking to the authorities, which it gave, to invest at least as much in Israel as the value of its sales there. In May 1970, in answer to a question in the Knesset, the Deputy Finance Minister said that IOS had sold $6.5 million worth of securities to Israelis, and had invested $14.6 million in Israel in return.*

The profile was maintained until October 1969. By that time the Arab boycott had happened, and in that month Bernie Cornfeld and Ed Cowett visited Israel. Bernie proceeded to make a series of spectacular gestures. He planned to buy a bank, and started negotiations to acquire one. He announced plans to build a whole chain of IOS hotels in Israel—Tel Aviv, Jerusalem, and Elath. And he tried to buy the Tel Aviv Hilton for a reported $14.5 million. (If that was his price, it is not surprising that the offer was unsuccessful, as it is less than the net value of the hotel, the stock of which belongs to the government.) He offered to provide expertise for the young Israeli fash-

---

*More than half of that was the Midbar oil-prospecting adventure. See Chapter 19, "John M. King: The Power of Natural Gas."

ion industry through his contacts with Oleg Cassini and Guy Laroche. And he offered to lend the government of Israel his private black executive jet for flying VIPs around.

Such friendly gestures did not, however, in any way have the effect of inducing the Israeli government to modify what remains a skeptical and cautious attitude to mutual-fund selling in general, whether by IOS or by its competitors. New and stricter regulations governing their operations are due to come into force at the time of writing.

• • •

"Talk about hot money!" Bernie Cornfeld said to our colleague James Fox. "We've got a million clients, and if any major proportion of those million clients represents hot money, there must be a lot of it about."

There is.

Cornfeld was cleverly evading the point. The proportion of the million *clients* that "represent hot money" doesn't matter, because a small proportion of IOS's customers provided a very large share of the money.

IOS always talked a great deal about "small investors." But in 1968 Allen Cantor became so convinced of the exceptional importance of individual large investors that he set up a "VIP department" to give them special treatment. It was run by Georges Gérard, a former professional interpreter for international organizations. IOS classified two kinds of clients as VIPs: those who—as heads of state (there were at least half a dozen of these) or finance ministers, or for some other reason—might be able to help IOS with influence or protection; and any clients who committed themselves to invest more than $100,000.

It is clear that a far higher proportion of the clients came from among the rich, as opposed to the merely comfortably off, than IOS publicity liked to tell the world. Gérard's department never had more than two thousand clients. That is 0.2 per cent of Bernie's million clients; and according to Gérard, they owned just under 20 per cent of the funds. Cowett told us that in mid-1969 some 8600 clients had investments of more than $40,000 each. Not much more than 1 per cent of the customers had about one-quarter of the money in the funds.

Phase Four, when IOS was profiting from capital flight from the underdeveloped world, only tapered off after 1966–1967 for two reasons. The first was, as we have seen, that government after government woke up with a bang to the fact that mutual-fund salesmen, and IOS in particular, were walking off with hundreds of millions of dollars' worth of their countries' slender supply of capital. This general tightening up of the currency laws coincided with a new stage in the internal logic of IOS's sales organization. Originally, the sales bosses were looking for rich, compact markets—a naval base, an oil field, a construction camp at a dam site—that could be mined by one or two men working from a hotel room. It was rewarding, but also exacting and even dangerous work. Once they had put together the necessary stake, it made sense for the early returners to put away their overnight bags and finance the largest possible groups of new salesmen, to work for them, sharing their commissions through the override system. They were tired of the road, of living out of suitcases. They wanted to settle down in a lakeside villa in Geneva, a London town house, or a Paris apartment, and turn themselves into bankers, executives, and gentlemen of means.

That was the beginning of Phase Five, when the markets in developed countries that had begun to open up when IOS first followed the European expatriates home became the main fields of IOS's activity. As market after market in Latin America or

Asia closed down or ran into difficulties with the authorities, Europe took over. By 1968, 60 per cent of all the inflow of money into the funds came from West Germany, Italy, Britain, and Holland. In 1969, almost three-quarters of sales were coming from Western Europe and Canada. That was Phase Five, and it was, as we shall see, so successful that well over half of all the assets under IOS management at the peak were brought in during 1968 and 1969.

But that does not mean that Phase Four was insignificant.

There is a tendency within IOS to suggest that the capital-flight business, while no doubt unfortunate and even deplorable, was more or less a passing episode, the venial sowing of wild oats in corporate youth—as if breaking the currency laws of poor and backward countries may be laughed off as a schoolboy prank. When the Brazilian fiasco was being discussed at a sales meeting, one executive quoted Marlowe. "Twas in another country, and besides the wench is dead."

The evidence suggests, on the contrary, that without the capital-flight phase, IOS would never have become an important concern at all, let alone "the most important economic force in the Free World."

It is important to be clear about the distinction between "black money" and "hot money." Black money was illegally invested in the funds, in the sense that currency or other laws were broken in the process. But a very large proportion of all the money invested in underdeveloped countries—and in some developed countries as well, as we shall see when we look at what happened in Italy—was "hot money"; it was flight capital.

Whether sales were technically legal or illegal is, from this point of view, irrelevant. What mattered was that such capital flight damaged the economies of the countries concerned. Some countries had laws against it. Others, often including those which most needed them, did not. In many cases, indeed, it was the activities of IOS salesmen that caused the laws to be introduced. What they were doing was not more harmful after it had been forbidden than it had been before. Is it possible to put a precise figure on the IOS hot-money business? Obviously a complete account can only be produced by IOS itself. (All its sales have been recorded on a computer since the early 1960s.)

When we first became aware of the scope of the question, we naturally hoped that the new management, which took over after Cornfeld's fall, would want to make a serious attempt to clear the matter up. The new President of the company, Sir Eric Wyndham White, a product of the British Treasury and then Secretary General of the General Agreement on Trade and Tariffs, and his chief information officer, Mr. Harold Kaplan, a respected former officer of the U.S. Information Service, took the position that IOS should be plainer and more straightforward about its affairs.

We therefore asked them to break the silence that had always covered virtually all details of the sales operation except, of course, for the loudly trumpeted total volumes. Sir Eric and Mr. Kaplan invited us to submit written questions, which we did. They were simple enough: essentially we asked for a breakdown of sales by year and by country, and for some indication of the proportion of cash flow that came in lump sums, and the proportion in monthly investment programs.

After some weeks, Mr. Kaplan telephoned to say that these questions could not be answered. It was not altogether surprising. IOS was in most respects a garrulous and gossipy organization. But there was one subject on which people were either studiously vague, or grimly tight-lipped: just where the money came from.

Parts of the sales organization functioned with all the elaborate secrecy of an espionage service. "Area desks" filtered contacts between the regions and the administrative HQ at Ferney-Voltaire. Contacts with clients in the Middle East and Africa were further filtered through secret processing centers, staffed with appropriate linguists, in the Swiss ski resort of Flims-Waldhaus and in Brussels respectively.

It was perhaps natural that many customers' accounts were kept under numbers. What was more extraordinary is that many territories were labeled with baffling code names, which altered from time to time. Israel was called Africa IIB. Cyprus was Europe III, and America 23 was actually in Italy. On one occasion IOS proudly published a photograph of a "Gold-Medal Award" being pinned on the Minister of Public Works in America VIE! Even more oddly, many of the salesmen were listed in the company's records under ludicrous pseudonyms, such as "Victor Hugo" and "Jacky Hotelplan." In spite of such heavy-handed precautions, the cloak of security can nevertheless be penetrated.

Up until 1962, the sales force was selling Dreyfus far more than IOS's own funds. The total amount actually brought into the IOS funds up to the middle of 1967, which may be taken as the end of Phase Four, comes in round figures to $700 million. So the crucial question is: where did that money come from in those five years from 1962 to 1967?

A director of IOS who resigned in 1965 told us that in his time Latin America accounted for about half the volume of sales. Several other officials who have left the company more recently have confirmed that Latin America continued to provide half of sales until the Brazilian debacle.

Sales in Brazil from mid-1964 until November 10, 1966, ran at around $5–6 million a month, face value. It means that even if selling was stopped then, the total amount IOS would have taken out of Brazil if all monthly programs had run their contractual course would have been not less than $135 million and possibly more. What is not easy to establish exactly is: what proportion of this was in cash? An IOS sales official who spent six years in Latin America has told us, however, that in Brazil cash was 30–40 per cent of face value (higher than in less dangerous markets) and that assets under management from Brazil reached $45 million at their highest point.

The same man said that assets under management from Venezuela came to $32 million and from Colombia, where sales had been going on longer than in Brazil, to some $40 million. If one remembers that Argentina, Chile, and Central America were also all major markets, and that sales were bubbling away busily all over the continent for six or seven years, it would seem that not less than $250 million of IOS's first $700 million came from Latin America.

A senior sales official in Beirut has computed for us from memory—the local sales records have disappeared—that total sales in the Middle East between 1962 and 1966, including both the Beirut and Tehran regions, came to some $80 million. In one year (1964), the Beirut region did $48 million in face value, a high proportion of which, perhaps as much as one-third, would have been in cash—a very large proportion of which was most assuredly flight capital.

From the very early days on, IOS held annual sales contests. They were important both as a way of boosting actual sales volume and, even more, as a way of giving men and women who were scattered all over the world a sense of belonging to one triumphant army on the march. At first, there was a pleasantly unpretentious and personal touch about these contests: George Landau remembers winning a large salami once. Later the big winners were given blocks of shares in the Fund of Funds, tape recorders, movie cameras, and other expensive consumer goods, including zebra skins and on one occasion a "seven-foot African leopard pelt."

This was appropriate for the 1964–1965 winter contest, which was called the "IOS Big-Game Safari." The official company report on it begins like this: "In a roaring windup, 1216 hunters hit the final clearing on the safari—and never in Big-Game history has there been such a jungle jangle jingle." (That was the sales organization's style. It hardly encourages one to take seriously the claim that the salesmen were really responsible, cautious "financial advisers." Hunters! Yes, indeed, that was much more how they saw themselves.)

The report lists the "contest volume" sold by the 1216 individual salesmen and breaks down "actual volume" between twenty-three regions, which between them covered every territory where IOS was then operating. Since the figures refer to face value, they do not show exactly how much money was brought in during the contest, but they do give a clear idea of the breakdown of sales between the different regions. (The proportion of cash did vary slightly from one region to another: broadly speaking, the more dangerous the operation, the higher the proportion of cash.) The figures turn out to fit very closely with the general picture we have described from other sources.

Brazil led the regions in the jungle jangle jingle, with $8.9 million out of a world total of $82.3 million. (Nor was this an isolated achievement: the Brazilians did even better the next year.) Latin America as a whole contributed some $34 million, or 41 per cent. The Middle East, counting the Beirut and Tehran regions, plus Sam Welker's personal fief, accounted for $11.4 million, in those particular six weeks, or 13.8 per cent. And Spain and Portugal between them, where the sales were largely illegal or at least depended upon illegal currency operations, provided another $2.7 million.

Not all the sales in Latin America or the Middle East, of course, were made to the nervous local rich. Some will have been continuing "Phase One," "Phase Two," or "Phase Three" sales to expatriates with external funds. But these were the years of roaring inflation and the fear of growing political instability. It does not seem farfetched in view of what we know of IOS operations world-wide, to assume that such sales as were made to expatriates in Latin America and the Middle East at this period were more than equaled by illegal sales elsewhere.

These were the five crucial years for IOS's growth. They saw what had been a modest sales organization, selling other people's funds, develop into a world-wide organization by the end of 1966, with more than $500 million under management. It seems safe to say that at least 40 per cent of that money came from the citizens of underdeveloped countries. Several $100 million was taken from those countries which could least afford to lose it, and put straight into that notoriously undercapitalized area, Wall Street.

"You must never forget," we were told by Eli Wallitt, a director of IOS, "that the company developed out of the illegal areas." That fact influenced its whole character and evolution.

They May Be Schmucks, but They're the Government

The clash between IOS and the Securities and Exchange Commission. A Cuban lady skindiver enters the stockbroking business. We examine some other matters that IOS never told the customers about, and a deal that "scared the hell out of the SEC."

Manuel F. Cohen was born in Brooklyn some twenty years before the Cornfeld family settled there. The district in which he was brought up, Bedford Stuyvesant, was much poorer than the Cornfelds' part. ("You had to have money to live there—at least, to us," he commented once.) Cohen went to Brooklyn College, and then on to Brooklyn Law School and a cum laude degree. After a short period in private law practice in New York, he joined the Securities and Exchange Commission staff in Washington, D.C., in 1942. Twenty-two years later, he became its fifteenth chairman.

Cohen, who is a Democrat, retired from the SEC in 1968 after Nixon's election and is now in private law practice in Washington. His clients include a fair number of mutual funds. It is hard to see in him a man dedicated to the overthrow of the American securities industry.

In the market gloom of early 1970, many people in the securities industry were easily seduced by Cornfeld's argument that the SEC was out to destroy them. The SEC had after all publicly advocated a reduction in many of the charges and commissions. The SEC is a small agency and its budget is not a generous one. Some of its methods as a result seem high-handed: brokers and investment managers tend to take offense when, after an SEC "request," they have to take a whole day to go down to Washington, paying their own fares, to be grilled by lawyers half their age.

Nevertheless, in at least one important respect the SEC is a considerable ally of the securities industry. If it were not for its existence as a buffer, the securities industry might well be prey to the potentially more ferocious attacks from the anti-trust section of the Justice Department. If the lawyers of that arm of the government were to be let loose on investigating the securities industry and were to attack, for instance, the minimum-commission agreements of the New York Stock Exchange with the same vigor as they attack the fixing of steel prices, then brokers and fund managers would really have something to worry about.

The brokers, investment managers, and security dealers to whom Cornfeld was speaking in New York in February 1970 were probably also sympathetic to his attack on the SEC, because they had been subjected to the constant blare of the IOS version of the dispute between the two. IOS tried to refer to the SEC case as little as possible at first, but, when it became unavoidable, they set the machine to work to present the interpretation which would do them least harm. It was not strictly in accordance with the facts.

The standard explanation of the SEC battle put out by IOS ran like this:

At the heart of the dispute was the SEC's demand that IOS supply it with a full list of the company's clients regardless of their nationality. This demand was made because of the SEC's contention that under U.S. law any company selling securities to Americans was compelled to open its records to the Commission.

The basic IOS position, as stated in court, was: U.S. securities laws do not apply to purchase and sales of securities which occur wholly outside of the United States. Transactions outside the United States, IOS contended, are subject to the laws of the countries wherein such transactions occur.

This statement is factually wrong in one respect: the SEC did not demand "a full list of the company's clients regardless of their nationality." In their own words, the Commission demanded that IOS "produce its customers' records *or* its records of all transactions or accounts effected by IOS with or for United States citizens or nationals, *whichever IOS preferred*." More important, however, are the subtle implications of the emphasis used by IOS: suggesting that the SEC was interested in the misdemeanors of IOS's clients (tax and exchange-control evasion for instance) and not those of IOS itself, and that IOS regarded its clients' rights to secrecy as a matter of principle.

There were undoubtedly many IOS clients, both American and otherwise, who would have been acutely embarrassed if the details of their dealings with IOS had fallen into the hands of the U.S. government. But no matter of principle was involved. The job of the SEC is to protect U.S. investors whether at home or abroad. It cannot, of course, stop U.S. citizens living abroad from squandering their savings on investments completely outside its control. But IOS, it felt with some justification, was not outside its jurisdiction. Investigation showed that they had ignored a number of the provisions of the securities laws, to the detriment of their clients; therefore the SEC had no alternative but to charge it with those offenses.

Like most people in the United States, even in the financial world, the SEC had heard little of Cornfeld or IOS before 1965—although Cowett and Cohen had met when Cowett was working on *Blue Sky Law* with Loss. What first brought IOS to their attention were the huge holdings that the Fund of Funds was building up in a selection of funds that were registered with the SEC and very much their concern. By the end of 1964, FOF owned over 40 per cent of one American fund, over 20 per cent of two more, and over $19 million each—or about 8.5 per cent—in the two giant Fidelity funds, Capital and Trend. So, early in 1965, the SEC decided to investigate IOS with two aims: to assess the impact of IOS and FOF on the American securities markets, particularly on registered funds; and to find out whether IOS or FOF had violated the federal securities laws.

The SEC investigation was started *before* IOS tried to invade the American fund market: it was not until the end of July 1965 that IOS took over IPC. (Cornfeld had bought out Walter Benedick, the man who had launched him in his fund career.)

The SEC investigators had precious little they could latch on to: the bulk of IOS's records were kept in Geneva, an arrangement which the SEC had ironically approved five years before without realizing the trouble they were storing up for themselves. But IOS had an Achilles heel. On the top floor of a converted brownstone on West Fifty-seventh Street, above an art gallery, there was an uncharacteristically shabby office belonging to a company called Investors Continental Services. ICS belonged to IOS, and it had been registered with the SEC as a broker/dealer since November 1958, and it was through this company that IOS sold to Americans abroad and serviced them when they returned home. ICS was also a member of the National Association of Security Dealers, the trade body in the United States which issues a set of Rules of Fair Practice which representatives of its members must comply with. It also has policing duties under the securities acts. That meant that the SEC could turn up at any time without warning and ask to see the books.

This is precisely what the SEC did. One day in late May 1965, a couple of SEC investigators, Dan Schatz and Hal Halpern, rode the rickety elevator to the top floor, presented their identification cards to Hy Feld, who ran the office for IOS with one secretary, and asked for the files. The two investigators were not quite sure what they were looking for. But the moment Schatz saw the following letter in a file in a back room he saw its significance:

February 10, 1965

Mr. Larry Rosen
Geneva

Dear Larry,

This is intended simply to illustrate an additional problem created by the entire ICS-NASD situation.

Whenever an incorrect commission statement comes into New York, whenever a letter written on ICS stationery by someone who is not an NASD registered representative finds its way into the New York office, or whenever there is any correspondence relating to any person who is not NASD approved, Hy attempts to remove such commission statement, letters, or other paper from ICS files. However, there is a strong probability that Hy will not be able to catch everything which should not be put into the ICS files. If Hy is not in the office and the matter is handled in his absence by one of the secretaries, there is an increased probability that an improper item will find its way into the ICS file.

As you know, the New York office is a very busy one, Hy attempts to do three or four jobs at once. The volume of paper work is staggering in relation to the number of personnel in the office. All of these factors only increase the danger of something slipping into the files.

As you are probably aware, the ICS files are always open to complete examination by the NASD or SEC. One improper paper in the file, if discovered, could lead to a complete investigation of the entire workings of ICS. Such an examination would include, in all probability, a review of all correspondence coming into the office over a protracted period. Since the correspondence in any period of three or four or five days is bound to include at least one damning letter, you can see that the results could be disastrous.

I do not mean to panic everybody involved by this letter and my letter of even date. I can ask no more than that each person involved do his part in cutting down the extent of our obvious violations.

Best regards,

c.c. Bernard Cornfeld
    Hy Feld
EMC:AW

The letter was clearly written by Cowett. Schatz took out a notebook and jotted down the wording of the letter. When he got back to Washington, there was great excitement. He was soon on his way back to New York for a second visit; this time he could not find the letter.

An employee of IOS in New York at that time who tried, for personal reasons, to find out whether the letter had been intentionally removed was unable to reach any firm conclusion. Cowett says that it was not taken out and that when the SEC men came back to fetch papers for Xeroxing for some inexplicable reason, they just missed it.

Cowett's explanation of the letter is that some of the commissions of salesmen were being recorded by mistake on ICS-headed paper. "I discovered that for three or four months the office had been sloppy with commission statements on business that was not subject to U.S. regulations. I got pretty angry and sat down and typed two letters myself—one to Lawrence Rosen and one to Kent Gordis, the head of the computer-processing department." In other words, it was purely a technical error.

The full text of the letter would appear to imply more than that. However, the SEC never proved that IOS had been selling its unregistered funds—FOF and IIT—to Americans *within* America, and ICS did not feature prominently in the charges. The principal impact of the letter was, frankly, in its publicity value to the SEC: because it did not form the basis of any of the charges, Cowett denounced its publication as "McCarthyism."

The real weakness of IOS's position is that Cornfeld had registered IOS *itself* as a broker/dealer with the SEC on June 10, 1960, shortly after he had incorporated the company in Panama. He had done this, no doubt to be on the safe side, because he was selling a U.S.-registered fund—Dreyfus—to Americans abroad. In cases where a broker/dealer has his main offices abroad, the SEC allows him to keep his records there and not in the United States itself, as long as he undertakes to produce them on request. IOS had given that undertaking.

Fairly quickly, the SEC discovered that IOS was not going to produce any of its customer records at all. The furthest they were prepared to go was to produce a statistical breakdown of them—which would have been virtually useless. So on November 29, 1965, the SEC formally demanded that IOS produce its books and records relating to customers who were U.S. citizens.

It also served a subpoena on the one branch of IOS that was within its grasp, that in Puerto Rico. Again the SEC asked for records of the branch's dealings with Americans.

IOS retaliated by filing an action on December 14 in the District Court of Puerto Rico. The company argued that Swiss industrial-espionage and banking-secrecy laws prevented it from producing any of its records, and claimed that anyway it was not under the jurisdiction of the SEC and wanted to withdraw its broker/dealer registration without prejudice.

After months of litigation IOS was to suffer a humiliating defeat. IOS produced the view of the leading Swiss lawyer, Robert Turrétini, to support their claim that they would be infringing Swiss secrecy laws. The SEC expert said they would not. Judge Hiram R. Cancio decreed, on October 3, 1966, that even if Turrétini were right, IOS was "nevertheless under an obligation to comply with the United States Law to which it has submitted." IOS's complaint to quash the subpoena on its Puerto Rican branch was also dismissed. IOS appealed and sought an injunction: the Appeals Court turned it down with the comment: "It is unthinkable that an administrative agency cannot even institute a proceeding until it has had, in effect, the permission of the district court and of the court of appeals whenever the parties to be investigated choose to deny its jurisdiction."

Our intrepid SEC investigator, Dan Schatz, spent a good deal of time on the air shuttle between Washington and New York in the early summer of 1965. On one of these trips he was dispatched to the offices of Jesup & Lamont, on Broadway, near Wall Street. He was not, at least as far as he knew, on the IOS chase. He was there to look into that firm's methods of handling institutional brokerage business. Schatz started with the usual interview with the senior partner, who told him that the firm had no branches. He then checked the list of the firm's employees, asking for addresses as well as names. He was struck by one name, that of Mrs. Gloria Martica Clapp, with an address in the Bahamas. So he asked for the details of her accounts and her commission statements.

Recalling the occasion, Dan Schatz nostalgically told us, "I remember after I asked for the information and before they brought me the files, I felt like Babe Ruth when he was playing in Yankee Stadium, and he pointed right over the middle flag of the bleachers to show where he was going to hit the ball out of the park, and the next ball he hit it right over the flag. When the files came, there it all was. I called Washington and they were so excited they told me to come right on down." It is one of the deepest regrets of the SEC investigators that they never got to meet Mrs. Clapp.

Gloria Martica Clapp is a Cuban who became a citizen of Bermuda and then went to live in the Bahamas with her first husband. He was an underwater diver in Nassau who guided visitors on walks over the colorful Caribbean sea bed, while Martica sat in the boat above keeping them supplied with air.

Her way of life seems to have changed considerably when she and her first husband parted and she married Sam Clapp, an astute Boston lawyer who was among IOS's tax advisers and who had set himself up in business in the Bahamas. Mrs. Clapp entered the securities business by becoming a registered representative of New York brokers: what Dan Schatz had discovered was that she had received $750,000 from Jesup & Lamont as her share of brokerage commissions that IOS had requested be "given up" to that firm.

Before the end of 1968 the practice of giving up commissions was common on U.S. stock exchanges. Many brokers found that they could buy or sell large blocks of securities so profitably on the minimum commissions set by the exchanges that they would rather part with a proportion of their commissions than lose the business.

The New York Stock Exchange strictly prohibited its members from giving up any of the commissions to the customers themselves; that would have meant its minimum-commission rules were being broken. They could only be given up to other brokers. This position was not fully approved either by some fund managers or by the SEC: their view was that anyone who ran a mutual fund had a fiduciary duty to keep the cost of that fund to a minimum, and therefore the funds should receive rebates.

Where the SEC and NYSE did agree was that in no circumstance should the management company benefit from given-up commissions. That would be abuse of the customers' money. The danger of this led the SEC to recommend the abolition of give-ups. This was accepted by the NYSE and they were made illegal as from December 1968.

Jesup & Lamont provided IOS with research services and kept half the commissions directed to them, allowing Mrs. Clapp to keep the other half. These she placed on deposit with Fiduciary Trust, a Bahamian company of which her husband was a director. IOS denied that the company or any of its principals benefited from these commission payments, and the SEC never proved that they did. Nor did the SEC ever charge them with violations of securities law on this count. The Commission merely listed the events under the heading, "With respect to the public interest."

The Clapps built a magnificent house on Paradise Island, whose psychedelic decorations and cathedral-like main hall have become part of the folklore—which values the house at $1.3 million. After the SEC episode, the Clapps' group of companies drew even closer to IOS. Their offices were on the same floor of the same building in Nassau. On January 2, 1966, Ed Cowett was elected a director of Fiduciary Trust. One of the Fiduciary companies changed its name to IOS Acceptances. And Fiduciary Trust began to run down its operations when IOS started up the Overseas Development Bank of the Bahamas (separate from, but naturally closely associated with, the original ODB in Geneva). Fiduciary was eventually wound up, and William Sayad, an associate lawyer of Sam Clapp's, who had been General Manager of Fiduciary, turned into the General Manager of ODB in Nassau, and the IOS bank bought up Fiduciary Trust's furniture.

IOS and Fiduciary co-operated in other little ways. For example, one company listed on the board outside IOS's offices in Nassau was called Lancaster Ltd. This company owned one share—there were only five issued—of the suitably named Palm Trees Ltd., which was registered at Fiduciary Trust's offices and of which William Sayad was a director. Such "shell" companies were occassionally needed as intermediaries in one deal or another. As Ed Cowett once remarked, "You never know when you may need a corporation."

There are all sorts of ways in which stockbrokers can effectively "repay" commissions to their big customers, from causing bank loans to be made at favorable interest rates to outright defraying of their expenses. Where such actions become an infringement of the rules is harder to determine. Arthur Lipper III, who became IOS's main broker in 1967, paid for the apartment at New York's Hotel Carlyle where Cornfeld often stayed. That was accepted. But his payment of commissions directly to Investors Planning Corporation during the months it was controlled by IOS was later challenged by the SEC. Like Cornfeld, however, Lipper has also been open about his position; he recently told the SEC flatly that he thought the level of brokers' commissions on institutional business was "unconscionably" high.

The IOS position on rebated commissions was simple and clearly stated by Cornfeld and Cowett in private interviews. If brokers were prepared to give up their "unconscionably" high brokerage commission wherever IOS wanted to direct it, even if back to IOS itself, then IOS saw no obligation to pass the benefit on to the funds they managed. After all, they argued with some justification, mutual funds under SEC control were not allowed to benefit from such give-ups. It is an argument with which the customers, whose money was creating the commissions in the first place, might not always have agreed.

Tracking down commission statements may have been the most exciting part of the SEC investigators' work but it was not the simplest. The most trenchant part of the SEC charges against IOS was derived from simple scrutiny of Fund of Funds prospectuses and reports.

Whether U.S. securities laws were actually broken because the prospectuses and reports of the Fund of Funds failed to make the disclosures that the SEC required was a question which turned on the larger question of whether the SEC could enforce the jurisdiction that it claimed over IOS. The SEC had, however, grasped the important point: the documents were so inadequate that they were misleading by any standards.

We described earlier how the Fund of Funds had only a small number of voting shares, all owned by IOS. Most of the inadequacies of the FOF prospectuses stemmed from the fact that IOS did not state in these prospectuses, nor indeed in the annual reports, that IOS itself controlled all these voting shares. As a result, no buyer of FOF shares who relied on the prospectus could be aware that IOS could change the whole structure and investment policy of FOF whenever it cared to do so. Investors could, and did, end up owning something almost unrecognizable compared to what they thought they were buying.

The crucial change came in 1965 when FOF stopped putting all its money in independently managed public mutual funds in the United States and started the proprietary system by which FOF also invested in funds IOS controlled. This was a fundamental change both in structure and in investment policy that could well have affected many people's decision to invest. Even after the transition, it was virtually impossible for anyone relying on the prospectus to discover what had happened as the slight, unexplained changes in the wording gave precious little clue, especially to anyone not versed in the intricacies of U.S. securities laws.

The SEC spelled out these changes. The most important was in the section dealing with what FOF could invest in. The FOF prospectus dated April 1, 1964—and earlier ones—stated that the FOF could invest in "shares issued by any open-end investment company (*mutual fund*) registered with the United States Securities and Exchange Commission which primarily invests in U.S. securities."

This section had been altered in the prospectus issued on May 3, 1965. The FOF could now invest in "shares issued by any open-end or closed-end investment company registered with the United States Securities and Exchange Commission under the *Investment Company Act of 1940*."

The effect of the alteration was dramatic. It meant that FOF need no longer invest in publicly sold mutual funds registered under the all-important Securities Act of 1933. While the Investment Company Act of 1940 gave important new powers to the SEC, privately controlled companies registered under this Act were still left free to do more or less what they liked in many areas.

No explanation was offered for the change of wording. Yet IOS was then about to invest $10 million of the FOF money in a new fund, called the York Fund, registered under the Investment Company Act: the controlling management company of which was half-owned by IOS itself; which would have no clients other than the FOF; which was going to levy a performance fee; and which was specifically designed to sell securities short. Yet the same prospectus still blithely told investors that the FOF was not allowed to sell shares short. Later in 1965 FOF poured money into four money funds which IOS itself controlled.

The SEC also objected to the fact that the prospectuses did not make clear just how IOS itself was benefiting from buying shares in U.S. mutual funds for the FOF portfolio. The same May 1965 prospectus contained this account of the costs that FOF incurred when investing. "The cost to the Fund with respect to each transaction will generally go at the minimum rate established by most mutual funds . . . , *and may not exceed an aggregate total of 1 per cent during any calendar year.* [Our italics.] If the total cost of all transactions involves costs to the Fund in excess of 1 per cent (including transfer taxes), Investors Overseas Services, exclusive distributor of the Fund, has agreed to pay such excess."

That sounded pretty generous. Yet if you plowed on through the next ten pages of the prospectus you finally found the following words. "The purchase and sale of securities for the Fund's portfolio will normally be placed through Investors Overseas Services as the investment dealer of record, and IOS will share in the customary charges, if any, relevant to such transactions." In other words, if any mutual fund was prepared to share its charges with IOS on the FOF investment, IOS would be quite happy to keep some for itself. Because of the enormous blocks that FOF invested there was plenty of room for a U.S.

mutual fund to split its sales charge with IOS, and for the FOF's cost of acquisition still to come out to less than 1 per cent. To give one example, in 1964 and 1965 FOF put a total of nearly $6 million into the Value Line Special Situations Fund, on which a sales charge of 1 per cent—over $59,000—was levied. The distributors of the Value Line Fund gave 80 per cent of that—over $47,000—back to IOS.

After dealing with all these failures to meet its disclosure standards, the SEC came to the section of the prospectus dealing with redemption of FOF shares. One condition in which sales or redemptions of FOF shares could be temporarily deferred was, it stated, if "the Securities and Exchange Commission of the United States government has by order permitted such suspension." The implication that the FOF was, after all, under SEC regulation must have been the last straw for the SEC.

• • •

Misleading investors was one thing. But what really "scared the hell out of the SEC"—as one IOS lawyer put it—was a deal which was put together around a firm called Ramer Industries, and in which Cowett and Cornfeld became involved. It was not a large deal in itself, but, to the Commission staff, it seemed to symbolize a whole set of IOS attitudes.

Ramer Industries was, and is, a Brooklyn firm making sneakers, cheap slippers, and shoes in competition with Japanese manufacturers. Early in 1964, the family controlling Ramer Industries decided that they wanted to sell a block of Ramer shares. They began negotiations with a group of prospective purchasers, all of whom were members of a New York law firm called Ross, Stamer, Wolf & Haft. (Robert J. Haft was the lawyer who had worked for Ed Cowett in 1962, and the firm had acted as counsel to IOS on a number of occasions.)

Haft, Howard Stamer, and two other members of the firm—all acting as individuals—made agreements to purchase a block of 447,000 Ramer Industries shares at just over $2 each. The agreements having been made, with the price fixed, the question of raising money to pay for the shares came up. In the summer of 1964, Ed Cowett was brought into the negotiations.

By this time, the American stock markets had more than recovered from the sickening losses of 1962. The steady rise of the market was beginning to accelerate, and the promoters were once again coming out into the sun. In Geneva, IOS acquired the Overseas Development Bank in 1964. It formed two more banks to specialize in investment banking, and in the underwriting of stock flotations. These were the Investors Overseas Bank in the Bahamas and the Investors Bank in Luxembourg. And, after its sad, early experiences with glamour stocks, "IIT, an International Investment Trust" was beginning to recover, although still overshadowed by its vigorous young sibling, the Fund of Funds. Cowett took the view that it would be a good idea for IIT to take part in the Ramer operation.

The first plan was that IIT and the Investors Overseas Bank should put up loans to finance the deal in return for options to buy shares. But for some reason this plan was dropped, and it was decided instead that IIT itself would take up some Ramer shares. (The actual mechanism here was that the four lawyers, in return for suitable "considerations," would assign to IIT the purchase rights which they themselves had acquired earlier in the year.) IIT agreed to take up 60,000 of the Ramer shares at just over $3 each. But this was not, in itself, enough to put the deal together, because Haft and his colleagues wished to assign more than 60,000 shares. Other purchasers were required, and approaches were made to the Banque Privée, a small bank in

Geneva, to one of the partners in Jesup & Lamont, and to a number of U.S. mutual funds.

The approaches to the mutual funds were made by Bernard Cornfeld, acting in his capacity as Chairman of the Fund of Funds. This was the aspect of the deal which alarmed the SEC: because the Fund of Funds was a substantial shareholder in several of the mutual funds to which Cornfeld went bearing Ramer shares.

In one case the Fund of Funds was actually in control, legally speaking, of a mutual fund which was persuaded to accept Ramer shares. This was the Value Line Special Situations Fund, in which IOS held more than 25 per cent of the capital.

Under the Investment Company Act, a holding of 25 per cent in an investment company is regarded as the controlling interest if there is no larger holding. The realism of this is obvious enough if one looks at the case of a normal mutual fund, whose shares will as a rule be held in many small parcels. If anyone holds 25 per cent of such a fund, that he can withdraw at will, he is in a position to inflict something not far short of disaster on the people who manage the fund.

Value Line Special Situations Fund agreed, on Cornfeld's approach, to buy a parcel of Ramer shares at $3.25 each. It was a reasonable enough purchase as Value Line had sold out of Ramer earlier in the year when Ramer's price was $4.50 a share. And the Value Line management maintained formally that they acted entirely independently when approached by Cornfeld.

Nevertheless, the sober fact was that IOS was floating off shares in which some of its own legal advisers were interested through publicly issued mutual funds, one of which, in terms of American law, was under IOS control.

In the end Haft, Stamer, and the other two lawyers assigned the rights to over 230,000 Ramer shares to IIT, Banque Privée,

Value Line, and the other mutual funds approached by Cornfeld. As the market price had risen since those rights were obtained, the lawyers, who had got in at $2 a share, were letting the end purchasers have the shares cheap, at a little over $3 each, and for this they got considerations of $218,000, of which $45,000 came from IIT.

IIT paid $188,000 for the 60,000 shares which it took, and, at the end of 1965, C. Henry Buhl III was able to report an increase of $89,000 in the value of this investment. But the increase didn't last. At the end of 1966 the Ramer holding, although it had been increased by another 1800 shares, had fallen in value to $146,800; by June 1967, when Ramer made its last appearance in the IIT portfolio, the value of the shares had recovered to $301,300.

No matter what Cornfeld and Cowett might say about the essential honesty and independence of all concerned in the Ramer deal, it was unrealistic to think that the SEC could tolerate such operations. The fact was that IOS was moving toward a position where it would be able to control the leverage of vast sums of money, put up by American investors, by virtue of the tactical concentration of the Fund of Funds' holdings in U.S. mutual funds. If IOS was going to start floating off promotions of its own on the leverage of such money, the possibilities were hair-raising.

To Bernie and Ed, the SEC men appeared merely as footling bureaucrats, interfering with the scope and grandeur of designs they could not even understand. In Cowett's case, a streak of quiet intellectual arrogance added to this effect: it is manifestly important to Cowett to demonstrate that his business and legal intelligence cannot be surpassed. And in Cornfeld's case, there was his remarkable capacity for turning his emotions to serve his interests. To judge by his savage public attacks on the SEC, and his even more bitter private remarks, Cornfeld managed to convince himself, as soon as the SEC tried to thwart him, that it was not merely wrong, but wicked.

Cornfeld was capable of making remarkable propaganda against the SEC. For instance, at the end of 1966 the Commission published its report, "Public Policy Implications of Investment Company Growth." Cornfeld said publicly that the report was "extraordinary" and "dangerous" and he suggested privately that people went to work for the SEC because they couldn't get decent jobs anywhere else.

But both Cowett and Cornfeld realized at some level that it was absurdly dangerous to let their differences with the SEC turn into a feud. As Cornfeld remarked, "They may be schmucks, but they're the government."

In the event, their more rational impulses were swept aside. Shortly after the SEC filed its charges against IOS in February 1966, and while the formal legal proceedings were grinding through the Puerto Rican courts, IOS and the SEC staff started negotiations to see if an agreed settlement might be possible. It was during these negotiations that the proceedings descended into something very near to personal abuse, and a bitter all-day hearing that culminated with a sharp exchange between Ed Cowett and Manny Cohen. After that, Cowett took no further direct part, and the other IOS lawyers were left to gradually sort things out.

Despite his remarks about the quality of people who work for the government, Cornfeld hired three former SEC staffers. There was Allan Conwill, who had been SEC General Counsel and then director of its Division of Corporate Regulation until 1964, when he became a partner in the New York law firm of Willkie, Farr, Gallagher, Walton & FitzGibbon. Conwill became IOS's main attorney, and a director of the Fund of

Funds—whose prospectus the SEC had found so profoundly wanting. Then there was Milton D. Cohen, who had been on the SEC staff many years before, and was to return to work on the Commission's Special Study of Securities Markets. And IOS's Associate General Counsel was David Silver, hired from the SEC in the summer of 1965.

Silver objected to the way in which Cowett was handling the case, and resigned from IOS in the summer of 1965. The principal credit for smoothing things out in the end, and getting a settlement, should probably go to Robert Haft. But it took a long time.

The Offer of Settlement submitted by the IOS lawyers was finally accepted by the SEC on May 23, 1967. The terms were on the face of it humiliating. In exchange for the SEC's agreement not to proceed with its charges and to allow IOS to withdraw its broker/dealer registrations, IOS agreed to wind up or sell off all its U.S. operations (that meant reselling IPC and a life-insurance company recently acquired, and liquidating the proprietary funds), to stop selling to U.S. citizens whether in the United States or abroad, and to offer those who had bought charge-free redemptions. In addition, the Fund of Funds was not to buy or hold more than 3 per cent of any U.S. mutual fund, while none of the funds were to take a controlling interest in any U.S. company.

In 1967 IOS was being swept out of country after country around the world. To be turned out of America was almost the final blow. IOS was quickly to turn the rejection to advantage and even use it as a springboard from which to bound to new heights, but this did not mean that Cornfeld could forgive the SEC. Yet his later outbursts should be considered against the fact that a number of the SEC staff men, once ranged against him, subsequently chose to join the mutual-fund business.

Looking back today, some people at the SEC feel privately that they should have made the settlement harsher, or perhaps not have settled at all. They particularly dislike any suggestion that they looked after U.S. investors, but did not bother about other investors. But even in 1967 it was easy to underestimate the sheer persistence and flexibility of the offshore monster that Cornfeld and Cowett had created. If the SEC thought that it had heard the last of IOS when the settlement was made, that was a mistake. As the speculative fever of the later 1960s intensified, the Commission's staff found themselves tangling, or at least shadowboxing, with the old opponent on several occasions.

The man who enjoys the reputation for being the most dedicated pursuer of IOS at the SEC, Alan Mostoff, was still there in early 1971 as an associate director of the Division of Trading and Markets. (He had once to give a talk to a professional audience immediately after Cornfeld. "Mr. Cornfeld is a hard man to follow," he started, "I've been following him for years.") Mostoff is terse when questioned on IOS: he was recently asked to comment before a committee of the House of Representatives on Cornfeld's statement, in that same speech to the *Institutional Investor*'s conference, that the SEC was mainly responsible for the unhealthy state of the American securities market. He answered, "It is impossible to comment on such a statement because it is obviously without basis."

• 10 •

A Little Question in Switzerland

In which IOS nearly gets thrown out of Switzerland, the vital base. After sparring with the Swiss Bankers' Association, Bernie makes a tactical but precipitate withdrawal.

On February 28, 1967, a deputy named Raymond Déonna tabled in the Swiss parliament what is technically known there as a "*petite question*." Déonna's "little question" was the one publicly visible point in a subterranean disturbance which came close to getting IOS expelled from the one country it could not afford to be thrown out of: Switzerland, the home base.

Taken together, the crises of 1966–1967 almost shook IOS down. But they also led directly to what was perhaps Bernie Cornfeld's most virtuoso achievement. He grasped the idea that if you couldn't beat the Establishment, then you must—if not join it—at least come to terms with it. And with every trick of the arts of lobbying and public relations, he succeeded in making his essentially piratical operation look like a passable simulacrum of a sober international financial corporation.

"Investors Overseas Services," Déonna's question began, "is making itself much talked about these days.

"This organization . . . is resident in Panama, but in all its propaganda . . . only the name of Geneva is mentioned. It would seem that in this respect there is an abuse of the name of Geneva and of Switzerland.

"Moreover, by its aggressive policy of soliciting individuals, door-to-door, especially small savers, the company would seem to be in breach of the rules laid down on June 6, 1931, to implement the law of 1930 on commercial travelers. In addition, it seems to be in breach of the regulations governing foreign workers insofar as it has registered some of its agents as students at the university.

"It is known that the company violates foreign exchange control regulations abroad. A scandal has broken out about this in Brazil. . . . Every time that these violations come to the notice of the authorities, the reputation of Switzerland suffers. The Securities and Exchange Commission of New York (*sic*) has just undertaken an investigation. . . . The Federal Council is requested to state . . . whether, and how, it proposes to take steps to insure that IOS conforms to the law in its activities."

Raymond Déonna is not what you would call a left-wing demagogue. He belongs to the Liberal Party, which is roughly the ideological equivalent of the Republicans in America or the British Tories. Such a question, coming from him, meant that IOS had run into trouble in the quarter where it could least afford it: the Swiss financial community.

There have been times when it has suited Bernard Cornfeld to stress his close links with the Swiss banks, and he has done so. There have been other times when it has been more to his advantage to portray himself as the victim of their jealousy and exclusiveness, and he has done that, too. Both pictures have a certain foundation in fact, perhaps. Certainly the history of the IOS sales operation in Switzerland suggests a certain ambivalence on the part of the banking community.

Since 1965 the Banque Privée in Geneva, which we met in the previous chapter buying shares in Ramer Industries, has been controlled by Baron Edmond de Rothschild, who keeps his huge personal financial interests separate from those of his cousins Guy, Alain, and Yves, who run the Banque Rothschild in Paris. (Edmond has the reputation of being the richest of the Rothschilds. He also has a reputation for more adventurous investing than the rest of the family: he has backed the Club Méditerranée and the ski resort, Megève. One of his more prescient speculations was the smallish sum he lent to a then unknown American engineer called Robert Vesco—whom we shall meet again as the Savior of IOS.)

Some time before Baron Edmond bought control of the Banque Privée, it had entered into a rather unusual arrangement with IOS. What had happened was that an IOS salesman named Alvin "Bud" Schleiffer had persuaded the Banque Privée to let him use it as a cover for his own selling in Switzerland. Schleiffer was so successful that the IOS sales organization pressed him to set up a whole sales group in Switzerland. The Banque Privée didn't like the idea of a whole school of Schleiffers using its name, and so it "lent" Schleiffer an inactive subsidiary company called Athold SA, which was then used as the IOS sales company in Switzerland.

In 1966, Athold was sold to IOS. The Banque Privée people had discovered, to their horror, that Schleiffer's men were now taking the name of Rothschild in vain to sell their funds.

On October 21, 1966, IOS, Athold, and the Banque Privée each received a letter from the all-powerful Swiss Bankers' Association, which is not an official body, but the gnomes' union, so to speak.

The letter was drafted in exquisitely feline French. Door-to-door selling of investment programs, it pointed out, was "not customary" in Switzerland. It might lead unsophisticated clients to have an inaccurate idea of the risks they were taking. Indeed, the bankers murmured, one might even ask oneself whether it wasn't contrary to the federal law on commercial travelers of October 4, 1930. . . . "Wishing above all to avoid any incident or controversy which might lead to an official intervention which would hardly be desirable," the Association suggested that IOS might wish to reconsider its policy.

This elegant missive was recognized at IOS for what it was: a warning shot across the bows. Allen Cantor was despatched to Basel about a month later, taking with him the lawyer Robert Turrétini. A compromise was worked out. IOS agreed to phase out direct selling in Switzerland. The bankers, for their part, offered to look favorably on the creation of a new company which would sell exclusively through the banks, who would offer IOS funds to their clients just as they offered any other investments. (Banks in Switzerland, as in Germany, Italy, and most other European countries, fulfill the function of stockbrokers for their clients.)

Once again IOS proceeded to try to twist the situation to its advantage. Just as they had used the Crédit Suisse's name in their publicity (although the Crédit Suisse was no more than a depository), and just as the most tenuous connection with the Rothschild name had been instantly exploited, so now even the trouble with the Swiss Bankers' Association was made to sound like an endorsement.

On June 23 the Association had to send its members a circular letter putting the record straight: "IOS representatives are interpreting the contacts their company has had with the Association to mean that we are backing their commercial activities and would recommend to banks to act as intermediaries for the sale of IOS programs and certificates. This is absolutely not the case." The Association added that it had approached IOS and invited it not to refer to the Association either in its publicity or in its contracts with banks and clients. In several other ways, in the course of 1967, the Swiss authorities started to make life tough for IOS.

The Federal Banking Commission wrote to ODB saying that analysis of its balance sheet showed that its lending operations were preponderantly with IOS and its subsidiaries, and that the Commission doubted whether ODB could be regarded as a bank in the strict sense.

What worried the Commission, of course, was that since virtually the whole of ODB's business was with either IOS, its subsidiaries, its officers, or its clients, ODB was not so much a true bank as a financial-service subsidiary of IOS.

What worried Bernie Cornfeld and the sales executives was the prospect that they might be forbidden to talk about their "Swiss bank." For in many "hot-money" markets, one of the chief appeals of IOS to the clients was the idea that their money would be going into a Swiss bank.

Cornfeld's reaction was characteristic. He appointed to the board of ODB a blue-blooded young Swiss lawyer, one of whose relations happened to be a president of the Swiss Bankers' Association. A professor from a Swiss university was also retained to argue the case with the Commission. The balance sheet was passed as satisfactorily diversified, and ODB was allowed to go on calling itself a Swiss bank.

In the meantime, the fall-out from Déonna's question continued. The Federal Council in due course handed down a formal reply confirming Déonna's charges. It summarized the steps that had been taken to stop IOS posing as a Swiss corporation in its publicity when it suited it to do so, and to control door-to-door selling in Switzerland. Third, it confirmed that IOS had indeed been breaking the rules by hiring foreigners without permission, and added ominously that "the authorities in Geneva have taken the necessary measures to bring the situation back into conformity with the law."

The situation was that IOS had some twelve hundred employees in Geneva, exactly eighty-seven of whom had work permits. For many reasons, the Swiss in general, and the canton and republic of Geneva in particular, do their best to restrict immigration. They would have to restrict it anyway: Geneva is a small and very attractive place. There is also a growing amount of quiet and sometimes not-so-quiet xenophobia. And the authorities are seriously worried about the economic dangers of an unlimited influx of foreign workers.

Like people elsewhere, the Swiss are particularly irritated by the spectacle of foreigners breaking their rules. Here was a large and conspicuous group of foreigners apparently going out of its way to break the rules. IOS people didn't bother to get work permits. They didn't bother to get residence permits. Some didn't pay taxes. And in order to get around the rules imposed by the *contrôle de l'habitant*, the department of the cantonal government responsible, they adopted a number of cheerfully unsubtle ruses. IOS office workers were registered as students at the university. Dummy companies were bought, and a dozen IOS accountants or secretaries would apply for work permits as employees of some mythical import-export business.

The civic bureaucracy and the police began to get cross. They started raiding the Budé apartments, behind the Intercontinental Hotel, which, being the most expensive in town, were naturally favored by IOS-ers. They found dozens of people there without valid papers.

What made things worse was the insouciant arrogance with which the IOS chiefs treated the Swiss bureaucrats. On one occasion, Cornfeld himself called an official of the *contrôle de l'habitant* a "son-of-a-bitch" and threw a handful of pens and pencils in his face. "They behaved exactly as if they were in a conquered country," one IOS lawyer told us. "I repeatedly made the point that if a Swiss company behaved that way in New York, the cops would come down and clear the building with their night sticks in two minutes flat."

In the end the Geneva police came within a whisker of doing just that. Early in 1967, Bernie Cornfeld hired Raymond Nicolet, perhaps the ablest criminal lawyer in Switzerland, when two government inspectors arrived at the front door of 119 Rue de Lausanne and got ready to lock it and physically shut IOS down. The first words Nicolet spoke on behalf of his new clients were, "*Où sont vos mandats?*" "Where are your warrants?" The two inspectors, as it happened, didn't have them, and things were smoothed over just short of catastrophe. For to be thrown out of Switzerland would have been a serious blow to IOS in several ways. The sales force found it an inestimable advantage to wrap themselves in the mantle of Swiss financial respectability.

A lawsuit in Germany suggests just how powerful a talisman this was. On July 19, 1968, a Düsseldorf court found for a plaintiff, Adelgisa Rentsch, and against "IOS Ltd. (SA), Panama City," expressly because "the accused concealed the fact that it is a Panama company and knowingly gave the impression that she was taking out the IOS program with a Swiss company." The judge upheld the plaintiff's contention that she would not have signed her investment contract if she had realized it was with a Panamanian company. "In Europe," he said, "and especially in Germany, there is no very great confidence in the stability of South American republics." In due course IOS modified its sales literature so that it could no longer be accused of misleading clients in this way. But it remained true that an address in

Switzerland was reassuring to clients everywhere: an address in, say, Nassau, would have had very different overtones.

In any case, the world-wide IOS sales force depended on communications with headquarters. Salesmen who didn't get their advances against commission on the dot would soon drift away to work for other funds. Clients who didn't get their certificates promptly would redeem. And all these communications depended on the IOS computer. (The staff who ran the computer were equally in danger of being expelled.)

The fact was, however, that no matter how outraged the Genevan authorities might be, they were reluctant to throw IOS out. There was the prosperity IOS brought to the town—all those Patek Philippe watches, and those dinners at the Richemond and the Chat Botté, the oceans of whisky and gasoline and perfume that IOS and its employees consumed.

And so the city fathers negotiated. But they did not do so in lenient or kindly spirit, and they had all the high cards. The settlement they imposed was appropriately tough.

First, they insisted that IOS set up a Swiss company with assets within the jurisdiction. They did not want to find themselves dealing with a Panamanian will-o'-the-wisp that might steal away across the frontier one dark night leaving them clutching an empty jacket. Then they confirmed the original quota of eighty-seven work permits—but only eighty-seven. And they agreed to waive fines and back taxes, or rather to commute them for a sum in the region of 1 million Swiss francs, or $250,000. IOS could stay in Switzerland. But the greater part of the IOS administrative machinery would have to go somewhere else, and go quickly.

Where could they go? Many places were suggested: London, Munich, Luxembourg. Then Monaco was chosen. An option was taken on a palace there, to be turned into office space. But Bernie had had a brighter idea.

The Geneva international airport at Cointrin is only a bare two miles from the main IOS offices in the Rue de Lausanne. But the high wire fence which guards the frontier between Switzerland and France runs directly along the far side of the airfield. The main highway from Geneva to Paris passes under the main runway in a short tunnel and then immediately emerges on the main street of what was then still an unreconstructed French village—complete with *café*, water pump, farm tractors, and mud on the road.

This is Ferney-Voltaire, which owes half of its name and the whole of its fame to the fact that the greatest of French writers, wits, and cynics spent the last twenty years of his life there, obeying his own advice to cultivate one's garden, and at the same time standing poised to slip over the border to safety in Geneva whenever one of his more waspish sallies got him into trouble with the French authorities.

Ferney is only three miles from the center of Geneva. All road traffic between Geneva and Ferney must stop at a border equipped with customs post and armed guards. Two telephone lines, in 1967, had to accommodate all the traffic, not just between Geneva and Ferney-Voltaire, but between Geneva and the French system as a whole. Ferney was totally unprepared in every way to absorb three-quarters of the head office staff of an international financial organization whose brain and nerve center were going to stay across the border in Geneva.

Yet this is just what Bernie Cornfeld decided to bring about. And he succeeded.

Voltaire's successor as the leading citizen of Ferney is a young businessman named Roland Ruet, who is also the mayor.

Ruet is a close friend of the mayor of the neighboring town of Divonne, Marcel Anthonioz, the major shareholder in a nearby casino, and the junior minister for tourism in the French government. (In March 1970 Bernie Cornfeld and Ed Cowett proposed at an IOS Board meeting that IOS should buy the whole Divonne hotel and casino complex and develop it in conjunction with Hugh Hefner of *Playboy*. The board turned the idea down.)

"I was very helpful in getting the IOS people their *permis de séjour* [residents' permits]," Mayor Ruet confided to us. "IOS was grateful, and made a grant of two million francs to help build a new school for the commune. They also made an interest-free loan of three million francs for a swimming pool, which is still under way. We haven't had all the money yet."

"Were there any other conditions?" the mayor was asked.

"No. And please note that these were not conditions. This was all a spontaneous gesture. IOS was very happy at the way they had been received here, and this offer was only made six months after the move. That shows there were no conditions."

"During the move," we asked M. Ruet, "did you act as a consultant for IOS?"

"Yes," he said. "I helped them. They had to get building permits and all sorts of authorizations had to be obtained."

"Did you do this in an honorary capacity, or were you paid for it?"

"Purely honorary."

Even when IOS had been guided with an expert hand by the mayor through the thickets of bureaucracy there were still other problems to be overcome. Land had to be bought. Compelled to negotiate with landowners, builders, and other shrewd fellows in a hurry, IOS found the move extremely expensive. Everything had to be provided: not just office space, but a restaurant, a club, bus service, housing, and a large loan to the postal authorities for improved telephone service. The whole bill came to over $4 million, not counting $128,000 for professional services.

For the architects, shopkeepers, contractors, and landowners of a remote corner of provincial France, it was like striking oil. For the rest of the citizenry of Ferney, the arrival of IOS was a mixed blessing. The population of their village doubled. Prices went up in the shops. Parking became a nightmare, and traffic accidents increased. There was a good deal of tension between the villagers and the new arrivals.

For IOS had already begun to affect a characteristic style, the key to which was the idea that the rules did not exist for them. You cannot import thirteen hundred foreigners of every nationality, mostly young and disproportionately single, into a small French village without creating powerful antagonisms. You couldn't import such a group into a comparable area in Texas either without stirring up similar resentments.

The move to Ferney was, however, an impressive feat. The contract for the Ferney buildings was signed on March 6. The first staff moved into their new offices on May 15. And by September 16 the whole complex of prefabricated buildings in plate glass and blue curtain-walling was finished.

Bernie Cornfeld and his men had certainly risen to the challenge. But it was a challenge provoked by his own indifference to the Swiss authorities and their reasonable sensibilities. It is an article of faith with IOS men that the Swiss establishment persecuted them. The record suggests that on the contrary the Swiss only reacted under extreme and repeated provocation, and that they acted in the event with moderation. Bernie Cornfeld had only himself to blame for placing IOS under the absurd handicap of having to split its head office in two.

11

Pacem in Terris . . . and Good Will to All Men

Great efforts are made to improve the image of Investors Overseas Services. Eminent international citizens are brought into the company. They are carefully excluded from real power.

I n 1931, shortly after he left Harvard, Franklin Delano Roosevelt's eldest son, James, was offered a job in the insurance business. The salary was $15,000 a year, a handsome sum in those days. The duties were not arduous; according to young Roosevelt they consisted mainly of sitting behind a large desk. He took the job.

"I wasn't being kidded," the President's son told *Collier's* magazine later. "I knew perfectly well that they were paying me for the name. . . . I was newly married, and I needed the money." He was hailed as a "young meteor" of insurance, but in the event he did not rise to great heights in the business.

There are always difficulties, it is said, about being a great man's son, and there were special difficulties for FDR's son. The thirty-second President made plenty of enemies of the sort who would not hesitate to attack the son where they feared to attack the father, and James Roosevelt's early years were studded with small but often damaging political controversies, which he did not always handle with the greatest tact. By 1966, when he went to work for Bernie Cornfeld, much of his career had slipped past in a pattern of bright hopes and disappointments.

He went out to Hollywood to work for Sam Goldwyn in 1938. Then he set up his own business to sell coin-in-the-slot movies for bars, saying, "I want to make motion-picture production my life work." But his interest in movies didn't last.

He built up a magnificent war record, winning the Navy Cross for "extraordinary heroism." Few of his brother officers in the Marines have forgotten the huge, enthusiastic man with the two big .45s strapped to his thighs. "When he came to us," recalled one professional Marine in affectionate reminiscence, "he didn't know his ass from a hot rock. But he was hot to trot."

Yet even this had started in an aura of controversy, because at first James had gone into the Army as a lieutenant colonel. It was an error, and he quickly resigned and joined the Marines as a captain.

After the war, he served as a liberal Democratic Congressman from California for ten years. He ran for Mayor of Los Angeles, and in 1950, for Governor of California, but he lost each time. His political career was marred by allegations that a savings-and-loan company in Maryland paid him a salary while he was in Congress.

Barney Rosset, President of the Grove Press, well known as the distributor of *I Am Curious Yellow*, has known Roosevelt for twenty years and his family had been in several business ventures with him. Rosset sums him up shrewdly as "a really nice guy and a courageous Congressman, who had a strange career: he always seemed to be just missing."

In 1966, when he was introduced to Bernard Cornfeld, Roosevelt was the U.S. Ambassador to the United Nations Economic and Social Council, a job which essentially involved dealing with the underdeveloped nations of the world. If he was feeling, at fifty-nine, any disappointment about the way his career had developed, he was not showing it. James Roosevelt is a hearty man, stands six foot four, wears horn-rimmed glasses, and is as bald as an egg. He remained unfailingly affable and sociable, a great party man, knowing everybody worth knowing between Geneva and Los Angeles.

Americans with a degree of political sophistication were perhaps not much impressed when Cornfeld "captured" James Roosevelt. But they underestimated Bernie's coup. Franklin Roosevelt may have had detractors as well as admirers within the United States: outside the United States he had, for practical purposes, nothing but unqualified admirers. Even in Communist countries, FDR's son carried a name taken as a guarantee of judgment, probity, and, perhaps most important, generosity. The benefits that Roosevelt brought to IOS could scarcely be measured.

Cornfeld originally asked him to be an outside director of the Fund of Funds, without quitting his diplomatic post. The recruitment did not go smoothly.

Roosevelt asked for time to consider the offer, and set off back to New York by boat. While he was still on the Atlantic, Cornfeld released the news of his appointment. The press in America, led by *The New York Times*, immediately questioned the propriety of a serving ambassador taking that particular job. Roosevelt, reached on the *United States* by a *New York Times* reporter over the ship-to-shore telephone, sounded unconcerned about his new associates' troubles with the SEC. "Questions are raised about the United States Steel Company too, aren't they?" he said. But the State Department, deeply embarrassed, had to concede that there did seem to be a certain possibility of conflict of interest. A small but nasty row blew up. "Ambassador James Roosevelt," thundered *The New York Times* editorially under the headline "Dubious Association," "has shown poor taste and judgment in becoming a director of the Fund of Funds . . . it is clearly a matter of national embarrassment for an ambassador to be a director of a company involved in litigation against the Government of which he is a part."

By the time poor Roosevelt's ship docked in New York, a small army of reporters, photographers, and television crews was waiting for him. Ed Cowett had flown to New York to do what he could to improve the image-improver's image. In a meeting the same day, Roosevelt agreed to resign from the Fund of Funds to satisfy the State Department. And Cowett proposed that Roosevelt should come to IOS as a full-time executive with a splendid salary, not to mention the benefits of the stock-option plan. Roosevelt accepted, and started work formally for IOS on December 16, 1966.

Cornfeld was delighted with his new personal ambassador to the international establishment, and quickly put him to work improving IOS's external relations, which sorely needed improvement at the time, as we have seen. But he also took good care that neither Roosevelt nor anyone else should get any wrong ideas about the true strength of Roosevelt's position inside IOS.

Soon after he joined, Roosevelt characteristically proposed to give a splendid party to celebrate his new functions. Cornfeld agreed, and put the company's lakeside villa, Bella Vista, at his disposal.

Roosevelt went ahead with the arrangements for a banquet in the grandest style. An impressive guest list of UN delegates, ambassadors, bankers, generals, and politicians was invited, and a distinguished chef was hired with an entire kitchen staff to do justice to the occasion. An hour after the time appointed on the invitation card, the Ambassador's party was in full swing. By ten it was still getting noisier, and by eleven the last limousine had disgorged the last general. Only one person was missing to make it the most glittering social occasion Geneva had seen for many years, the man they had all been invited to meet: Bernie.

By eleven-thirty, the chef was threatening to commit hara-kiri amid the ruins of his dinner. Roosevelt was frantic. Around midnight he surrendered, and asked the guests to take their places for dinner. "Gentlemen," he said, "I'm sorry, but Mr. Cornfeld will not be with us this evening. We work for an extremely brilliant man. A man with a peculiar personality. He may even be a genius, and we must give genius its due."

It is said that Roosevelt did not forget this first lesson.

. . .

One of the many countries where IOS was in bad odor at the beginning of 1967 was Iran. And Iran was also a place where the name of Roosevelt executed an even stronger magic than elsewhere, for the excellent reason that the Shah of Iran owes his throne to a man called Roosevelt.

In 1953, Kermit, or Kim, Roosevelt pulled off one of the most daring and successful of all the CIA's secret operations in the Cold War. The Shah was then at loggerheads with his left-wing Prime Minister, Dr. Mossadegh, who had expropriated the assets of Western oil companies, and assumed near-dictatorial powers, including the power to sell the Shah's estimated $50 million worth of jewels, and the Eisenhower administration sided with the Shah.

Kim Roosevelt slipped into Iran to help the Shah, who had fled to Rome. A few days later, Roosevelt infiltrated a large number of supporters of the Shah into Tehran disguised as a religious procession. At a prearranged signal, the "fanatics" whipped out arms from under their robes, and headed for various key points. By midnight Operation Ajax was completely successful, and Mossadegh was under arrest. Two days later the Shah came back to Tehran.

James and Kim Roosevelt are only remote relations. Kim is a grandson of President Theodore Roosevelt, who belonged to the Oyster Bay branch of the family. James's father, FDR, belonged to the Hyde Park branch of the family.

In 1965 Ira Weinstein, who became boss of IOS in Canada, handed over the flourishing IOS operation in Iran (and indeed in Afghanistan, Pakistan, India, Ceylon, and Nepal, all of which were controlled from Tehran). The man he chose as his successor was Bill Haller, a former schoolteacher who spoke Farsi, the principal language of Iran.

Weinstein admits that he had turned his attention from the expatriates to the Iranians as early as 1962. "The Iranian people are no different from any others; they want to make more than bank interest on their money, and to send their children to good schools in Europe and the States." While he insists that all the Iranians who bought IOS funds in his time had external accounts, IOS's own lawyer in Tehran, Dr. Chahin Aghayan, has confirmed to us that one of the reasons for IOS's troubles there in 1966 was "foreign currency transactions not made through the Central Bank."

It would seem that after Haller became manager the salesmen turned to less wealthy Iranians. The outflow of money became more noticeable, and the clients became less discreet. Some salesmen paid no taxes, for one thing. And Haller himself had a passion for clandestinity. He used codes and ciphers, and if a client's name appeared on a document he would snip it off.

Gradually his affairs got into a hopeless tangle, which was made even worse by what Weinstein called "some maniacal deals," one of which involved shrimping in the Persian Gulf. To cap it all, a large mail pouch containing checks to be invested in Geneva was handed to an Iran Air hostess who turned out to be an agent of SAVAK, the secret police.

At the end of 1966, the Iranian government had had enough. "They lowered the boom in the direct way they have there," one Geneva executive remembers. But Iran was a valuable market. With James Roosevelt's help, Bernie Cornfeld and Allen Cantor were determined to get back into it if they could.

We shall describe the Iran crisis in some detail because in many ways it was a model of the world-wide campaign by IOS's new "diplomatic service" under Roosevelt to deal with what were euphemistically called "sensitive areas."

The first step in this instance was untypical. Haller was summoned home and terminated. He was perhaps a little unlucky. True, he had made the supreme mistake of getting caught. But other managers—Tregea, Jessen, and Börlin in Brazil, for example—had been caught without losing status.

The next step was more imaginative. James Roosevelt used his contacts to get an audience with the Shah, who was having a skiing holiday at Saint Moritz. Roosevelt and Cornfeld went up to Saint Moritz to see the King of Kings, and succeeded in persuading him at least to allow them to negotiate with the Central Bank and tax authorities.

Cornfeld almost spoiled this promising beginning by bragging about his chat with the Shah. The Shah was understandably annoyed, but Roosevelt was able to soothe his ruffled feathers in time and, with Allen Cantor, he flew off to Tehran to talk to Iranian officials.

A whole series of meetings followed, with several negotiators involved on the IOS side. They enlisted the good offices of the Shah's nephew, Prince Shahram. IOS also promised to pay all the salesmen's unpaid back taxes and to give an undertaking of good behavior.

But IOS diplomacy in those countries where it was Roosevelt's job to improve IOS's relations with the government relied not only on promises to go and sin no more, or even on Jim Roosevelt's talent for making friends and influencing top people. The central argument Roosevelt used was designed to appeal to the host country's own economic advantage.

This was the "national fund" concept. Essentially the idea was that where it was objectionable, for balance-of-payments reasons, for citizens to buy foreign currency to buy foreign mutual funds, thus in effect exporting capital, IOS would provide a local fund which would invest a high proportion of the money it raised in the country itself.

The "national fund" was a sound enough concept in principle in a country with a developed securities market. It could be made to work in Britain, in Germany, in Canada, or even in Italy (where Fonditalia was being developed at this very time, and has been successful in spite of the limitations of the Italian stock exchanges). But the "Iranian Fund" that Roosevelt and his colleagues now proposed to set up as a *quid pro quo* for being allowed to go on selling in Iran was something else again.

There is a stock exchange of sorts in Tehran, but only a handful of Iranian companies are listed on it. Few have shares widely held by the public, and fewer still are large enough to offer any hope of liquidating in a hurry without heavy loss. If an IOS Iranian fund were to put half its money in Iran, which is what was proposed, what could it be invested in?

Here we meet one of the characters who was to play a leading role in the *dénouement* of the IOS story: none other than

John M. King, the Denver entrepreneur who was looking for "natural resources" to put his clients' money into.

We shall have to describe in greater detail later how King came to be so closely associated with IOS. What matters here is that he was very close, and that he was interested in a copper field in Iran. It was only in the exploration stage and would therefore have been an unsuitable investment for an open-ended mutual fund, especially one for small savers in a poor country. But several of those involved in the negotiations on the IOS side agree that the copper project was used as a providential answer to the question, "What will your Iranian fund invest in here?"

In the end, plans for an Iranian fund never came to fruition. Nor did plans for an Iranian insurance company, which were also discussed. On November 28, 1968, the Iranian government suddenly declared the activities of IOS and all other foreign mutual funds illegal. All foreigners connected with the company were given from twenty-four hours to two weeks to leave the country, and all Iranians were asked to sign a statement saying that they would have nothing further to do with IOS. The IOS men were impressed by the smoothness of the closedown. They were also impressed by its firmness.

"Could IOS or any similar organization ever operate in Iran again?" we asked an official of the Central Bank.

"No one in their right mind would ever buy anything from IOS now," was his reply.

• • •

SO Roosevelt's diplomacy failed in Iran in the end. But the scope of his efforts over the three years after he joined the company was breath-taking. The subsidiary he was in charge of was called IOS Overseas Funds Management Ltd. for a while. Later its name was changed to IOS Development Ltd. The assignment remained the same: to improve relations with the governments that had "lowered the boom," or threatened to, either because IOS had been selling illegally, or because it was taking too much capital out of their countries, or because of some other "sensitive area." In each case Roosevelt's prescription was the same: either an equity-linked national-insurance plan, or a national fund, or both. As a solution to the "sensitive area" problems it can hardly be said to have worked brilliantly.

The 1967 annual report stated that "at present"—*i.e.*, in the spring of 1968—"IOS Overseas Funds Management Ltd., under President James Roosevelt, is exploring the possibility of product introduction in developing countries." By "product," IOS meant a fund or an equity-linked insurance company. The countries where IOS eventually succeeded in setting up national products were Canada, the Sterling Area, France, Italy, West Germany, Sweden, Holland, Australia, and—on a tiny scale—Argentina and Cyprus.

The countries where the national-funds gambit or its insurance variant were seriously attempted without success included Iran, the Philippines, Spain, Portugal, Venezuela, Mexico, Israel, Lebanon, Scandinavia (as a whole), Norway (where IOS had a charter which has never been used), Japan, South Africa, and Yugoslavia.

The national-funds drive, of course, was backed up by a tremendous public-relations campaign, the thrust of which was to suggest that IOS was something altogether purer and more cosmically important than a mere business. Its ultimate goals, the campaign set out to convince the world, were not mere profits, but peace and economic development.

Here again, while the initiative for the most audacious projects tended to come from Cornfeld himself, Roosevelt's role should not be underestimated. It hardly mattered that in the end he proved to have little real power in the company. What mattered was that he cast over all that IOS did the magical aura of his parent's name, which is identified everywhere with the most disinterested achievements of American liberalism. And he was tireless.

No other mutual-fund group, possibly, would have had the audacity to sponsor an international peace conference, and then turn it into a commercial jamboree. No other mutual-fund group, certainly, could have produced someone to preside over such an occasion with the aplomb which James Roosevelt brought to the solemn farce of Pacem in Terris II.

In 1962, Robert M. Hutchins, the head of the Center for the Study of Democratic Institutions in California, had arranged what he called a "convocation" in New York, at which eminent private individuals from various countries were invited to meet and discuss the problems of war and peace. That was Pacem in Terris I. Such meetings are not rare, and most people think they are desirable, even if they do not lead to the millennium overnight. Inevitably, however, they cost money. On the previous occasion, Hutchins had been able to raise what he needed from various American corporations. Then someone introduced him to Cornfeld, who became not just the angel of peace on earth, but its impresario.

Four hundred people, many of them of the greatest eminence, were invited to Geneva from seventy countries. They assembled on May 28, 1967, in the Intercontinental Hotel, the setting of the famous sales conference. Much earnest oratory was heard from them over the next three days, though James Roosevelt's assertion that their "deliberations mark an important breakthrough for the cause of all humanity" sounds, in retrospect, a trifle exaggerated.

Three principal themes had been chosen for discussion: the

war in Vietnam, the threat of war in the Middle East, and the deadlock over the two Germanies. It was unfortunate that the meeting coincided with a resumption of American bombing in Vietnam and with the outbreak of the Six-Day War in the Middle East.

Bernie Cornfeld cannot be blamed for most of what was said on the chosen topics which were therefore ghoulishly inappropriate. What was characteristic was the way he did his best to get his sponsor's plug in whenever he got a chance.

The list of participants must now make embarrassing reading for some of the great men who attended, and for some of the innocent unknowns: for Senator Fulbright and John Kenneth Galbraith; the editor of *Le Monde* and the Swiss Cardinal; ambassadors, ministers, archbishops, and four Nobel peace laureates jostled shoulders there with a mob of Bernie's cronies, some of whom may well have thought Pacem in Terris was a stock traded over the counter.

The most exquisitely vulgar exploitation involved the octogenarian musician and pacifist, Pablo Casals. It had been arranged for his peace oratorio, *El Pessebre*, to be performed in connection with the conference in Geneva with the composer conducting. As it happened, Casals was prevented from doing so by illness. His brother took his place. But he did send a touching message of good will.

"Dear friends," the old man wrote, "my only weapon for justice and against war have been my cello and my conductor's baton; and though I cannot be with you, my music will speak for me of love and peace."

The music was recorded, and Cornfeld arranged for the tapes to be transcribed onto discs and handed out in glossy packages to the participants. This was duly done, and the albums were marked: "IOS presents *El Pessebre* by Pablo Casals."

Both at the time and in a lavish book he had produced, with himself naturally given precedence among the princes of peace, Cornfeld gave great play to the fact that the money for Pacem in Terris had come from the IOS Foundation. What he did not say is where the foundation had got it. It came from New York brokerage houses that were instructed to direct brokerage for this purpose.

James Roosevelt was not just Bernie Cornfeld's customer's man, trouble shooter, and ambassador-at-large. He was also useful as a recruiting sergeant.

It was Cornfeld's own idea, of course, to adorn the IOS Board with some reassuring names. Roosevelt himself was not quite the first acquisition. Wilson W. Wyatt, the jovial Kentucky lawyer and politico, joined even before him.

But a lieutenant governor of Kentucky, even one who has managed a presidential campaign, carries relatively little weight in Europe. A governor of California is more imposing. Roosevelt was able to persuade his old friend ex-Governor Edmund G. "Pat" Brown to join the Fund of Funds Board. And Cornfeld had recruited a useful man in West Germany: Erich Mende, head of the small Free Democratic Party.

But Cornfeld was after bigger lions. That summer of 1967 he made his first approach to the ex-Chancellor, Ludwig Erhard, reputed father of the West German economic miracle, and perhaps the most highly regarded economist-in-politics in Europe. For eighteen months, Cornfeld paid court to Erhard. He needed the most imposing figurehead he could get to offset IOS's public-relations problems in Germany. He needed Erhard badly enough to fly to Germany himself in mid-December 1968 to try to persuade the ex-Chancellor to join him. A month later Erhard was still talking to Cornfeld's emissary, Mende's man, Dr. Preussker. But in the end Erhard said no.

In mid-1968 IOS went shopping for some august names in

Britain, and came back with the Earl of Lonsdale; a Conservative MP, Sir Harmer Nicholls; and Anthony Montague-Browne, who had once been one of the late Sir Winston Churchill's secretaries. All three became directors of International Life Insurance (Luxembourg).

At about the same time, James Roosevelt also recruited an expatriate Englishman called Sir Eric Wyndham White, whom he knew socially. For some twenty years Sir Eric had played a leading role in administering the General Agreement on Trade and Tariffs, of which he became Secretary General, with his office in Geneva. Wyndham White joined IOS because he had been attracted by Roosevelt's talk about the potential of the national fund idea for providing development capital to underdeveloped countries. It is doubtful whether Bernie Cornfeld took as much notice of him when he arrived as he would have done if he had been able to read the future.

Early in 1969, IOS's first royal recruit was brought in—Count Carl Johan Bernadotte, of the Swedish royal family. That was IOS's last great success out lion hunting. But it was not the last hunt by any means. Bernie Cornfeld had almost certainly approached Adlai Stevenson and invited him to join the IOS Board shortly before Stevenson's death in London in 1965. He definitely did approach both ex-Vice President Hubert Humphrey (to whose 1968 presidential campaign he had been a moderately heavy contributor) and ex-Supreme Court Justice Arthur Goldberg. An approach to the present President of France, Georges Pompidou, when he was out of favor with General de Gaulle in early 1969, was also enthusiastically discussed by Roosevelt.

• • •

Pacem in Terris was by no means the only instance in which IOS sought to project itself as far more than a mere business enterprise. Sometimes it seemed almost to lay claim to the status of an independent power among the nations. On September 16, 1968, for example, to quote its own brochure, IOS "brought together over three hundred eminent jurists, philosophers and statesmen in Geneva to discuss specific action to be taken for the establishment of international peace and human rights through law." As the brochure, perhaps a trifle naïvely, admitted, "IOS contributed a major portion of the funds needed to be sure that the international observance" of World Human Rights-Law Day "take place in Geneva." That eminent jurist Edward M. Cowett was the host and sat on the right hand of Chief Justice Earl Warren of the United States, and the chief justices of Ireland, Italy, India, Denmark, Libya, Switzerland, and Norway occupied appropriate places of subordinate dignity.

It should be said to Cornfeld's and Roosevelt's credit that they did not stuff the boards of their companies with purely ornamental figures, but made an effort to acquire men with real, earned reputations. The effectiveness of the tactic, in any case, is not in doubt.

People looked at the list of eminent men who had associated themselves with IOS, and they said to themselves: "This must be a solid business." It was not only potential investors who had this reaction.

In April 1969, for example, a well-known British financial columnist, Kenneth Fleet of the *Daily Telegraph*, published a big feature on IOS. He raised several serious questions. But then he said, "Anybody who wants to substantiate charges of this kind has, among other things, to explain the towering presence in Geneva of James Roosevelt."

Even more important, perhaps, Roosevelt's own reputation and the big names he helped to bring in enabled IOS to recruit a wholly new kind of executive at those middle and upper-middle levels which become so important for an organization once it passes a certain size and degree of complexity.

In the end, it is quite true, the sales veterans, such as Allen Cantor, George Landau, and Harvey Felberbaum, kept the ultimate power in their hands, or rather such power as was not retained by Cornfeld and Cowett. But from the beginning of 1967 on, IOS began with Roosevelt's help to acquire able executives from backgrounds other than selling. They included lawyers such as the American Henry Carnegie or the Swiss Jean de Muralt; bankers such as Michael Sakellaropoulo of the Bank of Canada or the German Viktor-Emmanuel Preussker and a particularly strong contingent of diplomats and international civil servants. Jim Wine, former U.S. Ambassador to Luxembourg and the Ivory Coast; Murray Belman, who had been a deputy legal counsel at the State Department; and Frank Peel, former counsel to the International Labor Organization in Geneva were persuaded by Jim Roosevelt that economic development was what IOS was all about.

Gradually these new men, collectively, began to introduce an element of rationality—or of bureaucracy, depending on the point of view—which in time altered the company's style. Many of them—such as two State Department graduates, Hal Vaughan and Harold Kaplan—played important roles in the coming crisis. For professional men like these it came as a rude shock when they were first exposed to the freebooting reality of IOS sales operations. Take Colonel Gordon West's traumatic experience in Spain, for example.

West is a personal friend of Roosevelt's from Marine Corps days who had stayed on to have a very distinguished career of his own in the Marines. It included secondment to the White

House as an aide during the Kennedy years and a spell in the London embassy, as well as combat experience in the South Pacific, in Korea, and in Vietnam.

In the summer of 1967, as one of his first tasks with IOS, the colonel worked out detailed plans for a national fund in Spain. That autumn, he set off for Madrid for what he had been given to think would be friendly talks with Spanish officials.

"While I was there," he recalls with an inimitable wry gesture of all-embracing dismay, "they just went ker-choonk." The Spanish authorities locked the IOS offices, impounded the books, and jailed those of the salesmen who hadn't fled the country. For the colonel, who had outfought the Japanese, the North Koreans, and the Viet Cong, it was a new and humiliating experience—a rout.

It is possible to piece together the events that led up to the Spanish tragedy in precise detail from court records. IOS had been selling to American military personnel in Spain from the early days. But the first IOS sales company there was not set up until March 3, 1967—after the Roosevelt campaign against hot-money operations was supposed to have begun.

The management of the company, which was called Investors Iberia, was in the hands of a man called Emile Giubelli, a Canadian citizen born in Milan. The lawyer who advised Giubelli about setting it up warned him that "the money laws of 1938 are ironclad"; it was strictly illegal to sell foreign mutual funds to Spaniards under any circumstances, let alone to convert pesetas into dollars in order to do so. Giubelli ignored the warning.

But on July 7, 1970, the Special Judge of Monetary Offences in Madrid, Don Antonio Sanchez del Corral y del Rio, fined Giubelli a total of 22 million pesetas (about $330,000) and sentenced him *in absentia* to three years in jail for what was described in the judgment as "a monetary offense, committed and repeated, of a complicated nature." Nineteen other IOS salesmen and clients received lesser, but still severe, fines. All had fled the country.

What happened was that in the autumn of 1967 a savings bank in Barcelona, the Caja de Crédito Popular, had failed. A routine examination of its books showed irregularities, and the books were passed to the Special Judge's investigators. This is one of the most feared arms of the Spanish State, at least for those members of the business and professional classes who have opportunities of salting away money which they would like to take abroad. (The peseta is now convertible, but in 1967 convertibility was still forbidden under the Draconian laws passed during the Civil War.)

The Special Judge has his own fraud squad of trained accountants, and its head, Don Antonio, has a reputation for total impartiality and an invincible determination to ferret out the truth. IOS, its defense lawyer told us, "had run foul of the toughest law in Spain."

In January 1968 the judge announced that there was "a strong preliminary indication of criminal liability" on the part of Giubelli. The court eventually found that he had illegally converted no less than 50 million pesetas into dollars through a bank in Andorra. Some of his sales force had cottoned on and done the same, though on a smaller scale. IOS, in the meantime, found that Giubelli had cheated them, too. On March 15, 1968, Ed Cowett complained formally to the public prosecutor in Geneva that Giubelli had:

> Caused to be remitted sums amounting to at least US $132,785 by divers clients of our company, on the pretext of transferring them to IOS in Geneva. He then drew seventeen checks on his

own accounts with the Societat de Banca Andorrana, situated on the territory of the Principality of Andorra, representing a total of only US $21,715, which he remitted to Geneva. These checks . . . were subsequently returned for insufficient funds. . . . The balance of US $111,070 remains unpaid.

Giubelli left his wife behind in Spain to face the music, but she was found not guilty. His disappearance and the judge's preliminary finding of guilt induced consternation in Geneva. What frightened IOS most was that the Spanish authorities might take action against IOS's gigantic real-estate holdings, Playamar and El Rosario, on the south coast.

By the summer of 1968, James Roosevelt was down in Madrid to see if he could work things out with a little chat with the boys at the top. This time he was out of luck.

In July 1970 the verdict was finally handed down. Giubelli and seventeen other salesmen received heavy sentences, but IOS itself got off relatively lightly. It had to pay 10 million pesetas (roughly $150,000) in fines unpaid by the salesmen. And 44 million pesetas which had been illegally converted were quietly returned by IOS to Spain in dollars which were officially changed back into pesetas and returned to the original Spanish investors.

Giubelli was later expelled from Switzerland and briefly jailed in Nice. But he talked his way out of being extradited back to Spain, and is said now to be working for a rival mutual-fund group. In his fashion Giubelli, too, seems to have mastered the offshore idea.

12

Reminiscences of the Court of the Emperor Cornfeld

In which Cornfeld gives some views of sexual codes, and several of his followers show how to suppress a scandal in the court. We examine the loyalties of Cornfeld's old friends.

Geneva summer is green and sparkling blue: the green of the cool parkland that rims the lake, and the blue of its waters moving slowly south to join the Rhône. The sun lasts a long time into the autumn. Sails gleam on the lake till evening, and swans move quietly along the shallows.

The air is fresh and brilliant, banking being an industry that produces very little pollution. The Rue de Lausanne curves along the lakeside past demure eighteenth-century villas, new office buildings that glint with glass and metal, and open-air restaurants where boats sway gently alongside the tables.

Volkswagens, Cadillacs, and Fiats make orderly processions through the streets, and in the great days of IOS, salesmen visiting HQ could look out for Ed Cowett's blue Maserati, or perhaps the yellow Lamborghini of Ossie Nedoluha (one of the great chieftains of the German override system), or for any one of Bernie's cars—the Rolls, the custom-built Lincoln, the Cadillac, or the Sting Ray.

Almost incredibly, Geneva has the motorcar without the traffic problem. Superb auto routes curl away from the city toward Zurich, Paris, Munich, and Rome, and ten minutes away on the French border is Cointrin airport, with three planes leaving every day for New York. Perhaps no other place conveys so vividly the impression of having the pleasures of Europe at one's feet, with the conveniences of America within easy reach.

Bernard Cornfeld was certainly not the first man with imperial ambitions to find Geneva a useful base—he was preceded, among others, by Louis Napoleon. But few have played the imperial role with more enthusiasm than Cornfeld did. From the take-off of the Fund of Funds, through the final crisis, none of the alarms and triumphs of IOS affected the level of Cornfeld's personal existence (one that "a maharaja might envy," said *Time*) or the awe in which his followers held him.

Although Geneva remained a constant, the emphasis frequently shifted between alternative seats, of which there were an impressive number: the Villa Elma in Geneva, which belonged to Cornfeld; Bella Vista, which was the IOS villa; the Château de Pelly in the Haute Savoie; the apartment in Paris; the London town house in West Halkin Street; the apartments at the Carlyle Hotel and on Park Avenue in New York and a penthouse downtown; and, toward the end, a second château, the castle of Prangins, in Switzerland. As he acquired new environments, Cornfeld spent his time with rather different kinds of people. Mutual-fund salesmen became less prominent.

Cornfeld was seen more with dress designers such as Guy Laroche and Oleg Cassini, with actors like Laurence Harvey and Tony Curtis, Las Vegas casino promoters like Delbert Coleman, fast-moving U.S. businessmen like Gene Klein and Charlie Bluhdorn. The Emperor's tastes changed, and although he always liked to claim that "a good meal for me is at a hot-dog stand," he favored the Club dell' Aretusa in Chelsea, where they have better things to boast about than their hot dogs. But however it varied, the high Cornfeld style was always well suited to calibration in the media. He was usually depicted making luxurious informal progresses, at high speed, but receiving petitions and dispensing wisdom en route. Always, Cornfeld appeared as a man of imperative whim and incessant movement. Over and over again, he was seen converting the skeptical. The imperial pronouncements of the period make, in retrospect, strange reading:

"What I have done is apply socialist ideas about redistributing wealth in a free-enterprise context."

"We're in the business of literally converting the proletariat to the leisured class painlessly. . . . It's revolutionary and goddam exciting."

There were prophetic forecasts:

"I'm convinced that IOS is going to become the most important economic force in the private sector in the free world."

There were witticisms:

"I met a guy I trained with as a social worker, and he asked me what agency I'd gone into. I said, 'A preventive agency. We find our people before they're destitute, and do something about it.' "

There were excoriations of the heathen:

"Government agencies are full of half-wits and political appointees who can't get a decent job anywhere."

And there were, naturally, extravagant praises of the Emperor himself. John King, who helped Cornfeld and Cowett punt nearly $100 million of the customers' money into "natural-resources investment," declared that Bernie possessed "one of those types of minds that has an instantaneous grasp of any subject he chooses to be interested in." *Business Week* described him as "King of Europe's Cash," and said that the judgment of the financial world was that "Cornfeld can take IOS just about anywhere he wants." *Time* said that he was "part Peter Pan, part Midas."

Eli Wallitt, court member of much standing, and another ex-campaigner for Norman Thomas socialism, put the whole business on a less grandiloquent level in personal reminiscence. "Did you ever go to one of those parties?" he said. "There were heaps of caviar [a shaping gesture with the hands] like *this*."

The awe in which Cornfeld was held derived very largely from the frequently published tabulations of his wealth and his possessions, and the constantly growing estimate of his financial power. It was said that he was responsible, on some days, for 4 per cent of all the trading on the New York Stock Exchange, and that he was an important item in the American balance of payments. But the scarlet glow of his sexual reputation, although less often discussed publicly, also helped make him an object of fascination. "He certainly wasn't a one-woman man," said his cousin Hubert.

Two women have had durable relationships with Cornfeld: Sophie, his mother, who moved to Geneva in 1962 after a spell in Los Angeles; and his secretary, a red-haired German girl named Didi Fischer. But, by his own account, none of his sexual relationships have been designed to be so durable—and in the latter phase especially, there was a tendency for them to be conducted in parallel as well as in series. A survey can only illuminate a few highlights.

According to Cornfeld, he had one girl friend in Paris and another in Vienna within a few months of his arrival in Europe. Neither of these affairs, however, made a powerful contribution to the legend. In pre-imperial days, in Geneva, he is said to have paid court to a maid of one of his fellow directors.

After 1962, a more glamorous note is sounded. There was an affair with a Japanese actress, which was brief but dramatic: Bernie met her in Tokyo on a Saturday and invited her to drop everything and fly to Europe with him on Sunday, which she did. "But in the end," said Hubert Cornfield, "she couldn't put up with the all-night business meetings Bernie used to have. Maybe it was because she was different that he liked her. Bernie was always looking for something different."

He rather liked to theorize about sexual affairs, claiming to see the effects of Puritanism in the sexual attitudes of both Hugh Hefner and of most members of the hippie movement. These people, he said, were reacting against a Puritan upbringing, and this was shown by the fact that, although they rejected one code, they were always trying to build others. For himself, he said, he favored "the joy of anarchy" in sexual matters. Such discussions tended to include accounts of various tectonic orgasms experienced by the Emperor and this or that anarchist sympathizer.

Cornfeld liked to travel with a convoy of three, four, and sometimes more girls—conveying at times a rather harem-like impression. It was not, however, as Oriental as all that. To share the Emperor's airplane was not necessarily to share his bed, and he never said that his theories about sexual anarchy extended to multiple congress. So far as one could work out the dynamics of these groups, there was usually one girl who was the sexual partner of the moment, while the others would be along for their own amusement or curiosity.

The members of Cornfeld's entourage of young women were often associated with subdivisions of his business ventures, which were not easy to separate from his personal life. At their height, Cornfeld's multifarious interests included an acting-and-modeling school in Paris, and a piece of a model agency in New York. So, when there were "three lissome girls" in his escort, it might well be some of the girls taking a ride with the boss—innocent enough in itself, though perhaps a rather informal way of running a business.

The Paris operation, Studio 22, took its name from the address of Cornfeld's first apartment in Paris, 22 Boulevard Flandrin, and it was started after Cornfeld met a Parisian dentist and plastic surgeon named Pierre Albou, a celebrated expert at capping the teeth and modifying the profiles of aspirant actresses. This business enabled Albou to maintain a house in the elegant Rue de Tilsit, by the Place de l'Etoile: Bernie bought a floor of Albou's house, and installed there a modeling school which he had bought as a going concern, and it had about twenty-five students.

Studio 22 had an international flavor, with girls from Sweden, Israel, and Germany, and Cornfeld wanted to make it a base for his ambitions in the movies. He got as far as approaching the film director Jean-Pierre Mocky with suggestions that Mocky might like to make a series of movies employing the talents of the Studio 22 girls. But Mocky, while remaining friendly with the Emperor, seems not to have wanted him as a patron again. "Bernie told me," he recalled of the earlier collaboration on *Snobs*, "that I should make a film that was really way-out and different." The finished work was a very individual adaptation of Thackeray's book and Mocky says that Cornfeld was "horrified" when he saw it. (According to Victor Herbert, Bernie cried, "Where are the girls?") Mocky took the view that "if one acts as a patron and gives money to the artist, then one should accept the work he produces, as the great seigneurs did in the Middle Ages," and he declined the second offer.

Whether or not it was Bernie's lack of seigniorial tolerance that was to blame, Studio 22 does not seem to have built up a large show-business reputation.

Talent Management International was a model agency with offices on East Sixty-third Street, New York, and Cornfeld put some money into it. A deputation from TMI accompanied him on his journey to Mexico to confer with Hugh Hefner in Acapulco just before the crash of IOS. Julie Baumgold, reporting the progress for *New York* magazine, identified "The Darby," "Lorna," "Cedric" (also called "Rattlesnake"), and "Jackie, a nineteen-year-old model from a Scottish town." Possibly, the most revealing cameo from Miss Baumgold's cool report concerned the Emperor arranging rooms for the night. "Bernie organizes the rooms. He says to Jackie, 'You room in with me.' It is not a request."

The quotation encapsulates an attitude. Probably, most of the girls at Studio 22 and Talent Management International did not really understand Cornfeld's sexual philosophy—least of all, how bluntly egocentric it could be. Had they done so, they might have been more reluctant to lend their presence to his caravan. It was not that his patronage automatically included a sexual *quid pro quo:* indeed, he was capable of imperially unpredictable acts of generosity for which no return was expected. It was just that Bernie himself was so stridently liberated that he made it quite difficult for a woman to go around with him without making some people think she shared his views.

For all that, some of Cornfeld's women friends were the most loyal. On East Sixty-third Street, in the building that houses Talent Management International, Peggy Nestor runs a boutique. (It was originally set up, with Cornfeld's backing, for the girl called "Rattlesnake," but she didn't care for the business and sold out.) The décor includes a large picture of Oleg Cassini in Mexican dress, and several months after the crash it still included a picture of Bernie, fondling an ocelot. (By that time, it was hard to find a picture of him on Wall Street. Noticeably, his portrait had vanished from the wall in the office of Arthur Lipper III, the stockbroker who did most of IOS's business on the New York Stock Exchange.) And Cornfeld's most frequent companion of the latter years was a starlet named Vicky Principal, a slight, dark girl of about his own height. Her devotion remained for a long time unruffled by eccentricities in the Emperor's behavior. Certainly it survived the Acapulco diversion.

But while the joys of anarchy were no doubt apparent enough to Cornfeld himself, they do not seem to have been quite so plain to all of the girls who found themselves drawn into his orbit.

One of them described him in dramatic terms as a man who never had any idea of where to settle down—or where to go to; the kind of man who loved every woman he saw, but could not love anyone in particular; a man whose elaborate explanations were likely to mystify rather than enlighten. When he appeared to confess everything, he revealed nothing.

The joys of anarchy, clearly, carried their own special tensions with them.

And indeed, tension and conflict were natural to every level of the IOS court and its empire. Just as the people in Cornfeld's immediate circle could never predict the directions which his personal interest might take, so those in lowlier positions were afflicted by the turbulent and mysterious atmosphere of the organization which he ruled.

In the early years, when IOS was still a freebooting syndicate of more or less hardy spirits, the corporate unorthodoxies were merely amusing. But by the middle-1960s, IOS was a big company, with more than a thousand regular staff and eight thousand salesmen. Far from there being serious attempts to modify and stabilize the structure of the growing company, its internal competitiveness was reinforced. One of the major aims of the conferences for which managing salesmen were brought to Geneva was to refresh their "motivation," to show them the glories of life at the top. This was when the parties were given at Bella Vista, with the heaps of caviar "like *this*." After Cornfeld bought the Château de Pelly, sales conferences always included a visit by the managers' wives to the château, where they could be impressed by the advantages of a thirteenth-century dining hall and a twentieth-century swimming pool. Each year, the biggest party of all was the IOS Christmas party: the last one lasted from eight p.m. to dawn, consuming 3000 bottles of Moët et Chandon *brut*. It cost $500,000 and occupied senior executives' time for weeks.

Such celebrations must be viewed in the light of Eli Wallitt's grim retrospective estimate that "the majority of the salesmen were marginal," and made "a miserable living." Another piece of background is suggested by some physical details. At 119 Rue de Lausanne, Cornfeld operated from an office lined with raw silk, and Ed Cowett's was lined in red velvet, with a large telescope aimed across the lake to his villa. But the hastily erected buildings at Ferney-Voltaire were bleakly utilitarian—and the offices were cheerful compared to the concrete towers, planted in muddy open spaces, where the swelling crowds of office workers lived.

The official claim, repeated insistently, was that IOS was a happy family. But when Nina Kaplan, a social worker from New York, was hired to examine the condition of the IOS staff, she did not find it so. Miss Kaplan (a graduate, like Cornfeld, of the Columbia School of Social Work) found the basic problem simple enough; the company consisted of a small group of people living very well, and a large army of poorly paid juniors living in drab apartments. IOS was sufficiently concerned at her report to try to hire her (with stock options) to ameliorate the problems she had exposed. But Miss Kaplan, no doubt wisely, chose to go back to New York and get married.

Tensions were multiplied by the fact that the IOS command structure was largely a sham. Formally, IOS had a main board, over which Cornfeld presided, and which included most of the eminent world citizens brought in during the great public-relations drive. The IOS Sales Company was supposed to be a subsidiary, under Allen Cantor, of the main board. But one of the things that people like Ambassador Roosevelt, Count Bernadotte, and Sir Eric Wyndham White discovered was that in reality the sales company totally outranked the main board. "The sales company board used to meet first," said Wyndham White later, "and they would go on the whole day, maybe two. By the time they were finished there was no time for the main board to do anything except agree."

Sooner or later the imported excellencies made a further discovery, which was that, as in all courts, the true power did not reside in any formal structure, but in what people called "the chemistry" of the personal relationship between Bernie Cornfeld, Ed Cowett, and Allen Cantor. All other relationships had to take account of this "troika" as it was known. And however much he might be distracted by model schools, boutiques, and movies, there was no question that Cornfeld saw himself as the ultimate fount of authority. "Ed was running the company," he told us, reviewing the debacle. "I put him in charge."

People tended to see the Emperor's liking for having his own way in different kinds of light, and it depended a good deal on when they joined up with IOS. Thad Lovett, for instance, was of the first generation, and tells a story which begins with him typing out a scathing resignation letter after a stormy dispute with

Cornfeld. While Lovett is composing, Cornfeld comes in and delivers a fresh burst of denunciation.

Lovett jumps to his feet ("so fast my chair broke the glass in the window") and says, "Bernie Cornfeld, just you go out of that door and don't come back till you can learn to speak like a gentleman." Cornfeld rushes out, leaving Lovett to reflect that he didn't finish the letter of resignation, as he is obviously terminated.

The next day, Cornfeld walks in, bearing an exquisite Chinese porcelain lion. "What in earth is that?" asks Lovett.

"It's a cat," says Cornfeld.

"The hell it is," says Lovett, who has a passion for cats, which he shares with Cornfeld.

"Well," says Bernie, "it's the nearest I can get to an apology."

Robert Nagler, who was hired from Dreyfus to manage the Fund of Funds' investment policy, figures in a story with a different ending. Late one evening in his office, Nagler got a call from a fund manager in Los Angeles named Doug Fletcher, who suggested that the Fund of Funds put some money into his fund, because Fletcher thought the price was likely to rise. Nagler could not get hold of any other members of the Fund of Funds Investment Committee, so he put in $6 million on his own initiative, a normal enough decision for anyone managing a big fund.

In the morning, Cornfeld appeared in his office, dangling a copy of the Telexed "buy" order between two fingers. Very quietly, he asked Nagler, "What is this?"

Nagler told him, knowing perfectly well that Cornfeld didn't need to ask.

"Don't you ever do this again," said Cornfeld, "without consulting me." Nagler said that in that case he couldn't go on managing the fund—and suddenly it was a shouting match, with

Cornfeld screaming at the top of his voice. Nagler resigned or was fired on the spot, and in this case there was no apology on either side. Nagler, who did not admire Cornfeld's investment theories whatever he thought of his sales ability, departed abruptly, convinced that he had been submitted to an obedience test of some kind.

The fact that the Emperor liked to dominate his court was plain to anyone, but it was not so easy for an outsider to catch the flavor of the atmosphere behind the arras. Just how unsavory that could be is well conveyed by some details, from IOS's own documentation, on the "Gail Drew Affair." The file opens with a résumé signed by Gerald L. Berkin, head of the IOS Security Service, and it introduces us again to Richard Gangel, ex-socialist and international banker:

> On November 1, 1967, Dick Gangel contacted Bob King and told him to get the necessary equipment for recording telephone calls down to the Hotel Intercontinental in Geneva. Gangel explained that the above-named [Gail Drew] was trying to extort $200,000 from IOS on the basis of documents in her possession purporting to prove that IOS personnel in Federal Germany had rendered themselves liable before the German tax authorities by failing to declare their true taxable income.

The affair had begun a few days earlier, when a man named Eckhart Trenkle phoned Eli Wallitt, boss of the German operation. Trenkle, a former IOS salesman, warned Wallitt that "some people" had got hold of documents showing that Wallitt, and some other managers for Germany, received income under several code names and numbers. Unless money was paid over, these would be sent to the German tax authorities and to the magazine *Der Spiegel:* fairly rapidly, Trenkle admitted that "some people" really meant himself and Gail Drew, a forty-one-year-old American woman working for IOS in Geneva.

Perhaps to Trenkle's surprise, Wallitt reacted calmly. Wallitt admits he was paid under different code names—and that Gail Drew had the right ones. But as an American resident in Geneva, he did not consider himself liable for any German tax. As for the other managers, he didn't know whether they paid their tax or not, and didn't consider it his business. The reason he used phony names himself, he told us, had nothing to do with the German taxmen. It was to stop his own salesmen from finding out how much he was making in override commissions on their sales. "It might have caused resentment," he said.* Nevertheless, Wallitt informed Allen Cantor, the over-all sales boss, and Cantor called in Gangel.

They reacted like men thrown into acute panic at the idea that IOS security might be breached—and it scarcely matters whether they were more worried about tax inspectors or their own salesmen. Significantly, one response—which does not seem to have occurred to anyone—was to prove to the German authorities that everyone concerned was declaring their full income.

No one, of course, can justify blackmail. But Gail Drew was a lonely, rather eccentric woman, and in the beginning she seems to have been making a pathetic bid for attention as much as a serious attempt at extortion. Bernie Cornfeld was in New York when the affair began, but Cantor and Gangel kept him in touch by telephone. The matter was treated as a major corporate crisis, occupying the time of several senior executives, plus a Greek chorus of lawyers and security men.

Gangel's demand for recording equipment, with which the

---

* See Chapter 14, "Germany: The Super-Super-Supermen."

file opens, is made because Trenkle has agreed to betray his accomplice. Gangel's plan is to have Trenkle telephone her, and lure her into confessing her intentions on tape. This will be evidence that she is guilty of offenses under Swiss law (which takes industrial espionage very seriously).

Gangel, Trenkle, and an IOS Security Service man, take a room at the Intercontinental, from which the man telephones Gail Drew. The transcript of the conversation makes depressing reading. It is clear that Miss Drew regarded the ex-salesman as a friend, and shows no sign of suspicion while he probes for evidence of her motives and the strength of her information.

She can't understand what is happening to the company, she has only been given a hundred shares, when others have more . . . she has been moved without explanation from Thad Lovett's department to Allen Cantor's. She doesn't have any work to do, and is afraid of being fired. "I am tired of life," she says, "of going to the office every day, of coming back to the house and playing solitaire." In response to specific questioning, she makes it clear that she used to regard Cornfeld as her "protector" but feels that this is no longer the case.

Armed with this recording, Gangel, Cantor, and the security men feel that they can make Miss Drew sign papers giving them the right to search her apartment and her bank vaults—whichever necessary—to recover the override documents. They plan to confront her in Ed Cowett's office which is to be bugged for the occasion. Meanwhile, at Cantor's demand, surveillance is mounted over her apartment. The IOS Security Service seems to take a three-day surveillance in its professional stride: operatives Miller, Baud, Huguenin, Kunferman, Kiger, and Coeur are assigned.

At ten a.m., on November 6, Miss Drew is lured into the

bugged office on a pretext about her work permit and she is interrogated by Gangel, Berkin, and Miller. They play her extracts from the taped phone call, but she denies any crime, and refuses to sign anything. At eleven a.m., Berkin is sent to fetch the police; he comes back at eleven-thirty with two inspectors. The cops, possibly rather puzzled, say they will come back after lunch. At noon, Bernie comes on the phone from New York, and Gangel and Cantor report that the woman refuses to sign anything. Cornfeld has another idea, and after a break for sandwiches the woman is persuaded to fly to New York and hand the IOS documents back to him personally. But at this point, the police come back, and even though they are told that IOS withdraws the complaint, and that the woman has agreed to have medical treatment, they insist on taking her off to the Hotel de Police.

From this point on, the affair becomes yet more sadly confused. The police doctor finds the woman sane, the police release her without telling IOS, whereupon she goes home, locks herself into her apartment, and refuses to answer the phone. The IOS people scour the town for her and are apparently convinced she has fled—but then Cantor sights her entering her apartment block, and the police are persuaded to enter her apartment to see if she is all right. On the night of November 7, they get into Miss Drew's apartment via the balcony, where they find her in perfectly good health, but angrily accusing them of illegal entry. She declares that she doesn't want to go to New York, or to talk to anyone from IOS.

It is only after this, in a letter dated November 14, that she actually sends off the override documents to the German taxmen, with a copy to *Der Spiegel*. The IOS Security Service has meanwhile decided it wants nothing more to do with the matter:

but the affair is dramatically reopened when *Der Spiegel* contacts the IOS head office, saying that a special article is under consideration.

A legal conference is swiftly convened, and the assessment is made that there is no solution but to discredit the lady by "making known her instability and her mental state."

The file records that during the week of November 19–25 an IOS employee named Bob Walz has reported that Miss Drew is making threats to kill the children of Allen Cantor and another IOS executive if anyone should interfere with her plan. On November 29, Cornfeld sends word that he wishes to have legal process taken against the woman, and on the following day the police are informed about the threats.

The police seem to be impressed with the gravity of the situation, and request formal complaints from Cantor and the other father concerned. While these are being prepared, Walz comes back from a meeting with Miss Drew and says that this time she has threatened to shoot the police if they come to arrest her. This is passed on to the police, who decide to arrest the lady before getting any formal complaint. According to the file, she shoots at the police when being arrested, but misses.

IOS's secrets were safe. On June 10, 1968, Gail Drew and Eckhart Trenkle were convicted of attempted blackmail by the Correctional Court in Geneva, and given suspended sentences of eight months and five months, respectively. Gail Drew was also convicted of "abuse of confidence" and the suspension of her sentence was made conditional upon her undergoing medical treatment. She was, however, acquitted of having made threats against the children and also of a charge of having resisted arrest.

After her treatment, Cornfeld made himself responsible for seeing that Gail Drew had a roof over her head, and he did a good deal to help her out of her troubles. Many people in IOS who knew a little about the story thought that Cornfeld, and the company, had behaved generously toward her.

Yet the fact was that IOS had used tactics against this woman—the telephone tapping, the bugged rendezvous, the round-the-clock surveillance, the "turning-round" of Trenkle—more reminiscent of espionage work than of any ordinary business activity. To put it another way, a group of experienced and powerful men chose to submit an admittedly unstable woman to a series of pressures and harassments that could only worsen her condition. The episode shows all too clearly what wealth, fear, and years of clandestine operation had done to the atmosphere of the happy IOS family.

Cornfeld, of course, was a psychiatric social worker by profession. Apparently his early training did not help him to recognize the real nature of the organization he had created.

• • •

"I really don't see," Cornfeld said once, "why affluence should cause one to surround himself with ugly people, and gloomy surroundings. I think that if the affluence didn't exist, I'd also strive to surround myself with amusing, creative, if you like beautiful people, rather than gloomy, dreary people. And I really don't think it's a product of affluence, because I think that all of the same kind of people were around as far back as I can remember."

That was how Cornfeld saw it. Yet it did often happen that the amusing and creative people with whom he surrounded himself were linked, in one way or another, to his affluence. Oleg Cassini, a close friend, had been Jacqueline Kennedy's personal dress designer: he was author of the aphorism that "it is easy to be humble when things are going well for you, but the trick is to be arrogant when you are a flop," and a great believer in the dictum of his mother, the Countess Cassini, that "if you own a tuxedo, and are a gentleman, you cannot fail to make your way." Cornfeld used to give the IOS girls Cassini scarves for Christmas, and he put up money for more than one of Cassini's business ventures.

Jacques Lowe, the French-American photographer, who also had his Kennedy connections, was usually around at Bernie's parties. Lowe was in charge of producing the vast bulk of photographs that IOS used in its publicity material. (The IOS reports, prospectuses, and handouts were brilliantly laid out and illustrated, even if their contents were less than adequate.) The actual creator of most of Bernie's surroundings was the interior decorator Serge Mourreau, something of a specialist in ornate interiors; he did them for IOS as well as Cornfeld. Guy Laroche, the Paris designer, supplied dresses for the IOS receptionists and Cornfeld put money into one of Laroche's companies.

Cornfeld was openhanded with his fortune, as he had been even before he became affluent. When he was a fund salesman in New York, he would let his friends use his car. When he became a financier, he would let his friends use his bank account. This he did by guaranteeing them at the Overseas Development Bank, where he kept his cash reserves, and in this way Cornfeld became creditor for some very large sums, which he did not pursue for payment. In describing a deal which he did in partnership with Ed Cowett, Cornfeld once said to us, "Our relationship was one where, if he had the money he paid, and if he didn't he didn't, but I never asked." It was an attitude he applied to more than one deal, and to many people besides Cowett.

Perhaps the most attractive part of his reputation deals with his repeated acts of generosity toward IOS salesmen in financial distress. Thad Lovett told us a particular story about a Scottish salesman who suffered a prolonged nervous breakdown. The man's wife got a job in Woolworth's to make ends meet, and they were anxious to take an assisted passage to Australia and make a fresh start. But before a migrant can get a passage from the Australian government, he must prove himself free from debt. It turned out that the man owed IOS $3000 and he asked the company to let him off. Lovett took the matter up with Cowett and Cantor, and they were arguing about it when Cornfeld walked in. Cornfeld was shocked that there should even be a question about the debt. "What sort of company is this," he snapped, "if it can't help a man whose sales are in our funds under management?" There are many such stories; Cornfeld was especially generous with medical expenses when employees or their relatives fell sick.

Cornfeld reveled obviously enough in the pleasures of consumption that affluence brought him. He drank Coke, but he drank it out of a silver tankard, and he indulged his epicurean appetite for ice cream. But it was his view that there was little difference in standard of living between a man with half a million, and one with three million. And he told Hubert Cornfeld in 1962, probably accurately, "I could retire now, with $50,000 a year for life."

Perhaps nobody can say exactly why he went on. But the more money he had, the more he could have his own way, and he often did act as though it was worth almost any sum to gratify a whim. At one point, he wanted to hire as an adviser Rosser Reeves, the advertising man who "packaged" Dwight Eisenhower. (This was at the beginning of the image-brushing era.) Reeves didn't want the job, and it was hard even to persuade him to travel to Geneva. When Reeves did arrive, he swiftly concluded that Cornfeld didn't really want to do anything about his image—he just wanted to feel that he had done something. So

Reeves decided to get out of the situation and, employing a classic technique, he told Cornfeld, "You couldn't afford my fees."

"How much would you want?" asked Cornfeld.

After a pause for calibration, Reeves said (this was 1965), "A quarter of a million dollars."

"Fine," said Cornfeld.

"On contract," said Reeves, slightly embarrassed.

"Fine," said Cornfeld.

"With expenses," said Reeves, now groggy.

"O.K.," said Bernie.

Reeves signed his contract the next day, and found, exactly as he expected, that was virtually the last time that Cornfeld expressed any interest in his professional services. Reeves spent a week with Cornfeld, but Bernie changed the conversation every time it turned to business. Eventually, Reeves gave up and spent the time teaching Cornfeld to play backgammon. What Cornfeld eventually acquired for his money was an enduring passion for backgammon.

Reeves maintained a friendship with Cornfeld, and whenever they met, they would play three or four hours of backgammon for ten cents a point. He says of Cornfeld, "I like Bernie very much. In my life, I've met just about as many eccentrics as you could possibly meet. I'm like an orchid collector, and Bernie is the most exotic in the greenhouse."

Reeves also said, "I don't think Bernie could bear to be alone for more than two hours." If the Emperor Cornfeld wanted to avoid being alone, he succeeded most of the time. At any moment, he could fill his gilded rooms with bankers, journalists, actresses, artists, businessmen, politicians, designers, and specimens of the nobility and gentry of Europe. But the guests sometimes noticed that Cornfeld, at the center of the swirl, looked curiously inert. The gray eyes would become almost expressionless, and the soft, controlled voice almost inaudible. The pauses, between whispers, seemed interminable.

If Cornfeld had real friendships, it should have been with the veterans of the IOS sales drives, the men who joined him when IOS was only an idea and who rose to wealth and power with him. Yet a reporter, talking to these men, is likely to encounter the assertion of friendship more than its substance.

There is, for instance, Eli Wallitt, who on his own account owes his considerable fortune largely to Cornfeld. He described himself as a lifelong friend—indeed, for that reason, he said that he did not want to "psychoanalyze" Bernie. Then, in the context of discussing decision-making within IOS, we asked this man what were his feelings toward Cornfeld. Almost as though the answer were obvious, he said, "I'm terrified of Bernie."

He could not, it seemed, give any clear reason for this. But at last he said, "Mr. Cornfeld is a man who surrounds himself with a circle of people who are to do his bidding. One by one, these people make mistakes. Then Mr. Cornfeld picks the person up, the man, and castrates him, and he puts him back in his place in the circle."

Although it means a leap ahead of the narrative, that statement is most relevant when placed alongside something that another of the original circle told us about the events when Cornfeld was trying to retain control of his empire in 1970. This man, who describes himself with great warmth as a close friend and great admirer of Cornfeld's, held one of the bigger blocks of shares, and Cornfeld asked if he could rely on the votes of those shares in the battle he was planning. Firmly, the request was refused. Cornfeld was stunned. "Try and make me see," said Cornfeld, "why you have no loyalty." He received, according to the old friend's own account, this reply:

"Bernie, I'd give you my commissions, or my money, or my

shares—but I'm not going to give you my proxy vote, because I'm loyal to the best thing about you, which is the company you built up. You are the best man alive at sustaining and nurturing a sales force, but I believe that there is no such thing as universal genius."

The request was made by Cornfeld, at the crisis of his career, of a man whom he had rescued from obscurity and raised to wealth. The reply that he received was a salesman's reply. But a court, of course, is about power, not about loyalty.

• 13 •

The Off-White Cliffs of Dover

The boys find a way to beat the SEC—operating through the City of London. They go into the life-insurance business, and show the Bank of England a thing or two. In which it is shown how the Winston Churchill Close should be applied and generally how sales techniques became refined.

On April 14, 1967, a group of IOS executives met at the Savoy Hotel, London. They were there to thrash out the details of a system on which depended, it would be no exaggeration to say, the survival of IOS. However, the crucial members of the meeting were not the IOS executives, but two stockbrokers: one from New York, Arthur Lipper III; and the other, Henry Hely Hutchison, from London. On their co-operation would depend IOS's ability to evade the results of the SEC settlement and to continue buying and selling shares on the U.S. stock exchanges.

Arthur Lipper III had paid his first visit to the investment department of IOS in 1963. That was before he had ever done any business with this new force in the investment world; he got his first order in 1964. He was then with the New York firm of Zuckerman, Smith & Co., and in the next two years relations between Lipper and IOS grew close. He met Cornfeld in late

1964 and Cowett shortly thereafter; by early 1967, he was an important figure in the IOS structure. IOS business was sufficiently weighty for him to think it necessary for Zuckerman, Smith to set up a branch in Geneva. His partners disagreed, and Lipper left the firm.

Lipper set up his own brokerage firm in New York in March 1967. He did not get any direct help from IOS, but IOS guaranteed a loan made by the London bankers Guinness Mahon to Lipper's brother Michael, who became a partner.* One end of the problem was solved: IOS had a captive broker in New York, who would buy and sell shares for the funds. But the men who were actually taking the investment decisions for the IOS funds down in Wall Street would still not be able, under the terms of the impending SEC settlement, to place their orders directly with the new mid-town brokerage firm. That was where Henry Hely Hutchison came in.

Hutchison, a friendly, bouncy man, first came into contact with IOS when he was working for one of the City's more blue-blooded firms of brokers, Laing & Cruickshank. This firm made a specialty of unit and investment trusts, and Arthur Lipper called one day to exchange ideas on the possibility of creating a trust which invested in other unit trusts, as in the original conception of the Fund of Funds. He was put on to Hely Hutchison, who had done the firm's latest survey. Hely Hutchison was interested and went to Geneva, where he was told he would get a guaranteed amount of business for working with IOS. But the partners of Laing & Cruickshank decided they did not want to get that closely involved, and Hely Hutchison had to make up his mind: Laing & Cruickshank or IOS? He chose IOS, and af-

---

*The new firm, Arthur Lipper Corporation, is to be distinguished from Arthur's father's firm, Arthur Lipper & Co.

ter some months he found another City broking firm willing to accept him as a partner and do IOS business. The firm was called G. S. Herbert.

The problem, in the spring of 1967, was to find the most suitably located body to place IOS fund orders with Arthur Lipper in New York. It had to be someone outside the United States and it had to be someone who could be seen as independent of IOS. Hely Hutchison in London was the most sensible solution. At the Savoy on April 16 he was asked if he could have the operation set up by the end of May.

With the noble co-operation of the British Post Office he made it. It was one of the GPO's biggest jobs: Telex lines and machines were installed so that the London office would be in constant and direct contact with New York and Geneva. The GPO sprang to its task with enthusiasm, and the new London office in Old Jewry was ready even before those at the other end. But the plan met with a last-minute hitch: the officials of the London Stock Exchange decided they did not want G. S. Herbert, a member firm, to place the orders with Lipper directly. A further intermediary had to be found; IOS luckily already had an association with another City firm, the London & Dominion Trust run by Clinton Redgrove, a specialist in South African investment. It was agreed that one room of the offices, the one with the Telex machines in it, would have a plate nailed to the door saying London & Dominion Trust, so that the orders were actually placed in its name.

When the day of settlement came IOS was ready. The legal domicile of the FOF proprietary funds was shifted to Canada, but the managers stayed in New York and their other U.S. bases. They no longer placed orders but made "investment suggestions." These were collated by Arthur Lipper and Telexed through to London & Dominion's office in Old Jewry. From there they were passed on to Geneva for confirmation; once confirmed the clerks in the London & Dominion office would turn the suggestion into an order and pass it through an interconnecting window to the next-door office which had an Arthur Lipper label on the door. The London office of Arthur Lipper would then transmit the order to the New York office for execution. Hely Hutchison had an office the other side of London & Dominion Trust from which he supervised the operation. It was expensive, but Arthur Lipper's commissions were adequate to cover it and the SEC order was thwarted. So well did the electronics work that a "suggestion" could be turned into an "order" within forty-five seconds.

• • •

When the offshore madness reached its peak in 1969, London became the favorite base of a number of the wilder of IOS's competitors. Britain's laws, like those of many an offshore haven, are tolerant of those who want to use her facilities as long as her investors and her resources are left alone. But when, in early 1967, IOS showed how useful that tolerance could be, the company was no stranger to London. For, unique among offshore firms, IOS had found a way four years before to avoid both the U.K.'s securities laws and exchange-control laws. It was an operation conducted with the same audacity as those in far-flung countries in South America, Africa, and the Middle East, but with a much higher degree of sophistication. Britain was the first European country IOS systematically set out to convert to the cult of equity investment.

The Saint Augustine of this mission was a small, prematurely gray former lieutenant of the U.S. Air Force named Roy Kirkdorffer. He had been stationed in England before he left the Air Force in 1959 to join IOS in France. He returned to London in

October 1962 and took offices in Dover Street in the West End. Let the *IOS Bulletin* take up the story: "Five hundred miles away, in Geneva, Switzerland, two men are leading a small team working late into the night on a new, as yet unnamed concept of insurance linked to equity growth. Their names are Dick Hammerman and Barry Schwartz."

Hammerman was one of the few early IOS recruits with a professional financial background. He had worked for an American insurance company and was a chartered life underwriter (CLU). He was brought in to set up an insurance company for IOS which he formed in Luxembourg in early 1962, called the International Life Insurance Company. The Fund of Funds itself was launched just as Kirkdorffer was arriving in London.

But before Hammerman and his salesmen could get to work on the British investors, he and Schwartz had two major obstacles to overcome. First, in Britain no fund or unit trust authorized under British law may be sold by salesmen; second, no one in Britain can make nonsterling investments without incurring a heavy extra expense. British investors who want dollar shares must first buy "investment dollars." These can only be created by the sale of foreign shares by other British residents. They are traded at a substantial premium above the official exchange rate because the demand normally outruns supply.

Such obstacles should have been daunting indeed to any company whose business was selling dollar investments by door-to-door or cold telephone-call methods. But IOS engaged the services of Freshfields, one of the most prestigious firms of London solicitors, who also act for the Bank of England. Together, they came up with an ingenious solution to both problems by using the special status which insurance companies enjoy in British law. Ed Cowett said later, "We had very imaginative and very sound legal advice in Britain through Freshfields. I must give them full credit."

Getting around the salesmen's problem was easy enough. Although British laws do not allow salesmen to sell shares, it does allow them to sell life-insurance policies, and this is how they are traditionally sold by most leading insurance companies.

In Britain, as in many places, the concept of taking precautions against untimely death is inextricably entangled with the concept of making investments for use in life. Often, most of the money paid into insurance policies is used for investment, with only a small part covering the "life risks." So IOS dressed up the Fund of Funds as an insurance policy and called it the Dover Plan. The name, drawn simply from the street off Piccadilly in which Kirkdorffer had his offices, was nevertheless another inspired association of ideas, conjuring up the White Cliffs of Dover, security, and essential Britishness. A picture of the White Cliffs was used on the front cover of one annual report.

Getting around the investment-dollar premium required much subtler perception of the legal and financial status of insurance companies in Britain. No individual in Britain is allowed to take out a life-insurance policy with a company abroad. But London is a world center for insurance and earns a considerable income for the balance of payments out of it. Transfers of money between insurance companies in and outside the country are, therefore, not restricted. Any insurance company in Britain is allowed to "re-insure" its risks with a company abroad, even if that company is its parent. Normally, the payment sent abroad on any individual life-insurance policy would be small—commensurate with the small slice of the policy payments actually used for life risks. IOS had other ideas.

In April 1963, as Kirkdorffer's sales force was ready to swing into action, ILI Luxembourg spawned a British subsidiary. For two and a half years after that, ILI (UK) sent virtually all of the premiums paid to it to ILI in Luxembourg as "re-insurance." There the bulk of it was invested in the Fund of Funds, *i.e.*, in dollar securities without the prohibitive extra cost of "investment dollars." (Part of the premium, required to cover the death risk, was actually placed in London for re-insurance with an independent company.)

Thus, with the best of legal advice, the intention of the British exchange-control rules was frustrated. That was remarkable enough in itself: the insurance policy which enabled the money to be collected was no less cunning.

Its special qualities have much to do with the relationship in Britain between life protection and investment, which has always been particularly close because of the tax reliefs granted on life-insurance payments.

Until the early 1960s, the main way of investing through buying a life-insurance policy—in installments or otherwise—was the "with-profits endowment policy." The death benefit under such a policy is small in comparison with the premium taken by the insurance company, which is mostly invested in stocks, shares, and properties. The company pays bonuses to the investor out of the income from the capital gains they made with the money. Each policy runs for a set period of years, at the end of which the insurance company guarantees to pay back a certain minimum sum.

The fact that they must always have reserves adequate to meet such guarantees makes life-insurance companies of this sort inherently conservative in their attitude to bonus payments. During the 1960s, with the growth of stock-market prices, the bonuses paid out on with-profits endowment policies began to lag far behind the growth and income of the underlying investments. This opened up the life-insurance companies to the competition of unit trusts, the equivalent of American mutual funds, which began to grow rapidly even though they could not use direct-sales methods.

By the time Kirkdorffer reached London, a new breed of policy had been evolved called "equity-linked." Usually, this had no guaranteed maturity payment, and its value at any moment was determined by the value of the underlying shares—usually shares of a unit trust—bought with the premiums.

The lack of a guaranteed end payment naturally required special safeguards. On a with-profits endowment policy, the insurance company shares in the income and capital gains of the money under its control, taking a slice for its profits and leaving the rest for distribution to the customers in bonuses. It may fail to pay bonuses, but the guaranteed maturity value cannot be touched.

In normal "equity-linked" policies there is a different safeguard: the proportion of premiums that the company can take for profits and expenses is laid down in advance and written into the contract. Otherwise, it is clearly possible for the company to use up all the money in profits and expenses, leaving the policyholder with nothing.

The Dover Plan was drawn up and sold for some time with no such safeguard. There was no guaranteed maturity value on the policy. It was laid down that ILI should take a percentage of each premium payment before investing it in what it called the Equity Unit Account. But the size of the percentage was not laid down, and the wording of the document was so vague that it is hard to understand how it got the approval of ILI's legal advisers. All it said was that the company would invest "that part of each premium paid under this Policy which after deduction of expenses including investment costs is to be applied towards Equity Units." More plainly, any of your money that we don't keep for ourselves, we will invest for you.

For two and a half years the Dover Plan salesmen had everything their way. Equity-linked policies were still a novelty and few questioned the fact that the Dover Policy did not specify its charges. Questioned in 1964, Hammerman said that they were about 50 per cent of the first year's premium and 10 per cent of each year's premium for the remaining nine years of the policy. The front-end load of the investment program had been transferred to the Dover Plan, but this did not seem unfair when compared with the low surrender values of a "with-profits" policy in its early years.

In the summer and autumn of 1966 markets on both sides of the Atlantic dropped sharply by some 20 per cent. Investors generally grew restless, especially those who had recently been converted to the great equity cult. Dover Plan holders wrote in to find out the value of their investments. The replies they got frequently came as a tremendous shock. Many had just not understood the front-end load; they believed the salesman had told them they could get all their money back whenever they wanted, which, indeed, he sometimes had. But even those who had understood the front-end load on the first year's premium were a bit surprised to find that ILI was loading the second year's premium as well.

The load was not large by comparison with the first year's deduction, but it was nearer to 15 per cent than to Hammerman's 10. It came as a complete surprise to some Dover Plan policyholders, and to some salesmen too. Hammerman maintained that it had always been the intention of the company to load the second year's premium, but this had hardly become widely known. In December 1966, Barry Schwartz, Hammerman's executive manager, who had helped devise the Dover Plan, told a client who had decided to discontinue his policy that from the total amount of premiums received, £102 5s od had been deducted to cover all first-year expenses, including investment costs. In the subsequent years an amount of £11 14s od would have been deducted each year, Schwartz said. This clearly suggested that charges, after the first year, would be even, although in fact they were not.

Bluntly, the wording of the policy document left ILI free to increase the price of the product after the customer had signed up.

Criticism of the Dover Plan reached a peak in the winter of 1966–1967. Newspapers and financial advisers were deluged with letters from company directors, retired army officers, vicars, stockbrokers, accountants, bank managers. They had been promised a "hedge against inflation," and told that their money would probably double over ten years if they invested monthly with the Dover Plan, or treble if they took out "prepaid" policies (*i.e.*, invested a lump sum). Yet after two years or so, not much progress toward these promises seemed to have been made.

Some typical examples: a major started paying £9 1s od a month in August 1964; by March 1970 he had paid a total of £289 12s od, but his equity units were only worth £200 18s od. A company director found that 56.5 per cent of his first year's premium had been deducted by ILI, 22.1 per cent of his second, and that the company was proposing to take 18.8 per cent of third and following premiums. An old-age pensioner with heart trouble (what was anyone doing trying to sell him *life insurance* in the first place? The policy had to be put in his wife's name) had invested £2221 in early 1966 and by October he found to his dismay that his life savings had been reduced to £1760.

The small print of the Dover Plan was also discouraging: the extra accidental death benefit excluded eleven categories including, for example, death from "any poison or gas or fumes, taken, administered, absorbed or inhaled, whether voluntarily or involuntarily accidentally or otherwise." This clause alone would rule out many deaths from household accidents.

Eventually IOS had to abandon this method of getting around the British exchange controls, and under considerable pressure of publicity the International Life Insurance Company came more or less clean about its deductions. But by that stage, IOS had made a substantial beachhead in Britain: the whole exercise was an excellent example of the IOS dictum "write the business first, and fix the sweat later."

Tables were included in Dover Plan policy documents which detailed the allocations to the Equity Unit Account, showing the part retained by ILI. If the quality of the policy was not improved, at least by the end of 1967 it was easier to find out just how expensive it was. It might well be asked how the product could be sold, if it was inferior to other products on a market which swiftly became extremely competitive (within a short time even the mighty Prudential Assurance Company was selling equity-linked policies). The answer is that in direct sales, the enthusiasm of the sales force can be more important than the quality of the product. In the American mutual-fund industry, a study conducted by the Wharton School of Finance for the SEC found that sales of individual mutual-fund shares tended to increase as sales charges were increased—*i.e.*, as the product grew objectively *less* attractive from the customer's viewpoint. (The Wharton study found no evidence that funds with high charges had superior investment records.)

The methodology of selling somewhat unsafe investments, dressed up in the form of a mediocre insurance policy, is illuminated by a brief study of IOS sales techniques. These, as the company grew, were refined and institutionalized with an impressive skill, which showed to its best advantage in a glossy kit, with attached tape recording, called *Eight Ways to Close Sales*. The "close" is the move with which the salesman, having made his "presentation," brings the prospect to buy, and turns him into a client. The tape declares that knowing when and how to close "can put more money in your pocket than any other sales skill."

The closes recommended are embedded in the lore of the doorstep sales game under a number of names: IOS in this kit called them the Basic Close, the Alternate Choice Close, the Winston Churchill Close (a version of the Ben Franklin Close), the Eliminate the Negative Close, the Similar Situation Close, the Provisional Close, the Final Objection Close, and—as a last resort—the Lost Sale Close.

The techniques revolve around one idea, which is that sales resistance can always be beaten down by persistence. *Eight Ways to Close Sales* teaches a series of cunning verbal and emotional tricks, in which the salesman is taught to capitalize on the fact that people will be reluctant to hurt his feelings, to tell frightening stories whenever it seems necessary, and to whine for sympathy if all else fails to make the prospect "relax his defenses."

There is the standard injunction that the prospect must never be contradicted. "When the prospect states an objection, agree with him in your response and then go on to point out an advantage that meets his objection." But there is an even more revealing instruction: the prospect must never be asked to "sign" the contract. He must be asked to "approve the application" because "many people are hesitant to sign anything *without carefully reading it* and perhaps *discussing it with a lawyer* [our italics]." Apparently, only to their own salesmen did IOS admit that it might be bad if the customers had their lawyers read the contracts.

The closes themselves are in essence childish ploys, but their effect in a prospect's living room, in the hands of a salesman greedy for overrides, was obviously considerable. The Winston Churchill/Ben Franklin Close, designed to overcome "nonspecific objection," consists of telling a wavering client that Churchill, Franklin (any dead statesman will do), when uncertain whether to do something or not, used to draw a line down a sheet of paper. On one side, he would list all the "yesses" and on the other side all the "noes." Then he would add them up, and if there were more "yesses" than "noes" he would go ahead. The salesman, having got the prospect to draw the line, then enthusiastically helps in the composition of the "yes" list. To continue in the taped words of IOS's instructor:

> When he gets to the "no" column, what do you think our Associate does? Of course, he keeps quiet, as shown in Picture D. He lets Mrs. Smith list all the reasons for not buying, and, of course, she may have trouble in doing so. Our Associate then concludes that the decision is quite an obvious one, and closes the sale.

All the closes, essentially, are based upon the idea of "controlling" the prospect and forcing him to do things by offering either (a) two alternatives which are both attractive, or (b) by stating hypothetical reasons against buying that are couched in such form that the prospect has difficulty in expressing his or her objections. The principle is "never offer an alternative that in effect asks whether or not the prospect wants the program."

But the instructions for using the closes reveal even more than do the techniques themselves about the real nature of the "estate planning" and "financial counseling" that IOS was offering. First, recruits are informed that "successful" Associates on average have found five "trial closes" necessary to effect a sale. They are then asked to agree or disagree with this proposition:

> The close should be thought of as a hammer. If you don't make it the first time, you should keep hitting. If you do this enough

times, you will weaken the resistance of the prospect and he'll finally buy from you.

On turning to the "answers" part of his kit, the recruit would find this same remarkable proposition printed right across the page, standing out against a broad band of color, and with new emphasis added to the word "hammer." It receives, actually, more emphasis than any other statement in the chart—although careful examination shows that the more correct answer is to say that the close should be thought of as a "helping hand" to "guide the prospect to an affirmative decision." At this point, the tape recorder murmurs, "Don't worry if your words are not the same. It's the thought that counts."

When Bernie's hammerers went to work on British prospects after 1967, the Dover Plan policy which they persuaded people to "approve" was certainly rather more frank than it had been. It even said that the Equity Unit Account bore the costs of investment. But it did not reveal that these included a further deduction of one-half of 1 per cent taken off when the Equity Unit Account transferred the money into IOS funds. In early 1967, most of the Dover Plan money was going into a new device called the Fund of Funds Sterling. It had been born, as it were, in the back of a taxi, and suffered some disadvantages.

For the first two and a half years, Dover Plan money went into dollar funds via the loophole discovered by Hammerman, Cowett, and the imaginative lawyers. ILI was not keen that the means be publicized, but the salesmen, it seemed, began to mention it as an inducement to customers, and the Bank of England got to hear. The bank is charged with implementing British exchange controls, and in 1965, with the pound under pressure, the bank was as acutely conscious of the problem of capital flight as any South American country.

The traditional description of the bank's method of regulation is "by nods and winks." When the bank heard about ILI's re-insurance arrangements, it shook its head. ILI was not doing anything illegal, but the bank didn't approve.

In America, IOS was able to sue the SEC and win a measure of support: indeed, some Southerners appeared to approve the move of any outfits that tangled with the hated federal bureaucrats in Washington, and sales to them increased before the final ban. In London, however, you cannot sue the Bank of England; not if you want to stay in business.

On November 25, 1965, Hammerman blandly announced that ILI had made its first investment of £500,000 in a new device called the Fund of Funds Sterling. IOS, it seemed, had become convinced that there were good opportunities in British ordinary shares, well chosen. Second, they wished to diversify the underlying securities of the Equity Unit Account. . . . It was not until two years later, during the great "image-polishing" era, that IOS admitted publicly that the real reason for the change was the collapse of the "re-insurance" scheme.

To those British investors who had been buying the Dover Plan, because the salesmen sang the glories of dollar investment, Hammerman's sudden discovery of the London market seemed strange indeed. As luck would have it, it was a not unhelpful moment to switch new investment; the British market held on for a few months after Wall Street burst through the 1000 mark on the Dow Jones and then began sliding. But the reprieve was brief. By the end of the year, both markets were down 20 per cent, and the cries from Dover Plan purchasers were indeed dolorous.

The sag in the market was a passing phenomenon, but IOS must shortly have realized that the Fund of Funds Sterling was a serious business mistake in itself. This was because IOS, the great "tax-minimization" experts, had somehow managed to quite misunderstand some basic facts about the insurance business they had entered.

The Fund of Funds Sterling was registered in the Bahamas, which is part of the Sterling Area, and thus open to free-currency exchange to and from London. However, Bahamian funds escape British capital-gains tax. FOF Sterling was no more a true fund on funds than, by that time, was the Fund of Funds proper; all it did was collect money from the Equity Unit Account of the Dover Plan and channel it to investment advisers in London, clipping 1 per cent off the money in the process.

It did avoid capital-gains tax. But its British investments also produced income, as well as capital gains, and this was subject to a 40-per-cent tax in Britain. The great irony was that if the investment income had been received direct by ILI, without the gratuitous Bahamian fund intervening, the company could have offset expenses against the income and claimed substantial tax repayments. In fact, because of British tax law, the essence of the insurance business is to generate investment income and then claim tax relief on it. Even capital gains in an insurance company can be offset against expenses. ILI, having cunningly divested itself of investment income and gains, had nothing against which to offset its expenses, which were thus pure loss.

Showing characteristic IOS flexibility, ILI more or less dropped FOF Sterling by the middle of 1967, and reorganized their investment system to fit in with the real taxation advantages. The only remaining usefulness of FOF Sterling was that it could be sold to Sterling Area residents who did not want the life-insurance component of the Dover Plan. As far as most of ILI's customers went, it had no more significance—except that a half-per-cent charge survived it and still went to IOS. But the customers were not told about that.

The fact that the Dover Plan survived these mishaps and misjudgments was a tribute to the unresting acquisitiveness of the sales force. In early 1967, the plan was being subjected to a wave of hostile criticism, the British stock market to which its investments were committed was sagging, and the competition from British companies was increasing. The Board of Trade refused to let ILI buy a unit-trust company which was up for sale. Yet the salesmen, helped by a timely recovery in the market toward the year's end, brought in almost £10 million in Dover premiums, which was more than enough to cancel out the £1,673,000 surrendered by unhappy investors.

This was partly because ILI, existentialist as ever, had branched out. The six hundred Dover salesmen now spent less time persuading the English middle class who had been so vociferous in their objections, and were developing new markets among the immigrant communities in Britain—Indians, Cypriots, and Pakistanis especially. And, reversing an earlier trend, salesmen followed many of these people and their families *back* to the colonial lands from which they had come. Dover Plan operations flourished in Malta, Cyprus, and East Africa. (All these were Sterling Area countries, but the Kenyans wouldn't let the premium money go out, so ILI had to use it for property investment in Kenya.)

By 1968, ILI had resumed its position as one of the fastest-growing insurance companies in Britain, with a cash inflow of £24 million a year, and commitments by the end of the year of £250 million. Its main achievement had been to bring about a quantum jump in the sales pressure used by the insurance business, a somewhat ambiguous blessing. But at least the IOS sales force remained more or less under control in Britain. That was hardly the case in Germany.

14

Germany: The Super-Super-Supermen

In which the sales force finds the last great market and, under the re-remarkable Eli Wallitt, becomes a kind of chain-letter game.

I t was in West Germany that IOS's sales operation finally stood revealed in its pure essence: as an elaborate system for enriching the salesmen—or rather more specifically the sales managers, but advertised as a crusade to bring capitalism to the masses.

For a time the IOS German operation was a triumph. From 1966 to 1969, it shot up from being no more than one among a couple of dozen territories around the world until it was virtually half of IOS: almost half the clients, fully half the salesmen, and almost half the face volume of sales.

But the expansion in Germany was bought at a cost that contributed substantially to the sales operation's over-all loss. To compensate for that loss, management was driven to more and more speculative expedients. The discovery of those expedients caused the share price to collapse, and brought on the apocalypse. And an important strand of that fuse of causation led back to Germany.

There is a quality about those last extravagant years of IOS in Germany that reminds one of one of the great religious revivals. IOS was not spoken of there simply as an investment company among others more or less successful; both its supporters and its opponents discussed it in terms of ideology—as if Cornfeld's vague rhetoric about People's Capitalism really added a new thesis to Marx's dialectic.

The IOS salesmen, one German IOS executive wrote, "did not simply offer a product or a service. They offered a *Weltanschauung*." Eli Wallitt, who devised and controlled the German miracle, put it a little differently to us. Salesmen, he said sadly, are "fantasy-oriented." Their motivation lies in the future. It is a dream that keeps them working. Most of them, he conceded, made only a "marginal" living. A few—and Wallitt was one of them—made a fortune. Nowhere was the fantasy richer or more effective, for a while, than in Germany.

• • •

There were several reasons why IOS should have taken root in Germany with the vigor of an idea whose time has come.

In the mid-1960s, West Germany was almost completely unfettered with any regulations to hamper the foreign mutual-fund salesman. The West German mark, for a start, was freely convertible. "There is nothing to stop any German putting all his capital into 100 DM notes, getting into his car, driving across into Switzerland, and changing it all into Swiss francs," says a leading West German banker. "It's a *Ganovenwunderland*!"—a hoodlum's paradise.

German domestic mutual funds were carefully regulated by a law of 1957, in some respects more strict than the SEC regulations for American funds. But foreign and offshore funds in Germany were not regulated at all until 1969. So long as they did not distribute their profits as dividends, they were not even taxed, for no income was due when dividends were automatically reinvested to buy additional units.

West Germany is, as everyone knows, one of the wealthiest countries in Europe. What is not so widely known is that the habit of owning stocks and shares is less widespread in Germany than in any comparably wealthy country. In 1960, for example, fewer than one million West Germans owned any shares, as against three and a half million people who did in Britain, a less wealthy country. Two world wars, with revolution at the end of the first and the destruction of the economy after the second, and above all the traumatic inflation of the 1920s, have made the older half of the German middle class ultrawary of the stock market. The character of the German markets has reinforced this attitude. There are no brokers in Germany, as such. The banks act as brokers, and operate the markets between them. In the late 1950s, both the Christian Democratic government and the big banks tried to encourage small investors. The government denationalized Volkswagen on terms favorable to the small shareholder. The banks started their own mutual funds.

But in the 1960s, though the economy, by and large, went from strength to strength, the stock market emphatically did not. The new investors who had come gingerly into the market in the late 1950s burned their fingers when the market fell by more than 50 per cent in 1960–1961.

By the mid-1960s, more and more people had money burning a hole in their pockets, or at least deposited in 4-per-cent savings accounts. The net result was that by the beginning of 1967 IOS was ideally poised for a successful sales campaign.

More than one of the German bankers, officials, and journalists we talked to about the IOS phenomenon reminded us of another factor which cannot be ignored: the extraordinary trust in, and admiration for, all things American by the generation of Germans who had been young in 1945—the generation who had money saved by the 1960s.

More than anywhere else in Europe, the old values had been discredited in Germany. Germans turned to America and identified American ways with everything that was modern, democratic, progressive. Mutual funds were new, they were modern, they were American. Hundreds of thousands of Germans in the young-middle-aged generation were ready to believe that if mutual funds were criticized by the bankers, then that just showed how fusty or self-interested the bankers were.

Why was IOS so slow to realize that this huge market was waiting for it in Germany? It had, after all, been very active in Germany since 1957. Most of the leading individuals in the sales management—from Bernie Cornfeld down through Allen Cantor, Victor Herbert, Jack Himes, Eli Wallitt—knew Germany well from having sold programs to the American military there for years.

The truth is that for seven years Cornfeld was in the position of a man who doesn't realize he is sitting on a gold mine. In 1960, Cornfeld had actually sold the IOS dealership to Wolfe Frank (who had been the chief interpreter at the Nuremberg trials). He decided to buy it back in 1963. In mid-1963, IOS material was produced in German for the first time, and Cornfeld got into Germany in a big way.

It was Eli Wallitt who grasped the potential of the West German civilian market. After his first stint in the military market in West Germany, he had been back to New York to work for Investors Continental Services (the IOS subsidiary there) recruiting people to work overseas. He came back to Geneva in 1962 and worked as a sales executive. He guessed that there must be a lot of small savers in Germany who would be wanting to get back into the equity market again after the 1961 drop. He was right.

Wallitt is one of the most intriguing of the IOS inner circle and one of the wealthiest today.* He is not an obviously ambitious type. He is tall, with curly gray hair, and the suggestion of a scholar's stoop. He is highly intelligent; not merely shrewd, but given to speculative conversation like a born intellectual, and prone—like the social worker he was, for considerably longer than Bernie Cornfeld—to theorizing at length about human motivation, including his own. In business, Wallitt's style was to remain in the background, using his intelligence to control people and events indirectly.

When this adroit and interesting man set out to conquer Germany in 1963, he took with him one lieutenant and one recruit. The lieutenant was Ossie Nedoluha. The recruit was Raimund Herden, who became the IOS General Manager in Hamburg. Nedoluha is a broad, stocky, blond young man—not yet thirty at that time—of Czech descent and Austrian nationality. He joined IOS as an office boy in the earliest days, and then went to work in the mailroom to perfect his English and French. He started selling in Africa, but his first big coup came in the Canadian Arctic, where he found—not oil—but well-paid Canadian servicemen with nothing to spend their money on. They signed up as clients in droves. Next he moved on to Central America, where he learned Spanish and sharpened up his sales technique in a tough school.

Nedoluha has had little formal education, but he does have both formidable determination and what has been described as "a wayward Viennese charm." Many of the salesmen came back

---

*See Chapter 20, "The Book of Revelations."

from the road in the mid-1960s in search of a manager's more dependable profits. None timed their move or chose their territory so perfectly as Ossie, and only two or at most three others in the whole IOS sales organization—Wallitt himself, Felberbaum, and conceivably Werner Kunkler—earned as much money.

Raimund Herden had been out in Iran, not as an IOS salesman, but working for Brown Boveri, the big Swiss electrical engineering firm. Before that he worked for the Deutsche Bank. He had, in short, a thorough German business training: he had the performance figures of every mutual fund at his fingertips and was never at a loss for words, either in the office or at the dinner parties which he advised his managers to frequent as assiduously as he did himself.

Wallitt is quite open about his philosophy of management. He told us that he wanted his German operation to be as tight as he could make it administratively, and as loose as possible on the sales side. For a former socialist, he has an unusual belief in the merits of competition. He reasoned that strong personalities make the best salesmen, and that a strong personality is hard to direct. He was quite prepared to have four or five general managers treading on each other's toes in Munich, so long as they got on with the job of selling. And they certainly did that.

Wallitt and Nedoluha's organization multiplied like an amoeba. Cells were always splitting off, with a strong salesman as their head. As this man moved up the managerial ladder, he recruited more and more salesmen under him. And in the course of time they in turn split off and started their own amoeba-empire.

The best way of illustrating how this worked is to compare the structure of the West German sales operation in 1964, when Wallitt had had time to get it under way with the shape it had assumed by 1969. In this way one can also follow how individual early birds were wafted up the override tree by the efforts of the men underneath them.

In 1964 Nedoluha was the regional manager for West Germany. (Wallitt discreetly kept in the background.) There were only six branches in the region. Branch A was based on the Rhineland-Ruhr industrial area, and coming geographically closest under the eye of Nedoluha in Düsseldorf, it was divided between three managers: Gerhard Schicht in Cologne; a veteran of the IOS operation in South America called Bodo von Unruh, in Essen; and a third man called Jochen Freetown, whom we have been unable to trace.

Branch B was run by Raimund Herden, who had moved from Düsseldorf to Hamburg, and he spent a good deal of time disputing the boundaries of his territory with Ossie, who, however, retained an override on Herden's business. Herden was listed as having nineteen salesmen.

Branch C, with twenty-one salesmen, was managed by Larry Palmer, a former paratroop captain and ice-hockey goalie on the U.S. team that won the gold medal in the Squaw Valley Olympics of 1960. Palmer had his offices in Frankfurt.

The remaining three branches were all in Munich, under Wallitt's more immediate eye. Two of them, E and F, with fourteen and eleven salesmen respectively, were managed by Americans, Joseph "Bru" Brubaker and Pat Lucier. Branch D was run by Werner Kunkler, and already had forty-five salesmen.

Altogether, the one hundred fifty-six salesmen in Germany achieved $4.8 million of face volume in that 1964 contest, a little more than half the volume done by the twenty-one salesmen in Brazil, the champion region at that time. As a region, West Germany came eighth out of twenty-three regions in the world.

By 1969, West Germany sold a contest volume of $257 million, an increase of over 5000 per cent in five years! Eighteen separate regions sold more than all of West Germany had done five years before. One of Kunkler's 1964 salesmen alone, now a general manager, had five hundred twelve salesmen under him, more than three times the number of the entire German sales force in 1964. And each of the six branches of 1964 had swollen to a whole complex of regions and divisions with a dozen or more branches under them.

The geometric progression of the expansion shows up most clearly in Werner Kunkler's command. It was Kunkler who came closest of anyone to beating the Americans in IOS at their own game. He did it by relying on the classic German military virtues: order, hierarchy, discipline, and application.

Kunkler had been a doctor of psychology, an actor, and an insurance man, but before that he had lost several fingers on one hand as a tank captain on the Russian front in World War II.

He had been sold an IOS program by Bernie Cornfeld's cousin, Hardy Reisser. "When the fellow had gone," Kunkler explained afterward, "I worked out how much money he had made off me. And I said, 'If he can do that, you can do it too!' " At the beginning of 1964 he quit his job as an insurance-loss assessor and started his dizzy climb up the IOS ladder. In each of the three years, 1967, 1968, and 1969, the salesmen under Kunkler's orders did more than 10 per cent of IOS's entire business, worldwide. Kunkler's secret was not his personal persuasiveness as a salesman, but the methodical way he deployed his troops from Munich all over south Germany.

By 1969, eight of Kunkler's most successful salesmen of five years before had become managers. Several of them had worked up to the title, and the override, of a general manager.

Number one in the 1964 contest was Lothar Schwabenbauer, a master baker by trade and a former cinema owner. By 1969 he was the manager of a whole region known under the code name "MC," with his base at Regensburg. (M for Munich was the code for the whole of Kunkler's territory.) In five years, Schwabenbauer had built up a sales force of three branches and eight sections, with one hundred twenty-eight salesmen working for him.

The man who had been number three in 1964 had done best of all. This was Egon Schneider. His headquarters were in Offenburg, in Baden, and most of southwest Germany was his territory, known as Europe IV MA. Schneider had worked with Kunkler for the same insurance company before they joined IOS. At the peak, in April 1970, after only six years with IOS, he had two general managers, three divisional, nine regional, and twenty-three branch managers under him, with more than five hundred salesmen under them. With $16 million in face volume *a month*, Schneider was the top manager in all Germany for all of 1970. Another of Kunkler's protégés, Rudi May, a former industrial salesman whose MB region was centered on Würzburg, was not far behind. Managers like Schneider, May, and Schwabenbauer were taking an override on all the volume in their regions. And Kunkler was taking an override on them.

In Germany the pyramid structure of the IOS sales organization reached its most refined form. The aspiring recruit started as a trainee, hoping to progress to "basic" and then to "advanced" schedule. The crucial step was the next. When a man had sold $300,000 worth, he became a "senior" salesman. Then two good things happened for him: he joined the stock-option plan, with options on 50 shares; and he acquired the right to hire salesmen of his own, and to start to build his own pyramid.

Above senior status, the steps were from branch to regional to divisional to general manager. To become a branch manager, for example, you must be able to show "$500,000 of your own volume, plus three active associates on Advanced, or $300,000 of your own volume plus six active associates on Advanced, and group volume of $3,000,000."

And so on up the steps of the pyramid to general manager. To qualify for that title, you had to put in six unbroken months of more than $1 million in business or $10 million in twelve months. A general manager got options on 800 shares, and override of 0.5 per cent* on all the business done lower down in his "structure."

There were, therefore, several different pressures all working in the same dangerous direction: all tempting the managers to build up the number, as opposed to the quality, of the sales force under their control. To start with, the more salesmen a manager had under his control, the more he made on his own sales: the salesmen in his group pushed him up the schedule ladder. More important, the more salesmen a manager controlled, the more money he made because he was getting an override on their business. Third, the less experienced the salesman, the lower the proportion of the total commission that went to him, and, therefore, the more the managers on the structure above him made. Last, a "new-man bonus" was paid in cash for every new salesman taken on.

It might be, as one Hamburg manager said, "the most perfect system of slavery ever devised." But like most systems of slavery, it had the seeds of destruction in it. (It takes no exceptional acumen to guess what is likely to happen at the lower echelons of any army recruited on this system, however sincerely the men at the top try to maintain discipline.) Inevitably, both sales ethics and the quality of some of the sales force deteriorated under the

---

*As we shall see, this 0.5 per cent came to be divided between more than one GM in some structures, with important consequences.

temptations and pressures of breakneck expansion. The early sales tended to be made to fairly sophisticated investors, such as doctors and lawyers.

But, as the sales force snowballed, there was a tendency for less and less scrupulous salesmen to confront more and more innocent prospects. A farmer, for example, was persuaded to borrow money from the bank (to build a new barn), and then divert it into an IOS fund. The farmer, according to a West German newspaper which reported the case in detail, lost 60,000 marks on an investment of 200,000. One salesman got hold of a list of ladies from a marriage bureau and systematically worked his way through the lonely hearts. Instead of marriage, he proposed an IOS capital-accumulation plan.

One admittedly extreme case shows just how little IOS cared what sort of people it had as "associates" and "financial counselors." For three years IOS had a man working for it in Germany with a criminal record, which included fraud. Yet when the man's supervisor tried to warn top management about him, he was met by studied indifference over a long period.

The man used two names; sometimes he called himself David Crawley-Boevy, sometimes Ernest Richard Garnett-Smith. Tall, forty when he left IOS, with an English public-school manner and accent, Crawley-Boevy spoke no German, but sold IOS programs successfully under Ossie Nedoluha to the diplomatic community in Bonn and later to British Army of the Rhine personnel all over north Germany.

Crawley-Boevy's nominal supervisor—nominal because Crawley-Boevy was a hard man to supervise—found out that he had a criminal record. The supervisor went first to Nedoluha, then to Wallitt, to warn them of what he had found out and to complain of Crawley-Boevy's sales methods. Neither could be persuaded to take any interest. Finally the supervisor went to Geneva, and after several weeks got to see Cornfeld himself, who was charming but equally unconcerned.

In the end Crawley-Boevy was only terminated by IOS after he had been arrested more than once in Germany, taken back by IOS, and then rearrested for fraud by Swiss police in the Intercontinental Hotel in Geneva.

It turned out that he had been convicted in Britain for fraud, gross indecency, and several other offenses. He had been in trouble with the police in four or five other countries. In 1967 a London divorce judge found that two years before he had abducted a girl with a mental age of thirteen, gone through a marriage ceremony with her, and then asked her father for money.

An IOS salesman called Müller sold a program for 4000 DM to a German holidaymaker on Lake Maggiore. He then wrote out two contractual policies for a total of 240,000 DM ($72,000) and put the 4000 D-marks in as the down payments. Unluckily for Müller, his client was the well-known writer Henry Jaeger, who once did time in prison for robbing a post office. Jaeger redeemed his investment, but got only 2600 D-marks back. Jaeger made so much fuss that Bernie Cornfeld personally arranged to have him paid back in full.

If you recruit more than six thousand people in a few years, paying head money to those who take them on, and asking as their principal qualifications that they should sincerely want to get rich, then you must expect to find among your recruits a certain number as little qualified to act as financial counselors as Crawley-Boevy or Müller. But what contributed even more in the end to the instability of the German sales force was the widespread prevalence of practices that were relatively innocent in themselves.

For example, in their hurry to build up their own sales groups and so climb up the pyramid, salesmen would not only sell programs to their own family, they would hire their own relatives as salesmen. Even more serious, they would lend money to clients to invest in IOS.

Even five thousand dollars, split up as the down payments on five $60,000 capital-accumulation programs put in friends' names, would not only bring the salesman $1500 in commission, it would take him straight to senior salesman rank, which would allow him to hire his own salesmen under him. It would increase his personal rate of commission from 3.5 per cent to 4.5 per cent on his own sales. And it would win him options on 50 IOS shares. At that rate, he could well afford to redeem his friends' programs, pay them back the front-end load, and possibly pay them something for their trouble. Volume, everyone at IOS always insisted, was the name of the game. But volume and recruitment were interchangeable. The more volume you could get, the more people you could have working for you. The more people you had working for you, the greater the volume on which you shared in the commission.

Every few years, the world's teen-agers get caught up in the chain-letter craze. An ill-written, dog-eared letter arrives through the mail, covered with unknown names and faraway addresses. "Send a dollar"—or a pound or ten francs—"to the undersigned, then write to six of your friends, and they will each send you a dollar." It sounds too good to be true, even when you are fourteen. It takes only a moment's thought, even at that age, to work out that the only people who are sure to do well out of a chain letter are the people who get into it first.

IOS Germany was a refined version of the schoolboy chain

letter. It lasted as long as new people kept joining the chain, and sending in their dollars.

• • •

In 1967, Wallitt's planning, Kunkler's recruiting, and the missionary zeal of Ossie Nedoluha and Raimund Herden began to show visible signs of success. Sales in West Germany for that year reached 31 per cent of IOS's world volume—a contribution that was doubly useful because it came in time to replace the markets that had been lost through the SEC settlement and the troubles in South America.

But 1967 was also the year of James Roosevelt's drive to make IOS respectable by recruiting as many eminent politicians as he could persuade to join the colors. Naturally, this form of public relations was put into effect in West Germany too. We have seen how Cornfeld tried to recruit perhaps the most eminent available politician in West Germany, Ludwig Erhard, and in fact did not give up hope of getting him to join IOS until 1969. Attempts were also made to recruit other West German political heavyweights, Franz-Josef Strauss (whose wife was an enthusiastic IOS client) and a former finance minister, Fritz Schäffer, who died, however, in March 1967.

As a fourth choice, IOS had to make do with a political figure who had nevertheless through an accident of party politics come very close to the apex of the West German political system. Erich Mende was one of the founders, in 1945, of the Free Democratic Party, the small third party in the middle between the two giants of West German politics. In 1963, because Ludwig Erhard's Christian Democrats needed the FDP's bloc of seats to give it a working majority in the Bundestag, Mende became Vice Chancellor, and nominal number-two man in Erhard's cabinet. Mende lost that eminence in 1966, when the Christian Democrats got together with the socialists in the "Grand Coalition." At the same time Mende's standing in his own party was threatened by the FDP's shift to the Left. IOS came along at the right time for Mende, just as Mende came along at the right time for IOS.

Like so many before him, Mende first became involved with IOS because he bought an IOS program. It was sold to him by an FDP colleague, Dr. Reinfried Pohl. In the end IOS recruited not only Mende and Pohl, but also another former FDP Minister, Viktor-Emmanuel Preussker, partner in the small Bonn bank of Preussker & Thelen, and Josef Moll, Inspector General of the Bundeswehr under the Erhard cabinet. Preussker became the head of the IOS bank in Munich, Orbis Bank.

All in all, Mende's association with IOS was not a happy experience. Although he was the chairman of IOS Deutschland GmbH,* the main German sales company, he had been hired to be a figurehead. Wallitt and the other sales bosses had no intention of letting him discover what was really going on. They were often brusque with him to the point of rudeness. Werner Kunkler once reminded Mende in a restaurant that he, Kunkler, earned as much in a month as Mende earned in a year, which was probably a slight exaggeration, as well as being bad manners. The inner circle in Geneva never liked him much. They found him too good-looking, too smooth, too "German": surely an illogical objection in the circumstances. Poor Mende had to endure being shouted at by Cornfeld in his own home in Bad Godesberg.

After he left IOS, the whole episode left a bad taste in his

---

*The letters "GmbH" stand for the German words *Gesellschaft mit beschränkter Haftung*, "private limited liability company."

mouth. He busied himself with lobbying the government in Bonn for tighter regulation of mutual funds, and with organizing an association of former IOS employees, some of whom, he told us, had "suffered personal tragedy and hardship," and for whom he felt a sense of responsibility that does him credit.

Yet surely the inner circle did Mende an injustice; for he served IOS well and with an almost naïve enthusiasm. For two and a half years he zigzagged back and forth across Germany. He was ready to speak at any hall where the local manager could get together an audience to hear him preach the gospel of the mutual-fund revolution. He opened two hundred IOS branch offices, and made more than a hundred public speeches a year. It was calculated that in 1969 he had met more than 60,000 Germans on IOS business. No gathering was too humble, too provincial, or too remote for him. Like a politician on the stump for votes (and after all, perhaps that is what he was at the same time), Mende went to cocktail parties, football matches, wine tastings, press conferences, lunches, dinners, and any other functions where two or three people were gathered together in the name of IOS.

The result was that Erich Mende achieved, for a while, what IOS had never really been able to achieve anywhere else, certainly not on the same scale. He made IOS, as Manfred Birkholz and Wolf Saller* put it, *salonfähig*—"drawing-roomable," respectable. He did not achieve all this by himself, naturally. But he did more than anyone to establish the precondition for the sales boom by making IOS not merely respectable, but fashionable. Mende and the Germans came close to actually achieving what Geneva's publicity claimed for the company as a whole.

---

*Two IOS public-relations men to whose book, *Senkrechtstart und Absturz einer Erfolgsidee*, we are indebted for this adjective and for other details about IOS in Germany.

For in Germany, in 1968 and 1969, IOS for the first time came close to breaking into a genuine mass market of small savers.

Monthly sales figures tell the story. In mid-1967 they were running at around $25 million a month. That was before Mende began his itinerant preaching. By mid-1968 they had jumped to around $70 million a month. In the single month of June 1969 they hit $150 million. That was the high point. Sales went on rising after that: face-volume sales, that is, and the armies of salesmen went on swelling. But by mid-1969 the signs of danger were already there to be seen by anyone who could keep a cool head in the middle of all the rhetoric and the excitement.

On June 26, 1969, the Bundestag passed a new law to regulate foreign mutual funds, to take effect on November 1. What was noticed at the time was that it meant that the Fund of Funds could no longer be sold in Germany, though IIT could. That did not matter too much. IOS had founded its own national fund, Investors Fonds, in Germany at the end of 1967, and the sales force should have no difficulty in getting most of the investments that would be redeemed from the FOF reinvested in Investors Fonds.

What was far more serious for the salesmen was that as from November, the proportion of the commission that could be charged on the down payment of an investment program dropped from one-half to one-third. Given a constant level of business, that meant a one-third cut in the average salesman's income. The salesmen were not pleased at this. But even more dangerous tendencies were built into the situation.

The managers were, after all, professional optimists. They therefore invested heavily in the shares of IOS Ltd. itself. Their holdings were like an unexploded bomb in the basement. So long as expansion went on, all might be well. But at the first hint of serious trouble, those salesmen who had borrowed to buy IOS shares were likely to become bitterly disillusioned.

Again, it is worth underlining the contradiction between what IOS claimed to be, and what it was.

The most fundamental idea of IOS, indeed of mutual funds in general, is the idea of safety in diversification. These same salesmen and managers were persuading the clients to part with their money by preaching the advantages of having your money in as many different baskets as possible. And here they were plowing every penny they could lay their hands on, *not* into the IOS mutual funds but into the shares of IOS Ltd. They were hoping, of course, that they would "cash in" when those IOS shares became salable on the market.

Expenses in the meantime rose crazily. All over Germany, managers competed with one another for those intangibles which usually have English names in German—"prestige," "standing," "image"—but which cost millions of all too tangible D-marks. Managers built or rented luxurious office space. They furnished it with expensive antique furniture. Others invested in Ferraris, Maseratis, or Rolls-Royces. Ossie Nedoluha bought the most expensive car of all, a bright yellow Lamborghini. Kunkler, who already had a hotel on the Sorrento Peninsula, started building a luxurious villa in Rome.

As long as managers spent their own money, they were not hurting IOS. But several major projects started with corporate money at this time were conceived in the same lavish spirit. Perhaps the most disastrous expansion was the computer "preprocessing center" in Munich. In that city, IOS had eight office buildings, and plans went ahead for a stupendous complex which was intended to be the headquarters for the 1972 Olympic Games.

In that last wonderful year, it must have seemed as if it were raining money in Germany, and would never stop. In 1969 alone, Wallitt and Nedoluha both earned more than a million dollars each in overrides.

. . .

It was in Germany that IOS first had to face a problem that was a direct result of the speed with which sales and the sales force had expanded. It was a problem that IOS eventually had to face in every successful market, because it was an intrinsic flaw in the arithmetic of the commission structure itself. The solution the company found contributed in the end to the fatal shrinking of its profits, and to the instability of the sales force.

Over the years, the 8½-per-cent commission* which the clients paid had been split between IOS Ltd. and the sales force in the proportion of 2 per cent for the company, and 6½ per cent for the whole of the sales force. Roughly half of that 6½ per cent went to the man who had actually made the sale, and the other half was divided between the different managers.

For many years this was the scale. But a close reader of the 1969 IOS Ltd. prospectus would have noticed different figures: there the maximum commission payable by the client was still given as 8½ per cent. But the maximum percentage that could go to the sales force has risen from 6½ per cent to 7 per cent. Half a per cent, in other words, had been taken from the company's share of commission income, and given to the sales force. Half a per cent does not sound like very much. But it is one-quarter of

---

*This was a maximum figure. Since the commission you paid declined in proportion to the size of your investment, the maximum commission applied only to the smallest investments. On an investment of $1 million, the client paid only 0.5 per cent and the salesman's commission and managers' overrides would be correspondingly smaller. The principle remains the same.

2 per cent. IOS Ltd. therefore handed over up to one-quarter of its income from sales charges, the most fundamental source of its corporate revenue as a mutual-fund sales organization, to the salesmen.

This happened company-wide, as a matter of corporate policy. But the situation which brought it about first arose in Germany.

When, because of the volume of his group's sales, a man rose to be a GM in a structure which already had a GM at the top of it, the existing GM was bumped up, and became a "Super-GM." That, for example, is what happened in Germany when Ossie Nedoluha first reached GM status under Eli Wallitt in 1966.

But the German chain letter did not stop there. The amoeba continued to split. Werner Kunkler, in due course, became a GM under Nedoluha. Schneider became a GM under Kunkler. That made Kunkler, too, a Super-GM, and Wallitt became a Super-Super-GM.

And the process went further still. Schneider, too, acquired more than one GM under him, which made Schneider into a Super-GM, Nedoluha into a Super-Super-GM, and Wallitt into a four-times blessed Super Manager. At the apex, in 1970, as the whole organization took off into orbit, several structures existed where there were no less than four Super-GMs above a General Manager.

Long before that, as early as 1967, in fact, the financial incentive for the individual manager to go on building up the structure underneath him had begun to be eroded. A point had been reached—in Germany first, but soon in Canada, in Britain, and in other major markets, as well—where, if the returns had not actually begun to diminish, there was less and less reason for managers to help others to rise.

There was a cogent case, at that point, for revising the entire commission structure. But that was not what IOS did. It changed the rules so that in certain circumstances as much as 0.5 per cent could be lopped off IOS Ltd.'s share of commission: and it gave it all to the Super-GMs.

The increase was actually made in two stages. The first ¼ per cent was given to the Super-General Managers late in 1966, and a second ¼ per cent was added a year later in late 1967.

In March 1969* the sales company board fixed the override superstructure as follows:

A GM got ¼ per cent override.

Where there was one Super-GM, he got ¼ per cent.

Where there were two Super-GMs, they each got ¼ per cent, making ½ per cent in all.

Where there were three Super-GMs, they got ½ per cent divided by 3 = ⅙ per cent each.

Where there were four, they got ½ per cent divided by 4 = ⅛ per cent.

This formalized the taking of an extra 0.5 per cent from the company and the giving of it to the top echelon of the sales force.

It is quite easy to rationalize this decision to hand over part of the company's income to its highest-paid executives. One of the recipients, for example, told us that he thought of it not as something taken from the company, but as an investment made by the company in the future development of its own sales organization.

And, of course, even if IOS had not lived in the legal never-

*The extra ½ per cent was taken away from the Super-General Managers after the crisis in May 1970.

never land offshore, where there was none to say it nay, it would have been perfectly reasonable for IOS to take a decision to increase the executive's compensation at the expense of corporate income. That happens all the time.

But this case was a little different. It must be remembered that most of the Super-Super-GMs were members of the Board of IOS Ltd., or at least of the sales company, where the decision originated. At the time it was taken, the sales company's board meetings were the real forum of decisions: the IOS Ltd. Board met swiftly, almost perfunctorily, after the sales company's board had thrashed things out for many hours.

Some of the Super-GMs—Eli Wallitt himself, for example—were active in management. Others were less active. All benefited from the extra share of commission. What they did, as a group, was to take a decision to pay to certain of the highest-paid men in the company money that would otherwise have accrued to the company's profits and to the shareholders. There is no hint that this had happened in the IOS Ltd. prospectus. And nothing could more graphically illustrate the priorities inside the IOS sales management. For all the rhetoric about "People's Capitalism," when it came to the point, the inner circle came first.

• • •

And so the German balloon swelled and swelled, getting weaker in proportion to its expansion. When it popped, all that was left was the usual shriveled remnant. The managers rushed off to join other funds. The Super Managers went their various ways. And the salesmen marched off in whole companies, like mercenaries following their *condottiere* when the pay runs out.

A rump company remains in Germany, called Orbis-Finanz. But IOS's true monument in Germany is in the Königsallee in the financial district of Düsseldorf. It is called the Investors Club. It opened in December 1969, at the height of the IOS craze, as a sort of *café*-restaurant of the kind which is a pleasant institution in Germany. But it offered a most unusual double service to the burghers of Düsseldorf. They could order ox-tail soup, of course, or steak, or any one of a tempting selection of *torte*. They could sip Rhine wines such as *1967er Oppenheimer Krötenbrunnen spätlese natür*, or give themselves Dutch courage with an "Investors Drink" cocktail. But at the same time, without stirring from their leather-upholstered easy chairs, they could, on electric display panels, check price movements in 1600 German, American, British, French, Dutch, and Japanese stocks. Each table is equipped with an electronic Stockmaster, such as brokers' offices have, which flashes up the latest price of any particular stock. And a "Stockmaster hostess" is on hand to punch up the code of IBM or Royal Dutch for you between the pear and the cheese.

But the greatest wonder of the Investors Club is neither gastronomic nor electronic. It lies in the fact that it belongs to the Deutsche Bank, the largest of the three great banks that have dominated financial life in Germany since World War II. Before the advent of Cornfeld, Wallitt, and Nedoluha one would no more have expected the sober and reticent men who direct the Deutsche Bank to serve cake and cocktails to their customers than to run through the streets handing out hundred-mark notes at street corners.

The German banks in general were wary of IOS from the start. And IOS men, up to and including Cornfeld himself, were never slow to attribute the banks' attitude to mere competitive jealousy. In April 1970 Cornfeld gave an interview to the Sunday paper *Welt am Sonntag* in which he flatly accused the German banks of having helped to bring on the IOS crisis by selling IOS shares, and even selling them short. Other IOS spokesmen repeated the accusation.

The banks' answer was indignant denial. They were able to show that they could not in fact have done what Cornfeld accused them of. "The insinuation is so absurd as to be self-condemnatory," sniffed the Commerzbank. The Deutsche Bank was even shorter. "*Abwegig!*" ("incorrect") said an official spokesman.

It is probably not even true that the banks lost much business to IOS. Very few clients of the Deutsche Bank, for example, liquidated their holdings with the bank in order to invest in IOS. But one senior Deutsche Bank official admitted that in 1968 and 1969 he and his colleagues got thoroughly irritated by the number of customers who complained that the bank was not doing as much for them as IOS would do. The aggressive methods of IOS shook German banking to the roots. Even Establishment bankers are prepared to agree that this may have been to the good.

That is why the Investors Club, owned by the Deutsche Bank, is a monument to IOS. It may be a long time before the small savers of Germany recover their confidence in the magic of the stock market. It will be longer still before the German banks forget their small clients.

At its zenith, the IOS operation in Germany seemed to have taken as its motto the noble sentence from Schiller's "Ode to Joy": "*Seid umschlungen, millionen!*" ("We embrace you, oh ye millions!"). But there were those, even within IOS, who were never taken in. "Have you ever heard my personal formulation for the German operation?" Ed Cowett asked us. "I always used to say that it was built on a unique foundation of shit and quicksand."

15

The Bella Figura of Harvey Felberbaum

In which we show that IOS's good resolutions about currency smuggling were not always kept. How IOS went into business with an interesting bank.

Nowhere in the world was the double strategy which IOS adopted to cope with the crisis of 1966–1967 apparently more successful than in Italy. That strategy was based on two principles: national funds, and respectability. The setting up of national funds—where governments would allow them—enabled IOS to counter the main objection to its sales operations. They made it possible to argue that some, at least, of the clients' money would not be lost to the national economy. And as a prerequisite and a protection for the national funds, IOS, under James Roosevelt's tenure, pulled out all the stops to build up the best possible relations with governments, central banks, the press, and anyone else who might be able to lend a spot of elbow grease to the mahogany and leather patina of solidity that IOS needed to acquire. Both parts of the strategy succeeded brilliantly in Italy.

The IOS national fund in Italy—called Fonditalia—was incorporated in Luxembourg on September 26, 1967. IOS began selling it early the next year. By January 27, 1970, two years later,

James Roosevelt, in his capacity as President of Fonditalia, was able to give the investors a glowing report in his second year-end letter. Fonditalia was associated with blue-chip banks: the Istituto Bancario San Paolo of Turin, as its Depository for Cash in Italy, and the Banque Rothschild as Custodian and Banker. It now had 30,000 investors, and no less than $183.5 million under management. The net asset value of their fund, over a period of time in which the Dow-Jones industrial average in New York had virtually stood still, had gone up by no less than 21.5 per cent.

To succeed in business in Italy, even more than anywhere else, you must *fare bella figura*: put on an impressive front. IOS's front in Italy was not merely impressive, it was refulgent. Physically, Fideuram, the Fonditalia sales company, inhabited some of the most expensive-looking offices in Rome: marble-floored and air-conditioned, they had been modernized out of the Renaissance splendor of the Palazzo Orsini, itself carved in the sixteenth century from the ruins of the Theater of Marcellus, built by Julius Caesar himself in the very heart of the imperial city, between the Capitol and the River Tiber.

Fideuram moved into the Palazzo Orsini because its legal adviser and subsequent president had his law offices there. This was Avvocato Pasquale Chiomenti, who is not only one of the most successful and respected lawyers in Italy, but also a man who is plugged in to the sources of power in the country at half a dozen points. He is, for example, connected through some of his numerous directorships with both Fiat and IRI, the two great powers of Italian economic life.* And it was undoubtedly to

---

*IRI (Istituto per la Riconstruzione Industriale) is the major State-owned holding company which controls a large share of the Italian economy. It holds controlling interests in banks, shipping lines, shipyards, telecommunications companies, and, for example, Alfa Romeo. Fiat is by far the biggest private industrial corporation in Italy and is in many branches of the engineering industry besides automobiles, of which it is the biggest producer in Europe.

please his lifelong friend Chiomenti that Professor Guido Carli, Governor of the Bank of Italy, turned up to wish Fonditalia well at a widely publicized reception at the Hotel Excelsior in October 1968.

IOS was to receive a mark of signal favor from an even higher power. On December 10, 1969, Bernie Cornfeld was received in audience for thirty-five minutes by the Pope. This crowning accolade for IOS's new respectability was granted in recognition of the IOS Foundation's role in running Pacem in Terris. The meeting, in any event, was greatly enlivened by the presence of Bernie's mother, Mrs. Sophie Cornfeld. It had not been Bernie's idea that she should come, but she insisted, and it soon became plain why. In a very forthright way she tackled the Pope about relations between the Church and Israel. The Pope assured her that he was very sympathetic to Israel, but Mrs. Cornfeld pressed him, asking whether he saw any hope of improving relations between the Vatican and Tel Aviv. Again, the Holy Father politely insisted that relations were excellent.

Both Bernie and Mrs. Cornfeld were delighted to find that the Pope was not "austere and cold," as they had expected, but on the contrary "a warm, charming, and very human person," as Bernie later put it. As they left, it seems the Holy Father turned to Mrs. Cornfeld and said, "*Shalom, Shalom.*"

While Bernie Cornfeld, James Roosevelt, and Pasquale Chiomenti all did their bit to get Fonditalia under way and to make IOS known in the right places in Italy, the success of the Italian sales operation was almost wholly due to someone else: Harvey Felberbaum.

In 1967, according to the IOS prospectus, Italy accounted for only 1 per cent of sales. In 1968, according to the same source, that proportion had reached 10 per cent. By June 1970, according to Edward Cowett, Italy accounted for not more than 6 per cent of the skyrocketing expenses of the sales operation and only 7 per cent of the salesmen: but it was providing no less than 45 per cent of the cash flow.

Felberbaum's achievement was recognized on June 8, 1970, when he was named Vice President for Sales and Marketing of the IOS parent company: successor, in effect to Allen Cantor, and supreme boss of the worldwide sales operation. Felberbaum received the ultimate seal of respectability when, in October 1970, 51 per cent of Fonditalia and of Fideuram, were sold for close to $10 million to the Istituto Mobiliare Italiano (IMI), a government medium and long-term credit institution. Harvey Felberbaum, in fact, emerged from the disasters of spring 1970 as the champion survivor among the paladins of the sales force. Italy, we were told again and again in Geneva, was the one galleon in Cornfeld's armada which could be counted on to ride out the storm because "Harvey Felberbaum runs a tight ship." In June 1970, he gave an interview to the *IOS Bulletin*, the theme of which was that he had built his operation round the word "control."

Harvey Felberbaum ran a tight ship, all right, but not quite in the sense that he was generally supposed to. The real nature of the operation Felberbaum was running was very different from its Renaissance façade. Felberbaum himself operated clandestinely to the extent of using a false name over a prolonged period—he used the name of a real person for his own business activity without bothering to ask that person's permission.

In 1966 Sanche de Gramont, who had been the Rome correspondent of the New York *Herald Tribune* until it closed, decided to move to Tangier. He let his apartment in Rome to Felberbaum, who lived there until September 1968. In that month Mrs. de Gramont went to Rome to put the apartment back in shape. She was somewhat surprised when she went to

Felberbaum's office to be introduced by him to several of his colleagues with the words, "Meet the real Mrs. Sanche de Gramont."

Later Mr. and Mrs. de Gramont learned what this cryptic phrase meant. After Felberbaum moved out of the apartment, mail was forwarded to de Gramont in Tangier, addressed to "Sanche de Gramont" but meant for Felberbaum: the fifteen or twenty letters in question dealt mainly with IOS problems in Greece—which came under Felberbaum's jurisdiction—and the help that could be expected from certain Greek officials in sorting these problems out. Mr. de Gramont has, of course, no way of knowing how much mail might previously have been sent to Felberbaum under his name, or what it might have dealt with. He was, however, in no doubt that Felberbaum had used his name and that a large proportion of his business activity in Italy was illegal.

The entire IOS operation in Italy was obsessed with similar conspiratorial devices. A secret documentation center was maintained in the offices of an affiliate company called Servinter in Chiasso: even IOS managers were not allowed into one particular room there unless accompanied. Italy was known in IOS internal documents by a series of different codes, which changed approximately every six months. At one time it was "Asia 23." At another it was "America 23." Later it was "Asia VII." Salesmen were listed in IOS records under pseudonyms, including such brazen ones as "Leonard Vinci" or "Ben Disralli" (*sic*).

Felberbaum explained to us that this was done to prevent rival fund-selling organizations from tempting the salesmen away. It is a little hard to see why he should have needed to protect himself from temptation in this way. His General Manager in Milan, Roberto Alazraki, in an unguarded moment, put forward what sounds a more likely explanation. "We started using false names as a precaution after Brazil, when the operation there blew." In an even more unguarded moment, another of Harvey Felberbaum's GM's, Charlie Freeman, gave the whole game away in a letter: "As to the question of legality," Freeman wrote early in 1967, months before the establishment of Fonditalia first made it legal for IOS to sell to Italian citizens and residents in Italy, "there are very few large investors who would invest legally. They prefer to go through a Swiss bank. We are, however, establishing a legal operation here in Italy, with the participation of one of the major banks of the IRI group. This will enable us to have a vast new development, opening up the market of the small investor who doesn't know about Swiss banks and prefers to have his capital remain in Italy."

The truth is that long before Fonditalia was set up, the IOS sales force was selling the Fund of Funds and IIT illegally in Italy to Italians who wanted to change their capital from lire to dollars. This was done with the co-operation of one Swiss bank in particular, the Finter Bank, through its branch in Chiasso, which is just across the frontier in Switzerland, less than an hour's drive on the *autostrada* north from Milan.

The Finter Bank had been involved in similar business before. As we shall see, it had been implicated in one of the most celebrated of Italian financial scandals before IOS came in contact with it. But between them, the Finter Bank's Chiasso branch and the IOS managers in Italy helped to smuggle out millions of dollars' worth of currency by an ingenious method which we will describe in detail, on the basis of precise documents, below. And they went on illegally exporting currency out of Italy in this way into the IOS-dollar funds in Switzerland, long after Fonditalia had been set up with the Italian government's blessing.

The Italian operation, in other words, is a warning against misinterpreting the change that came over IOS after the crises of

1966–1967. What the IOS men in Italy learned from the Brazilian debacle was not that they must stop illegal sales but that they must cover them up, with tighter security and a more respectable façade.

For many years, some wealthy Italians have been shipping their capital across the frontier to Switzerland. This traffic accelerated sharply in the early 1960s after the so-called "opening to the Left" in Italian politics. This was IOS's opportunity in Italy, and it was equal to it. Once again, IOS's contribution was to make available to a broader share of the middle class the possibilities for capital flight that were the traditional prerogative of the rich. It is, we suppose, a kind of democracy.

• • •

Long after we started doing research for this book, we were taken in by the façade of the IOS operation in Italy ourselves. We had no reason not to believe the official line as it was given to us in Rome and in Geneva. This version can be summarized as follows:

There had been a very small sales force in Italy from the late 1950s since the ubiquitous Jack Himes began selling Dreyfus programs to U.S. Navy personnel at the big NATO support base in Naples. Naturally IOS sold only to foreigners and to the small number of Italians who for some reason had funds abroad which they were at liberty to invest in IOS. This meant selling to, besides American naval and military personnel, the expatriate community, including the embassies and the United Nations agencies in Rome; the American business community in Milan; and the considerable number of Italians who had returned with savings from South America (there are large Italian communities in Argentina and Venezuela, as well as in Brazil). IOS was naturally eager to get permission to sell in Italy, but this permission was not forthcoming, and sales to Italians were not made until Fonditalia was established.

This, with variations and *obbligati*, was the story we were told, and we believed it—at first. The first serious indication that all might not be quite so boy-scoutish in Italy did not come until September 7. And it came from the most unexpected of sources. Two of us were talking to a director of IOS Ltd. in his office in Geneva. Abruptly, he picked up a sheaf of papers from his desk. Waving them at us, he said (we paraphrase), "And there's another thing you don't know! The operation in Italy has been 'black' for years, and, what's more, according to these figures it's still black!" Eleven per cent of the sales Felberbaum's men were making in Italy even then, he assured us, were not sales of Fonditalia at all: they consisted of sales of Fund of Funds or IIT made to people who had no business having external funds, and the money came out "in suitcases" through Chiasso and Lugano. The same day another main board IOS director confirmed the story: he said that 11–13 per cent of all sales in Italy were still illegal. There seemed to be a point here to be checked, one way or the other.

It was not until a month later that a former IOS salesman told us bluntly that it was quite notorious that the selling in Italy was illegal on a large scale in 1965, 1966, and in 1967—before Fonditalia was set up later that year. He told us that at a time when all selling to Italians was illegal, there were "five thousand clients, all clandestine." And he mentioned the name of the Finter Bank. IOS managers had continued to use it to change lire into dollars until the spring of 1970, he said, when relations had been severed at Felberbaum's request.

By the end of the same week we had found three IOS managers in different parts of Italy, who confirmed the essentials of this story: namely, that to their certain knowledge illegal sales of the Fund of Funds (known in Italy as "la Fof," to rhyme with "cough") and IIT had been going on for years; that such sales had been a very important part of the operation in Italy before Fonditalia was set up; and that the Finter Bank had been involved in the necessary clandestine currency exchange. One of them also spelled out exactly how it was done, down to the way postal boxes were used for reasons of security in Chiasso and two neighboring villages.

We then visited Dr. Chiomenti in his sumptuous office in the Palazzo Orsini. He explained to us that he had resigned from the Board of IOS Ltd., the main company, "because I didn't know enough of what was going on." It seemed, however, that he knew less than everything about what was going on in Italy, where he remained President of Fideuram.

Had there been any illegal selling in Italy before Fonditalia was set up? Dr. Chiomenti said it had never occurred to him to inquire. Had he ever heard of the Finter Bank? He professed complete ignorance. He was, he explained, "the constitutional monarch" of IOS in Italy. Harvey Felberbaum was the "operational chief."

We accepted Dr. Chiomenti's repeated statement that he knew nothing of any illegal selling. But it seemed to be time to have a word with Harvey Felberbaum.

• • •

The operational chief of IOS in Italy—"Regional Vice President in Charge of Italian Sales Operations" was his official title—is one of the most attractive, as well as one of the ablest, of the IOS inner circle. He is strikingly good-looking, dark, slight, with a disarming grin. He looks a good deal younger than forty, which is what he was in 1970.

He joined IOS in 1957, and started out as one of Allen Cantor's personal trainees around the U.S. Air Force bases in France. For the next five years or so, before he settled down in Italy, he was one of the most successful of the peripatetic salesmen, clocking up thousands of miles round Asia and the Pacific. One catches fleeting glimpses of a man always in motion in the dashing little items about him in Cornfeld and Cantor's monthly *Bulletin*. In February 1960, for example, "When Eileen Felberbaum required an operation recently, Harvey spent hours in the hospital waiting until he could go in and see his wife. As soon as the medics let him in and Harvey made sure that Eileen was perfectly all right, he sold the patient in the next bed a program."

In September 1961, "Harvey Felberbaum, roaming the South Seas, has crossed the International Dateline so often that he isn't sure whether it's today, tomorrow, or the day before yesterday. On one of his stopovers on dry land, Harvey managed a spot of duck shooting with an Asian prince."

In June 1962, "Harvey Felberbaum, driving a friend's Mk II Gilby Climax, placed third in the Naples Grand Prix. Just to give an idea of the class Harvey was up against, the first and second place cars were factory Ferraris. . . ."

We met Felberbaum in London, in one of IOS's apartments in Park Lane. He was affability itself. His general position was that while there might have been a little illegal selling, it was insignificant in volume and had all stopped before Fonditalia was formed. He himself had given strict orders that it must stop, and he had in fact fired any salesman who was caught doing it. It was, he conceded, possible that individual clients might have been changing money illegally, but IOS knew nothing about that.

What about the Finter Bank? we asked. Yes, he said, he had heard of it, but neither he nor IOS had ever had any formal arrangement with it. In a telephone conversation a few days later, he restated this position: there had never been anything like a formal arrangement with the Finter Bank.

A few days later, one of us was going through a file of Brazilian newspaper clippings. A reference to the Finter Bank jumped out of the page. It was in the *Jornal da Tarde* of São Paulo for November 18, 1966. That was a week after the Brazilian police cracked down on IOS, and the name of the company was in the headlines. So when a boy of ten found a pile of letters and papers with the letters "IOS" all over them on a vacant lot in the Street of the Begonias in the São Paulo suburb of Morumbi, he took them straight to the nearest policeman. The cop was not interested so the boy took them to the newspaper, which was very interested. And a few days later the same boy, rummaging around the same lot, found another and larger pile of papers.

The newspaper established that they had belonged to an IOS Associate called Daniel Aharony, who had either jettisoned them in his haste after the police raid or had been using the vacant lot as a hiding place. There were letters, reports, and documents dealing with many aspects of IOS business. And among them there were several papers which mentioned the Finter Bank.

One of them read as follows: "Checks in lire. Make them out in any name you like. Should be crossed for greater security. Do not put the name of the place. Send check to Harvey Felberbaum, care of the Finter Bank."

Just why Daniel Aharony should have needed instructions about lira payments from Brazil is not clear—though there is, of course, a large Italian community in São Paulo. Two thoughts struck us. The first was that it was rather unlikely that anyone—let alone a man with a reputation for running a tight ship—would have had indefinite sums of money sent to him "care of" a bank with which he had no kind of formal arrangement. And the second was that we would like to know more about the Finter Bank.

• • •

The history of the Finter Bank is linked with the story of one of the most mysterious financial scandals of postwar Europe, the affairs of the Balzan Foundation. It is also inextricably connected with the flight from the lira.

Eugenio Balzan was an Italian journalist who in the 1920s became, and remained until he was beaten up and driven into exile by the Fascists, the business manager of the greatest newspaper in Italy, the *Corriere della Sera*. The job was very lucrative. Balzan negotiated a percentage of the paper's net profits for himself which enabled him to go into exile across the Swiss border in Lugano with a fortune of some 47 million Swiss francs, or say $12 million, in the money of 1934.

When Balzan died in 1953 in Lugano, he left his money to a daughter, Lina, whom he had scarcely seen. Shortly before her own death only four years later, Lina Balzan wrote a will in which the greater part of the Balzan millions were left to endow a foundation whose main purpose would be to award prizes, in the manner of the Nobel Foundation, for services to world peace, and to learning and the sciences.

It is clear that Lina Balzan was encouraged in this design by two remarkable men who were to be the principal actors in the Balzan affair. One was a lawyer of Italian descent and Venezuelan nationality named Ulisse Mazzolini. The second was Padre Enrico Zucca, who must be one of the most improbable of all the followers of the Franciscan rule of poverty.

Zucca first appeared in the headlines when he reburied Mussolini's body in 1946. He then established a Catholic cultural center in Milan known as the Angelicum, which operates on the most lavish scale, with its own orchestra, theater, cinema, and classical recording company.

Zucca and Mazzolini were not shy about the Balzan Foundation and its prizes. The first year they had the neat idea of awarding their own peace prize to the Nobel Foundation. Next year they had an even bolder idea: they gave the prize to Pope John XXIII. Their third attempt, which was frustrated by the outbreak of the scandal, was to give the prize to the United Nations. A check was actually handed to U Thant at a ceremony in New York. Unfortunately, it was signed by an unauthorized person, it was undated, and the amount in figures and the amount in words differed by 50,000 Swiss francs. U Thant sent it back.

That was the beginning of the end. The Swiss and Italian Presidents, who had been made honorary presidents of the Foundation, hastily withdrew. The Swiss government moved in and appointed a new board of directors to look after the Foundation's funds, which were naturally kept in Switzerland. The Italian government appointed a special commissioner to look into the Italian end. And in 1965 the Zurich authorities opened a criminal investigation. For four years they delved into the Foundation's convoluted dealings in Venezuelan land, on the Zurich Bourse, and in Italy. Zucca, Mazzolini, and their associates were eventually cleared of criminal embezzlement, but they were officially declared to have been "negligent" in their management of the Foundation's money and had to pay costs.

The name Finter comes into the story of the Balzan Foundation at every turn. It started as a company in Caracas, Venezuela, with the noncommittal name of Continuous Metalcast CA. In 1957 Mazzolini changed its name to Finter Inc. CA. And later, according to one of Mazzolini's fellow directors, half the Balzan millions were actually held to the account of the Finter Company.

The Finter *Bank* started as the "Westbank" in Lugano, but had become the Finter Bank by 1958. Though it later moved its head office to Zurich, it kept branches both in Lugano and Chiasso, conveniently poised in both places to do business across the Italian frontier.

The Swiss investigations showed that in some cases, at least, the gifts made to the Balzan Foundation were "donations" of a very special kind. The donors were paid back—sometimes in Swiss francs—a substantial proportion of the land or money they gave to the Foundation in Italy. Both in Switzerland and in Italy, the press pointed out that this looked very much like a way of enabling wealthy Italians to get their capital out of the lire into good hard Swiss francs, while at the same time avoiding death duty and other taxes.

On July 27, 1960, for example, two sisters in Bologna who had "donated" a plot of land to the Foundation received a letter from Finter Inc. CA. It informed them that almost 6 million Swiss francs would be placed to their credit, earning interest at 5¼ per cent. At the same time the Balzan Foundation would be debited an equivalent amount. They had given in *lire:* their reward was not only in heaven, but in Swiss francs. The letter was signed by one Beltraminelli and another employee of Finter Inc. CA, with Mazzolini's authority.

A few days after discovering the reference to the Finter Bank in the Brazilian newspaper, we visited Chiasso. There was no difficulty in crossing the frontier with a bulging briefcase which could have been jammed with ten thousand lire notes for all either the Italian or the Swiss frontier guards would have known. Chiasso has 8554 inhabitants, and there are fourteen banks listed in the phone book. All the banks list rates of exchange prominently in the window and quote the latest market price of leading stocks and of gold. Chiasso is in the capital-flight business the way Detroit is in automobiles, and people can even joke about it. When a fifteenth bank opened there recently, the head of the local Italian customs was invited to drink to its success.

There was no difficulty in finding the Finter Bank. It inhabits a handsome new building less than two hundred yards from the customs barrier in the main street. Nor was there any difficulty in obtaining access to the bank's executive offices—with a bulging briefcase and a muttered word about "a delicate matter" we were ushered in. We were received by none other than Stelio Beltraminelli.

Mr. Beltraminelli readily confirmed that the Finter Bank had been used by the IOS managers in Italy for channeling funds out of Italy and into IOS funds in Geneva. The only subject on which he seemed sensitive was the use of postal boxes. "It was a simple precautionary measure," he explained. Some of the money arrived in cash, physically brought over the frontier, he said, but the larger proportion arrived in the form of "bank transfers." He was, in short, vague about the mechanisms of the business the Finter Bank had been doing with IOS, but he was absolutely open in admitting that it had indeed been doing such business.

Beltraminelli also told us that, since the Balzan scandal, a stake in the Finter Bank had been bought by the Pesenti group. Carlo Pesenti is one of the wealthiest and most powerful industrialists in Italy. From his power base in Bergamo, not far from Chiasso, the Pesenti family controls Italcementi, one of the largest industrial corporations in Italy, and extensive interests in paper-making, banking, and real estate. Pesenti recently sold the Lancia automobile company to Fiat.

Later, in a two-hour interview in his enormous villa high above the lake of Lugano, Pesenti's representative on the board of the Finter Bank, a courtly old Swiss gentleman whose wife comes from Bergamo, refused to tell us just how large the Pesenti group's holding in the bank is, or who the other shareholders are. He would tell us only that the Pesenti holding is a minority, that it was bought in 1967, and that there *might* have been other changes in the shareholding since the scandal. There are two representatives of the Crédit Suisse on the Finter Bank's Board, and one representative of each of the other two major Swiss banks. (The Crédit Suisse has informed us that it has no shareholding in the Finter Bank, however.) Nevertheless, both before and after the eruption of the Balzan affair, the Finter Bank has been connected with some of the most influential figures in the social and economic life of Switzerland and northern Italy.

· · ·

Harvey Felberbaum told us that he had forbidden the key people in his organization to talk to us. But, double-checking, we had no difficulty in finding several more managers who were quite willing to explain to us more exactly than Mr. Beltraminelli how the illegal selling worked, and to give us an idea of the magnitude of the operation.

They also supplied us with documents which establish three points beyond any doubt:

1. Fund of Funds and IIT were sold illegally in Italy on a massive scale before Fonditalia was set up, and senior IOS management in Italy knew this well.
2. Illegal sales continued long after Fonditalia had come into existence, and this, too, was known to top managers.

3. The Finter Bank was deeply involved. It went to the length of having special stationery printed to handle the volume of IOS and Fund of Funds business it was doing. Indeed, on at least one occasion Beltraminelli wrote *to an IOS manager* asking him to visit the Finter Bank's offices "to have the mechanism of the IOS organization explained to you by one of our employees"!

Understandably, for a long time, Harvey Felberbaum insisted to us that he knew of no illegal selling in Italy after the setting up of Fonditalia. Eventually, however, confronted by the evidence to the contrary, he conceded that illegal sales "did continue." He explained that his earlier denials had been motivated by his concern for the sales force, for which he feels a strong sense of responsibility. "O.K.," he said, "I was playing games with you, but what would you have done?"

. . .

One prominent lawyer in Rome told us that he was called up so often by IOS salesmen offering to take his money in lire and pay it into dollar funds in Switzerland that he got in the habit of slamming the phone down whenever anyone introduced himself, or—as it often was—herself, as being from IOS.

Here is how IOS got around the Italian currency laws. When the salesman had found a client he would ask the client to make out a check to the salesman on his ordinary lira account. The salesman cashed this and asked his bank to make him out what are called "*assegni circolari*" for the equivalent amount. The *assegno circolare* in Italy is a banker's check for a given amount which can be endorsed on from hand to hand: because it is guaranteed by the bank, it is as good as cash. The salesmen were under instruction not to make out these *assegni circolari* in amounts higher than 5 million lire (about $8000) each. Higher denominations had to be registered in a way that could be traced.

These banker's checks were made out by the salesman to imaginary names, such as Giuseppe Verdi for example, and sent to the Finter Bank through a particular postal box in a village near Chiasso. (Correspondence relative to these transactions went through two other postal boxes, one in the Chiasso post office, one in another village.) The salesman then telephoned the Finter Bank and told them which client's account was to be credited with the amount that had been mailed to the false name.

Then came the trickiest stage of the operation, the actual shift from lire into dollars. It was done by means of an ingenious system of reciprocal accounts between the Finter Bank and certain banks, or branches of banks, across the Italian frontier in Como.

This is how it was done. The Finter Bank opened accounts with these banks in Italy—into which, naturally enough, it was perfectly legal to pay Italian checks. The Italian banks, in turn, opened numbered accounts with the Finter Bank, which, again, was perfectly legal. Naturally the Italian banks had checkbooks to enable them to write checks on these Finter accounts.

When the *assegno circolare* for, say, 10 million lire arrived from a salesman in the way we described, the Finter Bank would call up the bank in Como and say, "We are crediting you with 10 million lire," and it would send the check, made out in the name of Giuseppe Verdi or whoever it might be, to be credited to its account in the Como bank. At the same time the Como bank would call up the Finter Bank and say "we credit you with $16,000," the dollar equivalent of the client's 10 million lire. They would then send a check for this amount in dollars to the

Finter Bank: it was of course perfectly legal *for the bank* to transfer dollars in this way.

The transaction was thus finished with a minimum of risk for all concerned. The Finter Bank now had the dollars to invest in Fund of Funds or IIT, according to the instructions received from the salesmen. It would also handle the return flow of liquidations and "automatic withdrawal accounts" for the clients, and commissions for the salesmen. Sometimes the more successful salesmen had enough dollars in their Finter Bank accounts to carry out the exchange transaction on their own account. But the method we have described was the standard one.

The system had one refined advantage. On the back of an Italian *assegno circolare*, indeed of any Italian check, it says, "to be circulated only in Italy." This provided the IOS salesman with an escape hatch if he should be stopped and searched at the frontier. "I'm taking it back into Italy with me," he could tell the frontier police. "And anyway you can't say it's currency, because no one can cash it in Switzerland."

· · ·

HOW big was Harvey Felberbaum's black operation in Italy? When did it start? And how long did it go on?

Once again, precise figures could only come from inside IOS itself. We have only been able to glean certain specific indications.

Records for one individual IOS manager in Italy show that up to the same summer of 1969 he had sold in his entire IOS career (all of it after the setting up of Fonditalia) 32 per cent of Fonditalia and 68 per cent of illegal funds. During the period of illegal sales, $100,000 a month was considered only a respectable sales total for an individual salesman. The number of salesmen involved in illegal selling was given to us as 250–300 by several sources: of these, only a couple of dozen managers were in on the details of the method for changing money through the Finter Bank. The rest passed their business through their managers.

The lowest estimate any of the managers we talked to gave us for the volume of illegal business was $12 million a month in face volume for the whole of Italy during the peak years. One man stated with precision that the volume was $20–30 million a month in illegal sales, of which half was in cash. He added that this made IOS the biggest single illegal exporter of currency out of Italy.

It is clear that this business had started as early as 1965, and we were told by the two IOS directors in Geneva that it was still going on in September 1970. We have documents to prove that it was going on before February 1967; that new Fund of Funds' accounts were opened well after the establishment of Fonditalia; and that the Finter Bank was still servicing illegal accounts at least as late as January 1970.

What the Italian story shows is that the IOS sales organization did not change its spots after the shift in emphasis from the underdeveloped countries back to Europe.

It cannot be argued that, after Brazil, the IOS management in Geneva did not know that illegal selling was still going on. Apart from the fact that two directors told us that they knew about the illegal selling in Italy, there was a general discussion of the whole question at a meeting of the sales company board as late as March 12, 1970. The directors heard a report from the Sensitive Areas Committee, which dealt with illegal selling in the Philippines, Bolivia, Peru, Singapore, and elsewhere. "Sensitive areas" had been the euphemism for black operations since the days of Ed Coughlin's first birthday cables. Did the board reiterate a firm opposition to illegality? It did nothing of the kind. There was a general discussion of an "early warning system" through contacts with "highly placed people" in each country. The committee recommended that sensitive areas should not be closed down, but that controls and security should be tightened. Allen Cantor moved that this policy should be adopted, and the motion was unanimously passed. The sales company was thus formally committed to permitting illegal sales to continue.

If money was to be made legally, IOS was quite happy to make it. But if money could only be made illegally, that was all right too. After the new drive for "respectability" as well as before it, IOS remained indifferent to legality wherever the rewards justified it.

16

Good Evening, Comrade Prospect!

Before going on to see what they did with the customers' money, we look at some other markets: France, Scandinavia, Communist Europe. IOS is ready to assume almost any form and go almost anywhere so long as the salesmen can still collect.

For the revolutionaries, iconoclasts, and enemies of the Establishment that they liked to boast of being, the mutual-fund princes had a remarkable penchant for what used to be called "good addresses." In London, IOS was to be found in Mayfair, W.1, a neighborhood fit for any dowager duchess. In Rome, it was the Palazzo Orsini. But the Paris office was perhaps the most impressive of all—the house where Frédéric Chopin died in 1849, in the Place Vendôme, a few strides from the Rue de Rivoli and the Tuileries and just opposite the original Ritz Hotel. The only thing that you had to be was sharp-eyed enough to notice that the Paris headquarters of IOS had anything to do with IOS at all.

"Banque Rothschild, Division des Programmes d'Investissement," is what it says most prominently on the brass plaques outside the entrance to number 11 Place Vendôme. Underneath is the discreet annotation: *"Assistance Technique IOS."* In France, Bernie Cornfeld, scourge of the Establishment, hid behind the skirts of the most established financial dowager of them all.

This policy has certainly paid off in terms of sales, though not yet in terms of profits. France was the last major market in Western Europe that IOS had never been allowed to penetrate.* It was able to do so in the end only by suppressing its own name and to a great extent its own personality in a fifty-fifty joint venture with the Paris House of Rothschild.

It was a shrewd move. Two of the safer generalizations about the French are that they by no means share the Germans' predisposition to admire all things American—but that they do have a deep faith in the financial acumen of the Rothschilds.

The Rothschild link enabled IOS to get permission to sell in France. It helped the salesmen to get their foot into French doors. And it prevented sales in France from being damaged by the IOS crisis to the same extent that they were in countries where IOS was clearly identified.

Rothschild-Expansion did not come into existence until the summer of 1969. The sales force did not take to the road until October. Within three months the IOS-trained salesmen doubled the net asset value of the fund from $6.4 million to $12.7 million. And the volume of sales continued to flourish through the spring in spite of all the news from Geneva. In April, Rothschild-Expansion salesmen sold some $25 million face value, and by the end of 1970 the net asset value stood at $69 million. The salesmen themselves were in no doubt of the reason. "In France," said Jacques van ler Berghe, a branch manager, in the autumn of 1970, "we have had a different situation than in IOS generally, because the public was not directly af-

---

*Belgium is the most important market IOS was never able to penetrate: in Spain and Portugal as we have seen it did so only temporarily.

fected by the IOS crisis. Much of the public does not connect IOS with Rothschild-Expansion."

Nevertheless, however much it may have suited both IOS and Rothschild to pretend that IOS wasn't IOS, the origins of this respectable operation can be traced back to a typical rambunctious IOS hot-money, capital-flight operation in an underdeveloped country—the Philippines, of all places.

. . .

Rothschild-Expansion owes its existence chiefly to two men. One of them is Paul Vincent, the young managing director of the Banque Rothschild. Vincent has been very much the spearhead of the Paris Rothschilds' determination to modernize their gigantic business. One of the principal directions in which the barons Guy, Alain, and Yves de Rothschild and M. Vincent have decided as a matter of policy to move the bank is into what might be called the consumer end of banking. To this end, the bank has, for example, opened several new branches for the first time in its history. It has created an enormous new complex of modern offices in the Rue Lafitte, which seems to symbolize a desire to leave behind the image of conservatism and secrecy that is traditional with private banks in Europe.

Mutual-fund management fitted in with Paul Vincent's conception of Rothschilds' future development. And he was particularly attracted by what seemed to be IOS's impressive expertise in sales.

The Rothschilds were also aware of how profitable the purely banking business brought in by mutual funds might be. The Banque Rothschild had been acting as Custodian and Bankers to Fonditalia since it started in September 1967.

IOS had made previous attempts to register a national fund in France. An application was made in 1967 but was turned down by the French authorities. The French government in the days of Charles de Gaulle did not want investment companies in France controlled by foreigners. And that was that. There was also the additional problem that French law permitted no more than 4.75 per cent to be deducted as a sales load.

What had been impossible for IOS, however, was easy for the Rothschilds. They decided to go in with IOS in January 1969. They formally asked for official authorization in May, and they got it in July. Specifically, the arrangement was for IOS and Rothschild to split profits and losses equally, both on the sales side and on the management of the funds. It was also proposed to buy the Paris affiliate of the Swiss-Israel Trade Bank for 45 million francs (about $10 million) as the IOS bank in France.

The man who set up the sales operation was Alain Berrier; it was he who came from the Philippines. Outwardly, Berrier can show all the badges of membership in the French technocratic elite. Tall and thin, he is a graduate of the Ecole Polytechnique in Paris and the Harvard Business School. And he has the tidy mind and precise speech that these two institutions stamp on their pupils. But Berrier has an attractively unorthodox side to him. After graduating from Harvard he went around the world, doing odd jobs and playing the guitar to pay his way. In February 1965, he found himself in Japan, broke, and saw an IOS advertisement in the paper. He signed up as a salesman, and worked with the foreign business community in Japan for nine months.

He is an ambitious young man and when he saw that he could never hope to rise to be a GM in Japan, it was agreed that he should move on and try his luck in the Philippines.

When he arrived there, there was a small IOS sales force at work, doing $500,000–700,000 worth of business a month, according to Harold Becker, who was then the manager. They were selling mainly to the American military market at Clark Air Force base (one of the main rear bases for the Vietnam war). Becker made it plain to Berrier in their first conversation that in his opinion it wasn't even worth trying to sell to Filipinos; it was not clearly illegal to do so at that time, but most of the IOS salesmen were only in the Philippines on two-month tourist visas. Shortly after Berrier arrived, Becker had to leave, because his wife was caught overstaying a visa. A typical IOS row developed over the succession, with Cornfeld and Cantor called in by the rival factions.

Berrier had already discovered that his American colleagues were wrong: you could sell to Filipinos. "I refuted their hypothesis," was his way of putting it. In the end he solved the hierarchical dispute in a way which is not recommended at the Harvard Business School. He simply drove a truck down to the IOS office in the middle of the night—it was during a typhoon—and removed all his papers. In practice, from then on, the military market went its way, and Berrier and his group sold to the Filipinos. Over the next eight months, sales went up from $600,000 a month to $2.8 million a month. The more Berrier and his men sold, the more the Central Bank worried about the flight of capital involved and tightened up the currency controls. And the more the bank turned the screw, the more business boomed. Finally, early in 1968, the Central Bank put out a last circular which made the whole operation indisputably illegal.

"I decided to play a last throw," Berrier said. He pointed out to us that it was a considerable gamble, since not only was his operation illegal because of exchange control: he had only a tourist visa, and he was paying no income tax.

He went to the Central Bank, and explained to the director of foreign exchange that because of the front-end load, if all the Filipinos who had taken out systematic programs were forbidden to keeping them going, they would lose money on their investments. He succeeded in persuading the official to give him permission to continue to take in monthly payments on all programs initiated before the date of the meeting.

"It was a bluff," Berrier admitted to us. He simply made an arrangement with the IOS computer programmer at Nyon for all programs sold in the Philippines to be antedated to earlier months—and went on selling.

Clearly, the days of the Philippine market were numbered. It had always been Berrier's ambition to get back to France and set up an IOS operation there. It so happened that Henry Carnegie, one of the lawyers who had been taken on by James Roosevelt's IOS Development Ltd., came out to Manila. Carnegie was the man charged with examining the possibility of getting into France. Berrier urged on Carnegie his own conviction that the only way to get into France was to do it with Frenchmen. With the Rothschilds as partners and with a wholly French sales force,* Berrier argued, the French government's opposition would melt away.

And so it proved. The operation was enormously successful for Berrier. By May 1970 he was listed by Allen Cantor as one of fewer than a dozen IOS people who would be affected if no one was allowed to earn more than $100,000 a year. It has been satisfactorily successful for the Rothschilds too, and they are happy at the way it has turned out. But the connection between the highly respectable sales operation they run together today and the freebooting capital-flight phase of IOS's history is plain and direct.

Understandably, the Americans who ran IOS were used to

---

*Of the fifteen original managers, fourteen were French, and one Swiss. This contrasts sharply with the dominance of the American managers in Germany.

something relatively close to uniformity in the laws governing mutual funds as among the fifty states, and they found the diversity of the legal situation in Europe both puzzling and irritating. Holland and Belgium are a case in point.

In Belgium the law forbade any mutual fund, foreign or domestic, to sell its shares unless both the fund itself and its promotional literature had been approved by the Belgian Banking Commission. No offshore fund ever won that approval—though *Fortune* magazine found that no less than twenty-three funds followed up a coupon sent from a Brussels address in answer to their advertisements in an international newspaper.

IOS made repeated attempts to change the Banking Commission's mind, but the Belgians would not budge. They had sent to the SEC in Washington for all the material it could give them on mutual funds in general and IOS in particular, and having studied this material, they could not be persuaded to allow IOS to sell in Belgium.

Eventually, IOS accepted defeat on mutual funds and tried to make up for it with other "products." In March 1970, George Landau persuaded the sales company board to pass a resolution for "an all-out effort" in the insurance business in Belgium and also for a real-estate project there, "since we cannot sell our present funds." The crash came before anything resulted from those plans, and Belgium never experienced an IOS sales force.

In Holland, on the other hand, foreign mutual funds could be, and were, freely sold. Holland was, in fact, the first European country where the IOS sales force "followed the clients home": George Landau had acquired a substantial number of Dutch clients who worked for the Shell group or Unilever in West Africa when he was there, and he says it was they who first suggested to him the possibility of selling to Europeans in their own countries. It was a lucky contact: the prospects for IOS in

Holland, a country with a strong currency and therefore with no insuperable regulations against investing abroad, were as promising as anywhere in Europe.

A number of IOS men—Allen Cantor, Richard Gangel, the inevitable Ellenport—had made swift sweeps through Holland before 1961. But it was Landau who first organized Holland as a systematic sales operation. (It is a graphic illustration of the personal, quasi-feudal character of the IOS sales organization that Landau's territory ran literally "from Greenland's icy mountains" to "where Africa's sunny fountains roll down their golden sand." Nigeria, Liberia, Morocco, Holland, and Iceland have little in common. But because Landau had helped to bring the gospel to each of them, all continued to pay him tribute.) In 1961, the Amsterdam Bank H. Albert de Bary, whose dignified eighteenth-century bankhouse is reflected from the waters of the Herengracht canal, became custodian of securities for IIT. About a year later Landau got permission to sell in Holland.

The prestige of the de Bary Bank was tempting for the salesmen. "IOS constantly tried to use our name in their publicity," a director of the bank told us, and added that he was repeatedly obliged to insist on editing IOS sales literature to cut out subtle language intended to suggest that de Bary guaranteed the *quality* of the fund's investments, where in fact, of course, it merely guaranteed their physical self-custody.

Nevertheless, IOS sales continued both legally and profitably, having their greatest success, as in most places where sales were legitimate, with self-employed people such as doctors, dentists, and businessmen. The only problem was that Dutch law required that foreign shares be held, not by the client directly, but on his behalf by a Dutch bank. IOS got one of the large Dutch deposit banks to perform this role.

IOS ran into criticism in Holland from an unexpected direction. *Consumentengids* is the magazine published by the Dutch Consumers Association; it is roughly analogous to the British *Which?* or the American *Consumer Reports*. In its May 1966 issue, *Consumentengids* published perhaps the sharpest and most sophisticated critique of the Fund of Funds to be published in Europe before the spring of 1970. It began by pointing out the inherent dangers in any offshore fund. Where, for example, could an investor protect his rights? It quoted the SEC's doubts, and then cited seven examples of what it regarded as misleading propaganda used by IOS in Holland: on which it commented that "the least that can be said is that it is very one-sided." It tried to estimate the true charge structure on the Fund of Funds, and concluded that the Dutch government ought to forbid the selling of such funds, and that until it did, "we have only one piece of advice: hands off IOS and the Fund of Funds."

IOS immediately sued, claiming that the article was defamatory, inaccurate, insinuating, and unlawful. In The Hague, the court of first instance disagreed. On just one point it found IOS's complaint justified: it found that the article had gone too far in claiming that because of tax provisions Dutch investors would necessarily lose money. On that one point, the magazine was ordered to publish a correction. But IOS was sentenced to pay four-fifths of the costs. The lower court's verdict was an undeniable defeat, and IOS appealed.

The appeal was never heard, because the parties settled out of court. In January 1967 *Consumentengids* published an article which was the result of long conversations between Consumers Association staff and IOS management. It was noticeably less sharp in tone, and conceded several points to IOS. IOS in turn claimed to have reformed certain practices and improved its sales literature. The magazine did not, however, withdraw its serious over-all reservations about IOS: it ended its article by saying that it was impossible to make any prediction about the future.

In spite of this case, which received a good deal of publicity in Holland (far too much, in Landau's outraged view), sales continued satisfactorily. In both 1967 and 1968, Holland accounted for 2 per cent of IOS's worldwide sales, a handy contribution for a country with less than 13 million people.

In March 1969 IOS set up a Dutch subsidiary with its own "product." This was IVM Invest Management, organized, the reader will not by now be surprised to learn, under the laws of the Netherlands Antilles, and managing a fund which was used as the vehicle for insurance policies sold by a Dutch insurance subsidiary in Holland.

• • •

The logic of sales took IOS into Sweden in the person of Bret Davidson, another of the veterans who became weary of the adventures inseparable from "financial counseling" in undeveloped countries. Davidson asked Bernie Cornfeld for a solid territory to manage, and Cornfeld gave him Sweden, even though a market study suggested it would never be a very good market. There was an imperial simplicity about those years.

Davidson was living in some style on a yacht which he keeps in the harbor at Cannes on the French Riviera, and he at first proposed to run Sweden as an absentee landlord from there. Eventually he was persuaded that this might not be popular with the Swedes, and he consented to move to Stockholm.

Then he brought off a great coup. Late in 1968 he was introduced to Count Carl Johan Bernadotte, who is a cousin of the King of Sweden. The story is that Davidson asked for advice from the Count, who is a prominent businessman, about starting a fund in Sweden, and was astonished to learn that

Bernadotte would be happy to join the IOS Board. James Roosevelt was even more astonished to learn that Davidson, who had started life as a sailor, had netted a fish that had slipped through the meshes of his diplomatic skein.

In the meantime, two lawyers had been dispatched to the north and reported that prospects there were better than anyone had dared to hope. There was no problem with Swedish law, and for once the local Establishment was helpful. IOS found itself in association with all three of the big Swedish banks, Stockholm's Enskilda Bank (the one controlled by the legendary Wallenberg dynasty), the Skandinaviska Bank, and the Handelsbank.

A Swedish national fund was set up, called Interfond. But the long-term plan was for an all-Scandinavian or Nordic Fund. Individual national funds in each of the Scandinavian countries would, it was hoped by the planners in Roosevelt's Development Ltd., eventually merge to form this bigger fund. They actually got as far as getting a charter for a Norwegian Fund, which has never actually materialized. In fact, Roosevelt and his men exaggerated the speed with which the Scandinavian countries were moving toward Nordic Union, which would have included free-capital movement between the member countries. Nordic Union slowed down and stopped: so did IOS's plans for a Nordic Fund.

• • •

By 1969, then, Western Europe was not only staked out into sales territories. The prospectors had long done their work. Shafts had been sunk in all promising lodes, and the mining of savings had reached an industrial scale. The craft industry of the sales operation in Latin America and the Middle East, relic of the days when people in IOS still thought $5 million a month was a lot of sales, faded into insignificance in comparison with the volume men like Kunkler and Schneider were achieving in Germany.

One vast tract of utterly virgin territory remained to tempt the ambition of 119 Rue de Lausanne, where people were beginning to live in a world of strangely unreal dreams. In the final spiraling climb to the wild blue yonder, IOS began to dream of the last great untapped market: the 150 million inhabitants of Eastern Europe.

For some time, Bernie Cornfeld's own imagination had been tickled by the notion of bringing the benefits of People's Capitalism to the Communist countries. It appealed at once to his more high-flown ideological notions and to the impish side of him. As early as December 1964, the *IOS Bulletin* referred to an itinerant salesman who had sold a few investment programs to people in the Western embassies in Moscow as "the IOS man" there.

Our colleague Murray Sayle, visiting Cornfeld as an old friend in 1967, was given a demonstration of this. Sayle had just come back from Moscow, where he had been working solely as a reporter; Cornfeld hustled him into a meeting of IOS managers from various parts of the world and introduced him proudly, but to Sayle's considerable surprise, as "Our Man from Moscow."

It was some of the people in James Roosevelt's Development Ltd. who first thought they had found a way to adapt the national fund, their universal jimmy for levering their way into a closed market, to a Communist economy. One of the top people in Roosevelt's entourage met, by chance, a German businessman who had shifted some of his expensive modern plant down to Yugoslavia, where he was helping the Yugoslav economy, and at the same time improving his profit ratio because of the low cost of labor there. Checking, the IOS man found to his surprise that

Yugoslavia had recently accepted similar industrial partnership deals with several West German and Italian firms. Such joint ventures might provide the vehicles a national fund would need to enable it to promise to invest a percentage of its money in Yugoslavia.

Roosevelt was tremendously excited by the idea of a Yugo-Fund. In March, the IOS Board was told that there were a number of possibilities in Yugoslavia, including not only a fund but also "an underwriting." That would have been a notable "first" in a Communist country. On May 1, 1969, he announced publicly in the Bremen town hall that he had been down to Belgrade to work out a plan "which should contribute to solving some of Yugoslavia's problems. In Belgrade," the master diplomat went on, "we had to listen to an hour-long eulogy of socialism, but in the end even our colleagues in the Yugoslav government were all ears for our capitalist methods."

Roosevelt described how IOS through its Indevco real-estate subsidiary hoped to finance resort hotels and beach bungalows on the Montenegrin coast. And he talked, rather less precisely, about distributing road-building machinery and "improving the infrastructure."

The greatest appeal for IOS was that his investment in Yugoslavia would enable IOS to tap the savings of Yugoslav *Gastarbeiter* (temporary immigrant workers) in West Germany. But IOS apparently also hoped to get Yugoslavs inside Yugoslavia to invest in the IOS Yugoslav Fund as well.

As in Persia and Portugal, this strategy of penetration was to be sweetened by the activities of John M. King. As early as January, when Roosevelt first put up the Yugoslav project to the executive management committee, he was asked to find out whether King Resources were interested before discussing the matter with the Yugoslavs further. It turned out that King was interested, up to a point, in financing oil exploration in the Adriatic.

None of this came off, in the end. But Yugo-Fund, bizarre as it may sound, was seriously discussed, at least on the IOS side. Roosevelt managed to get some kind of a tentative green light from President Tito, and visited Belgrade more than once (taking several members of his staff with him) for talks with the Yugoslav central bank and economic planners.

That was the high tide of ambition so far as Eastern Europe was concerned. It is true that James Roosevelt eagerly discussed with his colleagues the possibility of setting up a national fund in Czechoslovakia in 1968. But the Russians moved in before he could. And although there was similar talk within Development Ltd. of setting up a Romanian Fund, that too never reached the point where any approaches were made to the Romanian government.

Yet, even unfulfilled, such flights of fancy were symptomatic of the vaulting mood in IOS as 1968 turned to 1969. One could hardly blame Roosevelt's men for dreaming dreams. For it was a time when the sales force was expanding in geometric progressions: and on the investment side, IOS had begun to move in a world where men seemed to believe they had repealed the law of gravity.

17

The Master Financiers

In which we investigate "the best investment advice $2 billion can buy." IOS and its stock-market speculations—stoking the flames of the conglomerate blaze. IOS goes into investment banking, which is bad luck for the customers.

I n 1966 Fred Alger received an invitation from Sam Clapp, tax adviser to IOS and husband of Martica Clapp, to spend a holiday at the Clapps' house on Paradise Island.

Alger, who was then in his early thirties, had reached New York from San Francisco a couple of years before. In San Francisco he had managed the investments of the Winfield Fund and within a few months he had become the hottest fund manager in New York. In 1965 the Security Equity Fund, which Alger handled, appreciated in value more than any other fund. The fresh-faced young investment expert, whose normal working garb is shirt sleeves and suspenders, was soon in great demand, and he was a natural recruit for IOS. At the end of 1965 Alger was approached by C. Henry Buhl III, the investment director of IOS, and asked if he would like to handle one of the ingenious proprietary funds through which the Fund of Funds money was now invested.* After a breakfast meeting with Bernard Cornfeld, Alger agreed to take on a slice of the Fund of Funds. "We'll call it the Alger Fund," said Cornfeld, "so we'll know the schmuck to blame if it goes wrong."

The stock markets were shaky in the year Alger got his invitation from Clapp, and so he had to stay in New York working to keep his funds high up in the charts. But in 1967 the markets rose again, and Alger decided he could take that Bahamas holiday.

Paradise Island is separated from Nassau by a strip of water just four hundred yards wide. The only way to get across in those days was by boat, and as Alger was being ferried across he saw that a large bridge was being built across the narrows. He asked Clapp who was building the bridge and what was it all about. Clapp told him that a company called Mary Carter Paint was going to develop the island, and was starting with the bridge.

Sam Clapp had a particular interest in Mary Carter Paint: in July 1966 one of his companies, Fiduciary Trust, had acquired $100,000 of Mary Carter's promissory notes. And a private fund run by Clapp, Fiduciary Growth Fund, also took up $100,000 of these notes, which carried the right to be converted into common shares at a rate of $5 per share.

Fred Alger was intrigued, and when he got back to New York he went to see the Chairman of Mary Carter Paint. Paradise Island, formerly Hog Island, had been purchased from Huntington Hartford. The little paint company was being used as a shell to acquire the island and turn it into a holiday resort complete with hotels, a golf club, and yachting marinas. The

---

*See Chapter 7, "The Birth of a Superfund" and Chapter 9, "They May Be Schmucks, but They're the Government."

cornerstone of the scheme was to be the development of a casino on the island, and the company had managed to acquire a license for this from the Bahamian government, then still controlled by Sir Stafford Sands, though he was nominally only the Finance Minister and Head of Tourism. On the strength of all this, Mary Carter Paint was going to change its name to Resorts International.

This was a classic hot-stock recipe of the period, and Alger decided that Resorts would be a good investment. In June 1967, he bought two large blocks of shares at $9.50 each: 268,000 for the Fund of Funds and 100,000 for his own Security Equity Fund. These were not registered shares: instead of being bought through the stock market, they were bought in a private agreement with the company. This meant that the Fund of Funds had a large investment—$2,546,000—which could only be disposed of in another private placement.

For its help in arranging the two placements with Alger and for agreeing to convert some of the notes it owned into shares, Fiduciary Trust (of which Ed Cowett was by now a director) received a "finder's fee" of $70,000. Fiduciary Trust was rather active in Resorts shares, and just before Alger's deal, it acquired a parcel of 56,000, also unregistered, at $7 each, acting as nominee for a private family interest and for Clapp's Fiduciary Growth Fund. (Nearly a year later the Growth Fund sold 25,000 Resorts shares to the Stamo Foundation, in which C. Henry Buhl III of IOS was a participant.)

The Fund of Funds' customers would have received a swift profit on their Resorts shares if the fund had only been able to sell them in 1968, when the price hit $50. But the stock could not be sold through the exchanges until it had been registered with the SEC, and registration was held up while the Commission looked into a couple of dealings in the shares.

The first trouble came in summer 1968. The SEC learned that some of the Resorts stock, which had been issued as promissory notes and then converted into shares, had been sold while still unregistered through the American Stock Exchange, the second and less prestigious of the New York exchanges. (This was done without the knowledge of the Resorts management, who was furious.) The Commission obtained consent injunctions against Fiduciary Growth Fund and Fiduciary Trust making any such sales in the future.

A larger row came to a head on March 10, 1969, when the American Stock Exchange suspended trading in Resorts shares for three weeks or so, while Resorts clarified some transactions in the shares of Pan American World Airways. Resorts was proposing to buy up two huge blocks of Pan Am shares, with options to buy still more which would have made it the airline's biggest shareholder. The take-over fever was still active in the stock markets when suddenly the story spread that Resorts International was going to make a bid for Pan American. At that time, it seemed just credible that a newborn casino company might take over the world's biggest international airline. Bills were quickly introduced in Congress to prevent anyone doing such a thing: the fuss only died down when Resorts management declared that it had no interest in acquiring Pan Am stock, except as an investment.

The story of Mary Carter's translation into Resorts International and its subsequent career is representative of investment business in the 1960s, and especially of that part of it which most fascinated IOS and its friends, advisers, and executives. Virtually all the elements are present: the ebullient young money manager, eager to make the value of his funds grow fast; the inside tip to a developing bonanza; the "special situation," in which a stock is created as promissory notes and then switched by complex means into shares; the expansive deals in unregistered securities; the network of private contacts and suggestions, with those "in the know" busily exchanging paper and "finder's fees"; the wild take-over rumors; and, as always, a "concept" at the heart of the enterprise—in this case, the idea that a gambling license bestowed by an acquiescent government would cause sensational adjustments to the value of a strip of sand and palm trees. There was also the problem of legislative and governmental interference, preventing the master financiers from reaping their full reward—although, as was mostly the case, the financiers did rather better than the customers.

After its rise to $61, and the suspension of trading, the share price of Resorts International was never quite the same again. Eventually, it emerged that the tourists were not quite as compulsively attracted to Paradise Island as had been anticipated, and a new government appeared in the Bahamas and decided to increase the dues on the casino license. By September 1970 Resorts International had fallen below $10, and the Fund of Funds' investment was worth less than half its purchase price. Still, there were times when the breaks, by accident or design, went the other way.

Fred Alger's interest in gambling stocks was not confined to Resorts International, and by the end of 1968 he had 20 per cent of his Fund of Funds money in gambling. He bought a large stake in Parvin/Dohrmann, the one-time Los Angeles supplier of hotel equipment which became the operator of three casinos in Las Vegas and one of the most controversial stocks of 1969.

Alger was introduced to Parvin/Dohrmann by Delbert W. Coleman, a lawyer from Ohio, who made a fortune with a juke-box and pin-ball company, Seeburg Corporation, which we shall encounter later in this chapter. In late October 1968 Coleman agreed to buy 300,000 shares in Parvin/Dohrmann, effectively the controlling interest. He was not acting alone, but with and for a group which included Allen & Co., the New York investment bankers; the actress Jill St. John; and a Chicago lawyer, Sidney Korshak. It was natural that Coleman should offer Alger, the purchaser of Resorts, the opportunity to take up some of the block of shares. Alger bought 81,000 for the Fund of Funds at $35 each: a $2,835,000 investment.

To run the company Coleman brought in William Scott, who had been the youngest partner in Arthur Andersen & Co., Parvin/Dohrmann's auditors. They bought another casino, the Stardust, for which Sidney Korshak got a finder's fee of $500,000. The stock took off—possibly those in the know on Wall Street were calling it "a moon job," in the jargon of the time. In spring 1969 it reached its peak of $141 per share.

Just before the peak, the Nevada State Gambling Board declared that the Fund of Funds must sell its Parvin/Dohrmann stock. The reason was that FOF had a large stake in another gambling company outside Nevada, namely Resorts International. The board did not want gambling companies in Nevada to have any connections with others out of state.

The forced sale meant that the Fund of Funds had to accept $90 per share, instead of the market price of $126, but this still left a tidy profit of $4,455,000 on the deal. And in this case, regulatory action had prompted a sound financial decision—because in May the SEC suspended trading in Parvin/Dohrmann shares for a week, complaining that Delbert Coleman had made insufficient disclosures at the time of his acquisition. When trading was resumed, the price slipped until it reached $65, at which point the SEC suspended it again, with the allegation that the stock had been manipulated. The charges were settled by means of a consent injunction, but early in 1970 Coleman resigned, in order to improve relations with the SEC and the American Stock

Exchange. By March 1970, Parvin/Dohrmann's price was still down at $71. The large profits made at various times on deals in Parvin stock remained a sore point with the SEC and with the company's new management, who proceeded to file suit against several people and institutions. The Fund of Funds was among them: Parvin/Dohrmann sued for return of the $4,455,000 profit on the ground that the deal involved insider trading.

There was little in the original concept of the Fund of Funds to suggest that it would turn into the kind of speculative investment that was epitomized in the stormy history of the gambling stocks. Originally, it was invested only in large, strictly controlled public mutual funds. We have already seen how this was changed with the introduction of the proprietary funds, with short-selling techniques, and with a system of performance fees. The IOS funds, which were virtually unregulated in comparison with domestic U.S. funds, thus became a magnet for every stock-market operator with a "special situation" to promote. But the commitment of IOS to the cult of "performance"—or to short-term capital gain, at all costs—went further than that.

As "Adam Smith" recorded in *The Money Game*, the idea of "performance" crystallized in the public mind at the moment when Gerry Tsai left the Fidelity Group of Boston early in 1966 to launch his own Manhattan Fund. The young investment adviser from Shanghai became the first of a galaxy of money-management stars: from that moment on, running investment funds was a matter of acute personal competition, in which each man strove to make the value of his fund rise faster than the next man's. The implications soon went beyond anything Jack Dreyfus had done with the Dreyfus Fund.

Fred Alger grasped the situation soon after he arrived in New York. He set out to promote himself as a hot money manager, and get his fund right to the top of the growth table: that was the only way to get the dealers to sell it. He succeeded—but it was a business in which new stars were continually being outshone by newer, brighter ones. There was Fred Carr, working from Los Angeles, applying an invention of his own which he called the "risk/return formula," and which looked marvelous while Carr was building up his Enterprise Fund from under $30 to almost $1 billion by the end of 1968. (It looked less marvelous in 1969, when the value per share of Enterprise dropped more than 30 per cent and Carr faded from the scene.) In San Francisco, David Meid carried on at the Winfield Fund. Meid once said that he could beat the Dow-Jones market average by 30 per cent in any given year; he did not specify whether he meant going up or going down, and perhaps it did not matter because he did both. The net asset value per share of the Winfield Fund increased by 80 per cent in 1967 and 13 per cent in 1968. (It dropped by 32 per cent by the end of 1969.)

Cornfeld and Cowett adopted the star system with unsurpassed enthusiasm. They hired a number of the hottest money managers, including both Fred Carr and David Meid, and made them compete with each other while working for IOS. Each was handed a chunk of money, and told that he had a free hand, so long as he produced large capital gains. The managers were not only rewarded according to how much gain they made: those who recorded the biggest gains were given more money to handle, while those who made smaller gains had it taken away.

"You cannot imagine the demands that were made on us for performance," said Fred Alger ruefully after he had been abruptly fired by IOS in March 1970. The effect of IOS's supercompetitive system was, of course, to eliminate any practical possibility of fund managers working for the long-term capital growth which IOS talked to its customers about. The only way to achieve "performance" was to buy into the right hot stock at the right time, sell out of it before its collapse, and then be on into the next hot stock before anyone else. What kept prices up was other funds buying, and what knocked prices down was funds selling. An actual company was behind each hot stock— but what that company was doing, if anything, ceased to matter.

One of Alger's competitors at managing a slice of the Fund of Funds said, "We bought stocks at $90, not because they were worth $90, but because we knew that tomorrow they would be at $120. When we went home nights, we just hoped the god-damned company would still be there the next morning." The real pressure fell on those who slipped behind in IOS's lists. One of their investment managers in London, where the same competitive system was used, said, "If you were bottom one year and knew you would have all your money taken away unless you came up with a real winner, the only thing to do was to punt it all on some outside chance, like Poseidon, in a last desperate attempt to catch up." (Poseidon was the classic share of the boom in Australian nickel mines. It went from 20 Australian cents per share to £140 on the London Stock Exchange, then fell back to a low of £15 per share.)

The life of an IOS fund manager certainly had its ups and downs. Alger was originally given $5 million of the Fund of Funds in December 1965. By the end of 1967 it had become $82 million, and by the end of 1968, $95.9 million. Then by the end of 1969 it was down to $40.3 million, and he was fired in March 1970. David Meid started with IOS in October 1967, and by the end of the year he had $22 million to handle. At the end of the next year it was up to $81.2 million. In addition, he later received a large chunk of the new special-risk Venture Fund International. By the end of 1969 Meid's piece of the Fund of Funds was just over $19 million. Dean Milosis and Carlyle Jones managed the first of all the FOF Proprietary funds, the York Fund, which had $61.3 million when they gave up. Martin Solomon, who ran the Hedge Fund Account of the Fund of Funds, had $48.3 million at the end of 1968, but only $9.3 million at the end of 1969.

Both Fred Carr, the man with the "risk/return formula" and Douglas Fletcher, his colleague at Shareholders' Management in Los Angeles, also handled money for IOS. Up to the end of 1968, anyway, the markets were mostly rising, and there was plenty of money for everybody. "It was a beautiful period," Fred Alger remembered. "We were impressed with the war babies. There was a new individualist sense, a greater sense of competitive enterprise, a sense of armies of entrepreneurs. You could *see* them.

"Of course," he added, "some of them were good, some of them were bad, like any people."

But no matter if some of them were bad, there were always new promotions, new hot stocks to take the place of the ones that turned cold. There were computer companies, leasing companies, and gambling companies. There were franchising, and fast food, and modular building, and prefabricated homes to beat the housing shortage. There were more nursing homes (shades of Geriatric Services) and even real hospitals, followed by environmental stocks and the antipollution companies. And of course there were the conglomerates, who were in everything.

The underlying cause of the euphoria Alger felt was the flood of money pouring into the markets from "institutional investors," of which the pension funds were the largest, and the "performance-oriented" mutual funds were the most aggressive in their investment policy. This certainly created a remarkable demand for shares. In 1950, institutional investors spent only $700 million on buying stock. In 1968 they spent $12.6 *billion*. According to IOS and the other enthusiasts for equity shareholding by the common man, this process was "investing in the development of American industry"—but it was not quite so simple as that. During 1968, when the funds put up so much money, American corporations bought back, or canceled, more equity shares than they issued, so that the number of shares available actually declined. Indeed, over the whole of the 1960s, institutional investors' purchases were greater than the net amount of new stock issued. Therefore, much of the trading consisted of existing shares changing hands at higher and higher prices, a process which perhaps contributed more to the development of the securities industry than of any other.

It appears that the funds were preaching the idea of the widest possible participation in equity shares, or common stock, at a time when American corporations were increasingly reluctant to raise money by issuing them. Many large corporations were able to finance themselves out of profits: in general, corporations preferred to raise money by issuing fixed-interest securities, or "debt" securities (such as bonds and debentures in various forms) while restricting the supplies of their common stock available on the market.

It was because of this desire for restriction that a substantial part of the equity shares that were available came out as "unregistered" stock, or "letter stock," of the kind created in Fred Alger's deal with Mary Carter Paint, and of which IOS funds were enthusiastic buyers. One advantage, from the viewpoint of a corporation issuing unregistered shares, is that it avoids the tedious and possibly embarrassing process of getting the SEC's approval on the prospectus necessary for a public issue. Another advantage arises from the dynamics of the market.

A company raising capital by the public issue of new shares obviously increases the supply of its shares on the market. The effect of the increased supply may be to cause the price of the company's existing shares to drop on the exchange: an acute embarrassment, when a high quoted price may be the index of corporate potency, and the crucial weapon on a take-over battle.

By placing a large block of shares with a fund manager, in a private sale, new cash is raised while the market price is left undisturbed. And this helps the fund manager, who cannot normally finish buying a large block of some attractive security without his own increased demand pushing up the price against him. In an unregistered purchase, the fund manager can buy a large block at an agreed price below the market rate. He then hopes to see the company's quoted price move up, through the effect of demand on a still restricted supply. All going well, the shares can be registered and sold at a profit.

The danger of unregistered shares is that until that moment the fund can only sell them in another private transaction—which may mean, in effect, not at all. Thus they can seriously compromise the basic liquidity of the open-end fund concept. (In December 1968, the Mates Fund of New York had to suspend redemption of its shares for some time, as a consequence of heavy investments in unregistered shares.) The managers of ordinary American funds, however, found letter stock an attractive idea, because it offered the rapid capital gains, or "performance" they were seeking. Of course, the other risk involved was that a collapse of confidence, while eroding the values of publicly quoted stock, might altogether destroy the value of letter stock, thus adding to the dynamics of speculative collapse. Despite this, it made a powerful appeal to any fund manager, aware that he stood to receive more investment from the public if he showed better short-term performance.

Letter stock was almost irresistible for an IOS manager. Not only was he required to outperform a number of other managers just to retain his position: also, he was directly rewarded by performance. IOS took "performance fees" out of the fund money, at the rate of 10 per cent of all gains recorded and passed a large slice of this to the managers. This money was paid even if the gain was purely in terms of book value. Alger, in other words, received a percentage of the gains on Resorts International, even though the Fund of Funds made a loss on the deal in the end. Performance fees of this kind are not permitted in publicly offered U.S. mutual funds: large-scale use of them was one of IOS's special contributions to the speculative atmosphere of the U.S. investment business.

The performance-fee system made a buoyant faith such as Fred Alger's a valuable commodity. In a single year Alger received over $500,000 for his achievements with the Fund of Funds.

With the passage of time, fund managers' appetites for letter stock grew, because it became harder to get swift gains out of orthodox stocks. The market of the latter 1960s was mostly high, but not easy. Having soared almost without interruption out of the pit of 1962, the Dow-Jones average index reached the magic 1000 at the beginning of 1966. But then it sagged, and took nearly three years to climb precariously back to 1000. The Dow Jones, of course, is only the average of thirty valuable but orthodox securities quoted on the New York Stock Exchange, and no doubt David Meid was right to say that it can be outpaced in terms of capital gains—but which were the securities with which to do it?

If there was one process that kept the market and the hot managers alive during that time, it was the wheeling and dealing, the tender offers, the mergers and battles of the conglomerates. Again, this was something into which IOS was drawn: partly because many of the smaller conglomerates liked to raise money by letter stock, but for other reasons as well. As in most things the IOS people did, the hectic pace of their operations helped to enlarge the limits of the possible or of the apparently possible.

The original justification of the conglomerate idea was that a corporation with striking financial and managerial expertise should deploy it in many different markets by acquiring numerous subsidiaries. Such expertise, it was said, could be applied equally to building typewriters, managing real estate, or selling life insurance: this was the concept of "synergy" and the belief that a properly constructed whole would add up to more than the sum of the parts. No doubt it had some validity, but the idea of buying other companies that would fit into a complementary but diversified group degenerated rapidly. If Resorts International had actually taken over Pan Am, there would have been more "industrial logic" in it than in many a conglomerate deal.

The process developed to a point where any company with a high quoted share price could take over one with a lower price: it merely purchased a controlling segment of the victim's stock by offering its own, more expensive, stock in exchange. And the price of the conglomerate's share was in turn maintained by the very rapidity of the growth it achieved through such maneuvers. Of course, it was part of the proposition that the companies taken over should be reorganized to achieve bigger profits, thus increasing the profitability of the whole. But in the rush of events, it was often hard to see whether that was happening. A good many conglomerates talked freely about computerized decision-making, "concentricity of interest," and "project redeployment of assets." Many people found their explanations of these terms as incomprehensible as their balance sheets. Existing accounting systems, according to Jimmy Ling of Ling-Temco-Vought, were inadequate to reflect what the conglomerates were about. "As for those who can't keep up with our changing financial structure," he said, "well, that's their problem."

The vital role of the conglomerate's quoted share price explains the penchant for unregistered securities when the need arose to find cash (and although shares could be used as a kind of "funny money," cash was eventually required if only in order to pay the bills). Tremendous efforts were made to augment the company's leverage—to restrict as tightly as possible the supply of public common stock with a right to share in the increased profits of the great expansion being engineered. To this end, huge bank loans were raised, and important executives spent their time hurrying from one bank to another, continually arranging new loans to pay off the last lot. And, where the smaller conglomerates resorted to unregistered share placements, the big conglomerates raised cash through fixed-interest debt securities, selling many elaborate breeds of bonds, debentures, and notes. These usually carried, like Sam Clapp's notes from Mary Carter Paint, rights to be converted into common stock at various rates and various times. Thus some compromise was made: new investors were granted the hope of eventual equity participation, while the first men in continued to enjoy leverage.

In this climate, it was the less conventional brokers and investment bankers who flourished: those who were prepared to stick their necks out that little bit farther to help some cash-hungry conglomerate place an issue of bonds that would enable it to maintain its necessary momentum. The shrewdest and quietest of them all was Charles Allen, a former Wall Street broker's runner who had started Allen & Co. in 1922. Allen's ability to back the right share at the right time was and is legendary. He backed Syntex, the contraceptive pill firm, right from the start, and he made a fortune out of the Grand Bahama Port Authority (also favored by the IOS funds). But Allen, though unconventional, approached the market as a sure-footed veteran of 1929, and he came through the collapse in better shape than many members of the financial establishment.

Not all of those who tried to emulate him were so sure-footed: the most spectacular case was, perhaps, Burt Kleiner of Los Angeles. Kleiner was a friend of Barry Sterling, the Los Angeles lawyer who headed the IOS investment-banking division. Barry Sterling's wife had been a limited partner in the brokerage firm of Kleiner, Bell & Co. for some three years until the end of 1965. Kleiner did business with IOS. But Kleiner knew and did business with almost everyone: he was the personification of the conglomerate market. Until his firm, Kleiner, Bell, went bust in 1970 it popped up in almost every deal the conglomerate wove, taking a finder's fee here, shifting a block of shares there. It was Burt Kleiner who performed one of the classic fast-food deals: he floated Minnie Pearl Chickens which changed its name to Performance Systems, and was bought by National General, the Los Angeles conglomerate and film distributor. He was known as a man of powerful enthusiasm. "That's beautiful, that's fantastic," he was once heard to say on the phone. "Listen, I can fly there without the airplane on that sort of situation."

Forces more powerful than Kleiner's links with Sterling brought the big conglomerates to IOS. In latter 1968, Washington began to grow unhappy about the ease with which fast-talking financiers could raise millions of dollars to swallow up important pieces of the U.S. economy. The Federal Reserve Bank put out a special request to the banks, asking them to stop making loans to finance take-overs. And the effect of the restriction intensified in 1969, as credit was further tightened in an attempt to moderate inflation.

The conglomerates, along with many other American concerns, began to look to Europe for money. There they found bankers who were delighted to purchase the convertible debt securities of American conglomerates, and for another nine months the spree continued. "Some of this was junk so bad you couldn't even sell it here," said one of IOS's New York money managers, evaluating the conglomerate paper that was still received eagerly in Europe at the very end of the boom.

Washington's regulatory effort was frustrated by the fact that years of deficit in the American balance of payments had built up a huge pool of dollars outside America. Its total size was uncertain: some estimates put it as high as $50 billion. What was certain was that IOS was the biggest fish in that pool. And when, at the end of the conglomerate invasion of Europe, the real "junk" came along, IOS was still showing an almost undiminished appetite.

James Ling first needed to raise money in Europe during 1966, when his company was in electrical contracting, electronics, hi-fi equipment, missiles and aerospace, telecommunications cables, meat-packing, sporting goods, and pharmaceuticals. His New York bankers introduced him to N. M. Rothschild and Sons* in London. Ling next needed cheap finance in 1968, when Ling-Temco-Vought had added insurance, real estate, car rentals, airways, and steel to its interests—or potential interests. Again his bankers called Rothschilds. A tour was quickly arranged. "In a period of one week, flying from London to Geneva to Zurich, Milan, Frankfurt, and Paris, we were able to place approximately $60 million in twenty-year convertible debentures at one hell of a rate, 5 per cent—exactly the opposite of the high-rate, tight-money situation in the United States," Ling told *Fortune* magazine later.

The Fund of Funds bought $1.5 million of that Ling-Temco-Vought convertible, and IIT bought $5 million.

If Marshall McLuhan's concept of the "global village" can be applied anywhere, it must be applied to the great conglomera-

---

*The bank run by the English branch of the Rothschild family. Independent of Banque Rothschild—but see Chapter 18, "A Very Long Way Offshore."

tors and their friends and business associates. Sometimes, it seemed that the whole vast world of American business had shrunk to three dozen men on first-name terms who spent their time getting in and out of executive jets in Los Angeles, Denver, Dallas, Mexico City, New York, the Bahamas, and Geneva, with occasional detours to Chicago, London, Zurich, or Montreal. Although Cowett and Cornfeld were never especially close to Ling, the head of one of Ling's important subsidiaries, Harding Lawrence of Braniff Airways, was on the Board of King Resources of Denver, which was so close to IOS that it was almost the same empire. Bernie himself ventured into the real-estate business with Troy Post, the Dallas millionaire who held a big piece of Ling-Temco-Vought stock and who briefly succeeded Ling when Ling was ousted from control. Post's company had a project for a club in Acapulco, to be called Tres Vidas and reserved for the use of leading American businessmen: Cornfeld was enthusiastic enough for the IOS real-estate fund, Investment Properties International, to put $30 million into this project. By the time IOS ran into trouble, $5 million of this had been paid over and its repayment was subsequently disputed.

The IOS men were even closer to the second most famous conglomerate empire, Charles Bluhdorn's Gulf & Western Industries. Bluhdorn, as well as Ling, went looking for big money in Europe in 1968—to finance digestion rather than further acquisition—and managed to raise $40 million by private placements of debt stock. The Fund of Funds took up a whacking $29 million of that, which was FOF's biggest single position at the end of the year. (G & W common stock was also IIT's biggest position at the end of 1968.)

Not all of the investments which grew out of such links were bad ones from the viewpoint of IOS's customers. (Although the value of the Ling-Temco-Vought bonds collapsed almost completely when Ling's juggernaut lost its momentum, the Gulf & Western bonds only slipped from $100 to $60.) The trouble was that the inhabitants of the "global village" were always "putting each other into things" that dangerously intensified the tendency, always strong at the top of IOS, to see investment policy in terms of inside information and special situations. Ed Cowett's idea about Famous Players was a case in point.

Gulf & Western owned the film company Paramount, which in turn controlled a company in Canada called Famous Players, which had cinemas and a cable-TV business. In 1967, IIT acquired $2.35 million worth of Famous Player shares, but in 1968 they were sold off by Jo Melse, the Dutchman who ran the Canadian and non-U.S. section of IIT. Then, in 1969, Melse came back from a holiday to find that a new block of Famous Players, bought on Cowett's instructions, had appeared in the IIT portfolio at a cost of $2.75 million.

Cowett's rationale had been that Famous Players had a "hidden asset," whose potential you could only assess if you had been shown, as he had, the list of cinema sites that Famous Players owned, and which were juicy prospects for redevelopment. On the strength of the list, Cowett had elaborated a plan in which IOS funds would buy Famous Players shares, while the IOS banks would put up money to develop the properties. IOS would reap the investment-banking returns, and the funds would benefit from the rocketing values of Famous Players shares. . . . After furious objections from Melse, who was not a performance theorist, the Famous Players shares were transferred to IPI, the property fund.

Melse's protests were justified when the great scheme sprang a leak, as such schemes often do. Famous Players was also a television company, and the Canadian government refused to have it remodeled by an American conglomerate.

Sometimes the chieftains of IOS pulled better deals out of the conglomerate whirl—as when Cornfeld caused the purchase of a block of Piper Aircraft shares. This was not a sentimental tribute to their role in Fred Börlin's successful escape from Brazil: it was because Cornfeld heard a whisper that a take-over battle for Piper was impending. Sure enough, there was a bid from Chris-Craft, the powerboat firm, followed by another from the richly named conglomerate Bangor Punta. This turned into one of the bitterest of all take-over battles, which reached a climax when Cornfeld flew dramatically to a meeting in Nassau and gave Bangor Punta the victory by selling them the block of Piper shares he controlled.

With American companies looking to Europe for cash, conditions were ripe for the development of the ambition set out in 1961, when the infant IOS had described itself boldly as, among other things, "investment banker." Raising $35,000 to back the movie *Snobs* was, in theory, the same transaction as the established investment banks perform in raising finance for industrial corporations. But it was a very small-scale model. Now, with $2 billion of their customers' money behind them and with a great hunger for money among the fastest-moving captains of American industry, Cornfeld and Cowett could assume something of the power and glamour attaching to the great investment-banking houses of Wall Street and Europe. Indeed, with the power of IIT, FOF, and the smaller funds, they possessed an advantage over concerns like Kuhn, Loeb, Baring's, or Wertheim.

Normally, even the richest of investment banks do not control the large-scale finance that they raise. They will use their own money when promoting a new company until it can be floated on the stock market. But when they help a big corporation to raise money, they become salesmen, although admittedly of a rarefied description. The classic mechanism is that in which the corporation offers its securities, which may be of the debt or the equity brand, for sale in an issue underwritten by the investment bankers; their underwriters' endorsement of the securities* attracts cash from the insurance funds, pension funds, mutual funds, and private investors. If the issue of securities is fully taken up, the underwriters profit by their commission on the value of securities sold. If it is unattractive, they are penalized by having to make up the deficiency with their own money. Just as the underwriters' power to attract cash depends upon their reputation for backing sound propositions in the past, so the theory collapses if the underwriters actually control large slabs of other people's money, which can insure the success of otherwise unsound underwritings.

Investors Overseas Services was both mutual-fund manager *and* investment banker. Large quantities of the securities whose issue was underwritten by the Investors Overseas Bank and the Investors Bank were taken up by IOS funds. Indeed, the banks' main function seemed to be to pick up underwriting fees and commissions or discounts on securities on their way into the funds' investment portfolios. IOS itself bore little risk and stood to suffer no obvious short-term penalties if its underwritings were poorly selected. In the end, its banks promoted and sold to the IOS funds an unrivaled succession of dud issues. Collapses in the value of such paper contributed some $200 million to the depreciation of the IOS funds in 1970.

The structure of IOS thus avoided the insulation which

---

*There is a difference between New York and London practice. In London, the underwriters actually undertake to buy all the securities in an issue not subscribed for by the public. In New York, the underwriters normally make sure that all the shares are bought before the offer is made public. In each case, the essential point is that the underwriters' responsibility is financially enforced.

American securities law* places between the investment-banking business and the managements of mutual funds. The history of IOS investment banking suggests that the insulation is a valuable one.

. . .

The first steps for an American company wishing to exploit the foreign dollar pool was usually to form a finance subsidiary in the Netherlands Antilles. (Forming such subsidiaries, which help to minimize taxes, is a useful trade for a small group of lawyers in Curaçao.) Then a bank, or perhaps a small group of banks, is found to manage a "public" issue of the securities of the Netherlands Antilles corporation, whose liabilities are normally guaranteed by the American parent. A prospectus is drawn up, describing the affairs of the parent company and the nature of the securities being offered, together with some account of the rationale for the raising of new capital. Having arranged for the securities to be quoted on some European exchange, often Luxembourg or Amsterdam, the managers invite bankers and brokers in general to take up blocks for resale to clients.

An alternative procedure is for the managing bank to place the securities privately. This dispenses with the need for a prospectus and means that the manager only has to find a few large investors who will take the securities on the strength of rather less formal explanations. IOS banks, acting on behalf of the funds, participated in many issues and private placements by

---

*The point has been made to us—by IOS men—that British merchant banks both run investment trust and underwrite issues, and that British law does not forbid this. But the Prevention of Fraud (Investment) Act of 1958 does place ultimate control over the investments of a unit trust in the hands of an independent trustee with statutory duties. In a different way, therefore, investors are protected against what IOS was doing with impunity offshore.

other banks. They also managed three public issues themselves, and arranged a number of private placements.

IOS took up very large slices of most American issues in Europe: nearly all of these investments subsequently had to be drastically written down. Two companies backed by Charles Allen, AMBAC International and Liberty Equities, were among them. IOS bought a lot of securities in Liquidonics, which distinguished itself, and enraged some Congressmen, by selling a large block of shares in a U.S. defense contractor to a Swiss bank. The IOS funds had heavy investments in Four Seasons, the notorious Oklahoma nursing-home company which went bankrupt amid a spate of fraud charges from the SEC, and they bought a large wad of bonds issued by Robert Vesco's International Controls Corporation. All these investments in issues managed by others were bad enough. But the ones that IOS found for themselves were something else again.

In December 1968, Morton A. Sterling, brother of Barry Sterling of IOS, bought 5000 shares in a conglomerate called Unexcelled. (Bruce Rozet, chairman of another conglomerate, Commonwealth United Corporation, also bought a block of 5000 Unexcelled shares at the same time.) They were bought for cash at $34 each. Half of the holding passed to the estate of Morton Sterling's wife, Marion, who died in January 1969: the shares were then held beneficially by Morton Sterling, Barry Sterling, and Burt Kleiner, who were trustees under Marion Sterling's will.

On February 7, Unexcelled formed a subsidiary, Unexcelled International N.V., in Curaçao, and on March 5 it entered into an agreement with the Investors Bank of Luxembourg. Barry Sterling, as President of IOS Financial Holdings, was in charge of the Investors Bank, having prepared for an investment-banking career by working as an attorney in Los Angeles, and being Treasurer of the Democratic Party of California under Governor Pat Brown. The Investors Bank agreed to manage the private sale of $10 million worth of guarantee debentures of Unexcelled International N.V., carrying an interest rate of 7 per cent. The Fund of Funds bought $3,037,000 of the $10 million, placed in two transactions, one on May 13 and the other on June 18, 1969.

Even before these bond placements, the IOS funds showed enthusiasm for considerable blocks of Unexcelled shares: it was the kind of outfit IOS liked. The company had once been related to Mary Carter Paint before Mary Carter transformed itself into Resorts International. In 1968, Unexcelled also experienced transformation. It came under new management, and it was intended to combine three principal interests: the operation of discount stores, the sale and leasing of machinery for meat processing and packing, and the conversion and operation of aircraft for outsize air cargoes. "The story on Unexcelled," said an ex-IOS fund manager, "was that it was going to be Burt Kleiner's own conglomerate, and Burt was going to really show what he could do."

It was the aircraft division which caused the most Unexcelled problems. The aircraft, bulging converted Stratocruisers, were called Guppies: there was a Pregnant Guppy, a Super Guppy, and even a Mini Guppy. The Guppies had been working for the National Aeronautics and Space Administration, carting pieces of rocketry since 1963. But, after several promising years, cutbacks in the space budget sharply reduced the traffic in this rather specialized cargo. In January 1970, Unexcelled reappraised the economics of its air-cargo business, and decided to write off $13 million in aircraft costs, thus reporting a heavy loss for 1969.

Then in May the Mini Guppy crashed while being tested,

and was totally wrecked. Although the plane was insured, there was by this time little left of the Kleiner charisma. In September the debentures of Unexcelled International N.V. became virtually worthless, when the company ceased meeting interest payments on them. That was a specimen of IOS's private-placement technique.

The three concerns for which IOS handled public Eurodollar issues were: King Resources Corporation, which was done with the help of John King's broker, Dempsey Tegeler (another brokerage firm which succumbed in the cold winds of 1970); Bruce Rozet's Commonwealth United Corporation, done with the help of Guinness Mahon of London, and Banque Rothschild of Paris; and Giffen Industries, handled by the same team.

The issue IOS did for King was quite small, and it was only part of the complex set of links between the empires of Bernard Cornfeld and John King.* But its special quality was that it made nonsense of IOS's stated position on investment banking, which was that decisions to underwrite came *after* the fund managers had decided that particular companies looked like good investments. "The participation of Investors Bank in underwritings" said IOS, "is frequently preceded by a determination of the Company's Investment Management Division that particular securities . . . are desired for . . . Company-managed funds."†

Investors Bank and Dempsey Tegeler underwrote the issue of $15 million in bonds for King Resources. IIT acquired a block of these bonds, with a face value of $8 million—but the fund paid a premium price, $9,724,000, for them. It was bad enough that the fund customers' money should be spent on securities that

---

*See Chapter 19, "John M. King: The Power of Natural Gas."

†In the prospectus of IOS Ltd. itself, dealt with at length in Chapter 18, "A Very Long Way Offshore."

IOS was floating to its own profit: but at least IOS might have put the funds in at the issuing price. If, in this case, there was any prior decision by the IIT management that King Resources was a good investment, it must have been accompanied by another decision—to hold off while the price of the bonds went up, enabling someone else to make a profit of $1.7 million, the difference between the issue and premium prices. (Not that it *was* a good investment: two years later, it was hard to sell those King bonds for even a tenth of their face value.)

Giffen Industries, a Miami-based conglomerate, raised $20 million through the Investors Bank in February 1969, a quarter of the issue being taken up by the Fund of Funds. Giffen had been backed by Allen & Co. in early 1968, after which it embarked upon a series of purchases that made it a prize example of diversification or, if you like, of "synergy" (which *Fortune* magazine once unkindly called "the two-plus-two-equals-five effect"). Giffen was in carpets, carpet-installation materials, resilient floor coverings, plastic laminates, metal moldings, aluminum extrusions, soft-sided luggage, electronic and electrical components, precision gears, carpet-seaming tape, sink rims, boats, snowmobiles, casual lawn furniture, and gypsum roofs and roof decks. Its synergy evaporated when the books of a floor-covering firm it had agreed to buy turned out to be not quite what they seemed, whereupon the Giffen common stock, which had reached $68 in 1968, fell to about $8. By the end of 1970, the bonds that IOS floated for Giffen were worth about a fifth of their face value.

But at least the King and Giffen bonds retained some value. That was not the case with IOS's biggest investment-banking deal, Commonwealth United.

In the same summer when Ling and Bluhdorn were looking for money in Europe, A. Bruce Rozet, a small, roundish, cheerful man, was staying in the South of France. From there, he arranged to meet Barry Sterling, who ran the IOS banks from Paris, so that they could discuss Commonwealth United's plans to set up a European film business in London. The meeting was prevented by the Paris student riots of 1968, but they met a little later in Geneva.

The Sterling family were part of the early history of Commonwealth United. Before his days as a Los Angeles attorney with Hindin, Sterling, McKittrick & Powsner, Barry Sterling had been General Counsel of an oil firm called Sunset International Petroleum, in which his family were large investors. In 1966, Sunset was merged with a finance company called Atlas Credit and the incipient conglomerate which resulted was named Sunasco. It was extremely unsuccessful, and rapidly built up huge debts, so the companies had to be disentangled again. "In hard terms," said a former executive, "Sunset had a negative value of $25 million. It was a question of putting together something worth zero."

The solution was to sell off Sunset International Petroleum, less a part of its real-estate assets, which were retained by Sunasco. Sunasco was then sold to Commonwealth United, which was itself the result of a merger between a film company and an insurance agency, and which had the important advantage of a quotation for its common stock on the American Stock Exchange. The deal left Commonwealth and Sunasco owning large blocks of each other's shares.

By this time Barry Sterling had left for Europe, and Commonwealth United was interested chiefly in survival. Investment bankers were not paying it any great attention, and although Kleiner, Bell had placed about $6 million in bonds for Commonwealth, Burt Kleiner was not active in its affairs. What Commonwealth needed was for something to happen to Sunasco to boost the price of the 800,000 Sunasco shares Commonwealth still owned. Right on cue, Sunasco decided to go into the fashionable computer-leasing business. As soon as the magic words got round, Sunasco's stock "ran." Commonwealth sold out at $10 a share, for $8 million.

Burt Kleiner now started to take a lot more interest in the company. He organized a bond issue for Commonwealth which helped them buy back the Commonwealth stock still owned by Sunasco.

Then Commonwealth set out in earnest on the take-over trail. The movie business was one of its earliest targets: in early 1968, Commonwealth had its sights on Metro-Goldwyn-Mayer and had gone so far as to make a first approach to Warner Brothers. But the first big deal resulted from Commonwealth's being introduced, by Burt Kleiner, to Delbert W. Coleman of the Seeburg Corporation.

Delbert Coleman had bought control of Seeburg in 1956, when it was only a juke-box manufacturer. Under Coleman and his partner, Lou Nicastro, the firm developed into a manufacturer of just about everything in the coin-operated amusement line. Its turnover at the time that Commonwealth United took it over was close on $100 million a year—more than double Commonwealth's. Coleman and Nicastro sold their Seeburg shares to Commonwealth for $12 million cash, plus warrants entitling them to purchase Commonwealth shares. Kleiner got a finder's fee of $400,000, plus some warrants, for making the introduction. Commonwealth shares were thought to be a coming investment by many people, including IOS and its investment advisers: by June 1968, IIT had invested $1.3 million in Commonwealth shares, and, by the end of 1968, the Fund of Funds held an $8-million position in Commonwealth, which was Fred Alger's second biggest investment after Resorts International.

On the FOF side, of course, Alger knew Delbert Coleman (and indeed held Seeburg shares in his funds). Since early 1968, IIT had also been well-informed about the great promise of Commonwealth, because a New York broker who was a friend of Henry Buhl's joined the Commonwealth Board.

Rozet's trip to Europe in 1968 led to an agreement that IOS would raise $30 million for Commonwealth United through a Eurobond issue in January 1969. The Investors Bank shared $750,000 of fees and discounts on this issue with Banque Rothschild and Guinness Mahon—but even before the securities were floated, Commonwealth was running into trouble. In December 1968, shortly after Commonwealth had acquired Seeburg, one of Seeburg's main banks said that in view of the merger it would not renew the line of credit it was extending to Seeburg. So, whatever plans had originally been made for the Eurobond money, $19.5 million had to go to pay off the Seeburg bank.

This setback did not inhibit Rozet from launching a series of ambitious bids to maintain Commonwealth's momentum. Toward the end of January, Commonwealth came out in the open with its bid for Warner Brothers, which it proposed to acquire by an exchange of shares. Also in January, Commonwealth spent $3 million on the securities of the large construction firm, George A. Fuller Corporation. This deal was a classic example of leverage: while the partners of Kleiner, Bell bought 80 per cent of Fuller's common stock for $1.75 million, Commonwealth bought fixed-interest stock—the whole of Fuller's 5½-per-cent cumulative preferred shares.* Then, in late February, Rozet signed a deal with a big industrial group, Dart Industries,

---

*An irony of this deal was that at the time, the most absurd of all the offshore funds-men, Jerome D. Hoffman (whose career is described in Chapter 18, "A Very Long Way Offshore"), was trying to persuade Fuller to co-operate with him in running a new fund. Through the Commonwealth deal, IOS almost picked up Hoffman for free.

through which Commonwealth agreed to buy the Rexall Drug Company, a Dart subsidiary, for $50 or $60 million. The deal was to be closed on June 30, but Commonwealth paid a $5-million deposit immediately.

The Warner offer was futile, for a lot of companies were in the hunt. Commonwealth withdrew on March 17, when the Warner Board gave their support to a rival offer. Rozet was not long discouraged: next day he bought 86,000 shares of Perfect Film and Chemical, whose main business was film processing, but which was branching out into all sorts of other things. Commonwealth paid nearly double the market price for the shares, which cost $7 million and were only a 6-per-cent holding. But on the strength of it, Rozet was elected to the Perfect Board, where he proposed a full merger of Commonwealth and Perfect.

Now it was clear that the $30 million raised in January would not be enough, so in March, back went Rozet to Geneva for more. IOS, with the ever-obliging help of Banque Rothschild and Guinness Mahon, produced another $10 million for him—this time a short-term loan, repayable at the end of the year. As a further fee, IOS picked up 112,500 Commonwealth warrants, then worth about $8 each.

By May 1969, Rozet could see the crunch coming. The terms of the Rexall deal had been modified and the closing date put off to August 8, but he still needed another $10 million for deposits on June 30, with another $15 million due on July 15. He now did a deal with the Gulf & Western subsidiary, Paramount, under which, in exchange for yet more Commonwealth paper (people still believed in it) he got the rights to the Julie Andrews musical *Darling Lili*, plus $12 million in cash. Kleiner, Bell picked up another $500,000 fee for arranging this deal. (Altogether, during 1968 and 1969, Commonwealth agreed to pay Kleiner, Bell $2,153,500 in underwriting discount, commissions, brokerage, and fees. Kleiner, Bell was also to get $150,000 a year as financial consultants for four years from January 1, 1969.)

The intention in the *Darling Lili* deal was to use the money to make the Rexall deposits, but $5 million had to go to repay bank loans, and the rest melted away in other directions. Naturally, Rozet turned back to the apparently bottomless bucket in Geneva, and, now, when Commonwealth was unable to find cash anywhere else, IOS offered to dip into the customers' money again.

This was perhaps the most extortionate single deal that IOS ever proposed—a jewel, in its way. It was agreed that Commonwealth could have a loan of $10 million out of the Fund of Funds, the money to become available on June 30. In return, Commonwealth was to give a five-year note, convertible as usual into Commonwealth stock. In addition, the Fund of Funds was to receive 300,000 shares of Commonwealth for free, plus warrants which would enable the fund to increase yet further its already heavy investment in the dubious future of Mr. Rozet's concern. The interest on this loan was, considering the risks involved, modest: Commonwealth was to pay only the going Eurodollar rate of 10¾ per cent. The FOF customers, therefore, were not to receive any great reward for acting, collectively and unconsciously, as bankers of last resort to this feverish conglomerate.

The rewards were to go not to FOF, but to IOS. Fees for arranging the loan were calculated at a staggering $1.35 million, nearly all of it payable to IOS banks. Put bluntly, the weakness of Commonwealth United was to be turned into yet another occasion for enriching IOS itself at the risk and expense of the fund investors. It was, of course, no concern of Rozet's if IOS chose to mistreat its customers—but from his viewpoint the money was desperately expensive, because he would only receive $8.65

million after paying IOS off. Although normally insouciant about the cost of his financing, Rozet reserved the right to withdraw from the loan in the event that he could find something cheaper. In that case, all he agreed to pay was a "commitment fee" of $250,000, payable to ODB, Bahamas.

At this point it looked as though Rozet would get away with his balancing act. In addition to his $10-million commitment from the Fund of Funds, he had informal commitments from a Los Angeles mutual fund and from a Chicago bank to put up another $10 million each. This would have enabled him to swing the Rexall deal. Then suddenly the whole crazy structure was knocked sideways by a deadly article in the *Los Angeles Times* on July 10, analyzing the profits of Commonwealth's real-estate division, which had contributed a third of the conglomerate's total profits the previous year.

In December 1968 the real-estate division had bought a block of undeveloped land in Hawaii for $1,656,800, which it had managed to resell in the same month for $5,450,000. From the gains made on this deal, $2,963,000 had been taken as profits for Commonwealth United. So far so good: the transaction had been recorded in the prospectus IOS had issued to raise money for Commonwealth in Europe.

But information which Commonwealth had been required to file with the SEC now revealed that the Hawaiian sale had not been done on the open market. The land had been bought and sold on the same day, December 31, 1968, and the purchasers were Burt Kleiner and his fellow principals in Kleiner, Bell & Co., Commonwealth's own brokers. What was more, although nearly $3 million had been taken as profits, Kleiner and his friends had only paid over $541,000 cash—the rest was in promissory notes. (The brokers' reasons for buying the land, apparently, was that it would help with their "personal tax planning.")

The news that a large chunk of Commonwealth's profits had been jacked up in this fashion cast no little doubt upon the whole concern. "Thanks to the *L.A. Times*, everybody ran for the windows," Rozet is reported to have said ruefully. The Los Angeles mutual fund and the Chicago bank backed out, taking their $20 million with them. Dart Industries called off the whole Rexall deal—while hanging on to $4 million of the original deposit. Commonwealth's quoted price halved before the American Stock Exchange suspended trading on July 22. It then halved again in over-the-counter deals, falling to $4 before the SEC barred all trading. One good thing happened: the Fund of Funds' $10 million was returned, with the collapse of the Rexall deal (Commonwealth forfeiting the $250,000 commitment fee to ODB, Bahamas).

Rozet held a series of frantic meetings in July. He flew from Los Angeles to Washington to see the SEC, then on to a board meeting in New York, then straight on to meet with Cornfeld and Cowett in Geneva. All sorts of rescue plans were discussed: Rozet reckoned he needed another $12 million for Commonwealth, but offered to resign. The incipient collapse of Rozet's conglomerate must have been a serious embarrassment for Cornfeld and Cowett, who were now proposing to float off IOS's own shares.* They could not afford an obvious disaster in their investment-banking division, and, to hold Commonwealth together, they produced $4.5 million immediately. Again, it was a loan from the customers' money, in this case from the new IOS fund, Investment Properties International, which was still flush with cash from its launch. It was also agreed that Howard Stamer should be

---

*The IOS flotation is described fully in Chapter 18, "A Very Long Way Offshore."

put in charge, with other IOS nominees. The IPI loan was made on July 31 and Howard Stamer took up his duties on August 1.

But the IPI loan was not enough, and the IOS banks themselves had to advance another $3.5 million even before the IOS prospectus was finalized. By October 27, 1969, Commonwealth's debts to IOS companies—excluding the funds—ran to some $9.5 million, at which point IOS tried unsuccessfully to back out. Yet more management changes were introduced as Commonwealth lurched into 1970, arguing with the SEC over the rewards that IOS and its friends wanted for the help they had given Commonwealth. IOS had originally negotiated for options on 300,000 Commonwealth shares at $2 each, which meant that if Commonwealth could only stay at $4 when trading resumed, IOS had a clear $600,000 profit. Complaints from the SEC got this reduced to options on 200,000 shares, or alternatively, a payment of $100,000. Howard Stamer and Robert J. Haft were originally to have got options on 75,000 shares each at $2 per share. This was moderated to 50,000 each at $6.

Stamer was paid at the annual rate of $65,000 for his stint in charge of the company from August 1 to October 27, and the fee to Stamer and Haft's law firm was $150,000.

The IOS fund customers were not so lucky: the funds still held $19 million face value of the $40 million of convertible paper that had been floated off in early 1969. A little over a year later, as Commonwealth slumped back to the humdrum business of trading real estate, backing movies, and making juke boxes, the whole value of the investment was written down to zero in the books of the IOS funds.

• • •

Far from being abashed at this grotesque fiasco, Ed Cowett spent a good deal of time in 1969 devising yet more daring ways to employ the leverage of the customers' money. The half-yearly report of the Fund of Funds on June 30, 1969, recorded, without a word of explanation, that in May FOF Proprietary had advanced $50,468,750 to "the Kensington Organization N.V." in exchange for a convertible note.

The Kensington Organization N.V. was the Curaçao offshoot of a New York company put together by some former partners in the brokerage firm of Burnham & Co. It was intended to buy working control of other companies, reorganize them, and then sell them off at a profit. It was supposed to be a "kind of conglomerate in reverse" which would scour the whole world for companies whose quoted share price was below the true value of their assets, and naturally Cowett could not resist an idea like that. The men behind the Kensington Organization were not too happy about being tied up with IOS, but they needed the money, so while the Fund of Funds lent $50 million, it was arranged that the Investors Overseas Bank should hold some 900,000 shares of Kensington common stock at only 44¢ per share.

The whole scheme was built, of course, around the power of the customers' money, but it was engineered so that most of the advantages would accrue to IOS. First, IOS got its shares at 54¢ each: although the Fund of Funds' loan was convertible into stock, the conversion could not be made at less than $12 per share. And then the capital of Kensington Organization was so designed that the cheaper shares would have special growth potential not available to the more expensive shares. Fortunately, the Kensington Organization failed to raise another $50 million which it needed and so the whole deal had to be unwound.

It was, however, characteristic Cowett. Where Cowett, in the great years of IOS's power, went in for grand mechanisms of the Kensington sort, Cornfeld often preferred a miniaturist's effect—such as he displayed in the deals spun around a little company called EON Corporation. EON had been formed by a dedicated medical researcher, Dr. Nicholas Anton. Using the principle of the Geiger counter, Anton had devised a sophisticated machine for detecting cancer, using isotopes to measure the growth of the tumor. Anton's company ran into difficulties, and he received some fresh backing from a family called Srybnik. One of the Srybniks in turn became acquainted with Oleg Cassini and then with Cornfeld himself.

Early in 1969, Cassini was planning to expand his business on the U.S. fashion market, and he needed a financial vehicle. It was decided that he should use the EON Corporation: in early 1969, people thought it perfectly logical to merge a medical-equipment firm with a fashion house.

In February 1961, Cassini sold 25 per cent of his U.S. business to EON, in exchange for EON shares. In June, IOS's new Venture Fund (International) invested $990,000 in EON through a private placement: Venture received 600,000 unregistered common shares at 40¢ each, and a note for $750,000 which was convertible into common shares at about $3. The market price of EON at the time was around $6.

Another investor was planning to put some money into EON at this moment—none other than Bernard Cornfeld himself. Cornfeld told us that Howard Stamer had received some EON shares at 40¢ apiece, as a "finder's fee" for introducing the Venture Fund to EON. Stamer offered some of these to Cornfeld, who was going to buy them for his own private foundation. For some reason or other, the transfer of shares never seems to have taken place, but Cornfeld's interest in EON was fired. He conceived a great plan for the cancer machines to be sold by the IOS sales force, on 30-per-cent commissions. Anton was summoned to Geneva, where a company was set up to handle the sales side.

There was a ready pool of salesmen available: IOS had just been tossed out of Greece, accused of illegal sales operations. Plans flourished further: clinics were to be constructed in which the EON machines would be installed. But then the plans were killed by the master salesmen, who did not think that the Associates would like to sell cancer machines, even for 30 per cent. EON's price wavered toward the end of 1969: by September 1970 the whole of the Venture Fund's million-dollar investment had been written off.

The EON purchase was negotiated for the Venture Fund by David Meid, who was found, when IOS itself crashed, to have a $250,000 personal loan outstanding from IOS. We asked Meid if he would care to discuss the investment decision with us. He replied, memorably, "My responsibility is not to see the truth printed; my responsibility is to keep my mouth shut."

• • •

In order to impress the customers with the soundness and wisdom of IOS investment policy, IOS advertisements used to tell people that to put money into IOS funds was to get "all the investment advice a billion and a half dollars can buy." However much that was, it clearly wasn't enough.

But this much could be said about the deals like Resorts International, Famous Players, Giffen Industries, Commonwealth United, and EON: they did bear, more or less, the outward appearance of orthodox investment situations. When Ed Cowett went into the natural-resources business with John McCandish King, the last semblances of orthodoxy were cast aside.

18

A Very Long Way Offshore

In which respectable financiers strip off their watch chains and leap into the warm offshore waters. The techniques and consequences of IOS's competition; IOS, on the basis of a very curious prospectus, becomes a public corporation at long last.

J ust as one can select different incidents as the symbolic high point of the conglomerate enthusiasm, so it is possible to select different moments as representing the offshore idea in its highest development. For sheer theoretical audacity, it would be difficult to surpass Arthur Lipper III's idea of towing away a section of the New York Stock Exchange itself to the offshore world. Mr. Lipper thought that if the NYSE stuck to its rules about commissions, the solution might be to arrange for New York-quoted securities to be traded in Beirut on a new exchange organized for the purpose.

This thought was put forward toward the end of 1968, when a potent magic was already beginning to attach to the word "offshore." But in terms of events, 1969 was the miraculous year of offshoreness. It was the year when, at long last, Bernie and the boys "cashed in": at the end of 1969 IOS Ltd., nine years after its formation in Panama City, sold off a section of its own shares, as distinct from the shares of the funds it managed. When that happened, as Cornfeld said proudly, one hundred members of the company became millionaires—not in terms of the theoretical "formula value" of IOS but in terms, at last, of stock-exchange prices.

It was also in 1969 that Keith Barish and Rafael Navarro went successfully to the international stock markets with the concept of "liquid real estate" which made their Gramco Management company for a while the hottest offshore operation of all. During the summer of 1969, for the first and last time, the volume of cash collected by Investors Overseas Services exceeded for one month the volume collected by the entire American domestic mutual-fund business.

Small offshore funds proliferated, and novel financial principles were advanced. Allen J. Lefferdink, for example, said that none of his funds would be examined by outside auditors "because the appeal of offshore funds is confidentiality."

The flavor of the international financial atmosphere in that year is best conveyed by some account of the offshore career of Jerome D. Hoffman, a veteran of the sleazier end of the New York mortgage trade. Hoffman set out, quite frankly, to emulate the success of Investors Overseas Services. And he was IOS's ultimate offshore competitor—the man who carried the offshore technique past the point of *reductio ad absurdum*.

On May 16, 1969, Reginald Maudling, deputy leader of the Conservative Party and one of Her Majesty's Privy Counsellors, launched in London a new offshore fund to be called the Real Estate Fund of America, or REFA. Mr. Maudling announced that he was President of the new fund, which would collect money from international investors and put it into real estate in America. The fund would be administered by its Executive Vice President, Jerome D. Hoffman. Mr. Hoffman said that REFA would also enjoy the services of a number of former officials of the U.S. Treasury and State Department, and of M. Paul-Henri Spaak, ex-Premier of Belgium. Hoffman described Maudling as "one of the outstanding financial minds of the world," and it was true that Maudling's cabinet appointments included spells as Chancellor of the Exchequer and President of the Board of Trade. (On the Tory return to office in 1970 he became Home Secretary.) When Mr. Maudling said that the Real Estate Fund of America was a "good and sound investment" it was a view that carried weight.

A rather different impression emerged some eighteen months after the launch of REFA, and about twelve months after Maudling resigned from it due to the pressure of his political activities. Hoffman decamped abruptly from his London base in November 1970 and arrived in Rome, pursued by ugly questions from the world's press concerning the fate of REFA, now supposed to be worth $100 million. In Rome, Mr. Hoffman held a hasty conference with some remaining executives, and demolished the last of his carefully cultivated air of financial statesmanship. If things got any worse, said Hoffman, he was "going to take the money and run." "You guys," he added, "can look after yourselves." The Real Estate Fund of America, and Hoffman's International Investment Group, which was supposed to administer it, consisted by then of little more than a couple of baffled telephonists and a series of heavily mortgaged properties in the United States.

Jerome Hoffman is a little man, aged about thirty-eight, with a restless manner and a high-pitched laugh. This laugh used to punctuate the vague but expansive answers he gave when questioned about his financial activities. "Don't worry about me," he would shout. "I'm growing like a weed. Ha-ha-ha-haaa!" Hoffman had been run out of the securities business in New York in 1968 by Attorney General Louis J. Lefkowitz, for offering mortgages in a "reckless, improvident, and fraudulent manner." According to Lefkowitz's staff: "His modus operandi when contacted by a prospective client was to require a payment of $500 for inspection of the property to be mortgaged and an additional amount ranging from $2500 to $25,000 for a 'feasibility survey. . . .' All of the fees totalled more than a million dollars. . . . Hoffman and his companies actually obtained mortgages for only three applicants in the last two years."

Part of Hoffman's elaborate corporate façade was something called the Institutional Monetary Trust, which was supposed to be making a $25-million securities offer in 1968. The trust did get as far as producing a serious-looking prospectus. This named Holmes Brown, a former Director of Public Affairs for the Office of Economic Opportunity, as a trustee, and recorded that the firm of Ross, Stamer, Wolf & Haft were special counsel to the trust. But before it could raise any money from the public, Attorney General Lefkowitz brought charges against Hoffman. Hoffman denied them all, but rather than fight he signed a consent decree which banned him from the securities business in New York. He then took off into the offshore world, asking (according to his later publicity material), "Anyone know where I can get two rooms in Paris and a 1956 Chrysler convertible?"

There was nothing in Hoffman's record and little in his manner under questioning to suggest that he could or would run a viable fund business. However, Reginald Maudling was not the only prominent man who joined Hoffman. Robert Wagner, former Mayor of New York, agreed to become Chairman of REFA's companion fund, the Fund of the Seven Seas, or FOSS. Both Maudling and Wagner became shareholders in the company formed to manage these two funds, called International Investment Group Ltd.

Both REFA and FOSS called themselves open-end funds, and

in doing so REFA ran counter to the regulatory principles of the British Board of Trade,* the governmental department responsible for investment companies. The Board of Trade, working in this case on similar lines to the SEC, says that no fund that promises to redeem its own shares can invest in land or buildings—on the ground that, unlike shares, buildings cannot be swiftly and objectively valued, and often cannot be sold expeditiously.

The prospectus REFA offered to investors was distinctly vague, and that of FOSS, which consisted largely of pictures of ships owned by other people, was possibly the most ridiculous ever put out by a financial organization. Yet both bore the name of a respectable firm of lawyers in the City of London, Joynson-Hicks and Co. The fact was that neither of the International Investment Group's funds were susceptible to British law or regulation, even though IIG proposed to administer them from London. The two fund companies were registered in Hamilton, Bermuda, and the management company—in which Hoffman made his distinguished colleagues shareholders—was registered in Liberia.

The head of Joynson-Hicks and Co., Lord Brentford, formerly a Tory MP, director of an insurance firm, and Chairman of the Automobile Association, served from the start on the Board of IIG Management. So did his son, the Honorable Crispin Joynson-Hicks, so did Maudling, Holmes Brown, Dixon Donelley (formerly an Assistant to the Secretary of the U.S. Treasury), John F. Lang (a New York lawyer whose firm represented the British government in the *Torrey Canyon* oil-pollution dispute), and other respectable folk.

If the structure of IOS was flexible, that of IIG was primitive.

---

*Renamed the Department of Trade and Industry in 1970.

The arrangements for safeguarding the customers' money were so sketchy that late in 1970 Hoffman was able to admit breezily that he had shifted "a couple of million dollars" of REFA money into the Investment Bank, Zurich. This was a very small Swiss bank which Hoffman was about to take over personally. (In the end, he never finished paying for the shares.) The nature of the IIG sales operation, a rough-and-ready copy of the IOS model, was made plain by Guillermo Gutierrez, IIG's Latin American sales director, and an IOS veteran. Asked how many countries his sales area covered, he said, "Twenty-nine." Asked in how many it was legal to sell the fund shares, he said, "Only two." Gutierrez said that one of his salesmen was accustomed to getting money out of Brazil by canoeing across the river into Paraguay.

In July 1969 one of the present authors revealed the facts of Hoffman's background in New York to Mr. Maudling. Some of these facts were apparently known already to Holmes Brown and John Lang in New York. Yet neither Mr. Maudling nor the others chose to resign. Maudling remained a shareholding director of IIG Management, the basic Hoffman company, for another two months, and when he did resign, he did not express any doubts about the IIG operation. On the contrary, Maudling gave Hoffman an open letter *repeating* that REFA was a good, sound investment. John Lang, Holmes Brown, Lord Brentford, and Crispin Joynson-Hicks remained through most of 1970.*

Without his eminent supporters, it is difficult to believe that Hoffman could ever have floated his enterprise. As it was, he kept it swimming long enough to collect $9 or $10 million, which was parlayed via some hefty mortgages into an alleged

---

*M. Spaak's position is that he wrote a letter of resignation which Hoffman ignored.

$100 million in American real estate. How was it possible that Hoffman could be taken seriously at all?

It was possible in general terms because Bernie Cornfeld and Ed Cowett had more than $2 billion under their control by then, and had been in business for ten years without their company blowing up. Financial experts were willing to admit privately that IOS's fortunes were probably built upon flight capital, and much of it illegal at that. Few of them found that worrying. Even fewer were impressed by the complaints of the SEC staff, who were widely regarded as kill-joys. And beside the general inspiration of the IOS spectacle, people were beginning to understand just how profitable a business it could be to run a company managing offshore mutual funds. From that realization proceeded the idea that the shares of such fund-management companies might be very interesting propositions indeed. It was, as it happened, Gramco rather than IOS which first drove home to the international financial community the attraction of the mathematics involved. At the same time, the Gramco story—and the careers of some other newcomers—drove home a rather different point to IOS. This was that one of the things that was unregulated offshore was the competition.

The funniest effect of the appearance of people like Hoffman and Lefferdink was the suggestion that the offshore funds should get together and form their own voluntary regulatory body. This offshore "Securities and Exchange Commission," predictably, never got beyond the discussion stage.

Even Gramco, which collected $250 million in three years, did not become big enough, as had IOS, to make a significant difference to investment markets and foreign-exchange balances on its own. But IOS's competitors were important chiefly because of the effect that they had upon the self-confidence of IOS. Hoffman was the crudest of them. Gramco was the slickest, and the one that worried IOS most.

Gramco's best-known director was Pierre Salinger, John Kennedy's friend and press secretary. Salinger was joined in the Gramco promotion by several lesser eminences from JFK's administration. There was Richard K. Donahue, once special assistant in the White House; William P. Mahoney, former Ambassador to Ghana; Ivan A. Nestingen, one-time Under Secretary for Health, Education, and Welfare. And the rhetoric of its principal promoters, Barish and Navarro, made Gramco sound more like some crusading political party than a financial concern.

Gramco's publicity said that Rafael Navarro possessed "a breadth of vision on the social problems of today that is astonishing in a man so completely devoted to his work." Barish was described as a man "who wants to put money to work for people, and who glows when he talks about it." "I like to think," he said, "that we are engaged in a system that used money for social good . . . to prevent economic injustices, and make the world a better place." Barish, it was said, had "larger goals than merely making a lot of money."

He did, however, make a lot of money. Barish made his start in business at eighteen, when some friends of his were trying to start a bank in a Miami suburb. The Banking Commission thought that the district already had enough banks, but Barish persuaded the Commission otherwise. A clue to his powers of persuasion lies in the fact that he had already served a term as a White House "intern," traditionally a job for a youth who has some influence in his state and aspires to more. The upshot was that Barish became a shareholder in the new bank while he was still so young that his mother had to attend shareholders' meetings on his behalf.

Together with some associates from the bank, he formed Gramco, under its original name of the Great America Management and Research Corporation. But Barish developed ambitions that outran the visions of his former banking colleagues. He parted company with them, teamed up with Rafael Garcia Navarro, and abbreviated Great America, etc., to "Gramco." The Gramco literature asserted that Navarro had previously been a "high-ranking career diplomat," when aged only twenty-one. (His father was a Prime Minister of Cuba in the declining years of Batista.)

Barish and Navarro were obviously impressed by offshore possibilities. When they started business in 1967, they employed some of the same devices as IOS: the salesmen were called Associates, were graded in a similar fashion, and were offered a similar stock-option plan. The technique of decorating the operation with eminent names was reminiscent of IOS—and a certain number of the Associates were people tempted away from Bernie.

What tempted these men was the prospect of selling Gramco's "product," one even more audacious than anything which IOS had produced. According to their own account, Barish and Navarro toyed with the simple mutual-fund principle and with a fund on funds before they decided to concentrate on the idea of "liquid real estate." The pitch on this, put over with great polish, was that it offered safety, coupled with steady capital growth—and by 1967 there had been enough ups-and-downs on the world's stock markets to make the pitch attractive.

The straight legal problem of offering an open-end fund with nonliquid investments was overcome easily enough. Barish and Navarro's basic company was Gramco International SA, registered in Panama. It controlled Gramco Management Ltd., a Bahamas company, which was the sole distributor of shares in the "United States Investment Fund," also registered in the Bahamas, and known usually as "USIF Real Estate." The administrative HQ of Gramco Management was in London, which was handy for banking services, but no sales were undertaken in Britain. The main sales efforts were in West Germany (which had no developed fund law when Gramco started business), the Middle East, and Latin America.

Overcoming customers' doubts about the liquidity of a real-estate fund might have been more difficult than the legal obstacles. Much solemn hocus-pocus, some of it untruthful, was addressed to the problem.

Gramco carried to a high pitch the device of baldly reconciling opposites. For instance, they assured the public that USIF valuation methods were "at the same time orthodox and revolutionary." But the main reassurance was that Gramco promised to keep a proportion of fund assets in cash, ready for repurchases. The ratio of cash to real estate was supposed to have been settled after "careful analysis of liquidity requirements of U.S. and international funds on an historic basis." However, having started out with a promise to keep 30 per cent in cash, Barish and Navarro quietly adjusted that downward to 20 per cent while pretending that such had been their idea in the first place.

This growth was aided by a quintessentially offshore device. Real estate was *depreciated* for U.S. tax purposes, and then written back when calculating the fund's growth. Thus assets which were losing value in one set of books were gaining value in another. Price Waterhouse, the USIF auditors, did not put their name to this device.

Doubts about liquidity were overcome so successfully that by 1969 Gramco could claim that its fund was the largest single buyer of American real estate. USIF, directed by Gramco, bought the NUS building in Washington, D.C., Clermont Towers in Manhattan, 1000 Lakeshore Drive in Chicago, Troy Towers in New York, the Arizona Title Building in Phoenix, and that conglomerate shrine the Ling-Temco-Vought Tower in Dallas, Texas.

The Gramco salesmen claimed to be selling the "perfect investment," and, suitably enough, one of the Gramco sales contests was called the Best of Both Worlds Contest. The pitch even had a pleasing ingredient of caution in it, for the customers were told that, although their money would rise in value with the inexorable rise of the U.S. property market, there could be no pretense that it would rise as fast as the hottest shares on the stock exchange. They were not told that they were paying for a structure which gave Barish, Navarro, and their friends an investment of a sort which would rise considerably faster than the fastest stocks on a boom market.

A sales load was taken, of course, to feed the Gramco sales force, and there was also a management fee. But, far more important, the customers' money had to bear a brokerage charge of 5 or 6 per cent of the value of all properties bought in the United States. And as Gramco did not use real-estate brokers but made its own direct purchases on behalf of USIF, Gramco Management Ltd. appropriated the brokerage itself.

At this point, leverage was applied to the customers' money. USIF, like most property purchasers, bought on mortgage, borrowing between three and four dollars for each dollar of fund money. But Gramco took its brokerage fee on the *full* price paid for the property. Thus if the fund bought a building for $5 million cash and $15 million borrowed, Gramco took 5 per cent of $20 million, or $1 million. In this way, over the three and a half years to June 1970, Gramco Management took $43 million out of the USIF Fund for its own profits: roughly 17 per cent of all the money the customers put in—after the deduction of sales loads. The result was that Gramco Management Ltd., so long as the flow of cash continued, was a sensational money-making device. And as if the basic dynamic were not enough, USIF's growth was stoked with another ingenious application of leverage: Gramco arranged for its customers to buy USIF shares on credit.

The finance for these loans was obtained from the same banks in which the famous liquid-cash reserve of the fund was deposited. Indeed, the banks were persuaded to make the loans by the inducement of receiving the deposits. Security for such loans was, of course, the new USIF shares which were bought with them.

A number of observers pointed out the hair-raising circularity of this arrangement. In the event of redemption demands, Gramco would have to take its deposits out of the banks to meet them. Would not the banks then call in the loans they had made—and as the security for those loans were USIF shares, would this not lead to further redemptions? It was the financial equivalent of what electronic engineers call "positive feedback."

Both Gramco and their banking expert, Michael Gillies of Sassoon Banking in London, maintained this was not so. Despite their protestations, the suspension of bank liquidity closed the USIF Fund in the end. But, until that happened, it did look as though Barish and Navarro had devised something that made Cowett and Cornfeld look like savings-bank managers. Gramco Management Ltd. was able to claim, for the first quarter of 1969, profits at a rate of nearly $1 each per share per year—on shares with a face value of 50¢ apiece. And that rate had *doubled* over the same period in 1968. Of this income, 86.6 per cent had come from "fees for services performed in connection with the acquisitions of properties," and as Gramco was expecting the value of USIF properties to shortly top $1 *billion*, it seemed that the rate of return must continue to double, or more, every year.

Now was clearly the time to sell off a slice of Gramco Management's own magical shares, as against those of the fund. The results of the sale are recorded best in Barish and Navarro's own words, reviewing the progress of their parent Panamanian company at the end of 1969.

> In the course of the year we have passed many historic milestones. Perhaps the most noteworthy was the public offering, in May, of 10 per cent of the shares of Gramco Management, a subsidiary of International, and the impressive response aroused . . . in the international financial community. The shares of Gramco Management were initially offered at $10, and the company has now been given a value by the market of $170,000,000. Since 90 per cent of Gramco Management is owned by Gramco International, we believe this constitutes a sound basis for the continuing prosperity of International. . . .

The launch of the Gramco Management shares was managed by Sassoon and by Crédit Commercial of France. The price of $10 per share was underwritten by seventy banks and the list included many distinguished financial names. From London, there was the Westminster Bank, one of the "Big Four" British banks; there was Reginald Maudling's firm, Kleinwort Benson; there was S. G. Warburg, Samuel Montagu, and N. M. Rothschild and Sons (the London Rothschilds). There were big Wall Street names, such as Loeb, Rhoades and Bear, Steams & Co. There was Julius Baer International, controlled by the biggest private bank in Zurich and there was Banque Lambert of Brussels which had once declined to act for IOS's "International Investment Trust." There was Fleming-Suez, representing the combination of the Compagnie de Suez with the fortune of Robert Fleming, pioneer of the investment company. There was Banque Rothschild from Paris, the Berliner Handelsgesellschaft, Slavenburg's Bank from the Netherlands, the Vereinsbank from Hamburg, and fifty-three more. All of them were able to take up Gramco Management shares at $10 less the underwriters' discount of 20¢, and resell them almost instantly. At one point, these Bahamian shares were trading at $20 each.

Eighteen months later, they were worth $2, if you could shift them. But that was after the hurricanes had blown through the offshore world. At the time it was done, the cashing in of Gramco was a triumph. It gave an air of credibility even to the absurd Hoffman, who, it was thought, might manage some similar feat. It cast some magic on almost every one of the seven hundred fifty-odd international funds that were listed in the Fund Guide directory, from the Antilles Mutual Fund of Saint Thomas, Virgin Islands, and the Casino Fund of Curaçao, to the International Whisky Fund, conducted by Highland-Dunes Scotch Investors, of Great Neck, New York.

But for IOS men it was galling to have to watch Gramco sprint from launch to cashing in within two and a half years. And what made it worse was the knowledge that Barish and Navarro owed much of their credibility to the very existence of IOS.

One effect on IOS was to make Cowett and Cornfeld search even more eagerly for new investment devices that would rival the astonishing proposition which Gramco was offering the customers. The threat of being outbid in the offshore competition forced IOS to look for yet bigger, therefore yet riskier, advantages to offer to its prospects. In the offshore world, if someone else offered the investors the moon, you had to offer them the sun.

Also, Gramco shook IOS confidence because a lot of IOS salesmen had been waiting impatiently to "cash in" with their shares. They were angry that someone else should get in ahead—and it was clear that unless IOS men were able to cash in soon afterward, the bonds of loyalty might start to fray. (In 1967, IOS had to damp down impatience by offering to buy back 10 per cent of any shareholding at the "formula price.") How did it come about that the upstarts from the Caribbean were allowed to get to the market before the pioneers?

It sounds paradoxical to say that this was because IOS was near to financial collapse in 1966–1967. But it is strictly true: when Gramco made its dash, on the figures IOS was in no condition to sell off, to other than its own salesmen, the shares of the parent company, IOS Ltd. (SA). That year, as IOS was tossed out of country after country around the world, sales of IOS funds fell, while the decline in stock prices further eroded what was left. Nevertheless, the sheer bulk of the IOS funds remained impressive. But while even sophisticated financial minds tend to assume that where there is much money gathered there will be profits also, this is not inevitably the case. There may well be no profits of the sort that can be set out in accounts, and sold off in a share issue.

When Gramco started operations at the beginning of 1967, IOS was reeling from a series of blows: the series of expulsions; the loss of Brazil, the biggest market; the trouble with the Swiss and the hasty, expensive move to Ferney-Voltaire; rescuing salesmen, bringing them back to Geneva, and, in many cases, supporting them till new field operations could be mounted—all this was an expensive business. And there was also the costly process of bringing in James Roosevelt's lawyers and ex-civil servants. Operating expenses (as distinct from commissions paid to salesmen) took a 74-per-cent jump in 1967, while revenue from sales went up by only 11 per cent (it had been 40 per cent the year before).

By the end of that year, as we have seen in Chapter 14, IOS was giving away one-quarter of its net income from sales operations.

Like many developments in the IOS saga, the Latin American disaster shows up in the history of the sales force. The force almost doubled in size between 1964 and 1965, went up 50 per cent in 1966, but during 1967, increased by only 16 per cent.

The result of the mid-career crisis was that IOS lost money in 1967, on the item it called "sale and management of mutual funds." The loss was quite small—$635,000—but it was only recouped by the profits of the insurance companies, the banking operations, and the revenues IOS appropriated from the FOF Proprietary Funds system. This last came largely from "performance fees"—*i.e.*, IOS's slice of capital gains made with the fund money, rather than the regular fee for managing the money anyway.

Sales volume expanded again as soon as the machinery of stock options and overrides could be applied to new markets. And the rate of increase of the sales force recovered also: 28 per cent in 1968 and 50 per cent in 1969. The great discovery, of course, was Germany, and by 1968 the sales, in terms of cash and commitments together, had risen to $1.7 billion, with an even more astonishing rise in 1969 to $3.2 billion. But sales volume alone, especially in terms of "face value" of programs sold, would never make IOS Ltd. itself enormously wealthy, because the greater part of the revenue from sales loads would always go to the salesmen in commissions.

Indeed, the simple expansion of sales carried great dangers, because as time went on the override system became more and more heavily laden with sales bosses, who were drawing large sums of money on other people's commissions. Between 1967 and 1969, the percentage of sales charges going in commissions rose from 61 per cent to just over 70 per cent. As IOS's Canadian brokers, J. H. Crang & Co., put it, "The progressive build-up of a structured sales organization involving multitiered management levels increases the proportion of total volume subject to maximum commission rates."

Yet even if the sales expansion was becoming progressively more dangerous, there was no possibility that it could be controlled—at least, not before "the Apocalypse," as IOS men later called the events of 1970. By the later 1960s, the working of the stock-option plan had put powerful blocks of IOS shares into the hands of men whose personal income was related very precisely to the sheer volume of sales. Toward the end, in early 1970, there was an attempt to have a "self-denying ordinance," under which personal commission incomes would be limited to $250,000. But even though the roof was falling in by then, the idea was killed by the sales bosses. And in the logic of sales, they were right, because the whole motivational structure depended upon the idea that any sacrifice was worth while to achieve an override structure: that if you sincerely wanted to be rich, you could win a source of wealth which would be limited only by the size of the new markets you could find and exploit.

This was the other side of the feudal structure of IOS. Like barons, the sales bosses remained loyal, in return for grants of territory and income: they were not interested in obeying the sort of rationalistic, bureaucratic rules that are necessary if a modern corporation is to control and organize its profits. They were not likely to be impressed by the suggestion that dividends could be paid on IOS shares only by reducing commission structures. For the most part, the sales bosses *were* the shareholders, and in a choice between commission income and share income, commission income would always win.

Until the Apocalypse, Cornfeld remained much the largest single shareholder. But this gave him the power to punish and reward only as between individuals: he could not impose unwelcome restraints upon a whole class of men. Cornfeld could exercise the sort of control that a medieval prince could when leading a crusade. He could indicate the rough direction in which the crusade should head. He could furnish an inspiring personal example and help to build up a lot of ideology about overcoming the infidel, rescuing the Holy Places, and so on. When the crusade happened upon some succulent piece of territory he could apportion it to this baron rather than that one. But he could not afford to suggest—even if it occurred to him—that there should be any restraint upon the acquisitive process as such.

But however expensive the IOS sales force might grow, it could provide a huge *bulk* of money for Cornfeld and Cowett to operate with. Surely, the weight of hundreds of millions of dollars must be able to produce profits for IOS, more than enough to compensate for the cost of the sales force. It was only a question of organizing the right leverages.

One basic approach was to search for exciting short-term capital gains with the funds, and to appropriate "performance fees" as a reward. This was done at first by putting money into stock-market operations, under conditions which virtually forced the managers to speculate.* When it became harder and harder to wring short-term capital gains from the stock market, IOS reacted in several ways.

---

*See Chapter 17, "The Master Financiers."

One was to launch a new stock-market operation, which was frankly labeled as involving "more risk" than previous ones. The new vehicle was Venture Fund (International), launched in April 1969, partly as a response to salesmen who were clamoring for a new vehicle to sell, because they were worried by the rise of Gramco. Venture International quickly attracted over $100 million and within eight months it had spent $23 million—a quarter of its investments—on unregistered securities.

Another reaction was to get into real-estate promotion, but, whether from pride or caution, IOS would not emulate Gramco in building an open-end fund around real estate. Indeed, Ed Cowett went so far as to expound the dangers of the practice, and said that it was because of it he was at odds with his Harvard friend Lew Kaplan, who was General Counsel to Gramco. IOS's answer to "liquid real estate" was launched on June 20, 1969: Investment Properties International, a closed-end property company with a capital of $100 million in nonredeemable shares. (IOS, characteristically, kept all the voting shares for itself.) Investments were already on hand for the new fund, because IOS was building a series of costly apartment blocks at Playamar in Spain and Hallandale in Florida. The idea on the birth of IPI was neat: the fund investors would own the developments, and the apartments in them would be sold for the fund by the IOS sales force. IOS proposed to take off a 22½-per-cent commission for selling each apartment—and on the $46 million involved in the biggest development, the Hemisphere in Florida, that came to a handy $10 million for IOS. Out of that, expenses had to be paid, but it was action that even Gramco could hardly sneeze at.

The company's own auditors pointed out that this was twice the usual commission. And Martin Seligson, who was in charge of IOS real-estate operations, consulted his lawyers to make sure that the level of commissions could be kept hidden from buyers.

Although the IPI shares were received with heated enthusiasm by the sales force in summer 1969, the operation was predicated a little too heavily on there being no limit to the numbers of wealthy Americans anxious to rent retirement homes in the sun, owned by unsuspecting German, Lebanese, and other IOS customers. The shares did not take long to become virtually unmarketable, and few of the customers can have made much money from their association with IPI. Martin Seligson, the boss of IPI, had a happier experience—especially in connection with the Florida land bought by the fund.

Next door to the Hemisphere in Hallandale, there was a tract of 173,000 acres of unimproved inland waterfront called the Waterways, a 60-per-cent interest in this land was owned by IPI, and the other 40 per cent was owned by certain "junior partners," including Martin Seligson, Chairman of IPI itself. (Seligson explained that when he joined IOS as a real-estate expert, he arranged with Cornfeld that he should be allowed to participate personally in such developments as he fancied.) In early 1970, IPI decided to buy out the junior partners, whereupon Seligson made a profit of $80,000 on a $110,000 investment. "Things like this can be made to sound terrible," says Seligson, "but I disclosed my interest. Everybody knew about it." The value, he maintains, was independently determined. Everybody did not include the shareholders. The transaction was not thought worthy of mention in IPI's 1969 report—which, indeed, did not even reveal the existence of minority-interest holders in the Waterways.

When the price of IPI shares began to collapse in the fall of 1969, IOS's stern line on the evils of liquid real estate first wavered, then broke. The open-end Fund of Funds began to buy up IPI shares in an attempt to keep up the price, and so FOF acquired in short order nearly half of all the IPI shares. Thus were real-estate holdings stuffed into an open-end structure.

• • •

Real estate, however, was only a sideline, although one that fascinated both Cornfeld and Cowett. Their most important response to the thirst for profits was to carry the search for "performance" beyond the stock market. They organized a section of FOF to invest in "communications media" and they tried to work out schemes for an art fund, and even a commodities fund which would speculate in cocoa, coffee, rare metals, pepper, and so on. The commodities and art funds were still talking points when the crash came, but they did expand into "natural-resources investment" where the performance of the investments, and, therefore, the profits accruing to IOS became a matter of their own heady estimates. (This is fully described in the next chapter.)

Nothing was overlooked that could turn a percentage on the customers' money: brokerage was scooped up, and arrangements were made to make money on lending out fund securities. Although not one of the biggest operations, this was, in a way, one of the most audacious.

It exploited the fact that a stockbroker may find himself short in a particular security, when he needs to make a delivery. This means he needs to borrow a supply of the shares, and in 1968 securities from FOF Proprietary Ltd. began to be loaned out to brokers. The collateral for the loans was cash, and of course interest was earned on the cash. If such loans—which would have been illegal for an American mutual fund—were to be made, all the proceeds should have gone back into the fund.

But naturally IOS kept a slice of this income (called a "fee for advice") for itself. By 1969 the system was refined, and the fund "agreed to make its securities available for loan" to an IOS subsidiary. The IOS company then held the collateral cash when brokers borrowed the securities: so, in effect, IOS transferred fund money into its own hands. By this time IOS was keeping more than a third of the proceeds from the operation, getting on for $1 million a year.

Such devices were useful, of course, but the great hope and opportunity lay in the grandiose plans for investment banking, the ultimate expression of Cornfeld's dictum that "if you want to make money, don't horse around with steel or light bulbs—work directly with money." This was what lay behind convoluted deals like Commonwealth United: the idea that the IOS investment banks could underwrite gigantic financing operations, and take heavy fees for doing so, in the knowledge that the power of the IOS funds lay behind them to guarantee underwriting success. Something like a third of all the value of the bond issues underwritten by the IOS banks found its way into the investment portfolios of the funds. More bluntly: the customers' money was used to float securities promoted by Investors Overseas Services itself.

When, after its long hesitation, the market collapsed at last, the securities which the IOS banks had promoted were revealed, as one watcher in Geneva put it, to be "an unparalleled set of dogs." Still, short-term, the policy paid off. Profits from IOS Financial Holdings, the subsidiary which ran the banks, were under $1 million in 1966. They doubled in 1967 to $1.6 million, and more than doubled in 1968 to reach $3.4 million. In the first half of 1969, they seemed to be on their way to something like $10 million.

Just at the moment when the sales operation was about to

become hopelessly uneconomic, the banks saved the day. By early summer of 1969, even though Gramco had stolen a march, IOS Ltd. (SA) was able to present itself as a fairly orthodox corporation making substantial profits.

It was a finely poised moment. IOS could not have cashed in before 1966, because the international financial community was still suspicious of the offshore game. The latter part of 1969 was the first moment that cashing in became possible: but it was also the last. The short-term problems were the greed of the sales bosses and the consequences of speculation. There was also, however, a problem of a more general nature.

The end of the first decade of the IOS Investment Program was now in sight, when large batches of ten-year programs would reach payout stage. Nobody who was aware of the set of charges which had been applied to those programs could be confident about the reactions which would follow. Proceeds from those charges had gone to support the lavish and erratic administration of IOS, and to help provide capital for IOS banks, insurance companies, and real-estate ventures. The search for performance had in part been an attempt to find gains such as would cover the effect of the charges. It had succeeded only partially, and time was running out.

Nevertheless, in the last blue summer of the offshore years, the great ramshackle golden galleon was still afloat, and still had steerage way. It should be possible to sell off a part interest in her fortunes, and experts were invited aboard to sound the well.

• • •

The underwriting and public offering of the shares of a major corporation is one of the great ceremonies of capitalism. There is a flavor of priestly observance about the sonorous titles of the underwriting banks which are attached to the offer documents and listed in "tombstone" advertisements on the day of issue. One hundred and twenty-two underwriters, from New York, Tokyo, London, and most of the financial centers of Europe, put their names to the Investors Overseas Services offer in September 1969, and the list made an incomparably grander impression than Gramco's.

There was, however, a name missing, and its absence made the list unique in financial history. Although Banque Rothschild of Paris appeared as one of the six managing underwriters at the head of the list, the name of N. M. Rothschild and Sons of London did not appear at all.

The financial interests of the French and English Rothschilds are independent, but powerful ties of family and tradition remain. Nobody could remember an occasion when one Rothschild house had declined, as a matter of policy, to take part in an offering to which the prestige of the other house was publicly committed. The decision was taken only after a long and unhappy partners' meeting at New Court in London: it was one of the indications that the flotation of IOS Ltd. was not quite the stately financial occasion that it appeared to be at first sight.

Part of the trouble was the scope of IOS ambitions. Gramco only offered a million shares, and although the prospectus quoted some wondrous profits, it was reasonably plain that the thing was fairly chancy. "It seemed like a good speculation for our own account," said one London merchant banker. Few of the banks which underwrote Gramco actually sold the shares actively: they merely waited for inquiries, which as it happened were plentiful.

But where Gramco came along with a few hot shares and a terse fourteen pages of prospectus, IOS appeared with a sixty-seven-page tome in various editions on the strength of which they proposed to sell a total of 11 *million* shares. At $10 apiece, that meant the offer was intended to raise $110,000,000. And when Ed Cowett declared that this was the biggest public offering of shares since the Ford Motor Company went public in 1956, and was the second biggest on record, he was virtually asking you to agree that a large part of the future of capitalism lay somewhere out beyond the continental shelf. For some people, that was too much to swallow.

The Gramco operation might be little more than an agreement to "make a market" in some shares. But there was no getting away from the fact that the IOS operation was presented as a proper underwriting business. The six banks whose names appeared on the cover of the main prospectus were supposed to have made a thoroughgoing investigation of IOS and its affairs. On the strength of the reputation, and the inquiries of the principal underwriters, the other one hundred and sixteen underwriters accepted and represented that IOS was a serious, well-organized financial concern whose shares were worth $10 apiece in their opinion.

The London Rothschilds were not alone in refusing to underwrite IOS. A number of important London banks refused, including Warburg's and Hambro's. And although some big Wall Street names came in, Kuhn, Loeb—normally part of any important underwriting—did not appear. None of the big German banks came in, although Commerzbank Aktiengesellschaft had unbent so far as to join in the Gramco fun. But despite such exceptions, the big list was an imposing one.

There were twelve French banks, including the Banque de l'Indochine, Banque Worms et Cie., and the Banque de Suez et de l'Union des Mines. There were thirty-four British banks and financial concerns—the biggest contingent—which included major stockbrokers (Cazenove & Co., Panmure Gordon & Co.), two of the biggest banks (Westminster and Barclays),

Lloyds Bank Europe, J. Henry Schroder Wagg & Co., Samuel Montagu & Co., and Slater, Walker Ltd. There were twenty-five American firms, including Bache & Co.; Bear, Stearns & Co.; Loeb, Rhoades & Co.; and Goldman, Sachs & Co. There were four Japanese securities companies, and banks from Sweden, Norway, Switzerland, Finland, Denmark, Belgium, and Australia.

Yet the prospectus for the offer was marred by misrepresentations and inconsistencies. Its different editions did not even agree as to the arithmetic of the number of shares being offered, and the company which was under offer was actually so ramshackle that within six months its shares were barely salable.

Accidents happen in the best of underwriting operations, but this was a very big accident. General responsibility may be ascribed to the offshore euphoria of the year, but particular responsibility belongs to the six banks which were principal underwriters for IOS, and which, therefore, received principals' portion of the $3.2 million, plus expenses, which the offering produced in fees and discounts. As ranked in the prospectus, they were: Drexel, Harriman, Ripley Inc.; Banque Rothschild; Guinness Mahon & Co. Ltd.; Hill, Samuel & Co. Ltd.; Pierson, Heldring & Pierson; Smith, Barney & Co. Inc.

Drexel, which led the principal underwriters and therefore bore the chief responsibility for investigating IOS, was at that time a new amalgamation of a New York house with an old-line Pennsylvania house. The amalgamation changed almost immediately after bringing IOS to market: several partners departed and the bank changed its name to Drexel Firestone, with an insertion of capital from the tire firm Firestone.

Banque Rothschild, of course, ranked as one of the most eminent investment-banking names in Europe. But before the public offer, IOS and Banque Rothschild were working on the joint promotion of IOS's first French "product," the mutual fund called Rothschild-Expansion. Granted this, Banque Rothschild could scarcely decline to underwrite the offering of IOS itself.

Similar considerations applied to Guinness Mahon, first-named but smaller of the two London merchant banks. Since 1966, Guinness Mahon had been handling a block of IOS investments on the London Stock Exchange. Martin Brooke, a Guinness Mahon director, was also on the IOS Board. In effect, both Banque Rothschild and Guinness Mahon had taken the position that IOS was a sound concern before the underwriting inquiries began. The latter three principals played somewhat lesser parts. Pierson, Heldring & Pierson is a distinguished Amsterdam concern which is affiliated with Rothschild interests—on IOS, they agreed with the French, rather than the English, branch. Hill, Samuel is a London bank with a taste for large, international deals, and Smith, Barney, the last-ranked principal underwriter, is a well-known New York investment banker.

If, from time to time, any of the underwriters were worried by any antic of Cornfeld's, they found relief in the suave, masterful person of Ed Cowett—easygoing, tireless, with every figure at his fingertips. "All the underwriters liked the look of Ed," said one IOS accountant.

There were actually three different but simultaneous offerings of IOS shares. What the international banking group underwrote was the selling, to investors at large, of 5.6 million newly minted common shares of IOS at $10 apiece. After underwriters' commissions, this put $52 million of new cash into the IOS corporate treasury.

At the same time, people who already held existing IOS shares offered parts of their holdings at the same price of $10. Through J. H. Crang & Co., IOS's Toronto broker, 1.45 million shares were offered to the Canadian public. Through IOS's own

Investors Overseas Bank another 3.95 million shares were offered to salesmen, customers, and employees of IOS itself. These two offers, totaling 5.4 million shares offered for $54 million, constituted the long-awaited "cashing in." That sort of money seemed to have been worth waiting for.

There were some doubts about the wisdom of IOS going public, especially among the staff, as against the salesmen and big shareholders. Essentially, all these doubts were about whether IOS could stand the searching glare of public examination and the obligation to publish detailed accounts. These were misgivings, of course, which were amply justified, but they were only expressed at the time in disguised form. Another objection was that the markets were generally in poor shape. Cowett simply replied to this that a poor market would make the IOS offer look all the more attractive.

He had an inspiring example to offer, because in November 1968 IOS had floated off 600,000 shares of one of the principal subsidiaries of the empire, IOS Management Ltd. This was a Canadian-registered concern through which IOS channeled the straight management-fee income from three funds: the Fund of Funds, IIT, and the Canadian Regent Fund. In effect, IOS was selling off part of the income from its large funds, and the markets certainly appeared to think that this income was going to increase. The little parcel of IOS Management shares was formally offered at $12.50: trading began at $75 and in March 1969, when anything that could be called "offshore" was at a hectic premium, IOS Management shares stood at $180 each.

• • •

The prospectus for a public offering of its shares is perhaps the most serious document a company ever produces. There must be no puffing, no concealment, and no misrepresentation. The prospectus must give investors a truthful description of the company, whereby they can make rational estimates of its capacity to earn profits. Drexel, Harriman, Ripley and their legal counsel in New York, Shearman & Sterling, were acutely aware that IOS, because of its past history, was something of a tricky proposition for them, and in the early summer of 1969, they spent a good deal of time trying to get some kind of blessing for their project from the SEC. They made eloquent assurances that they would conduct a thorough investigation of IOS, and would make sure that the prospectus was up to SEC standards. The Commission officials, however, were noncommittal. They merely said that the project was not illegal and that if Drexel wanted to go ahead, it was up to Drexel's own business judgment. As none of the IOS shares were to be sold to American citizens—what Drexel was underwriting was an *international* offer—the SEC ban on IOS did not apply.

At one meeting, in June, the men from Drexel and Shearman & Sterling suggested that the underwriters might be able to get to the bottom of things at IOS that the SEC had not been able to do. According to IOS's own records of the offering, Allan Mostoff and his SEC colleagues were amused. Laughingly, Mostoff said they would be interested to see the prospectus when it came out.

Throughout the summer of 1969, a team of IOS accountants labored at calculations with the team from Drexel, Harriman, Ripley, and with another from Price Waterhouse, the accountants retained to advise the underwriters. Cowett commanded every aspect of the work, and in mid-July he personally directed the maneuver by which IOS Ltd. (SA) of Panama City turned itself into a Canadian corporation, with the same shareholders and officers, ready to have its shares listed on the Toronto and Amsterdam stock exchanges.

The basic IOS prospectus which emerged from this process ran to some 45,000 words, dense with legal definitions and statistics. It appeared to portray, if read with sympathy, a mighty and fast-growing international financial empire; twelve mutual funds, five insurance companies, eleven banks and financial-service concerns, four real-estate management companies, a construction company, a computer-service company, and a couple of small publishers. The injection into the treasury of the parent company of another $52 million capital would enable new expansion to proceed. And it was surely no less than proper that those who had built this great edifice so rapidly should be rewarded in separate share offerings.

Yet looked at with careful skepticism, there was much information in the prospectus which would produce a second, quite different, picture. This was of a company scarcely profitable, if at all, in terms of its rationally predictable income, which was from the sale and routine management of mutual funds. This was a picture of a company whose profits were increasingly cobbled together from a series of on-off deals and speculations. It was the general quality of the prospectus that the first picture was more easily visible than the second. There were particular omissions which contributed to that effect.

And there was something more than mere omission involved where a very considerable body had been stuffed under the carpet. The process left a couple of ruffles, which nobody noticed at the time of the offer. But they were clues to a misrepresentation which had its origins in the history of IOS and in the careers of Cowett and Cornfeld, and which affected the validity of the proposition on which IOS offered to sell its shares.

The reputation of IOS, as a manager of mutual funds, was firmly pinned to the idea of "performance." At the time that the offering was being prepared, the IOS performance flag was moving from the Fund of Funds over to IIT. And by the time of the offering, IIT had nosed past FOF and was again the biggest of the funds, with some $640 million under management. The reason that IIT attracted more mutual-fund investors in the late 1960s was that it appeared to have a better rate of investment growth than the Fund of Funds, which had begun to fade somewhat. The records on which IOS sold IIT said that the shares of the fund had been worth $3.53 in 1962, and by the autumn of 1969 each IIT share was worth $8.82. It thus appeared that the fund's shares had increased in value by 150 per cent over seven years under IOS's management—an impressive record.

It was also an *untrue* record, because the life of IIT began in December 1960, not autumn 1962, and at a value of $5 per share, not $3.53. The fund's shares fell to only $3.53 during 1962, under the impact of a series of investment disasters, including the collapse of a number of Ed Cowett promotions.

On the true record, IIT had not increased 150 per cent. Over nearly a decade, it had increased by 76.4 per cent. As "performance" that was mediocre, to say the least. Taking the sales load into account, a customer would have done better—with much less risk—by getting into a fixed-interest investment at 6 per cent and reinvesting in his returns each year.

The usual rationalization advanced by IOS executives to justify selling IIT on incomplete records was that the fund management had been reorganized in October 1962, when IIT was first offered under the IOS Investment Program. The accompanying implication—though misleading—was often that IIT had not been managed by IOS before then, even if IOS sold its shares. It was a rationalization which avoided the whole purpose of fund records, which is to help investors discover whether a fund has suffered from just such afflictions as would require its management to be reorganized.

Sometimes, IOS men suggested that the point was "unimportant." The suggestion that it didn't matter if most of the customers of one of the world's biggest funds had bought after receiving false information scarcely requires comment. And it hardly squares with the devious means which were used to obscure the facts at the time of the IOS offering.

There were three editions of the IOS prospectus: a Drexel edition, which bore the names of the principal underwriters; an Investors Overseas Bank edition, which generally followed the Drexel one, and a Crang edition, containing information required by Ontario securities law. They differed on the IIT point.

DREXEL EDITION

A table on page 15 encapsulated the history of the IOS funds. One column gave the year when each of them had been "organized" or "acquired"—but without saying which word applied. Against IIT's name, this column gave the year "1962."

On page 17, this statement was qualified in the text. IIT was described as "an open-end mutual fund, *organized* in December 1960 as a unit investment trust under the laws of Luxembourg, which *came under the company's management in 1962*." (Our italics.)

Taken together, the two statements could have only one meaning. Since the second said that IIT was "organized" before 1962, the first could only mean that IOS had "acquired" it in 1962. Therefore, IIT had been organized and run for some time by someone else, who sold it to IOS in 1962.

This was a plain misrepresentation, in the main prospectus, but so worded as to seem to fit in with the rationalization usually given for IIT's incomplete record. It suggested that IOS had had *nothing* to do with the sad early history of IIT.

The falsehood is exposed by placing alongside the prospectus IOS's Annual Report for 1961 (a document which it took us some time to find). The report records plainly that IOS "organized" IIT in December 1960, and that IOS owned 100 per cent of the stock of IIT Management Company. The 1961 report is confirmed by company registration records in Luxembourg.

CRANG EDITION

This was the prospectus in which misrepresentation would be most dangerous—IOS being by now a Canadian company offering shares to Canadians. Even so, there was some blurring of the IIT date. On page 4, giving a history of IOS, the prospectus said it was in 1961 that "IOS sponsored its first mutual fund . . . IIT." On page 9, in a table, the prospectus gave the correct year, 1960. (IIT, it should be noted, was never sold in Canada.)

INVESTORS OVERSEAS BANK EDITION

An early version gave, correctly, 1960 for the start of IIT. But the final version repeated the Drexel formula—thus suggesting, in its table on page 15, that IIT was not acquired until 1962.

Interestingly enough, Arthur Andersen & Co., the auditors to IOS and to IIT from 1960 on, specifically assured the underwriters that they had read page 15 of the prospectus. They took no specific responsibility for the accuracy of the prospectus at this point, but they did not report any omissions or distortions.

The misrepresentations over IIT not only allowed IOS to exaggerate its success in its basic line of business, namely, managing investments, but also obliterated clues pointing toward a discreditable but still recent episode in the history of Ed Cowett—the architect of the public offering and the man on whose personal standing the company was brought to the market with the imprimatur of the international financial community.

Another corpse was buried at the point where the prospectus implied that IOS was actually making profits on its sales operations—when, in truth, it was making whacking losses. At the top of page 10, a table declared that "sale and management of mutual funds and related income" provided 37 per cent of the company's profits during the first half of 1969. The text then said: "The Company does not allocate operating expenses between the sales and the management of mutual funds."

Considering that the essence of the mutual-fund business is to control sales costs, while making profits on management fees, this was not a very enlightening accounting policy. The text went on: "Although revenues from mutual fund sales are significantly higher than mutual fund management fees, the company believes that management activities currently provide a much greater contribution to net income." ("Net income" = "profits.")

This implies quite clearly that sales are making *some* contribution to profits. Yet by turning to pages 6 and 7, the reader could make a tortuous calculation, and deduce that the reverse was the case. On these two pages were the *Statements of Consolidated Income and Retained Earnings*. From this, the reader could extract the earnings of IOS Ltd. from all sources *other* than sales between January and June 1969: "management and service fees, interest, etc."; "earnings of unconsolidated subsidiaries"; and "income from Proprietary Funds." Altogether, these three items added up to $14,392,000. Yet the "net revenue," or profits, were much less: $9,521,000. Something, somewhere, was losing the difference, that is $4,871,000. Realistically, it could only be the sales force. And in the "Apocalypse," of course, it emerged that the sales force, far from making any contribution to profits, was losing money heavily.

"If you took a look at the profits for the first half of 1969," said an IOS accountant who worked on the prospectus, "the alarm bells were ringing all over the place." Maybe they were: but you had to know how to listen. And even if you did wonder whether IOS might not be losing momentum, there was a note on page 8, a sort of reassuring caveat which might dispel some fears. It was expected, said the note, that net income would decline in the third quarter of 1969. But the experience of previous years showed that IOS's last quarter was usually the best.

Just as the early history of IIT was eliminated, and the cost of the sales force covered up, so the prospectus minimized the evidence of IOS's injudicious investment-banking operations. The Crang prospectus did not even mention Commonwealth United Corporation, and the Drexel edition dealt with it in a footnote. This (repeated in the final IOB edition) merely said that Commonwealth had become "illiquid," and that IOS had caused Investment Properties International to lend it $4.5 million from fund money.

But before the completion of the prospectus, the IOS banks lent another $3.5 million to Commonwealth—a corporation which, since June 1969, had been unable to raise credit anywhere else. These advances put IOS Ltd. itself at a risk in the affairs of the sickly conglomerate. But there was no way purchasers of IOS shares could know that. (Eventually, IOS had to take over the IPI loan, advance still more money, and establish a $7-million reserve against Commonwealth commitments.)

Cowett, subsequently, claimed that the Commonwealth loans were left out of the prospectus because IOS regarded them as "normal banking transactions." Yet Commonwealth have since admitted that the only reason they agreed to IOS's abnormal terms* was that no one else would handle the transaction.

Possibly the most basic requirement in a prospectus is a de-

---

*See Chapter 17, "The Master Financiers."

scription of the share capital of the company being offered. Yet the different editions of the IOS prospectus did not even agree on that. The Crang version makes a simple arithmetical error in one section, which overstates by 100,000 the number of shares being put up by selling shareholders. As to the total share capital of IOS, the best calculation one could make, on the documents available on September 24, was that the total number of IOS shares outstanding was not much less than 48 million and not much more than 49 million. Thus, an investor could not even compute the book value of his shares precisely.

This was the prospectus which Drexel, Harriman, Ripley together with Shearman & Sterling set out to make the equivalent of those written under SEC regulation. Apart from other omissions, it told the investors remarkably little about what the company was going to do with their money. There was nothing more than an airy reference to making time deposits, and to expansion in "banking and insurance areas."

Having completed their investigation, the banks haggled with Cowett over the price at which the IOS shares should be launched. Great interest was being expressed in the offer, and in London it was reported that the investment-dollar premium was forced up by the eagerness of would-be investors. In Geneva the rights to IOS shares "when issued" changed hands for as much as $28 per share.

The directors of IOS were euphoric. Many of them thought that Cowett should ask the underwriters to set the launching price at $15, even $20 per share. Their attitude was that they weren't going to give IOS shares away to a lot of bankers at bargain prices: if the underwriters didn't like it, then let them drop out—IOS would sell the shares themselves. With some difficulty, Cowett, who was the realist on this occasion, got the board's authority to settle for $10. Even this left the underwriters unhappy. Guinness Mahon thought the price should be $7, and Drexel, Smith, Barney, and Banque Rothschild thought $8. Late in August, there was a long and difficult meeting in Geneva, and Cowett managed to get the underwriters to come up to $9.50. Complaining bitterly, the IOS Board accepted the price. Bernie was telephoned in Paris, and he too assented, rather reluctantly.

The underwriters were already dispersing toward their homes, and toward the Swiss mountains, when late in the afternoon Cornfeld called Cowett again from Paris. He wanted to talk to the underwriters himself. With some difficulty, Cowett reassembled them and Bernie flew to Geneva to make the new pitch.

"He talked to them about the mystique of the company," recalled Cowett, "and he talked to them about the mystique of ten dollars. And goddam it, he convinced them. Of course, within half an hour, they were unconvinced again—but they had done the deal." It was the conceptual salesman's finest single achievement, and so he closed the deal for a single sale with a face volume of $110 million.

Of that money, roughly half went to the selling shareholders, and the influx to the IOS corporate treasury from the sale of new shares was $52,400,826, after deductions (for underwriting commissions, etc.).

If ever a company needed to raise new capital, it was IOS: on the day the proceeds came in, the effective cash position of the IOS parent company was $1 million. But the respite for the treasury was short-lived. The new cash was rapidly disposed of in a series of intricate and profligate schemes. In order to understand the inner beauty of the grander ones, it is necessary to become better acquainted with John McCandish King.

John M. King: The Power of Natural Gas

In which we introduce Ambassador John M. King and describe an industry built on tax avoidance. Together with their new chum, our heroes get mixed up in the Middle East crisis, hunting oil in Arab waters. Ed Cowett discovers the Arctic; NOPIs and other strange animals appear; Handley Page Aircraft becomes a casualty.

T he IOS issue was a hot one. Investors were disposed to believe Ed Cowett when he said that the public offer was inspired essentially by a desire to demonstrate the maturity of IOS, not by a wish to cash in. "We don't need the money, that's for sure," he said. Wise financial heads were inclined to accept that the offshore problem child had grown up, and could make a serious contribution to the workings of international capitalism. The feeling induced by the public offer was admirably summed up by a writer in the *Financial Post* of Toronto, the city in which, formally, the Fund of Funds had its home. IOS, said the *Financial Post*, was becoming "increasingly conscious of its public image, and is perhaps becoming a bit more conservative. At the same time, the financial Establishment is becoming a bit more daring and innovative—and the two might meet soon in the center." Journalistic appreciations of IOS, in most parts of the world, were moving rapidly from the guarded to the fulsome: a conviction was spreading, in the words of the London *Observer*, that "the world needs IOS."

The general financial climate was ambivalent. The Dow-Jones index, having declined most of 1969, was wallowing. But people looked forward to an upturn in 1970: surely this was the bottom of the cycle? IOS appeared to be busying itself respectably with ways of protecting investors against the sluggishness of the stock market. And then on the very last day of the year, IOS displayed a sudden flash of the Old Adam. It was inspired by Ed and Bernie's fatal fascination with the schemes of John M. King, the resident djin of Denver, Colorado.

. . .

People used to find it very difficult to understand just what type of business John King's companies were in. Even in a basically laudatory article, a baffled newspaper in Denver had to admit that the city's fastest-moving businessman tended to use "a lot of words to reveal very little." In reply to a puzzled shareholder, King once said the King Resources Company was "a technological service company, oriented toward development and management of natural resources, with superior human resources to do the job. We are a body shop. We create ideas and cause those ideas to be well-financed—then we go out and do the work."

C. Henry Buhl III, the investment director of IOS, was among those who found this sort of language difficult to penetrate. In November 1969, when IOS was investing large sums of money with King Resources, Buhl went out to Denver and spent three days talking with King's executives. Buhl admits to having been convinced by some very unfortunate propositions during his time with IOS, but when he left Denver for Los Angeles, he told the King men, "You know, I don't understand this company."

No sooner had Buhl reached Los Angeles than he received a call from John King himself. "Henry," said King, "I don't think you understand my company."

"You're damn right I don't," said Buhl. "I'll fly out and explain," said King.

John King was going somewhere in one of his private jets, and he arranged to touch down at Burbank airport. Buhl spent two hours on the rush-hour freeways getting to Burbank, where they sat together in the back of a car while King delivered a two-hour lecture.

It must have been a curious scene. Henry Buhl is a slight, worried-looking man whose only concession to flamboyance in his business dress is a tiny CHBIII monogram on his shirt. John King stands six foot four and weighs two hundred thirty pounds: he affects cowboy boots, hats with a "K" on the side, and is reputed to own three thousand pairs of cuff links. He has a big, domelike head, piercing blue eyes, and a booming voice.

"He kept talking about the 'use-of-money factor,' " Buhl recalled. "He said King Resources didn't have any projects that were paying less than 60 per cent a year. I said, 'John, I never heard of any investment that always paid 60 per cent a year.' And he said, 'You know what I mean, we cut off the least profitable ones.' When King got out of the car, I still didn't understand his damned company."

King did make at least one very clear financial statement, apropos his connections with Investors Overseas Services. "I'm very hot for international monies," he said. "It is so much easier to do business with those people. . . ."

John McCandish King was born in Illinois in 1927, the same year that Bernard Cornfeld was born in Istanbul. King suffered from asthma and other illnesses during his youth, which meant that his education was upset, and he did not graduate from any of the three universities he attended. He left his last one, Northwestern, not from illness, but because he wished to further his political ambitions.

King was a Democrat until he was eighteen, when he switched to the Republican Party, and at twenty-three he was elected to the Illinois House of Representatives. At the end of his first two-year term, the young legislator found that he had about $1500 left over from his pay. He sank it all in a wildcat oil well.

As a number of his customers were to discover later, the chances of hitting oil with any well drilled in the United States are one in four, but only one in eleven hits oil in commercial quantities. The chances of a wildcat striking are one in thirty, but King's first wildcat, drilled on a friend's farm in Oklahoma, did strike oil. "I've always been lucky," he said. "I get into difficult situations, but I always manage to come up smelling like a rose."

The success of that Oklahoma wildcat decided the direction of John King's career. In 1955, King went into partnership with a man called Ben Stevenson in Chicago and formed the King-Stevenson Oil & Gas Co.

But John King did not become an oilman in the same sense as, say, Paul Getty. Nor did the companies he organized do the same kind of things as Standard Oil or Shell. In that sense, John King was not really an oilman at all. He was in the fund business; only his funds were drilling funds, not mutual funds. While Cornfeld owed his power and prosperity to the outflow of dollars beyond the United States, King owed his to features of the taxation system inside the United States. King's business consisted primarily not of exploiting oil fields, but of exploiting the taxation advantages available to those who look for oil fields.

Despite Congressional attacks which have progressively

whittled away at those advantages ("inept laws and historic emotionalism," said John King), it remains official policy to allow people to claim tax relief upon money invested in the search for oil and upon any income arising from oil discovered. The potential of this system as a "tax shelter" was widely exploited for the first time in the 1950s. Highly paid film stars, sportsmen, and other folk in need of tax relief could not go out and drill their own wells. But there was nothing to stop them getting together in partnerships, pooling their money into a fund, and hiring a manager to handle the drilling. It was then natural for the managers to turn into promoters, actively selling pieces of such partnerships. Fees increased, and since the manager tended to have little or none of his own money at stake, it often became questionable whether he cared whether his wells struck oil or not. Some wells were thought to exist only on tax returns. Others had to do service for more than one partnership, so that it would have been an embarrassment to strike oil, because accounts would have to be produced. There is said to have been some trade in "dry holes" to meet such difficulties.

Abuses of this sort came to a head in the late 1950s, when a couple of drilling funds collapsed and a cloud settled over the whole business. It suffered a further blow in 1964, when the maximum tax rate was cut, eliminating some of the demand.

At the end of the 1950s, John King moved from Chicago to Denver. The King-Stevenson partnership broke up, and in January 1961 King started up a new concern, King Resources, which took over the oil and gas properties of the old firm. For the first six years of its life King Resources made little mark on the business scene. Then in 1966 John King started up with a new kind of drilling fund, and within three years, *Forbes* magazine reckoned that $300 million would be "a low guess" for King's personal wealth. As to the amount of money his companies controlled, "nobody other than King would dare put a figure on the total. . . ."

The corporate structure that King assembled contained some of the most incestuous intercompany relationships which have ever been attempted, and it was this complexity of relationships that caused people to be puzzled about just what King Resources did. The companies that King formed to manage the new set of drilling funds were not subsidiaries of King Resources Company, but were all owned by John King personally. These private companies managed the funds, but they also contracted most of the oil-exploration work—geological surveys, drilling, pipeline laying, and so on—to King Resources, which in turn often passed on the contracts to independent concerns. An investor's money was subject to many charges in its progress through the corporate layers. Indeed, the prospectuses issued for King's drilling funds had to warn the customers that once John King had taken his cut, they might not get back their original investment.

"It's simple," said King. "You put $100,000 into an oil well and you can expect to make 30 per cent a year if it hits—but you might have to spend a lot more to get that oil. We'll sell you the property, drill the well for you, manage the production, do all the work. If we strike oil, you will make the 30 per cent, but we may make as high as 60 per cent." (Was this the "use of money factor"?)

King succeeded in making this package attractive—at least while there was a lot of money around—through two important innovations which he built into the old concept of the drilling fund. Previously, these had been thought of as suitable only for the very wealthy. King said that it "annoyed the hell" out of him that "only rich people could invest in oil drilling," and with populist fervor he set out to create tax shelters for the common man. His customers in the end were not exactly dirt-common— doctors were probably the largest professional group among them—but King was prepared to aim for lower-paid people.

First, he introduced an installment plan, which allowed people to invest in one of his funds for as little as $150 down and $50 a month. More important, he took a leaf from the mutual-fund book. In old-style drilling funds, an investor would have to wait until the drilling partnership had run its term before he could get any money back. King promised to arrange for the repurchase of his customers' shares on demand. This innovation was the equivalent of the mutual funds' feature of redemption of shares on demand. In the case of King's funds, the level of repurchase price the investor received was to be determined by the "market value" of the fund's drilling operations at the time of repurchase.

Repurchasing brought a new dimension to drilling funds. An investor in oil gets the relief on the "intangible" cost of drilling a well: locating and preparing the site, transporting the rig, and so on. This can amount to three-quarters of total drilling expenses, so that a man putting $10,000 into the operation could deduct $7500 from his taxable income. Assuming he were paying tax at 70 per cent, that means he would enjoy total tax relief of 70 per cent of $7500, which is $5250. Therefore, the *real* cost of his $10,000 stake in the funds' drilling enterprises is only $4750 ($10,000 minus $5250).

Suppose this is a King drilling fund, and after eighteen months the investor asks to take his money out. King may say that the "market value" of the drilling enterprise is only 90 per cent of the original investment—*i.e.*, some oil has been found, but not enough to make such profits as would recoup all the money put up. But even at that "market value" the investor gets out 90 per cent of what he put up, so he gets $9000 out in hard cash. And as the real cost of his investment was only $4750, he has made a profit in eighteen months of $4250, which is nice going. This explains the attraction which John King's operation had for people in high-tax brackets. On top of it was the added advantage that any income derived from oil gets a "depletion allowance," which means that no tax is levied on the 22 per cent of it.*

Nevertheless, people found it difficult to grasp the idea that a major corporation could be built around tax avoidance. Those who did grasp it occasionally overlooked the point that *some* oil had to be found—or anyway, the "market value" of the drilling enterprise had to be maintained—if the investors were to come out on top.

King ran into two main drilling funds: Imperial-American, which was supposed to drill mainly in proven territory, and Royal Resources, which was a "wildcat" fund. Each of them had an intricate inner structure; the investor did not become a shareholder in the whole fund as he did in the mutual-fund system. Instead, a King drilling fund was designed as a series of "partnerships," with a new partnership being formed within the fund every quarter. Each investor was given an interest in the first partnership to be formed after his joining the fund. But despite the partnership structure, all the investors' money was "commingled" into one large pool.

When an Imperial-American investor demanded repurchase what happened, formally, was that his partnership interest would be sold to a new partnership. The reality of this was that money coming into the pool from new investors was used to pay

*The theory is that income from oil arises from an asset which is being depleted, and that the investor should be entitled to recover his capital. The idea is to encourage reinvestment.

off old investors. And the most alarming feature of the system—
if its long-term stability were to be considered—was the method
of fixing the level of payouts. The "market value" of the underlying drilling enterprises, which set the level of "redemptions"
(or in other words, the price which new partnerships paid for
old partnerships), was determined by appraisals from independent oil experts. King however reserved the right to "adjust"
these appraisals.

An article in the Denver *Rocky Mountain News* in July 1970
analyzed the nature of the adjustments made. It dealt with eight
quarterly partnerships of Imperial-American, from the third
quarter of 1967 to the second quarter of 1969. King was quoting
on these partnerships an average repurchase value of 80 per cent
on face amount invested—which would require the "market
value" of the underlying oil ventures to be about $52 million al-
together. But the independent appraisers, Lewis Engineering,
had valued the lot at just $7 million. King Resources made no
comment upon this remarkable "adjustment." It was difficult to
escape the conclusion that only a flow of new money was making such repurchases possible.

The article dealt only with the more conservative of the two
funds, Imperial-American. Similar analysis of Royal Resources,
the "wildcat" fund, shows even less real return on money. From
the last quarter of 1967 to the third quarter of 1969 inclusive, investors put $20 million into Royal Resources. All this money
was expended for a return of only $2 million—most of which ac-
crued to one lucky partnership. And out of that $2 million had
to come royalties, taxes, operating expenses, and a "net
operating-profits interest" for King.

The effect of such unkind revelations on King Resources was
not unlike the effect of the *L.A. Times* article on Commonwealth United's profits. There was a good deal of running for

the windows. King resigned from the chairmanship of King Resources, and the whole concern was able to stagger on only because the creditors feared they would lose even more by forcing liquidation. But by the time the article appeared, King and his companies had made some enormous profits on the flow of money through the funds. "It is probable," said *Dun's* magazine, "that no man, including Henry Ford or John D. Rockefeller, ever made a fortune faster than John King."

The first way John King made money out of the funds was by causing them to make interest-free loans out of their cash pool to King's companies. (At one stage, he borrowed $500,000 of the money personally, though he did pay 6 per cent.) For some time, the money borrowed from the customers was used to pay the commissions of outside brokers who sold the fund shares in the first place: an interesting system, which was abandoned after a year or so.

King's personally owned management companies made money from the funds in two further ways. First, they took 25 per cent of the "net operating-profits interest" on fund operations. Most people think of a profit as what remains after all costs are deducted from income: King's definition of his own profit left out so many costs that it closely resembled a straight royalty on all income. Second, King's companies trimmed 5 per cent off all net-cash receipts from any successful drilling operations, before the cash was reinvested in new ones.

But the real leverage effect was achieved through the sales that King Resources Company made to the drilling funds. The funds, which had reached $100 million by the end of 1969, and were swelling rapidly, purchased many of their oil and gas properties, their geological surveys and technical services, from King Resources Company. There was a blatant conflict of interests in this arrangement. Its effect upon the sales, the earnings, and, in turn, the share price of King Resources, was dramatic.

In 1968, King Resources had an income of nearly $38 million from the sale of goods and services to funds managed by King. These were not only his own drilling funds: he had another customer, none other than the Natural Resources Account of the Fund of Funds itself. In 1969, $64 million came from such sales, and in this year, FOF became a more important customer than the King funds. King's private companies also earned juicy commissions for selling the oil-exploration skills of King Resources: more than $3 million in 1969.

King Resources made much more money out of these services than from actually producing oil and gas. In 1969 when the company received $110 million from selling its properties and abilities to funds, it only brought in $6 million from the exploitation of oil and gas resources.

Still, even if it was not rich in real oil, John King's operation, just like IOS, was rich in distinguished names and noble rhetoric. The private empire that was organized under the Colorado Corporation had four main arms: (a) the oil-drilling funds; (b) a real-estate division called General American; (c) a group of companies under the title of Regency Management designed to arrange the leasing out of oil-well completion equipment (pumps, storage tanks, pipeline gear, and the like) not to mention aircraft and many other things; and (d) the Denver Corporation, which was responsible for selling the funds, the real estate, and the leasing contracts.

The Denver Corporation was headed by Dr. Edward Annis, ex-President of the American Medical Association, and the man who led the battle against John F. Kennedy's Medicare program. Together with Hal Azine, the script-writer who helped him in the Medicare campaign, Dr. Annis prepared drilling-fund propaganda to be beamed especially at doctors, whose average income topped $32,000 nationally in 1969, but who tended to "lack adequate knowledge of investments" as King publicity noted.

The astronaut Frank Borman served on the King Resources Company Board, and another astronaut, Walter Schirra, headed one of the Regency leasing companies. Like Richard V. Allen, a former foreign-policy adviser to President Nixon, Schirra was hired to devote himself to King's international aspirations. Captain Schirra said that "one of John's basic philosophies that drew me into this complex is that whenever you develop something in a country, you pump monies and know-how back in . . . bootstrap a country as I would say it." He said that he and King had often talked about something called "the high-protein concept of feeding the world." Helping undernourished nations, said Captain Schirra, was high-risk business. But it was also "humane, compassionate, and exciting. . . . That's what it's all about. The people here. The ideas. Every once in a while Ed Annis and I meet in the corridor. I say, 'What the hell are you doing here, Doctor?' and he'll say, 'What the hell are *you* doing here, Astronaut?' "

. . .

In early summer 1967, John King sent a couple of men to Europe to look at the chances of selling drilling funds there to Americans, who still pay U.S. taxes when abroad, and they duly visited IOS in Geneva. But as IOS was about to agree with the SEC not to sell anything to American citizens anywhere, there was nothing to be done.

The next contact came in December 1967, when Ed Cowett was in New York and got a message saying that King would like to meet him. The introduction was made by Myer Feldman, a Washington lawyer who had been a back-office brain in John Kennedy's presidential campaign of 1960 and had then spent three years in the White House as the President's deputy special counsel. His acute mind was one of the first to spot the possibilities of expanding the fund idea beyond securities.

"I organized one of the first art funds," he told us, "one of the first real-estate funds, and one of the first shipping funds. Natural resources had more potential than any of them." Feldman was already a director of some of the King drilling funds, and he knew Cowett. "One of my dubious claims to distinction," he says wryly, "was to introduce Edward M. Cowett and John M. King."

Superficially, the two men seemed to have little in common. Ed Cowett lives in a mansion overlooking the lake of Geneva, drives a Maserati, and relaxes over the backgammon board. John King's style is a specially stretched black Lincoln with a sunshine roof fixed so that he can shoot from it, and a million-dollar ranch at the foot of the Rockies. But Feldman's introduction brought about a true meeting of minds.

King's first suggestion was that he might buy Investors Planning Corporation, the American subsidiary that IOS had bought from the Benedicks but which it was necessary to sell under the terms of the SEC settlement. The deal fell through, and it is hardly likely that the SEC would have approved it. But the attraction of the two firms for each other was powerful enough to survive this setback. The more money King could "manage," the more profits he could make. And IOS was eager to invest money in situations where spectacular "performance" might be created.

This was sufficient to account for the Fund of Funds becoming, through its Natural Resources Account, the biggest customer of King Resources. And there was another congruity of interest to develop. In 1968, IOS was eager to send its salesmen back into those underdeveloped countries from which they had been so unceremoniously expelled. So a new "concept" was born: IOS and King together would create systems of natural-resources investments.

One of the first countries to be selected for the privilege of being "bootstrapped" was Israel, whose government had regarded IOS with a cool and skeptical eye almost from the first.* And the result was John King's Midbar venture—which ended with a small international incident, the intervention of the State Department, and the loss of many millions of dollars.

In the summer of 1968, King formed a little company named Midbar Ltd., after the Hebrew for "wilderness." It was registered in London, and was not much publicized. Midbar's audacious purpose, which had the approval of the Israeli government, was to search for oil and gas in the territories and neighboring waters captured from the Arabs during the Six-Day War. The IOS parent company—not the funds—lent Midbar $1 million, and it went to work on seismic studies of the area, which proved encouraging.

King then sent a maritime drilling rig, the *Star I*, out to the Mediterranean, and a land-drilling team to the Sinai Peninsula. The land well was a "dry hole"—but the *Star* struck oil. Unfortunately though, she was drilling in a very exposed position in international waters: thirty miles off the one-time Egyptian port of El 'Arîsh, which is west of the Gaza Strip. (The safer waters off Israel had been taken by another American company.) The *Star's* well had to be "capped" and kept quiet, because the Israelis could not guarantee protection for the rig. The problem was that the Israeli Navy had been relying upon the delivery of

---

*See Chapter 8, "The Jungle Jangle Jingle."

five new gunboats from France, and de Gaulle had blocked the sale. Before the Israeli Navy managed to commandeer the boats in their celebrated raid of Christmas 1969, the political heat had turned on the Midbar project. The heat was generated by the adventures of a second rig that King sent to go around the South of Africa and drill in the Gulf of Suez itself.

The rig, drawn by a Dutch tug, berthed en route at Abidjan on the Ivory Coast, where a group of Arab saboteurs arrived one night and hung some sticks of dynamite around it. They were not very efficient saboteurs, and the three explosions did little damage—although some members of the rig crew had to spring naked into the water. But by the time the rig had been repaired and was under way again, the incident had focused the attention of the established oil companies upon the implications of Midbar's enterprise.

The oil companies were naturally frightened that the Arabs might take reprisals against U.S. oil investments in Libya and other places, if American companies went on helping Israel search for oil in disputed territory. The State Department was called in, and that was the end of Midbar.

King Resources had to write off nearly $7 million on its Middle East operation, and private investors who had bought participations for $8 million or so, also lost. IOS Ltd. was not a loser: it got $1.3 million back on its $1 million, and was left with a free 25-per-cent interest in Midbar. But that was IOS's own money. The same good fortune did not apply to most of the IOS customers' money that went into other King ventures.

The Natural Resources Account of the Fund of Funds was started on March 4, 1968, and it was rather different from those subdivisions of the Fund such as David Meid or Fred Alger ran. First, until March 1970, IOS never announced who was running the account. As a result the relationship with King was not widely known even within IOS. Second, there was no formal management agreement, and no charge was contracted. The manager of the account was IOS Ltd. itself, and it was handled personally by Ed Cowett. Third, none of the reports of Fund of Funds Proprietary ever gave a breakdown of what Natural Resources Account was invested in.

Although no fee was fixed formally, IOS proposed to reward itself for running the Natural Resources Account by taking 10 per cent of any appreciation in the value of the account's investment whether that appreciation was realized in a sale, or simply entered in the books. Ten per cent of the income from investments, less an expenses allocation, would also accrue to IOS.

The great point about natural-resources investments, however, was that unlike stocks and shares, there was no widely quoted and established market to put a value on "unrealized appreciation." It was up to IOS itself, with the aid of King Resources, to assess increases in the value of any oil-drilling leases or gold mines purchased with the aid of John King's companies. The higher the values estimated, the more profits IOS would receive.

In May 1968, a Fund of Funds prospectus quoted one of the celebrated maxims of the Duc de la Rochefoucauld: "The greatest of all gifts is the power to estimate things at their true worth."

• • •

By the end of 1969, $60 million from the Fund of Funds had flowed into John King's companies. This was by far the most important destination for new fund investment. Yet no list was published showing the disposition of this cash until March 1970—and even then it did not go out to the investors but appeared as a footnote to an article by John King in the *IOS Bul-*

letin, aimed mainly at salesmen. "Geologists tell us," wrote King, "that there is an infinite amount of natural resources—the earth itself, the treasures found within it, upon and in the skies above it." King Resources, which he called "a merchant banker of natural resources," was burrowing away in search of these treasures, with special emphasis upon the underdeveloped world, where "the old exploitation approach" was being avoided.

The subsequent brief note on the FOF money in his care showed that little had gone to the poorer parts of the world, except for $3 million spent on oil and gas exploration in Gabon and Liberia. More than 45 per cent of the money had gone into King's companies operating in the United States, chiefly to acquire oil and gas prospects. Another 39 per cent had gone to Canada, $11 million having been spent on oil-exploration rights in the Arctic. Eleven per cent went into South Africa and its colony, South-West Africa, where it was divided between a titanium and a diamond prospect. (After the Apocalypse, an IOS executive said he found the Fund of Funds' stake in the diamond business especially hard to assess. "I have looked at this," he said, "and I have looked at it for some time. The result is that I have no way of knowing whether it is a highly valuable investment, or whether it is the biggest heap of bull-shit I have ever seen.")

The real action, the source of hope, was in the Arctic. When the Atlantic Richfield company struck oil at Prudhoe Bay on the North Slope of Alaska in January 1968, a great glamour spread over the 550,000 square miles of North American Sedimentary Basin stretching between Greenland and Alaska. That glamour was much intensified when rights to exploit the new Alaskan oil fields were auctioned off for an average of more than $2000 per acre. It obscured in many minds the fact that the North Slope is only a small part of the whole area—which consists mainly of the Canadian Arctic islands and their seas between. People naturally assumed that here was a bonanza in which the shrewd or fortunate might buy frosty territory cheap, and sell it dear upon the discovery of gushers. But the financial realities of oil exploration are rather more complicated than that.

As long ago as 1931, an explorer named Parry noted that rocks in the Canadian Archipelago smelled of gasoline when broken. A geological survey in 1947 disclosed that the rock formations in the area strongly resembled those of major oil fields, but at that time oil companies were put off by natural hazards. The special nastiness of the Archipelago is that it is *warmer* than the mainland, because its winds come from the Greenland Sea. The snow cover is never thick, and in the twenty-four-hour summer days, when the temperature can reach 65°F., it melts—turning the land surface into a sloppy layer of mud on top of 1500 feet of permafrost, while most of the sea remains frozen. The difficulties of searching for oil there, and of extracting it if found, kept most people's attention fixed on easier exploration prospects.

A few wells were drilled in the early 1960s, after the American nuclear submarine *Nautilus* sailed under the polar icecap and gave rise to the notion that the problem of extracting oil from the Arctic might be solved by giant submarine tankers. But no oil was found, and the Archipelago might have been abandoned to the caribou had it not been for a dedicated geologist named Sproule. After much campaigning, the Canadian government announced in December 1967 that it would back Panarctic Oil, the company Sproule created. A few weeks later came the Alaskan strike: the demand for new prospects was higher than in 1947, and suddenly oil companies were rushing into the Canadian Arctic. Optimists reckoned that perhaps half the Canadian area might have potential to equal the North Slope of Alaska. King Resources joined the rush, taking its customer, the Fund of Funds, along with it. And if they found nothing else, they certainly found "performance." By the end of 1969, Cornfeld was telling his salesmen that the Canadian Arctic was "our most spectacular investment"—and if you took IOS's own estimates at face value that was certainly the case. According to their calculations, properties acquired for $11 million had increased in value to $156 million within a few months.

Probably a good many salesmen and investors thought that what IOS was doing in the frozen north was something roughly analogous to buying and selling ordinary real estate. This impression was naturally strengthened when Cornfeld referred to the investments as "leaseholds." But mineral exploration rights in the Canadian Arctic islands are properties of a very complicated sort, with little resemblance to ordinary leaseholds. Ironically, the system was designed to minimize speculation.

What the Canadian government distributes are "permits," usually lasting six years, to explore blocks of territory for oil, gas, or any other agreed-upon mineral. No charge is made for the permits, but they are issued on the condition that a certain minimum amount of money is spent on exploration over the term of the permit. This "work obligation" may be discharged by drilling, by making seismic surveys, or even by researching improved means of Arctic transport. The requirement is expressed as a cost per acre and the sum depends on the location of the permit area. As an earnest of his intention to spend the money, the permitholder must either make deposits with the Canadian government or find an acceptable financial institution to put up a bond on his behalf. This money can be reclaimed by submitting bills to the government as exploration costs are incurred. The idea is to stop people taking up permits and sitting on them: to keep the permits "in force" exploration work must be undertaken.

There is nothing to stop a permitholder from selling his permits, or an interest in them, to third parties, and, if the territory looks promising, people may be willing to pay a cash price for the privilege of participating in possible eventual profits, in addition to taking on their share of the work obligation. Alternatively, the permitholder may decide that a certain area is worth particularly close exploration and may draw up a drilling program whose cost may well exceed the minimum government work requirements for the area. The permitholder may then decide to "farm out" the work to a third party to whom he will give in exchange an interest in the permit. The planned cost of this program can then also be expressed as a cost per acre, although no cash changes hands. Again, however, in order to "earn" his interest the third party must complete the contracted work, which may take some years—although he may pass on to yet another person a share of the work. In the Arctic, you don't own a thing until you earn it.

Even then it is not that simple. Normally you would not turn a permit into a lease until you have found oil in commercial quantities. At that point it becomes advantageous to convert a six-year permit into a twenty-one-year lease so that you can continue to benefit from the production of that well. Nevertheless, at that point also you run into fresh regulatory complications. In the first place the Canadian government reserves the right to keep for itself half your permit acreage. Second, only Canadian citizens, or companies half of whose capital at least is owned by Canadians, may own leases. King Resources would, therefore, have had to float off a separate Canadian company to own leases while the FOF itself would have been, in the words of a

Canadian government official who investigated the position, "very hard pressed to hold a lease in its own name."

King's invasion of the Arctic is even now hard to chart with any precision although its broad outlines are clear enough. King Resources' first move was made in the autumn of 1968 when the company took out a number of permits in its own name. These covered about 4.5 million acres and were recorded in the prospectus which IOS helped King draw up for the Eurodollar issue at the end of that year.* The acres, it said, were "scattered in and around the Sverdrup Basin in the Queen Elizabeth Islands" and were described as having "only speculative value." Examining the Arctic enterprise around that time, Neil MacKenzie, boss of King's Canadian operation, said, "We're going to have to be lucky. The mineral-resources industry is a calculated gamble, but if you go into it on a big enough scale, the odds are in your favor."

King's next big deal came in March 1969, when he took a 50-per-cent interest in permits covering roughly 20 million acres. These permits had been taken out by two companies called Transalta and Siebens, who had pooled their Arctic interests. The great bulk of this acreage was offshore, some of it outside the Sverdrup Basin in the Arctic Ocean. Such permits carry only a small government work requirement, for at this stage of the game permits covering big slices of frozen sea are not much desired. It is not drillable in the present state of the art.

King took on an obligation to spend only 20¢ an acre in the first four years of these permits: according to Transalta, King did not earn his interest on them until February 1970, when the necessary money was deposited with the Canadian authorities.

---

*See Chapter 17, "The Master Financiers."

King's third main Arctic stake—and by far his most important one—was a series of complicated farm-out agreements made with Panarctic, the company backed by the Canadian government. They covered some 4.5 million of the more promising onshore acres in the islands. King stood to earn varying interests by undertaking a drilling program of five wells, to be started at various dates before September 1971.

King was maneuvering in the Arctic throughout the summer and autumn of 1969. By late August he had interests, or the right to earn them, in 29,700,000 acres. But in addition to these three main moves, he acquired a number of other interests in return for undertaking to do seismic work or drill wells. King Resources also took out more permits in its own name, including some covering remote sections of Ellesmere Island, the farthest north of all the islands, which he filed in September. By December 22, the acreage in which King had interests had climbed to 35,710,000: the interests varied between 100 per cent and 30 per cent and the average was 63 per cent, so that King's "net" acreage in the Arctic was 22,380,000. It was a half-share in that twenty-two-million acres which was Bernie Cornfeld's "most spectacular investment." It was hardly prime oil territory, four-fifths of it being undrillable, frozen ocean. In Arctic slang, it was mostly "whole pasture and caribou turd."

Supposedly, the Fund of Funds went into the Natural Resources Account on a 50–50 basis with King and his companies. Cowett later tried to tell the IOS Board that King Resources was in effect money managers for the Natural Resources Account— but the relationship was not like that at all in practice. At least, money managers are not usually allowed to sell properties of their own to the funds they manage, which was what King Resources was doing. The Natural Resources Account was built up by the simple device of King companies selling to the FOF half-interests in properties already owned, or about to be owned. And King decided that this was a sales situation in which the philosophy of *caveat emptor* should apply: his companies took markups on sales to the FOF, and it was up to the FOF to object if the prices were too high.

Cowett claims to have been "naïve" about these arrangements, and, as dismayed IOS investigators found later, they resulted in some spectacular markups for King companies. In some cases, King's private company, the Colorado Corporation, bought American oil and gas properties and resold to the FOF within days at markups of 1000 per cent more. And that was mild compared to what happened in the Arctic.

The Fund of Funds paid King Resources Company a total of $11 million cash for the privilege of participating in his Arctic interests. And King Resources paid virtually no cash price when taking up the interests—the costs being computed in terms of work obligations assumed, totaling some $20 million. Half of that burden of work obligations was transferred to the FOF at once.

So what the FOF bought, for $11 million, was the right to expend *another* $10 million on permit interests which were in the name of King Resources, most of which had not yet been earned, and which FOF would only be able to hold itself with great difficulty in the event King Resources should fail to perform its obligations.

The Fund of Funds got the right to keep 50 per cent of any profits from any oil or gas which might eventually be exploited—but King Resources arranged to keep a 12½-per-cent overriding profits interest on even that income, should it ever arise, from the FOF part of any individual holding. As King Resources paid virtually no cash purchase price for the Arctic permits, the $11 million paid over by FOF made a truly impressive markup.

Nothing in the conduct of an open-end fund is more important than the regular—usually daily—calculation of its net asset value per share. On this is based both the price of fund shares to new investors, and the redemption price to old investors. The total value of the fund's assets is determined by reference to quoted stock-exchange prices, and the total is divided by the number of fund shares outstanding.

It is not so easy to check the value of investments like oil-exploration permits. They are not quoted on any exchange: if the objection to real estate in any open-end fund is that its value is a matter of opinion, the objection to oil permits is that their value is a matter of the most esoteric opinion. Nevertheless, both Ed Cowett and Bernie Cornfeld were determined that the Arctic holdings should not be undervalued—it would, they said, be unfair to the investors. Surely, the value must have increased in 1969, the year of the Alaskan oil auction, the year when the tanker/ice-breaker *Manhattan* broke through the Northwest Passage?*

One technique of revaluing a natural-resources holding is to sell part of it: if the buyer pays, proportionately, more than you paid in the first place, it may be fair to apply the increase to the complete holding. But the validity of the technique obviously depends upon the independence of the buyer and the scope of his purchase: when IOS used it in 1968 to revalue another oil and gas holding, doubts arose in the minds of their auditors, Arthur

---

*The *Manhattan*'s voyage led, at the time, to large hopes of improved access to Arctic oil fields. Later, however, the sponsors of the voyage concluded that a pipeline to the Arctic might be more economic.

Andersen & Co. Only 10 per cent was sold on that occasion, and it was sold to a broker.

In early November 1969, Arthur Andersen (who are also auditors to King Resources) found themselves examining the same technique again. They suggested to King Resources that an increase could be allowed if supported by an arm's-length sale to knowledgeable outside parties. If King Resources Company sold a 25-per-cent interest in all the Arctic permits to Texaco or another major oil company, the auditors believed it would be appropriate to give proportionate value to the 75 per cent retained. Where to draw the line was the problem: the auditors at this stage regarded a 10-per-cent sale as a bare minimum.

Cornfeld clearly had no such reservations about the approaching coup, and he gave his followers several broad hints in the fall months. On November 14, he addressed the German sales managers at Bad Godesberg. Stock markets might be sagging throughout the world, he said, but fear not: IOS now had an investment policy to transcend such problems. Watch out, he advised them, for a special 10-per-cent jump in the Fund of Funds before the year's end.

Then on December 19, the Fund of Funds published its accounts for the first half of the year: Cornfeld's accompanying report said that there was a "strong possibility" of a partial Arctic sale and, "in such an event, the over-all holding will be revalued." The letter, on top of the Bad Godesberg hint, implied that the thing was virtually in the bag. Salesmen (who were absolved from sales loads) rushed into the Fund of Funds. One IOS accountant estimated to us that more than $10 million went into the funds in special transactions during December, and most of that could probably be ascribed to Arctic enthusiasm. Much confusion was caused because salesmen were having the computer run stopped so that their last-minute "buy" orders could be accepted.

Overnight, from December 29 to December 30, the Fund of Funds' net asset value jumped 12 per cent—and on December 31, Cornfeld sent a jubilant letter to his sales managers. The increase, he said, occurred because just 10 per cent of "our overall interest" in the Arctic had fetched $15.7 million in a sale to three independent oil companies on December 26. Four pages, and a map with the Sverdrup Basin vaguely indicated, were devoted to what Cornfeld called the "enormity" (*sic*) of the Arctic venture. Investments acquired for $1 per acre were already worth $8 per acre on "conservative" estimates, said Cornfeld, and he ventured that the Canadian Arctic might surpass the Alaskan bonanza, with its values of $2000 per acre.

Oil is an unpredictable commodity, and the Archipelago may turn out to be drenched in it. Even so, the letter would still be an investment fantasy. At the time that Cornfeld wrote, FOF had not in fact sold anything to anybody: the actual events of the Arctic "sale" were very unlike Cornfeld's description.

The idea of revaluing the Arctic permits developed while the acquisition was still going on. At least the FOF accounts say that a $3.6 million increase was recorded at June 30, 1969: that was over two months before the permits had been taken out on the lonely Ellesmere Island (covered by a permanent icecap, according to the Geological Survey of Canada). It was, in fact, before one-third of the joint interests had been taken up, according to the King Resources documents filed with the SEC. It was also before the interests had been earned. This revaluation occurred before the spectacular auction of Alaskan rights, and before the *Manhattan*'s hopeful voyage. During the summer of 1969, it is claimed, IOS was negotiating to sell part of its interest, but the deal fell through. IOS made it clear to King Resources that a sale of some part of the interest was desired as soon as a buyer could be found.

The transaction which was eventually used to justify the complete revaluation was not negotiated by IOS. It began with a game of golf between Rowland Boucher, President of King Resources, and Harry Trueblood, Chairman of another Denver firm, Consolidated Oil & Gas. King Resources owned interests in several wells operated by Consolidated: during the game, Trueblood said that he would like to buy into King's Arctic action.

Harry Trueblood and John King, who met in 1959, are neighbors in Cherryville, outside Denver. Over the years their various companies have exchanged with each other many deals in oil, natural gas, and other things. By 1969 their affairs were considerably intertwined. For instance, Holiday Airlines, controlled by Trueblood, had just leased an airliner from King's Regency Income Corporation to serve Lake Tahoe, in the Sierra mountains, where King's real-estate arm was developing a project called Innisfree, "dedicated to the total recreation concept." Indeed, there was a joint project with King which actually stood in the way of Consolidated's Arctic ambitions: this was a plan to redevelop part of downtown Denver, at considerable expense. Because of this Consolidated was strapped for cash and any Arctic deal would have to be specially tailored.

However, the negotiations begun on the golf course ended with a deal on December 26, 1969. Consolidated Oil & Gas agreed to take over 1/32nd part of the whole Arctic package—which then consisted of permits applying to 22,264,000 net acres. Consolidated agreed to pay a price for being let into the action, and also agreed to assume a proportion of the work obligations.

The price was $5,218,242—but only $443,550 was cash. Consolidated did not have to pay any of the balance of the price until June 1973, and that was only to be the first of a three-year series of installments. Yet, even on these easygoing terms, Consolidated did not find the deal an easy one to sign. Harry Trueblood's company was unable to make the down payment until someone from King Resources found a bank in Oklahoma that was ready to lend the necessary cash.

In addition to this *price*, Consolidated agreed to relieve King of a part of the *expenditure* necessary to keep the permits active. Consolidated assumed $5,218,242 of the total obligation of $20,872,564. So, in order to get into the Archipelago, Harry Trueblood had assumed liabilities up to a total of $10,426,484. As this brought him only 1/32nd of the whole net interest—or 3.125 per cent—you could say that he would be laying out, over six years, $15 for every net acre of interest which would accrue to Consolidated. Insofar as Cornfeld's rhapsodic letter to his salesmen bore any relation to reality, his price of "$15 per acre" was based on this kind of computation.

The sale to Consolidated was too small and too intimate to pass muster on its own for revaluation purposes. It was, however, buttressed by certain other transactions.

At virtually the same time as the Consolidated deal, King Resources sold another small slice of the Arctic to John W. Mecom, one of the more colorful oilmen in Houston, Texas. Stewart Alsop once reported that the industry credited Mecom "with a sort of magical intuition about what lies below the surface of the earth," but Mecom's truffling instincts do not seem to have been vastly excited on this occasion. He took up only 1/64th of the whole. Mecom, like Consolidated, undertook total liabilities which could be worked out to $15 per acre. But he also did the deal on the same "never-never" terms.

Even these two sales only disposed of 3/64ths of the Arctic package. But on December 30, with time running out a little concern called Lake Shore Associates entered the bidding, and took another sliver of the Arctic off King Resources' hands. On terms similar to Mecom and Consolidated, Lake Shore Associates took up 1/128th part of the Arctic.

The sales to Consolidated and to John Mecom could be squared approximately with Cornfeld's talk about sales to independent oil companies—even if Consolidated's independence might leave something to be desired in terms of a revaluation sale. But Cornfeld's account does not square in the case of Lake Shore Associates. It is not a company at all but a private partnership, including among its members John M. King as well as Bennett King (who happens to be no relation to John M.), who was the man who signed the contract for Lake Shore.

These three fractional sales could be totaled up to make 5.46875 per cent of the Arctic package. It was still a long long way from looking like a 25-per-cent sale to Texaco. But at this moment, another purchaser came forward to improve the figures.

This was none other than John M. King, acting this time in his personal capacity. On December 31, 1969, John King bought from King Resources Company a 1/64th part of the Arctic permit package. Once again, very little cash changed hands: there was a small down payment, plus a set of obligations for the future.

This set of maneuvers made it possible to say, in the last hours of 1969, that 9/128ths—or just over 7 per cent—of the Arctic interest had been disposed of. Half of the purchase price consisted of a series of easy credit arrangements. The other half consisted of undertakings to relieve King Resources Company of obligations. There was no certainty that those undertakings would ever be carried out, in which case the work obligations would have to be assumed by King Resources if the permits were to be kept alive. (And within twelve months, as it happened,

John Mecom and his companies were in deep financial trouble, and Consolidated was in dispute with King Resources over the deal.)

This pantomime did not remotely resemble the "arm's-length" sale of 25 per cent to a major oil company—which was what the auditors had suggested in November. It was not even the 10-per-cent sale which had then been called a bare minimum. But it was enough for Bernie and Ed.

IOS promptly transferred a flat 10 per cent of the FOF Arctic holding—that is 5 per cent of the whole package—back to King Resources. They then said that FOF had sold 10 per cent of its holding to "three independent oil companies." On that basis, IOS re-estimated the "true worth" of the FOF's remaining interest in the mixed bag of permits. The whole thing had been taken up virtually for nothing by King Resources. IOS now decided that the 45 per cent which the FOF retained had increased in value to a staggering $156 million.

The figure was not actually taken out of the air, but the computation upon which it was based was more involved than was suggested by the subsequent explanation in the FOF accounts. Altogether, it must have been a difficult judgment for Arthur Andersen & Co.—as hard as any they faced in ten years of auditing IOS Ltd. and its funds.

When, rather belatedly, the FOF accounts appeared in summer 1970, there was a note which said that a sale of 10 per cent of the Arctic interest had been made to King Resources, the "operator" of the interest, on "the same bases and terms as a December 1969 sale by such operator of a 9.375-per-cent interest to outside third parties." The percentage 9.375 per cent of the "operators" half-interest is the same thing as a 3/64th part of the whole—namely, the slice taken up by Consolidated Oil & Gas plus John Mecom. Apparently, these two purchasers were the only ones who could be used in actual accounts as "outside third parties." The other sales to Lake Shore and to John M. King simply helped to give color to the claims by Cowett and Cornfeld that an important sale had been made.

Although they shyly declared themselves "not competent" to pronounce upon the actual valuations produced on the basis of these sales, the auditors did say that they had checked over the procedures involved to make sure that they were as described in the accounts. Even so, the description does not tally properly with the actual events of FOF's sale back to King Resources.

The accounts say that "sales proceeds consisted of $779,300 cash down payment and $7,570,000 payable in six semiannual installments beginning in 1973. . . ." These figures would have been correct if King Resources had contracted to pay the FOF for its 10 per cent in exactly the same way that King Resources was to be paid by Consolidated, Mecom, Lake Shore, and John M. King personally. This was not so. King Resources was proposing to take the same credit, but the payments were different.

King Resources' down payment to the Fund of Funds was actually $606,618.59 rather than the $779,300 given in the accounts. And the amount that King Resources contracted to pay off in installments was not $7,570,000—but $5,795,726.96. The difference sprang from the fact that King Resources had a 12½-per-cent "net operating-profits interest" on all the FOF holdings in the event oil should be found. When buying back, King Resources "lost" this interest on the FOF customers' investment, and a valuation was added to the price to account for this loss.

For the purpose of revaluing, however, IOS and its auditors assumed that King Resources had actually paid FOF the same price as it had received when selling to Consolidated. The Fund of Funds' remaining 45 per cent was declared to be worth $14.1 per net acre—and it was this which produced the new gross value of $156 million. This was then solemnly discounted: first, by taking off an apparently arbitrary $17 million to account for King Resources' 12½ per cent on the holdings retained. Further allowances were made to allow for the interest FOF would lose by not collecting the full purchase price for six years, and for the fact that the work obligations would only be paid over three years. These were reckoned at around $20 million, which reduced the new "valuation" to $119 million.

These mathematical gymnastics were taken to mean that the Fund of Funds' investment had appreciated by a sum of $102 million, prudently discounted.* At this point there occurred the first serious cash transaction in the whole enterprise. IOS took $9.7 million out of the Fund of Funds and paid the money to itself as a "performance fee": a reward for having procured the increased value of the Natural Resources Account.

Elaborate as it was, the whole operation was not really an adequate excuse for removing nearly $10 million of the customers' money for the profit of IOS itself. And the effect upon the Fund of Funds was so dire that it requires a special brand of chutzpah to defend it in the name of "fairness to the investors."

Although the net asset value of the Fund of Funds was bumped up 12 per cent on December 29–30, 1969, the actual transfer of 10 per cent to King Resources did not occur until early January. The object of this maneuver was to avoid taxation, but all the same provision against a tax of about $18 million had to be put on the books. This chopped the "revaluation" down to $74 million—IOS, naturally, having taken its fee on the larger sum—and as a result the Arctic permit interest was left on the books at a figure of $8.01 per acre. This meant that the Nat-

---

*A small part of the Arctic interest had been placed in the IOS Growth Fund, a new promotion in Germany. It was allocated $2.7 million of the appreciation.

ural Resources Account, having paid out a large sum of cash for the privilege of recording notional gains, jumped to 22 per cent of the whole valuation of the Fund of Funds. Within eight months, that whole section had to be removed from the Fund of Funds and closed to redemptions.

It was understandable, in the aftermath of this grotesque deal, that Cornfeld and other IOS luminaries should scan the Arctic horizon eagerly for signs of gushers. During 1969, the most exciting event had been a "blowout" of natural gas encountered by a Panarctic team on Melville Island: ironically, King/FOF drills nearby found oil seepage, but the permits held there were only for sulfur exploration.

By summer 1970 King Resources was frantically trying to raise money on its part of the Arctic interest—or even just to get rid of its work obligations. But the major oil companies, the only ones with ready money, were in no mood to speculate indiscriminately. British Petroleum took over, for a small sum, King's obligation to drill a well on Graham Island, one of the more promising spots. BP also took an option on another set of permits, but even so the total acreage involved was minute in comparison to the total King/FOF interests. Sun Oil came in on this deal, and took on additionally some of King's obligations on much wider acreages. But Sun still avoided the large, undrillable offshore acreage, which was left to King and the IOS investors. The terms of those deals do not justify, in retrospect, the extraordinary liberties that IOS took with the investors' money: even a real discovery of oil would not do so.

• • •

The version of the Arctic deal that IOS announced to the press did not contain anything like the same details as Cornfeld's glowing dispatch to his sales managers. "IOS Funds Receive

Late Yule Present From Polar Regions," was the *Wall Street Journal* headline, and the story said that IOS had declared a sale, but refused to reveal the identity of the purchasers. The news delighted the IOS Associates, but not the international financial community. Those doubts about IOS, which had been smoothed over by the public offering, began to creep back into people's minds.

Once the elixir of confidence evaporated, abruptly, at the end of March, the Arctic deal became a magnet for bitter and destructive questions—but in February, it did not spoil Bernie Cornfeld's last triumph before the *Institutional Investor* seminar. At that point, the inner ruin of IOS was still held back behind the gleaming façade, although it needed all of Ed Cowett's cool nerve to keep it so. At the beginning of February, it was suggested in the Canadian press that the Arctic deal showed that IOS was "not afraid to generate a little controversy," and Cowett had to deploy bold denials. "If anything," he said, "we feel that we are being too conservative, and the natural resources fund is still an undervalued account." He asserted disingenuously that "the sale was made to three large companies, two of which were publicly held."

Once the break did come, it became clear that the manipulations of the Natural Resources Account were only part of the financial symbiosis between the empires of John King and Bernie Cornfeld. Other links, growing out of rather more individual schemes of self-enrichment, had existed back in 1968 and continued through the astonishing year of 1969.

During that year, it must be said, Ed Cowett maneuvered with the ubiquitous velocity of a financial Superman. Casual visitors to his office in Geneva saw only a quiet, bespectacled Clark Kent. But all and any of the terrifying financial problems which swirled around IOS were brought to him, and he eliminated them with dispatch. It was as though he slipped behind a filing cabinet and peeled off his business suit to reveal a magic cloak and a glove-tight body tunic—except, presumably, that the "S" on Superman's chest would be replaced in his case by a large dollar sign. Then Super-Ed would leap into action faster than the eye could follow. Zap! new triumphs of conglomerate financing were achieved. Powee! the underwriters' fears were assuaged and IOS's own public offer was assured. Bam! the natural-resources invention produced new vistas of speculative investment. Wham! Kerchunk! new investment "products" were produced for the hungry salesmen to sell.

• • •

In between, Cowett undertook another labor, the importance of which, in IOS values, could scarcely be overstated. This was to eliminate his colleagues' tax problems—an undertaking which was bound to lead back to John King, who was in tax avoidance on an industrial scale.

The incomes IOS generated for its chieftains brought problems because most of them were Americans, subject to the U.S. government's unique habit of asking its citizens to pay tax even if resident abroad. Although it is possible to defy the Internal Revenue Service, an American abroad who wishes to keep his citizenship in working order is well advised to make some obeisances to the taxmen. Adroit avoidance, naturally, counts as well as payment.

During 1968, Ed Cowett agreed, on the request of George Landau and other colleagues, to investigate systems of personal tax relief. Landau heard nothing more, he says, till the Overseas Development Bank told him that he had a debt of several thousand dollars, which had been written into his account on Mr. Cowett's orders. Taken aback, Landau told Cowett to inform him next time before putting him in debt to the bank. Cowett said it was "no problem": he had just been putting George into a little tax-avoidance scheme.

It was called Foundation Equipment Associates, and Landau was in it along with Cowett himself, C. Henry Buhl, Allen Cantor, Richard Hammerman, and some other big IOS earners. The "Associates" were to borrow money with which oil-well equipment would be bought and then leased out. They would then be able to claim tax relief both for the depreciation of the equipment and for the interest on the loans used to buy it. But that was only the start: the real attraction of such schemes sprang from the fact that the U.S. government was still allowing investment credits against tax on purchases of oil equipment. Where ordinary taxation reliefs merely diminish the proportion of an income which is assessable for tax, investment credits acted as straight deductions from an actual tax bill, thus providing the most attractive tax relief of all. And few groups of people have been more passionately attracted by it than the top brass of IOS.

Foundation Equipment Associates was quite a modest scheme, rather like those used by a number of American companies to assist valuable executives. The fact that IOS itself had lent $500,000 to the project was scrupulously recorded in the prospectus when IOS went public. The same could not be said of the schemes which followed—and which were too late to be noted in the prospectus. They were not modest at all: by now, the needs of the masters of IOS for tax relief were so pressing that the necessary devices soaked up nearly all the free cash in the company which had not been diverted into more orthodox follies. It was not just a question of override incomes: by early summer 1969, the people who had big shareholdings which had been acquired cheap under the stock-option plan faced appalling capital-gains tax liabilities as the moment of cashing in approached. George Landau was now only one of a large and slightly desperate crowd when he asked Ed if he was "going to have anything for us this year"?

To deal with this large problem, Ed Cowett recruited the help of a New York lawyer named Joel Mallin. The first difficulty was that the investment credit, that useful concession, was due to be abolished in the summer of 1969, which meant that any scheme following along the lines of the previous year's Foundation Equipment Associates would have to be devised well in advance of the public issue in order to claim the investments.

Cowett and Mallin rapidly assembled Beta Foundation Equipment Associates—the alphabetical flavor of the name perhaps conveys the eventual scope they had in mind. The participants included themselves; Henry Buhl; Arthur Feder, a lawyer on IOS's real-estate side; Dick Hammerman, the insurance boss; Barry Sterling, the investment banker; Ira Weinstein, the former Iranian chieftain, now in Canada; and Allen Cantor. Ed Coughlin, the "Happy-Birthday" trouble shooter, had a small piece, and there was a large participation for Bobby Freedman, who had no formal connection with IOS at all and was usually known just as the Tennis Player. According to Mallin, he was put in "as an old friend of Bernie's and Ed's, who had rendered them various services." The aim of Beta Foundation Equipment Associates was to acquire and lease oil-well "foundation equipment": the pumps, tanks, and associated gear required in an actual working oil well. The equipment it was to buy was already to hand: it was already installed and operating in various wells being run by King Resources Company for the uncertain benefit of investors in the Colorado Corporation drilling funds.

Beta promised to provide some useful tax relief for its hard-pressed members—but the problem now was to find the necessary money. There is little point to such a scheme if one only uses one's own money, for the whole idea is naturally to "gear up" the size of the investment credit obtained by putting in borrowed money, thus covering as large a section as possible of one's original income with tax relief. And as the interest on money borrowed can also be taken off taxable income, the system possesses a great structural elegance.

Could a bank be found in time to lend the money for Beta— $4.7 million was required—in time to catch the investment credits? American banks that had once been willing, even eager, to lend money for such devices were becoming less and less so as the credit squeeze tightened during 1969. There was nothing for it but to turn to IOS's own banking system, and on July 24 the Overseas Development Bank (Geneva), acting as agent for ODB (Bahamas) advanced $4.7 million to Beta Foundation Equipment Associates. Reviewing later the havoc caused by the liquidity of the IOS group by the demands of Beta and similar schemes, Joel Mallin said sadly that "the company was the victim of Nixon's credit squeeze"—in other words, if the President had not been so unsporting as to tighten up U.S. bank credit, it would not have been necessary to remove so much cash from IOS to rescue its officers from their tax problems. Even in those tight times it might have been easier to find an outside bank but for the fact that Beta wanted to operate on terms that would give the maximum possible comfort to its participants: the Beta financing was to be repaid over eight years in level installments of interest and principal. This would have the effect that in early years the repayments would be virtually all interest, and thus tax deductible.

Oil-well foundation equipment was far from being the only avenue of tax avoidance available to the men at IOS, for John King, IOS's great ally, was looking into virtually every kind of tax advantage that might be obtained by purchasing equipment, from bottling machines to airliners, and leasing it out again. This, indeed, was the "humane, compassionate, and exciting" business which the astronaut Walter Schirra undertook as President of John King's Regency Investors Company. "Leasing," said the King publicity material, "is the new economic way of life." Ed Cowett and his friends at IOS seem to have been enthusiastic converts to it.

Airplanes—with which John King was always fascinated—entered into many of his leasing projects, and IOS became involved in an especially complicated one, which concluded with the bankruptcy of a British aircraft company, and left Eli Wallitt, Harvey Felberbaum, and Roy Kirkdorffer (head of IOS's British sales force) stuck with one expensive and unwanted miniature airliner apiece.

These plans were made by Handley Page Aircraft, a pioneer aviation company and the first ever to go public. Handley Page, having made thousands of wartime Halifax bombers for the RAF, had fallen upon hard times with the regrouping of the British aircraft industry, and by 1969 its whole future depended upon one new plane. This was the Jetstream, an eighteen-passenger turboprop aimed at American commuter airlines. On the basis of an order for eleven Jetstreams from the U.S. Air Force, and promises of large further orders which were made by the U.S. distributors, a firm from St. Louis, Missouri, called International Jetstream, Handley Page committed itself to tool up for production. (International Jetstream was owned by a man named Kenneth R. Craven, a friend of John King's.)

During 1969, International Jetstream sold just ten Jetstreams: all to John King's Regency Income Corporation. Regency planned to lease them out to a little West Coast airline called Cal-State and got as far as finding three investors to finance a Jetstream each at $530,000 a time, including conversion costs: Wallitt, Felberbaum, and Kirkdorffer. The three sales bosses, who had never seen the planes, bought them on credit again supplied by the IOS banking system. The advances were made on July 23, the day before the Beta advances and came, with interest, to $1.65 million. The advances were to be repaid out of leasing income on the planes—which was unfortunate for the liquidity of the IOS banks, because, as it turned out, the investment depreciated all too abruptly and there was no income.

Handley Page, being very short of cash, fell behind on the development program that was required to bring the Jetstream up to its original specification. Jetstream performance was not matching requirements, which was awkward for Regency and for International Jetstream. During the autumn of 1969, hectic attempts were made to keep at least the Jetstream section of Handley Page alive: at one point John King himself made a midnight flight to consult with International Jetstream backers, the Craven Corporation of St. Louis. Kenneth Craven himself was willing to put up $5 million to try and save Handley Page, but King did not join in the rescue bid.

Then Kenneth Craven fell seriously ill, and the U.S. Air Force, growing skeptical about the Jetstream's performance, canceled its order. Cal-State ran into financial trouble and into difficulties over its Civil Aeronautics Board license. Toward the end of 1969, it emerged that the IOS banking system was in the position of having lent out $1.65 million against three of a batch of ten unwanted airplanes, while their manufacturer, Handley Page Aircraft, swooned gently into the hands of the Official Receiver.

• • •

George Landau was not a beneficiary of either of these deals, but Cowett still "had something" for him. Landau, along with several other members of the IOS elite was to become a part owner of that interesting beast, the Colorado NOPI.

A NOPI is a Net Operating Profits Interest—we have met the idea before—and John King had a specimen for which he was anxious to find a good home. King, with the approval of his fellow directors, had determined that King Resources, the public company which he effectively controlled, should purchase Colorado Corporation, the private company which he owned. King was to receive King Resources shares in exchange for his Colorado shares, and a deal had been roughed out which would make his new holding worth around $200 million. In effect, this deal would put a market valuation on the Colorado Corporation without all the tedium and disclosure involved in making a public offering. But the precise details of the scheme were to be fixed up in 1970—and the higher Colorado's 1969 profits, the more John King would get. He therefore wished Colorado to make some profitable sales, and so he turned to the "net operating profits" which the corporation extracted from the funds under its management.

These, it will be recalled, had been designed to exclude so many costs that they closely resembled a 25-per-cent royalty on all drilling funds operations. Colorado's problem, however, was that most of these interests were in properties which had yet to be explored for oil and gas; their value, therefore, could not include such interests in its 1969 income. If, however, those interests could be sold off, then the proceeds *could* be included.

And purchasers were on hand. Late in 1969 Ed Cowett, using IOS's Investors Overseas Bank as agent, agreed to buy a total of $45 million of Colorado NOPIs: $15 million for each of 1969, 1970, and 1971. It was arranged that 25 per cent of each year's NOPI would be paid in cash and the balance would be paid off in four annual installments.

The NOPI was then divided up among a number of the IOS people confronted with terrifying capital-gains liabilities, a predicament in which a piece of NOPI is very useful. American capital-gains tax rules allow an investor to include half of a year's gains lumped in with his ordinary income, and have this half taxed as income. Meanwhile, taxable income may be reduced by setting various types of losses against it. One such permitted offset is the loss involved in abandoning oil and gas properties which have been explored and found to contain no resources.

The charms of the Colorado NOPI thus become apparent: the more dry holes Colorado drilled, the better for the IOS investors. In the event, the NOPI performed heroically, recording abandonment losses of something like 70 per cent of the face value paid over.

Actual production of income from wells need not be totally embarrassing in a NOPI deal, because the investor can then have recourse to the depletion allowance. Indeed, some income must be made in the end, whether the deal be done on borrowed money or in cash, if the investor is to come out ahead in the end. There is a delicate balance between "sheltering" income and merely pouring into the ground money that would otherwise have gone to Uncle Sam. The evidence is that in the euphoric days of 1969, most people in IOS were more interested in finding some way of protecting their immediate wealth than in thinking out the ultimate implications of dry-hole operations. Cowett was able to assemble an impressive team of NOPI hunters fairly rapidly. There was Landau and his partner Don Q. Shaprow; Harvey Felberbaum and Roy Kirkdorffer (whose problems could not be solved by Jetstreams alone); there was Allen Cantor (who also had a piece of Beta Foundation Equipment Associates); there was Gladis Solomon; Ambassador Roosevelt; Martin Seligson, the real-estate expert; and there was Bernard Cornfeld himself, who took the biggest bite of all, with $5 million of Colorado's 1969 NOPI.

The Investors Overseas Bank paid out the 25-per-cent down payment required to secure the NOPI, amounting to $3,540,000. (A small part found a separate home in New York.) Some of the IOS participants, including Cornfeld himself, paid the IOB off for their pieces of NOPI, so that by the end of the year the bank only had $1.6 million of the original $3.54 million outstanding. Nevertheless, the IOB found itself stuck with $1 million worth of NOPI on its own account, because the whole of the purchase had not been taken up. And the bank issued a promissory note for $10.6 million to cover the balance of the $15-million price for purchase of 1969 NOPI.

The general strain of financing the tax-avoidance devices was telling rather heavily on the balance sheets of the IOS banks during the latter months of 1969. Formally, the Overseas Development Bank (Geneva), the Overseas Development Bank (Bahamas), and the Investors Overseas Bank were all separate entities under the holding company called IOS Financial Holdings Ltd. In practice, they were handled during 1969 simply as different taps on the same pool of credit.

This was shown clearly in the history of the Beta Foundation Equipment financing. The money was advanced first by ODB (Geneva) as agent for ODB (Bahamas), which then accepted the loan. By October, the whole system was suffering a little from the demands of Commonwealth United Corporation, and some fresh liquidity was required. On this occasion, IOS abandoned subtlety altogether, and as Cowett told us, they turned to Investment Properties International, the real-estate fund which had just been launched and that was flush with cash, and caused it to deposit $6.5 million of its cash reserves with ODB (Bahamas), the bank bearing the Beta and Jetstream loans. This was putting the customers' money to work very directly for the bosses of IOS.

Cowett later defended this maneuver by saying that IPI was not an open-end fund. It was a defense which ignored the fact that IPI shares were at that time being stuffed into the Fund of Funds at such a rate that IPI was becoming little more than a real-estate subaccount of FOF—which certainly *was* open end. But anyway, when he said it, Cowett must have forgotten that he had inserted in the IOS prospectus for the public offering a firm declaration that IOS banks "do not make loans to, or accept deposits from, Company-managed investment companies." That promise was abandoned almost as soon as it was made.

However, the depositing of IPI cash at ODB (Bahamas) aroused the ire of the Bank of New York, which was Depository of Cash for IPI. The bank was also Custodian of Securities for FOF, and it had not been disturbed to see the fund's investments being lent out to brokers.* Nor had the shenanigans with the Natural Resources Account disturbed the officials of the bank, so far as we can discover. However, the shifting of the IPI deposit was thought objectionable.

This problem came to a head at the very end of the year, when Ed Cowett, together with Bernie, had retired to Acapulco for a well-earned rest (leaving the Arctic deal to mature). Cowett was forced to spend a good deal of time on the phone from Mexico to Geneva, trying to sanitize the various balance sheets involved before "twelve thirty-one," as accountants call the

---

*See Chapter 18, "A Very Long Way Offshore."

year-end balance. The International Credit Bank* was asked to help but declined to do so. Money, however, had to be found, because the commitment to the Beta and Jetstream financing remained. So, when the IPI cash went back to New York, money had to be taken directly from the IOS corporate treasury in order to cover the position. First, IOS Ltd. put a deposit into ODB (Bahamas), but this was found to have some esoteric tax drawback. Therefore, the money was hastily inserted into a new bank, ODB (Curaçao) formed in the Netherlands Antilles, but actually existing in a ledger in Geneva. This new bank assumed the Beta and Jetstream loans.

In 1970 a brief respite was found. The Beta loan was placed with the European offshoots of American banks, Wells Fargo and Western American. The agreement, however, was conditional: at the end of April 1970, Wells Fargo and Western American declared that the Beta funding would only be continued upon receipt of a compensating deposit of $5 million from IOS Ltd. itself.

This was, in financial circles, a moment of no little panic. In New York, the Dow Jones was under 700 and falling like a stone. And at IOS it now emerged that, in the blunt words of an IOS accountant, "there was nothing left in the pot." Just over five months earlier, in its public offering, IOS had raised $52 million from the investing public. Suddenly, only one question was being asked around 119 Rue de Lausanne. Where the hell had all the money gone?

---

*See Chapter 8, "The Jungle Jangle Jingle" and Chapter 15, "The *Bella Figura* of Harvey Felberbaum."

• 20 •

The Book of Revelations

The people who "sincerely wanted to be rich" are rich! A tally of millionaires and multimillionaires. Joel Mallin and the "lifetime system of tax deferral." Cowett buys some shares, and the money runs out at last.

O n October 15, 1969, a young woman in a mini-cab arrived at the City of London offices of the Bank of New York and handed over to a small crowd of visiting bankers certificates for 5.6 million common shares of IOS. The bankers had actually been expecting a rather more high-powered deputation, but they paid over $52,400,826 to the IOS treasury in exchange. It was almost certainly the largest single sum which ever belonged to IOS, and constituted the stake in the last great IOS business game.

The statement may seem an odd one, but it must be remembered that the $2 billion in IOS funds belonged to other people. The safeguards over the investment of that money were pliable—but it remained true that the power of that cash could only be used by the IOS men themselves through the adroit use of leverage. The $52 million from the share issue was subject to no such restrictions: the previous chapter began to indicate the spirit in which IOS approached the task of spending it.

The investors were promised, in the prospectus, that the money raised would be used "to develop and expand the Company's activities, primarily in the banking and insurance areas." If that promise was made seriously it was rapidly abandoned. Apart from tax-avoidance schemes and the like, more than $8 million of the money raised was used almost immediately to buy stock from Cornfeld, Cowett, Cantor, and the rest of the shareholders who were cashing in.

Drexel, Harriman, Ripley, and the other distinguished underwriting banks were disposing only of new IOS shares. They did not want anything to do with the selling off of existing shares by members of IOS—the long-awaited "cashing in." J. H. Crang, the Toronto brokers, sold 1,450,000 of the existing shares to the Canadian public, and IOS's own Investors Overseas Bank was lined up to sell off 3,950,000 to some 25,000 employees, salesmen, friends, and customers of the firm.*

It was Cornfeld's claim that at the public issue one hundred members of IOS would become millionaires—and this claim, at least, was no exaggeration. Our own inquiries into the "cashing in" traced eighty-seven millionaires, and, because of the confusing nature of the records available, we probably missed a few. Of course, not all of them remained millionaires for very long: those who did were, on the whole, the ones who made the most thoroughgoing use of the right to sell shares, which had so long been denied to them. Cornfeld himself, who had always been able to sell, disposed of just 10 per cent of his holdings, which netted him $7.8 million cash, bringing his total proceeds from sales of IOS shares to some $14 million over nine years. (That, at least, is his own account.) After this sale he was left with holdings worth around $90 million on paper.

---

*See Chapter 18, "A Very Long Way Offshore."

Among the high command of IOS, there was some agonizing over the question of the exact proportion of his or her shares that each shareholder should be entitled to have freed from restriction in order to sell. It was necessary to put up a reasonable number of shares in order to make the offer worthwhile. But at the same time, if too many were offered, it would spoil the price. Indeed, to float off the entire IOS shareholdings as it existed in 1969 would have required, at $10 per share, about half a billion dollars: a demand which would have utterly exhausted the international investment market.

The other tricky point was that the offerings of existing shares, via Crang's and the Investors Overseas Bank, would have to be made at whatever price Drexel and the other underwriters settled for the new shares. There was great reluctance among the big shareholders to sell any more of their own shares than they had to at prices fixed by people they regarded as a crew of mean-spirited bankers. They thought that the share price was going to boom: their idea was to get a market established and then they would be able to sell when the prices were far above the issue level.

In the end, a rule was agreed upon that everyone inside IOS who had held their shares for more than ten years must sell at least 10 per cent, and no more than 50 per cent. The rest could sell up to 10 per cent of their holding.

The general pattern was that big shareholders who had retired and were no longer active in the company, sold very large blocks and often the full 50 per cent. Those who were still involved stuck mostly to 10 per cent. This was not simply because they were involved in the boom mentality generated in the IOS Board room in the late 1960s. Another reason was that most of them were beneficiaries of Joel Mallin's "lifetime system of tax deferral."

Joel Mallin is a New York lawyer who favors pink shirts,

wide plaited-silk ties, and heavy jewelry. He did a good deal of commuting to and from Geneva as the moment of offering approached. He designed a mechanism to vanquish the capital-gains tax as thoroughly as IOS's other arrangements had been designed to vanquish income tax. The first step was to erect a large batch of foreign, discretionary trusts in the Bahamas, using IOS banks, and the faithful International Credit Bank, as trustee. Then each big shareholder became a beneficiary under one of these trusts. "It was a kind of tax-avoidance supermarket," said one of the beneficiaries. "We didn't bother with guys who had less than 10,000 old shares," said Mallin. As the flotation of IOS was accompanied by an eight-for-one series of stock splits, that meant they did not bother with anyone who had less than 80,000 shares in the new setup: in other words they didn't bother with anyone who was worth less than $800,000.

The next step was for the shareholder to transfer his shares at a relatively low price to the trust. The trust would sell 10 per cent of them in the public issue for $10 each. Out of the proceeds, the trust would pay the shareholder for his shares in installments spread over five years. The trust would not, of course, be subject to U.S. capital-gains tax, and although the installments would have to be reported, they would be spread over a considerable period. The theory was that the trust would sell another 10 per cent each year, again with payments to the original shareholder to be made in installments over five years.

"This was deferral of tax, rather than avoidance," said Mallin. "True," he added, smiling finely, "in this case it might be lifetime deferral—coupled with absence of liability to estate duty."*

---

*Whether the Internal Revenue Service would have accepted this ingenious scheme was a matter eagerly debated by the shareholders and their legal advisers. In the end, the matter became academic: the collapse of the IOS share price solved most people's capital-gains problems for them.

Combining these advantages with the attractions of an orderly—and as they hoped, rising—market, men like Harvey Felberbaum and Roy Kirkdorffer elected to take 10 per cent of their shares out of restriction in 1969, with another 10 per cent to come in 1970. For this reason the biggest cash sums in the offering, after Cornfeld's own, were mostly taken by men who had been away from 119 Rue de Lausanne for some time. Lester Hayes, the one-time ballroom dancing champion, a veteran of the Boulevard Flandrin days, sold half his shares, and received $3.5 million cash. John Templeton, an American fund manager who put up some much-needed capital for IOS in 1962, received $2 million; and so did John Curran, the old rewrite man from the *Herald Tribune*. Eli Wallitt received $1.5 million—but he sold more than 10 per cent, not because he was about to retire from the IOS Board, but because he was financing the purchase of a lakeside mansion in Geneva.

Just behind him came an almost equally wealthy group: George Landau, now chief administrator; Don Q. Shaprow, overseer of Africa; Gladis Solomon, head of the IOS Foundation; and Richard Hammerman, the insurance expert. Each of these received $1.2 million for selling a tenth of their shares. This left each of them with another $10.8 million of salable shares at $10 per share.

There were 490 shareholders who put up shares for the "cashing-in," raising altogether some $52 million from the market, roughly the same sum as was raised by the new shares. Very much the richest of these pickings went to Bernie and his grand old veterans: indeed, just fifteen people, all of whom took $1 million apiece or more, accounted for $26 million of the cash between them. The list of sellers that IOS sent to J. H. Crang in Toronto reads like a wonderful, golden version of all those early sales-bonus lists. George Tregea, the man who left Brazil so hurriedly, took $1 million cash. Ben Heirs, who started his training alongside George Landau in Geneva almost exactly ten years before the public offering, sold shares to the tune of a little over $1 million: that, after underwriting discounts, brought him $988,000.* Allen Cantor took $1.1 million. Bob Sutner, another veteran of the early days in Latin America, took out $1 million. Hy Feld, a quiet man who ran the New York office during Bernie's ill-fated attempt to crack the U.S. market, took $1 million. The men who sincerely wanted to be rich were at long last rich—and in nearly every case, the cash that they took seemed to be merely an hors d'oeuvre, as it were, for the real feast which was to follow.

Even those who did not take the magic million had some impressive sums to their name. Ambassador Roosevelt received $684,000 and Barry Sterling, the investment banker, $691,600. Roy Kirkdorffer took $489,000 and Harvey Felberbaum took $605,416. As both of them were selling 10 per cent through the trust system, that placed their fortunes at $5.1 million and $6.3 million apiece. (And we have records only of IOS shares: other investments could well have been made out of the override riches.)

It may seem odd, at first glance, that Cowett was only recorded as cashing in for $658,692, placing his fortune at just under $7 million. But Cowett, as we said earlier, was playing the game for its own fascinating sake. He liked being rich—but sincerely, he wanted to wheel and deal.

There were solid rewards too, for lesser characters in the saga. Howard Stamer and Robert Haft, the New York attorneys, made sales worth $389,120 each. Eric Scott, head of Crang's, the Toronto brokers, sold a comfortable $136,800

---

*All our figures are for amounts received in cash, after underwriting discounts.

worth. Sameera Abou-Haidar from Beirut got $163,000. Ray Tabet, Sameera's boss, took $378,480. C. Henry Buhl III sold $457,000.

Going through the list of selling shareholders, it is possible to count eighty-seven people who sold $10,000 worth or more of shares. Assuming that their sales were in each case 10 per cent of their holdings, then this meant that each of them had a share-holding worth $1 million at the price of $10 per share—more, if the price rose.

• • •

Bernie Cornfeld was busy assuring everyone who would listen that the shares were a fine investment. Secretaries, cleaning-ladies, and messenger boys at IOS were exhorted to get in and buy while they could. Visiting reporters were offered shares. Much euphoria was generated, but at the end of the formal offer period, the Investors Overseas Bank, which was selling on behalf of existing shareholders, still had an embarrassing block of 800,000 shares on its books. Was the sale to be incomplete, leaving the men who were cashing in to go short of $8 million?

A charitable body came forward to prevent any such distress: none other than the IOS Foundation, promoter of Pacem in Terris. There was a slight problem: the Foundation lacked the necessary money. But IOS had just received $52 million for its new shares. So IOS lent the Foundation $8,344,000 to make the purchase and complete Phase One of the cashing in. Thus $8 million of the money that had been put up on the promise that it would go into the "development of banking and insurance" actually went to help develop the personal fortunes of the chieftains of IOS and their followers.

Amid all the intricate devices of the latter years, this is the one which shows most clearly that IOS had become, at heart, just a series of deals in the minds of Ed and Bernie. In this series of transactions they finally lost touch with even the fictional legalities of the offshore game.

Taking up 800,000 shares left the IOS Foundation with a huge debt which it could not possibly pay off unless it resold the shares. No problem: Cowett had another useful little Bahamian company called The IOS Stock Option Plan Ltd. He switched the block of shares to this company and decreed that the transfer amounted to a repayment of the loan, which was simply canceled.

The maneuver depended on the protean nature of The IOS Stock Option Plan Ltd. It had been formed to get around a problem which resulted from the shifting of the home of IOS Ltd. from Panama to Toronto, Ontario. Ontario securities law prohibits a company from buying its own shares. But in order for the stock-option plan to work, IOS had to be able to buy back its own shares at any time. Answer: turn the plan into a Bahamian company whose voting shares were owned by three private individuals, Cornfeld, Cowett, and Cantor. IOS itself only owned nonvoting shares and, therefore, according to IOS lawyers, it was not a subsidiary of IOS and could buy IOS shares. For Cowett's purpose, however, the stock-option plan was considered such an integral part of IOS that a loan made by IOS could be canceled out when "repayment"—in this case the transfer of IOS shares—had been made to The IOS Stock Option Plan Ltd.

What IOS had really done was simply to pay out $8 million of its newly acquired $52-million cash to the selling shareholders. They got their money all right, although someone, at some point in the series of book entries which constituted the transaction, lost track of events. It emerged that the bank was acting improperly in being a trustee of the Foundation, because it did not have the proper Bahamian trustee license. The whole deal thus became quite improper, and attempts were still being made to sort it out in the middle of 1970. By that point, The IOS Stock Option Plan Ltd. had been exercising the powers of its ambiguous nature to the full, and had become a major stockholder in IOS Ltd., playing a crucial part in the downfall of Bernie and Ed.

• • •

Although the new shares in the hands of the one hundred twenty underwriting banks were snapped up eagerly on October 15, it soon became clear that a sizable number of the outside investors had bought shares, not to hold, but to resell for a swift profit. Without its being widely realized, the long speculative cycle was running out of steam. There were many IOS salesmen who were "fantasy-oriented," in Eli Wallitt's phrase, and who believed Cornfeld's estimate that the price would hit $25, even $50. Many of them borrowed all they could get to buy IOS shares far beyond their means. But the fact was that the sophisticated people inside IOS, like Wallitt himself, were more interested in selling IOS shares than in buying them.

Whatever euphoria may be generated, the price of any share is eventually determined by the earnings it is expected to produce. Cornfeld was declaiming that IOS profits would be $30 million for 1969 and by 1975 there was going to be $15 billion under IOS's management. . . . He was not exactly disbelieved, but experienced investors were feeling cautious.

After a flurry on the first day's trading, the IOS share price stabilized briefly at $14. On the earnings per share calculable from a $30-million profit for IOS that meant the market was giving IOS a not ungenerous multiple of twenty-three times 1969 earnings for each share. Yet even so, there was a drift down.

It was clear that a hideous chain reaction must follow from

a drop in the IOS share price. First, the fierce motivation of the sales force depended on the idea that salesmen should desire the shares available under the stock-option plan. Formerly, the share price which spurred their efforts had been fixed by IOS itself, under the "formula value"* system. But now there was a quoted market value. If the price collapsed the efforts of the sales force would slacken, whereupon profits would again decline further. . . . If the downward drift should turn into a collapse, it would bring down with it the whole of Cowett's finely balanced edifice.

Almost immediately after the issue, Cowett began, secretly, a heavy program of buying up IOS shares. It continued, at varying intensity, until April 1970, and it had the effect of propping the price up above $10. Then, at the end of the first week of April, reality broke in and the price collapsed through the $10 level. Within three weeks, the shares were virtually unsalable.

Commercial moralities vary in detail upon the question of companies buying their own shares. It is, for instance, a cardinal offense in British law, although permitted to a limited extent in the United States. But no commercial code permits a company to manipulate the price of its own shares, creating a "false market." The buying of IOS Ltd. shares, including those taken up by The IOS Stock Option Plan Ltd., sucked back more than 15 per cent of the shares on the market. This undoubtedly created a false price.

Cowett himself denies that the program was begun as a price-support operation, whatever it looked like in the end. And indeed, there was such a tangle of purchases, in Cornfeld's name, in the names of Cowett's and John King's family trusts, and by The IOS Stock Option Plan Ltd., that it is difficult to as-

---

*See Chapter 5, "Early Travels in the Offshore World."

cribe any one purpose to the operation. During the months it went on, it may have had different emphases at different times: it could have been part of an attempt by John King to become a dominating shareholder in IOS; sometimes, as when the "profits" of the Arctic performance in December gave a brief fillip to the market price, it may have been a program of speculative personal investment. In retrospect, Cornfeld told us, as in 1962 "Cowett fell for the delusion that he could support stock prices through leverage."

Cowett says that some time in October he and Cornfeld, in Geneva, had a conference phone conversation with John King in Colorado. King was in the bar at his ranch house. They all agreed that IOS shares were a fine investment at $14 each, and that they should form a pool to buy them. The idea, said Cowett, was to buy the shares in Cornfeld's name and divide them up afterward. A special account was created at the ODB to handle the purchases.

If in October 1969 you still thought that IOS Ltd. would actually produce the $25-million profit on which its public offer was predicated, and if you knew that a $10-million profit boost would come with the announcement of the Arctic maneuver in December, then you might have thought IOS a smart buy at $14. However, if that was his motivation, rather than price support, then Cowett was committing a commercial sin of an opposite nature. Directors of public companies are certainly not supposed to buy up their shares on the strength of inside information that they have not given to the investing public.

Cowett says that what he was doing was not insider trading, because Cornfeld had mentioned the idea of Arctic revaluation to a conference of IOS salesmen in the summer. The trouble with that is (a) a talk to his own salesmen was scarcely a public disclosure and (b) why wasn't the information in the prospectus, finalized September 24, 1969?

In any case, though Cowett may have believed that the IOS shares ought to be rising, the reality was that they were going down. The price slid from $14 on October 15 to $11½ by the end of December. Then it recovered briefly to $13½, when speculators computed the results of the Arctic performance fee on IOS profits. The price would certainly have fallen much faster had Cowett not spent roughly $11 million buying back IOS shares from the market during November and December.

The market in IOS shares had little to do with any regular exchange. Essentially, it consisted of deals done with and between a group of banks scattered around Europe. One of the leading lights of this market was Mel Rosen, an old friend of IOS's New York broker, Arthur Lipper III: Rosen had left New York to work for an offshore fund group, and helped to set up the Deposit & Finance Bank in Luxembourg, a specialist dealer in the so-called "Euro-equities," like Gramco Management shares. Shortly before the IOS offer, Cowett brought Rosen into IOS, and under Rosen's guidance the ODB became a leading dealer in shares of IOS Ltd.

Rosen and the ODB worked closely with Banque Troillet, another Euro-equity specialist, owned by the large Swiss Banque Romande: together ODB and Troillet led the dealing in IOS shares in Geneva and Luxembourg, where both had branches. In Amsterdam, the dealing was led by the Slavensburg bank, and in London by Guinness Mahon. This market, which Cowett himself had helped to set up, was strikingly free: just a few bankers with busy Telexes, arbitrating between supply and demand rather like bookmakers making book. There were none of the minimal stock-exchange rules on, for instance, disclosure of buying-in operations. Cowett's operation could therefore be conducted in great secrecy.

Indeed, Cowett did not even tell the IOS Board what he was doing, and Cornfeld himself claims not to have known until February just what was happening. Cornfeld admits to remembering some general talk about a pool with King and Cowett in the autumn of 1969, but says he heard no more until February, when he was in New York to address the *Institutional Investor* seminar. Allen Cantor, he says, called from Geneva to say that big blocks of IOS shares were being bought on Bernie's ODB account, and did Bernie know?

It seems unlikely that it would have occurred to Cornfeld at this point—with the applause of half Wall Street ringing in his ears—that IOS shares could even need supporting. On the strength of the gigantic but deceptive sales inflow of the previous summer, he was now predicting that IOS would become the most important economic force in the world. And on his own account, he was at that time less interested in present details of the business than in certain plans to set up a chain of hotels in Latin America in collaboration with *Playboy*. As he put it to us later, this was another far-sighted attempt to create investments which would transcend falling stock markets: Cornfeld reasoned that "people would always go to the Playboy Hotel, in the hopes of getting laid." However, he diverted himself from this, and from his denunciations of the SEC, for long enough to tell Cowett that he would not have all the volume of IOS shares put on his account. The better part of a million shares had now been bought in.

Cornfeld eventually agreed to keep about 30,000 shares, whereupon large blocks had to be shifted to the Bahamian trusts set up for the Cowett and King families. These trusts financed their purchase with the aid of loans from that gallant but now wilting institution, the Overseas Development Bank (Bahamas). Altogether, Cowett borrowed $2.8 million to finance his family trust, and the King trust probably had rather more than $5 million by mid-February. (The King trust did a last burst of buying just before the collapse in April, which brought its loan up to $6.7 million.)

Whatever names originally footed the bill, all this money came in via credit from IOS banks. King and Cowett ended up with 600,000 common shares between them, but Cowett also wheeled out The IOS Stock Option Plan Ltd. which bought another 270,000 common shares of the parent company which owned but theoretically did not control it. These purchases cost the IOS treasury $3.75 million, taken in this case directly rather than via ODB credit. Cowett's share-buying program thus sucked back 900,000 shares out of the market, at a total cost of $12 million, which together with the Foundation purchase from the Investors Overseas Bank, meant that IOS Ltd. expended over $20 million on buying its own shares.

A point can be reached at the height of a speculative boom when transactions become so complicated that they baffle the very minds which devised them, so that men—and companies— end up swindling themselves. That point had now been reached: IOS was now supporting itself into a state of collapse.

Curiously enough Cowett's program was not the only case of IOS money going into its own shares. Late in 1969, an IOS director paid a visit to one of the IOS investment banks, the Investors Bank of Luxembourg. He suggested that IOS shares might be a good buy, and the bank, which had been dealing in them for its customers, now started buying them direct for itself. In this case, there was no stock-option plan to separate the Investors Bank from its parent. The buying was therefore simply illegal. But no one found out until 1970, when the value of IOS shares was largely hypothetical. Some $300,000 had to be written off.

• • •

Presumably, Cowett must have hoped that if a bold front could only be maintained, IOS might yet declare those luscious profits that Bernie was predicting. Granted, anyone who could engineer the Arctic deal might reasonably assume that while confidence endured his ingenuity would be equal to any occasion. (Cowett and King were busily planning a whole new fund to be devoted to natural resources.) But even while the money was being poured out to buy IOS shares it was becoming less and less likely that IOS would be able to turn in anything other than notional profits for 1969.

Cornfeld, Cowett, Cantor, and several other IOS luminaries have consistently declared that they only discovered things were going wrong when it was too late. This, they say, was because the IOS financial system was archaic. It takes some nerve, after the corporate boasting they had done, to *excuse* oneself by saying that one was looking after $2 billion of other people's money with archaic accounting services. But it wasn't ever true. The IOS accounting services were competent enough to produce a weekly cash report which showed with fair clarity how fast the money was being siphoned off. Nobody, however, seems to have been much interested in these reports until the final process of revelation.

This occurred at two sets of IOS Board meetings. There was a traumatic but relatively orderly double session on the weekend of April 11–12. This was followed by a strident, frequently comic, sometimes bitterly emotional set of meetings running from May 3 to May 9, 1970, which brought the regime of Bernie and Ed effectively to an end.

As New Year 1970 began, a process of revolt was under way inside the empire, confined at first within the IOS bureaucracy. As the scope of its operations expanded, IOS had inevitably acquired a force of professional accountants and investment managers to conduct its routine affairs. It was not intended that they, any more than the distinguished outsiders on the board, should share any part of the real power residing in the "troika" of Cornfeld, Cowett, and Cantor. None of these professionals possessed the emotional subtlety of Cornfeld, the hectic intellectual brilliance of Cowett, or even the superlatively pompous presence of Cantor (who, with his beard and pipe, looks like some infinitely reassuring Polar explorer turned businessman). But many were men of ability, and some of them retained throughout their sense of underlying reality.

Jo Melse, the Dutchman who managed the non-American investments of IIT, forced the first confrontation. In December 1969 he became desperately worried at the mass of conglomerate bond issues like Giffen Industries, Gulf & Western, and Commonwealth United which IIT had bought up after the "investment-banking" operations of Cowett and Barry Sterling.*
Mel Rosen, Cowett's new lieutenant, was handling most of this investment, and Melse demanded an interview with Cowett to ask for more information about why it was happening. Melse spent two hours in Cowett's office, but as Cowett was on the telephone for all but fifteen minutes, Melse learned very little. Furious—and he is a powerful man, some six feet six inches tall—he stormed in to see Cornfeld at home in the Villa Elma, and threatened to resign: Cornfeld, pacifically, promised that Melse should become President of IIT, with over-all control of investments. Although this came too late to protect IIT from se-

---

*See Chapter 17, "The Master Financiers."

rious damage, there was now some institutional barrier between Cowett and IOS's biggest fund.

The Treasurer of IOS was a young American accountant named Melvin Lechner, who had come from the auditors, Arthur Andersen & Co. Lechner was enough of a believer in IOS to have bought IOS stock heavily with borrowed money: but by January 1969 any hopes he entertained as a stockholder were being rapidly contradicted by his professional knowledge as an accountant. "On the day before we received the proceeds of the public offer in October," he told us, "we had in effect a cash position of $1 million for IOS Ltd. During the entire period of October you didn't have to be a blooming genius to see the cash position going down. The reaction of people in management was that the cash reports were wrong."

After the public offer, in fact, all but a few people in IOS followed Cornfeld's example, and took time out to luxuriate in the future. Allen Cantor's sales company had brought $135 million into the IOS funds during July, the high-point month of 1969—and Cantor claimed earnestly to us that he had not the slightest idea that the sales company could have been making a loss on its operations at the time. By Christmas 1969, Cantor and his salesmen were predicting that their sales for 1970 would reach $4,500,000,000 in terms of "face value." The vast sales, although generating a golden shower of commissions, were destroying profits, because cash sales were actually becoming a smaller proportion of the face volume. Commissions were calculated on the face volume, and the override burden was becoming heavier all the time as more and more men became Super-GMs.*

In January, while the 1969 profits were still being computed, Mel Lechner wrote a four-page memo to Cowett which he said

---

*See Chapter 18, "A Very Long Way Offshore."

was intended as a diplomatically phrased warning that profits would be "lower than we have been talking about." Cowett, having returned from his holiday in Acapulco, received this warning with equanimity. He was contemplating the one important piece of expansion that was actually mounted with IOS's new capital. This was the purchase of the Canadian Channing fund group. Effectively, it was Ed's last deal.

To assume the management of the three Channing funds and become the biggest fund operator in Canada, IOS paid $7 million cash. But then Cowett did a very odd thing. He caused IOS Ltd. to switch the ownership of Channing to IOS's own subsidiary, IOS Management—the entity which IOS floated off before going public itself, and which drew its income from fees on the proprietary funds. In payment for Channing IOS Ltd. received 400,000 shares of IOS Management, and the funny thing about this was that on the ruling market price, 400,000 Management shares were worth $14 million. It was a deadly error: market operators instantly assumed that IOS itself thought that IOS Management was overpriced, and therefore that income from the funds was falling.

On February 4, Cornfeld informed the admiring institutional investors of New York that IOS was "experiencing a net cash flow of over $100 million a month," and, having accused the SEC of plotting the overthrow of the stock market, departed for Acapulco with Hugh Hefner and a team of bunnies. Seven days later, Mel Lechner and his staff finished their preliminary computation of the 1969 profit. As we have seen, it was not $30 million or even $25 million; it was $17.9 million.

Nobody then knew that closer examination would bring that figure down to $10.2 million—meaning that without the performance fee on the Arctic deal IOS would have made virtually nothing. But the figure Lechner had, in terms of the current IOS share price, was disaster enough: he took it at once to Cowett's executive assistant, an ex-State Department man named Hal Vaughan. It was Wednesday, February 11, and Cowett was in Tokyo looking into a real-estate fund project. Together, Lechner and Vaughan put in a call to Cowett and gave him the figure over the phone. He said, coolly, that he would fly back to Geneva, and that Lechner should come to his villa on the following Sunday with the papers.

The Sunday meeting precipitated an almost continuous round of meetings between Cowett, Cantor, Vaughan, Norman Rolnick (Controller of IOS), George Landau, now in charge of administration, and Lechner and his accountants. By the end of February the accountants were able to predict, correctly, that IOS was going to lose money in the first quarter of 1970. And at the same time, it was impossible not to see that sales operations were in the red. Allen Cantor concedes that in February he began to get a little worried. Cowett's version is that there was a conference, at which Cantor reported that sales were 17 per cent higher than in February 1969, only to be told brutally by one of his own executives, "Shit, Allen. That's face volume. Cash sales are down 40 per cent."

Yet the "winter series" of board meetings, beginning on March 9 and ending on March 13, passed off, ostensibly, in peace and harmony. Cowett, to Lechner's amazement, told the IOS Board that profits for 1969 would be $25 million—and when Lechner asked, afterward, why he had not given the $17.9 figure Cowett said blandly, "Those were preliminary figures. Right, Mel?" There were two main items on the agenda for these meetings. The first was to approve "aggregate investment of $44 million of company money" during 1970. The directors did not commit themselves to "any specific projects," which was wise, because by this time a 44¢ expansion would have taxed the corporate treasury. Second, the directors conferred promotions upon some of their number.

Cornfeld remained Chairman of the Board, but Cowett took over from him as President of IOS, and Allen Cantor became Vice Chairman. Eli Wallitt was elected Executive Vice President, and James Roosevelt Senior Vice President. Ossie Nedoluha and Malcolm Fox, from Hong Kong, joined the main IOS Board. This, said Cornfeld, "realigned corporate titles to clarify . . . actual responsibilities." What it really showed was that unease was spreading among the directors, beginning to take the form of personal dissatisfaction with Cornfeld.

It was not just his penchant for bell-bottom trousers and the beard that he had been sprouting since the previous year. Cornfeld was now frequently absent from Geneva, and was increasingly less effective in his once-crucial role of inspiring the salesmen. Late in 1969, for instance, he missed an important meeting which was designed to boost morale in Germany, and instead of the magic presence, the Germans had to make do with an hour's talk about boutiques and other investments, amplified from the transatlantic telephone. In January, Cornfeld was diverted by a CBS project to make a TV documentary about his life: much energy went into mounting an eighty-first birthday party for Sophie Cornfeld, which was filmed by CBS at the Villa Elma. Such was Cornfeld's obsession with the movie that Sir Eric Wyndham White, who was threatening to resign because of the difficulty of discovering what was happening inside IOS, found himself discussing his resignation in front of the CBS cameras. Granted, all this was eccentric behavior in the President of a financial institution. But it was ironic that the directors should have chosen to augment Ed Cowett's authority as a means of curing the ills of IOS.

Cowett's own eccentricities were not to be hidden. The original agent of revelation was Professor George von Peterffy, one of the more colorful members of the faculty of the Harvard Business School. The professor joined the IOS Board in September 1969, having decided to spend a year developing his interests outside Harvard. Von Peterffy is not the cloistered kind of academic. He is a powerful young man, standing around six-four. He was to cause some consternation at one tense board meeting by telling Cowett that he had a gun with him—having just returned from the Middle East where, he felt, it was *de rigueur* to carry side arms. Nevertheless, he was distinctly unhappy about IOS by the beginning of 1970: apart from anything else, he did not care for the fact that part of the Italian operation still appeared to be illegal.

Late in February, Cowett admitted to von Peterffy that the 1969 profits would not match the prophecies, and after the March board meetings, he gave von Peterffy, together with a small group of executives, the task of examining IOS's profitability. The history of von Peterffy's exercise suggests that Cowett did not mean it to make any significant discoveries, but that by this stage the pressures inside the much-abused professional bureaucracy were at bursting point.

Lechner declares that as Treasurer of IOS he received no details of ODB loans, and that the ODB manager Phil Doubre had strict instructions to respect Swiss bank secrecy. However, Lechner claims that in the last days of March he deduced the extent of the loans from the IOS cash position. In the first week of April, von Peterffy got down to his task, and on the 7th met with Lechner, who described the meeting in these terms:

Von Peterffy turned to me and said, "What is the current cash position of the company? Give me a number. Is it $100 million? $20 million? $5 million?"

I said, "George, I have not been authorized to make this information available. Talk to Ed. Get clearance."

He blew up. He said, "This meeting is adjourned," and he stomped out of the door.

Then, says Lechner, it came to him four hours later that "maybe George is the guy to talk to. Maybe he can be the link." The Treasurer found von Peterffy in the office of a young IOS executive, Abe Carmel, who had been a student of von Peterffy's. "He wouldn't see me at first, he was so pissed off. I said to him, 'George, I have to talk to you—it's not only the cash position.'"

The Harvard Business School trains its sons well. Von Peterffy walked to the door, locked it, and said that no one was leaving the room until the truth was known. "I talked for three hours," Lechner recalled. "I explained to him about everything, including the banking transactions. He listened, sort of shocked and fascinated."

Lechner's disclosures burst upon an atmosphere which was thick with rumor. Henry Buhl told us that all through January he "kept hearing from Swiss bankers that we were lending people money to buy our own shares." Mel Rosen told Jo Melse that he was having to buy wads of IOS shares—for purchasers whose identity he didn't know. And the boasts about "expansion" had dismayed the accountants at Ferney, who knew enough to know that IOS could not conceivably find $44 million for expansion.

But whatever financial links existed in the mind of Ed Cowett, the clandestine tradition of IOS had divided the company into a series of separate compartments. A great many people knew that particular things were going wrong. "But what could you do?" said one of Lechner's assistants. "Ed Cowett was the guy running the company. Suppose you went to him. You know the bit in the Western, where the guy goes in to tell the sheriff that the baddies are in town? And while the guy's talking, you see the sheriff opening the desk drawer with the gun in it—because the sheriff's the chief of the baddies?"

Lechner had now bypassed the "sheriff." The train of events he set in motion was later dubbed "the Apocalypse" by the *IOS Bulletin*. It was a suitable title, the Apocalypse being "the revelation of that which hath been hid." The Four Horsemen, in this case, were von Peterffy, C. Henry Buhl III, Richard M. Hammerman, and Sir Eric Wyndham White.

After his session with Lechner on Tuesday, April 7, von Peterffy talked urgently with Henry Buhl. Buhl says that although he had not seen the weekly cash reports, he had already heard some disturbing whispers from the accountants. Next Friday, April 10, a meeting of the Executive Committee of the IOS Board was due: Buhl decided that a secret cabal must meet first. He spoke to Sir Eric Wyndham White, who promised support. Next, Buhl called Hammerman at the London office, and asked him to arrive quietly the day before the Executive Committee meeting was due. Then, on Thursday, April 9, the Four Horsemen met Lechner: not at 119 Rue de Lausanne, but privately in another set of IOS offices at number 147. Lechner said that if they promised to defend his right to speak, he had "a lot to say."

In other words, it was necessary to mount an intrigue before the company's cash position could be discussed by its own directors.

At three thirty the next afternoon, the Executive Committee met, with Cornfeld in the chair. The scene was Ambassador Roosevelt's office, draped with a large Stars and Stripes. Buhl's horsemen were all there, and so were Cowett and Cantor together with Roosevelt, Ed Coughlin, Wallitt, and a few others. Lechner was ready with "twenty copies of everything."

After half an hour, Cornfeld turned to Lechner and said, "What is your cash position?"

Lechner took out a five-page report.

Cornfeld said, "Just give me a number!"

Buhl and von Peterffy said together, "Let Mel speak!"

And then Allen Cantor weighed in with, "Let's get this on the table."

So Lechner spoke, for the next six hours. "I went all through the loans," recalled Lechner, "the integrity gap. I pointed out that Cowett had been talking about $25-million profits, when the goddam number was $17.9 million. Cowett spoke from time to time, sinking lower in his chair. They tried to shut me up at first, but I wouldn't let them. That was my day in court."

It was an unnerving set of sums that faced the Executive Committee. For in the six months since the public offer all the $52.4 million raised in the public offer, and more, had been spent. This must set some sort of record for commercial profligacy.

What follows is as close as we can get, from the weekly and monthly cash statements, checked with interviews, to the financial facts which emerged at the Executive Committee meeting. (The proviso should be made that in the shock and confusion of that Friday night, not all the details were clearly grasped.)

There was, first of all, the money which had been spent to buy shares of IOS Ltd. and IOS Management:

	Millions of dollars
Loan to stock-option plan to buy 834,000 shares of IOS Ltd.	8.3
Cowett trust loan to buy IOS Ltd. stock	2.8
King trust loan to buy IOS Ltd. stock (just increased)	6.7

	Millions of dollars
To stock-option plan for 270,000 shares of IOS Ltd.	3.7
Buying IOS Management stock	3.2

There were some transactions which would be put in a more orthodox light, although they consisted largely of much-needed additions to the capital of the sorely tried IOS banks:

	Millions of dollars
New offices, etc.	2.5
Increase in capital for ODB	2.3
Increase in capital of Orbis Bank (Germany)	1.5

There was the money paid over to keep Commonwealth United going, and to buy the Canadian fund group in February (which eventually made a loss).

	Millions of dollars
Loans to Commonwealth United	8.0
Purchase of Canadian Channing	7.0

There was then a disturbing batch of personal loans to IOS insiders, or to their tax-avoidance vehicles, and loans to King personally, besides those to companies and connections of King's. Also Bernie had decided that he would like to have a BAC 1–11 airliner fitted out to rival Hugh Hefner's Douglas DC–9—the all-black Big Bunny—and this cost was being guaranteed by the ODB:

	Millions of dollars
Loan to John King personally (apart from family trust loans)	2.0
Loans to Beta Foundation Equipment Associates, NOPI purchase, and three Jetstreams	8.3
ODB guarantee on purchase of aircraft by Bernard Cornfeld	4.9

Loan to Colorado Corporation	1.7
Loan to William White (a Denver business associate of King's and a Midbar investor)	1.6
Loan to David Meid (Venture Fund Manager)	0.2
Loans to IOS Associates and employees	3.3
Loans to officers and directors of IOS, other than already noted	3.4
Other guarantees	3.3
Grand total of transactions:	75.0

The members of the Executive Committee were as shocked and fascinated as von Peterffy had been in the first place. Cornfeld himself proclaimed throughout that he had been ignorant of the havoc wrought. "I apologize, Mel," he muttered, more than once. "I just didn't know." Some of those present, like Wallitt and Hammerman, must at least have known that Cowett had been organizing loans for their tax-avoidance projects. Others had had their suspicions. But perhaps even Cowett himself had never looked, until then, at anything like the whole picture. For the Executive Committee, the experience was akin to the one suffered by Dorian Gray when he uncovered his own portrait after years of self-indulgence. The stunned gathering did not break up until ten-thirty p.m. By that time most of them realized that IOS could scarcely survive unless outside help could be found. It is the memory of Eli Wallitt that supplies the apt phrase. "We realized," he said, "that we had all been blinded by greed."

The Feeling of the Meeting

How the minutes came to record that "Mr. Cornfeld voluntarily tendered his resignation."

April 11 was Ed Cowett's fortieth birthday, and it came at the end of a doubly eventful week—because the first fatal break in the IOS share price had now occurred. The price was standing at just under $11 when Lechner talked to von Peterffy. On Thursday, the day before the Executive Committee meeting, the shares opened at the Banque Troillet at 10¼. The price then fell under $10 for the first time, and by the end of the day the Troillet dealer, M. Plomb, had marked IOS Ltd. down to 8. On Friday, the price wavered between 8¼ and 8⅝: it was now firmly below its issue price, and financial journalists began getting on the line to 119 Rue de Lausanne. Cowett was suavely unshaken. It was a momentary setback, he said. A Swiss bank had tossed 30,000 shares into the market.

There was, almost certainly, such a block: it may have been the shares purchased in 1969 by Leonhard Lang, an IOS regional manager in Karlsruhe. It was Lang's personal disaster that he had taken Cornfeld's financial euphoria seriously and had bought this considerable block of shares for himself and some of his customers. Half the purchase price was lent by the Basel, Switzerland, branch of the United California Bank, and in April the bank decided, sensibly enough in view of the shaky appearance of the IOS price, to call in its loan—which meant selling off Lang's shares. They were offered first to IOS for purchase. IOS refused.

Speaking in memorably righteous tones, Cowett informed one of the present authors that weekend that IOS had refused to buy because "a company such as IOS, registered under Canadian law, may not trade in its own shares." It was a great speech from a man who, secretly, had caused IOS to spend $12 million on trading in its own shares, and had only stopped when there was no more money left.

The collapse of the IOS share price which followed the end of the buying program struck an immediate blow at the customers' assets, already depleted by the world-wide decline of stock markets.

When IOS's own shares fell, fund managers everywhere began to unload those inflated securities which were so heavily represented in the IOS funds: Giffen Industries, Four Seasons Nursing Homes, Unexcelled Line, Gulf & Western Industries, and the like. Jo Melse, the manager of IIT, estimated that this cost the funds around $50 million, because once it was realized that IOS was in trouble, the IOS fund managers were quoted knockdown prices whenever they tried to get rid of their shakier holdings. He was, understandably, furious that he had not been warned that the IOS share price was being supported.

And IOS was certainly in trouble. On Monday, April 13, IOS shares opened at 8½, and on the 14th they rallied briefly to 9½. On the 16th they fell back to 8. On the 17th, they opened at 7⅜—and they closed that day at a disastrous 5½. By the end of the month Guinness Mahon in London were quoting $4 per share.

The first response of Cornfeld, Cowett, and their immediate henchmen was to try to brazen things out. Once, it might have worked. But the collapse of the IOS share price was taking place against a background of generalized financial panic to which IOS itself had contributed in terms of general policy and particular actions. In April 1970, ghosts which had not been seen since 1929 were climbing out of coffins in Wall Street, in the City of London, and around the Place de la Bourse in Paris.

On February 4, when Cornfeld addressed the New York investment community, the market had been slipping steadily downward for rather more than a year. Having briefly scraped the 1000 mark at the end of 1968, the Dow-Jones average moved down from 950 during 1969, to stand at 750 in the first week of February 1970. It was, however, thought—or frantically hoped—that this was a low point, after which the market would embark on another long climb upward, as it had done in 1968. Surely, after a year's decline, the market must turn the corner? After an awful hesitation in February and March, it did. It turned the wrong way. All the stock markets in the world, with the temporary exception of Italy's, cracked at the same moment, and the cult of performance was discredited in a matter of days.

When hiring Fred Alger in 1965, the Emperor Cornfeld had declared that he would "know the schmuck to fire" in the event that things went wrong. In March 1970, IOS fired Alger: the $60-million portfolio of investments he had been handling was taken over directly by Geneva, and most of them were dumped immediately in return for cash. In point of time, Fred Alger was fired just days before the real break came, and David Meid, the other superstar of the IOS hot-fund team, departed a little later. Symbolically enough for IOS, the true collapse of the Dow-Jones index was just gathering speed on the day that Lechner talked to von Peterffy. On Tuesday, April 7, the Dow Jones was pitching down toward the 700 mark and seemed to be gathering velocity. Investors Overseas Services ran out of money in the week of the worst stock-market panic since World War Two.

On Sunday, April 12, the IOS Board met at the Villa Bella Vista. Saturday had been spent in splinter groups, discussing Friday's revelations: now, they were to be examined before a wider group. Not all the board were there, but although Mende from Germany and Bernadotte from Sweden were missing, Martin Brooke of Guinness Mahon had arrived from London, and Wilson Watkins Wyatt from Louisville, Kentucky. Lechner went through all the figures again, speaking for something like ten hours, with a break for a buffet lunch. Strangely enough, the mood of the meeting, although shocked, appears to have been essentially restrained. "The feeling was that Bernie and Ed were facing up to the situation," Lechner recalled.

Their "facing up" took a remarkable form. Now that vast injections of the company's own money had failed to keep the IOS shares alive, IOS tried the effects of a thunderously orchestrated propaganda campaign. Propaganda, after all, was what they had always done best. By the weekend after that first traumatic meeting, Ed Cowett's line about the 30,000 shares dumped on the market had been elaborated into a wicked plot against IOS. After a careful examination of the evidence, Cowett informed the *Frankfurter Allgemeine Zeitung*, it was possible to say definitely that *the market had been manipulated!* Speculators, he said, were trying to force down the IOS price by systematic selling. Trumpeting shrilly, Cornfeld rushed into battle with yet wilder allegations. He convinced the London *Observer* that IOS was a victim of "the biggest concentrated bear raid that Europe has seen in a generation." It was, he said (producing no shred of evidence), the jealous German banking establishment, getting together to sell IOS short. But they would fail.

"At present market prices," he said (and he must have taken figures from the air), "we have enough cash in hand to buy back all the existing stock fourteen times." For one of the present authors, he produced the claim that he had enough money in his personal bank account to buy back all the shares. That, in the light of later knowledge, was a remarkable statement, because until he objected in January, his account at the ODB had indeed been used to buy almost a million IOS shares.

Yet the tale was told with such matchless assurance that it was hard to disbelieve it. Henchmen pitched in to help, and in the melee taste and accuracy were early casualties. "I feel," said Ambassador Roosevelt, "like I did in 1933, when my father and I had meetings to sort out the problems of the United States. Then, we all pulled together, and none of the terrible things happened." Allen Cantor stated that a mighty consortium of banks stood ready to buy IOS shares, force up the price, and crush the speculators. Cantor spoke glowingly of this consortium, which existed only in his own mind. "When we give the word," he said, "they are all prepared to pile in and buy the stock." Harvey Felberbaum said that people in the know were already "piling in to buy the shares." It was, he said, "a real battle of the giants," adding compassionately, "the tragedy is that it is the little man who will get murdered."

Any little man who took that professional investment advice would have halved his money inside a month. Bernard Cornfeld, however, was not such a one. Privately, on April 20—in the same week that he was suggesting he might personally buy back all the shares—Cornfeld sold a block of 450,000 IOS shares. Of this total, he sold 60,000 on Cowett's behalf. They got $4 each for their shares, which made a total $1.8 million, and it was a very good price for such a huge block of shares on April 20, when the price had opened at about $5.

Cornfeld did have one inspiration about purchasers for IOS shares. Why shouldn't the customers of the IOS funds be lumbered with them? He went to Jo Melse, and told him to use IIT money to buy IOS Ltd. shares. When Melse refused to buy IOS with fund money, Cornfeld lost his temper: whether it was contrived or genuine rage is difficult to say. "Mr. Cornfeld," said C. Henry Buhl, who supported Melse, "was not feeling himself just at that time."

Perhaps not, but he was still selling concepts as diligently as ever. Both he and Cowett had another and subtler line to back up the "bear raid" story. Off the record, they were prepared to make frank, manly admissions that a few things had perhaps gone wrong at IOS. Profits, perhaps, were not going to be quite what had been expected. Cornfeld spoke of IOS executives flying economy class, and suggested that lights would have to be switched off when people left their offices. With a convincing appearance of humility, he admitted that perhaps success had gone somewhat to IOS's head. "We felt very rich last year," he said disarmingly.

Meanwhile, the IOS publicity machine churned out declarations to the effect that only irresponsible conspirators could possibly allege that IOS might be short of cash. Thus, on April 22: "One of the most persistent misstatements which have been bandied about in the past two weeks is that our Company [is] short of cash. . . . These statements are untrue."

It will not be a surprise to learn that IOS lamented that "the small investor" was the person who would be most harmed by these malicious rumors. One would hardly have expected IOS to admit they were broke: by the conventions of business life, some delicate misrepresentation is permitted to those who find themselves in tight corners. But there was nothing delicate about IOS's account of its own cash position: "As for our own liquidity, the IOS group of companies . . . presently has a cash position in excess of $30 million being held at interest."

The statement did not disclose that the figure of $30 million, given as evidence of the company's liquidity, included blocked time-deposits and blocked cash. In effect, therefore, IOS was citing as evidence of its liquidity the very sums that had been advanced to its executives! The company's true liquid-cash position was scarcely more than a third of the sum that was claimed.

The press were not the only recipients of such manufactured optimism. On April 20, M. Paul Vincent, Director General of the Banque Rothschild, called from Paris. Vincent asked Cowett, "As it is my job to ask as an underwriter, what has happened to the share price?" Cowett said it was all right, it was just some speculators, and produced his forecast of the profits: $25 million in 1969, $50 million in 1970. Not that M. Vincent was entirely deceived. Three days later, he informed his boss, Baron Guy de Rothschild: "*C'est foutue, l'IOS.*" This might fairly be translated as "IOS is screwed."

For the whole of April, although the share price fell relentlessly, keeping pace with markets around the world, the IOS façade held together. The version that the press, and the financial community, accepted generally was that IOS had run into some budgetary difficulties, but was "basically sound," and was facing up to them with courage. Cowett's bland assurances, Cornfeld's new humble mien, were produced with admirable polish: before the crisis burst openly in May, only the tiniest clues could be glimpsed by outsiders. Leaving Geneva airport on April 20, one of us caught sight of Cornfeld, seeing Cowett off.

Until they realized they were being observed there seemed to be some curious urgency in their attitude, which contrasted with the debonair calm they were projecting in their offices. Cowett was looking pale and weary.

Nobody was more horrified at the turn of events than the six distinguished underwriters who had brought the IOS public offer to the market. In the blunt words of one of IOS's own directors, the underwriters' reaction was that they and their clients had been had. On April 30, there was a somewhat acrid meeting in Geneva, when Bert Coleman of Drexel, Sir Kenneth Keith of Hill, Samuel, and a party of underwriters confronted the Executive Committee of the IOS Board, including Cornfeld and Cowett. If the underwriting team had taken Cowett at face value before the offering, they did not do so now. How could it be, they wanted to know, that Ed Cowett could have predicted IOS profits of $25 million as recently as mid-April? How were the loans to the collapsing Commonwealth United to be valued? And Sir Kenneth asked an especially nasty question: the prospectus, he pointed out, had suggested that cash from the offer would be used to expand banking and insurance activities. Did the IOS men think that the actual fate of the money squared with that promise?

Allan Conwill, the ex-SEC lawyer working for IOS, replied as best he could. The promise had been accurate when it was made, he said. And at least the Canadian Channing purchase represented some corporate expansion. Admittedly, some of the ways in which the IOS cash had been exhausted did not square with the prospectus. But you might well argue that some of the tax deals had been paid for with revenue cash, not the offering cash. Sir Kenneth and his colleagues do not seem to have been impressed with this line of argument.

They suggested rather brutally that the company needed to get rid of both Cornfeld and Cowett in order to save itself—but this suggestion was too much for the IOS men. John Templeton, one of the big shareholders invited to the meeting as an observer, declared that the company needed the creativity, the imagination that Bernie and Ed brought to its affairs. But after ten years, the alliance between the imaginative pair was beginning to crack up. Cornfeld was careful to point out to the underwriters that the tax deals had been set up by Ed Cowett, and that Cowett was the only man who knew that company money was used in them.

Although the IOS façade remained intact, there was now nothing behind it but a shifting pattern of factions, struggling with each other for control and secretly canvassing sources of outside help. The organizing principle of the company, Cornfeld's personal authority, had lost its true potency at the moment that the company ceased to be IOS Ltd. (SA): in the new public company, he no longer controlled the price of shares and he could no longer pretend to control the process of cashing in. All his manipulative skills could not replace that blunt power: it was now only a matter of the time and the issue, before someone would face him down.

By hints, allusions, and discreet allegations, Cornfeld tried to divert the emotional weight of the crisis onto Cowett. He professed ignorance of the immediate process that had brought IOS to the edge of ruin: although if anything in IOS escaped his knowledge, it did so only because he did not wish to know. Both in business convention and in terms of his long complicity with Cowett, Cornfeld's responsibility was inseparable from Cowett's—but it is a measure of Cornfeld's emotional adroitness that he did succeed in shifting some measure of responsibility away from himself. That did not, however, rescue him from

the new and uncomfortable status of being only one exceptionally powerful member of a gallery of rivals.

• • •

The arrival at the gate of the armies of disaster was the signal
for a savage power struggle to begin among the courtiers. The
determining consideration over all the rescue attempts mounted,
or half-mounted, for IOS was that the man, or alliance of men,
who could bring rescuers in on acceptable terms could expect
power and survival in return. There were, naturally, rival
groups with different candidates for the role of rescuer; and,
with the hierarchy of the company shattered, it was not easy to
be sure how acceptance was to be ratified.

The passions generated by the struggle came to their climax
during an extraordinary meeting of the IOS Board, which began
at ten a.m. on Sunday, May 3, and did not break up until nearly
eleven p.m. on the following Saturday. The meeting, submeet-
ings, cabals, and personal confrontations which accompanied it
were by turns bitter and furious, or inexplicably euphoric. During the week, emissaries and plenipotentiaries came and went incessantly, with offers of rescue or requests for information.
Cornfeld, Cowett, and John King all addressed the meeting with
explanations and suggestions. In between times, long periods of
sullen, ashen bickering supervened.

The Villa Bella Vista made a suitably theatrical setting. Long
before IOS bought it, the villa was the Swiss home of the Col-
gate family. It is a building of great, roughhewn gray stones with
heavy roof beams of dark wood; sprawling beside the lake, at
night it conveys a sense of Gothic melodrama. While the directors inside were lectured by members of their own company or
by visiting speakers as various as Meshulam Riklis of the Rapid-
American Corporation, and George Ball, late of the State De-

partment, now international banker, IOS employees and newspaper reporters milled around outside.

The tang of panic was in the air. In New York, the Dow-Jones index was down to 700, and nobody dared to guess where it might stop. "Years of speculation are coming home," said Sidney Lurie of Josephthals, summing up the general Wall Street feeling that a jealous god was wreaking some overdue retribution. There was genuine fear that Investors Overseas Services might simply disintegrate and dump some $2 billion worth of holdings onto the American markets. Already, the firing of Alger and the hasty dumping of his account was being blamed as one of the triggers that set off the break in March. The effect of IOS and its funds upon the market was not so simple and direct as that—but this was one of those times when the precise facts matter much less than the sudden terrors of the market. The irony was that although IOS itself was going broke, the frightened men gathered by the lakeside still had enough investments under their hands to initiate a devastating chain reaction of selling which could turn the market break into a genuine crash— and they were answerable to no one and to nothing except their own collective fears, ambitions, and desires.

Inside, at the meeting, the scenes were played by a distinguished cast. Together with special effects and noises off, there were contributions from nearly all the important protagonists, with styles and accents as varied as the history of the company itself. There was a group of sales bosses who shared the sleekly youthful air which is apparently conferred by selling international mutual funds: Ira Weinstein of Canada; Malcolm Fox, the ex-Davis Cup player from Hong Kong; Roy Kirkdorffer from London; Ossie Nedoluha; and Robert Sutner. There was Allen Cantor himself, sucking his pipe. Two impressive presences were George Landau, rangy and elegant, like a Russian poet dressed by Brooks Brothers; and Eli Wallitt, with his long prophetic face and a halo of white hair. There was Ambassador Roosevelt, towering and booming; Count Bernadotte; Martin Brooke, the English banker; Pasquale Chiomenti, the Italian lawyer; Wilson W. Wyatt, the Kentucky politician; and Professor von Peterffy, bulking even bigger, physically, than Roosevelt. Erich Mende, bouncy and red-faced, came in with a PR man to translate his German into English. Including Cornfeld and Cowett, twenty-two IOS directors were present when the meeting opened. Arthur Lipper III, the IOS broker, was there by invitation, and so were Allan Conwill and Mel Lechner, the Treasurer. Harold Kaplan, the new head of public relations, attended: no doubt finding it quite a change from his previous assignment, which was handling the Vietnam peace talks for the State Department.

Proceedings opened with Cornfeld in the chair, executing some delicate maneuvers. He was aware that Cowett was trying to promote a take-over of IOS by John King: this he was determined to resist, to the point of a personal break with Cowett. He reasoned, correctly, that the arrival of King would be the end of his own power. Cornfeld gave the meeting a résumé of the condition of the IOS shares, whose price was then wavering around $4 and said redemptions were up sharply. He acknowledged that IOS was suffering from a liquidity problem, and then went on to discuss in some detail the loans which had been made to the King and Cowett family trusts. What Cornfeld did not acknowledge was the idea that IOS needed rescuing, or taking over. In his opinion, all the company needed was some interim finance.

Was it possible that the six banks who had underwritten the offer might be a source of help? Ed Cowett reported on the abortive and acrimonious meeting with them: little was to be expected from that direction.

It was then Allen Cantor's turn. While Cowett had been talking to his friend John King, Cantor had been to Paris and talked to Paul Vincent at the Banque Rothschild. Cantor had discovered that if they could team up with the London Rothschilds, Banque Rothschild might be interested in a rescue bid. He was now able to report that Rothschild's were prepared to meet a deputation in Paris next day. However, he said, they would require the resignations of Bernie and Ed. Neither were they prepared to co-operate with John King.

C. Henry Buhl weighed in with "expressions of interest" from the Banca Commerciale Italiana, Lehman Brothers, and Warburg. Mention of so many important banks excited Cornfeld's incontinent optimism. Perhaps he said, this was IOS's chance, at last, to join the Establishment?

Mel Lechner then reported that IOS would probably lose $7–$13 million in the first half of 1970.

There was an unhappy speech by Dr. Mende, about unrest among salesmen and investors in Germany. It was decided that Mende and Roosevelt should go to Germany, and the meeting got down to discussing John King and his plans in some detail. Cowett had flown to America on a secret mission on April 20. He was looking for help: in New York he saw Charlie Bluhdorn of Gulf & Western and canvassed the possibilities of Bluhdorn's taking up some of the Commonwealth United strain. Ultimately, that initiative came to nothing. He went straight on to Denver, where he had found John King willing, even eager, to come to the rescue. This was less than amazing, since it would by now have been difficult for the King companies to survive the death of IOS. A possible deal had been lashed together, under which King would produce two sums of $20 million to get IOS out of its cash problems. Harding Lawrence of Braniff Airways, who was on the King Resources Board, would become President of

IOS, and King believed that he could get Gustave Levy, formerly Chairman of the Governors of the New York Stock Exchange, to become Chief Executive. It was certainly hard to see where Cornfeld might fit into the new system. But Cowett argued at Bella Vista that the deal would solve certain urgent problems, such as the fact that IOS was losing money, and that many of its salesmen and executives were insolvent because of the collapse of shares bought with borrowed money.

Arthur Lipper said that he doubted that a total of $40 million would be enough to bail IOS out. Richard Hammerman made the cogent point that King seemed to have been rather closely involved in most of the problems that were afflicting IOS. Was it therefore wise to rush into a deal with him? Cornfeld also thought that the whole thing was being done in rather a rush, and that it would not be easy to negotiate with anyone else once King had announced that Harding Lawrence was going to take over as President.

Buhl then suggested that King be asked to come to Geneva, and the meeting fell to discussing an embassy to meet the Rothschilds in Paris next day. Hammerman, Buhl, Barry Sterling, and George von Peterffy were selected to accompany Allen Cantor. Roy Kirkdorffer suggested (feeling perhaps that the group would need a native guide) that Sir Eric Wyndham White, as "a European," should join them.

The day's session closed with some sharp questions from Pasquale Chiomenti. What, he wanted to know, had happened to the cash from the public offering? Cowett, in reply, did not make himself quite clear. Dr. Chiomenti, on his part, made it very clear that he would like to resign from the board as soon as decently possible. In the evening the meeting closed, and the envoys departed for Paris.

Cornfeld opened up on Monday with a long exhortation to

the board not to be stampeded into the King deal, or any other. The thing to do was to get back to running the company, while looking for "partners." He thought there might be several possible sources of short-term money. He mentioned Mr. Meshulam Riklis, of that splendidly named conglomerate, the Rapid-American Corporation.

At this stage, the Paris delegation telephoned an extremely bleak situation report. The London Rothschilds, it emerged, were behaving in a lamentably unsympathetic way. They had kicked off by demanding that IOS be handed over to them as if in receivership. After discussion, they had broken this down to say that they would accept 51-per-cent control, and would offer a dollar a share. They wished to have nothing to do with King, and both Cowett and Cornfeld must go at once. They would bring six or eight of their own people in to run IOS and the funds. Besides the immediate resignations of Cornfeld and Cowett, they wanted everyone else's resignations "in the desk drawer." Furthermore, neither Rothschild house would move without the other.

From the viewpoint of that battered individual the "small investor"—and he did exist, especially in Germany—this would have been an excellent solution. The Rothschild name, of course, would have restored at once the confidence that IOS required. And that in itself would have gone a long way to lessen the depletion of the customers' money. But the Rothschilds were not about to have their name used to rescue a parcel of adventurers from the consequences of their own greed. Much offense was taken among the IOS directors at the Rothschild attitude, which was deemed to be insulting.

What really made it impossible for such an offer to be accepted was that the offer was only worth $1 per share. To the directors—and big shareholders—gathered around the table at

Bella Vista, the attraction of John King, however much they might fear him, was that he was offering, in effect, $4 per share. There was a large blackboard in the conference room on which the vital figures for the two deals were being chalked up at opposite sides. At some point in the debate, one of the directors took up the chalk, and added a comment at the foot of each column. Under the King figures, he wrote "Rape," and under the Rothschild figures he wrote "Murder." The meeting chose to accept a fate worse than death.

Martin Seligson, the IOS real-estate expert, moved, with Ed Cowett seconding, that the negotiating team be withdrawn and that a message be sent to John King accepting his offer. The motion was passed: of the men in Bella Vista, only Cornfeld voted against, and in view of the personal animosity he later expressed toward Jacob Rothschild, he did not vote out of any desire to accept the offer. Rather, he doubted that any organization would have room for two such conceptual salesmen as himself and John King. Voting by telephone from Paris, Richard Hammerman and Eric Wyndham White opposed the motion to deal with King. The meeting adjourned for the evening.

Tuesday was largely Cowett's day. King had replied with enthusiasm, saying that he was on his way to Geneva to consummate the deal in person. The board fell to discussing details of the King offer, such as escrow arrangements, and the timing of the second slice of $20 million, exactly as though John King were a serious financier. Cowett was active in drafting texts and suggesting legal safeguards, discussing the possibility that the Bank of New York might be brought in along with King.

It seemed possible that Cowett might pull it off. The only serious diversion was when Cornfeld's friend, Mr. Riklis, of the Rapid-American Corporation, addressed the board. There seems to have been some thought that Rapid-American, which controls Schenley Industries, might consider a rescue bid. But although Riklis made an inspiring speech, it was mainly concerned with exhorting those present to rescue themselves. He recommended to them a cunning stroke of leverage. The problem was that the earnings per share were not high enough, right? Well, why not convert the majority of the shareholding into debt securities at 4 per cent, thus leaving the earnings to be distributed over a smaller number of shares? As IOS just then had no earnings whatever, the suggestion was of uncertain value. Having made it, Mr. Riklis uttered words of cheer, and left.

• • •

ON the record of the Dover Plan, Richard Hammerman is not the idealistic type of businessman. But he now brought to bear one personal quality not often found in the upper echelons of IOS: realism. He continued to object passionately to the idea that IOS could be rescued by the natural-gas wizard from Denver. On Tuesday, the best he could do was get himself appointed to the subcommittee to negotiate with King. But on Wednesday morning, with King in the air and nearing Geneva, he mounted a cogent attack. He managed to get it across to the board that King was proposing to rescue from illiquidity a company to which King personally owed the best part of $10 million. If King just gave that back, Hammerman pointed out, IOS's immediate problems would be solved, and it would no longer be necessary to rush into King's arms. Malcolm Fox and C. Henry Buhl now came out against the King deal. Hammerman continued with some details of the Colorado NOPI deal, which moved Wilson Wyatt to suggest that in the future, any deals between IOS directors and IOS companies should be discussed by the board. This was presented as a new thought.

After this point Ed Cowett, who had already proffered his

resignation, took virtually no further part in the proceedings. He withdrew up the road to 119 Rue de Lausanne. His version is that "someone had to go back and run the company." Others suspected that his withdrawal perhaps had something to do with the rather critical responses he was now drawing from colleagues who had worshiped at his financial feet a very little time before. At some time during the week, a man who went briefly back to headquarters returned with a slightly awed word-picture of the great architect in retreat. "It's incredible. There he is, the man who singlehanded has just about brought down the economy of the Western world. And he's just sitting there, stroking his beard, and saying: 'The fools—they won't listen to me.' "

The "fools" had a great deal on their minds, but business discussion broke off for a moment while Bernie and George Landau expatiated upon the wonderful support the board was getting from the humble employees. Immediately after this an accountant entered the meeting to ask if (a) there was any information that could be given to the staff, and (b) could he check that the executives who were firing people had the board's authority to do so. No information was given, either to employees or to the reporters who were now besieging Bella Vista. Firing of employees continued.

Discussion resumed. It emerged that doubts about King were spreading. Ira Weinstein returned to the suggestion that IOS should try to borrow some more money, without offering anyone control.

Then Martin Seligson, who had been dispatched to meet John King's plane, came back to report the great man's attitude. King, it appeared, had expressed much admiration for the "mystique" of Bernie Cornfeld, which he felt was necessary to IOS, anyway for some time. But King had also made the point that nobody except himself was likely to give IOS any more money until an audit had been done.

Cornfeld made a speech about the need for the men who had built IOS to stick together in the face of disaster. From this category he apparently excluded Ed Cowett, however. Cornfeld said that while no doubt Cowett was doing his best and had everyone's interests at heart, that wasn't enough. Cowett, he thought, should resign. He, Cornfeld, should remain. If they wanted to chop his head off too, of course, they were most welcome to it, but, he suggested, they should wait until they could get a really good price for it. This argument—that they should only trade off his head for a good price—was used heavily by Cornfeld over the next few days.

Cornfeld wound up his speech with an appeal to all the directors to follow the dictates of their own consciences, whereupon Wilson Wyatt moved successfully that John King should be asked to address the meeting.

The vast figure of John M. King now emerged from a black limousine outside Bella Vista, and strode into the long board room. In view of the fact that King Resources itself was virtually bankrupt within months of this meeting, and that there was a sharp liquidity squeeze in the United States at the time, it may seem remarkable that King should have been able to scratch up the finance to answer Cowett's call for help. However, King Resources had increased its liquidity in several ways during the past few weeks. First, the company had conducted a thorough review of all the sums owed to it by the IOS funds, principally the Fund of Funds. Through what Ed Cowett called "a strict and full interpretation of all obligations," by the end of April King Resources had been able to obtain a total of $20 million from the cash resources of the Fund of Funds. This money was earmarked for Arctic and other exploration costs, but even so it substantially improved the liquidity of King Resources. Second, King had just discovered an oasis in the American credit desert. Although rather exclusive, this oasis was frequented by his own companies, by Harry Trueblood's Consolidated Oil & Gas, and by that IOS investment favorite, Four Seasons Nursing Homes. It was refreshed by funds from the Treasury of the State of Ohio, and from the Disabled Workmen's Compensation Fund of the Ohio Industrial Commission, whose monies were handled by the State Treasury. King's access to this cash had been arranged via money brokers in California, Miami, and Ohio: before the SEC declared the loans to be "illegal,"* this seemed a promising source of cash. On April 17, King Resources borrowed $3 million from the Ohio Treasury, and on May 1, the day before King left for Geneva, the company borrowed another $5 million. And King, who was then being described by *Forbes* magazine as "an American Croesus," was confident of getting more cash from orthodox banking and insurance sources. (King probably did not notice the story that *Forbes* added, apropos his attempt to take over IOS. Croesus, about to attack the Persians, was told that he was about to bring down a mighty empire. The empire in question was his own.)

King now made a wondrous speech to the IOS directors. He counseled everyone to look to the future, and abjure negativism. His own companies, he said, had passed through hard times in the past, but had risen to higher things. He said that everyone should adopt a positive attitude and work together. At the same time, he thought that he should be in control, because who else would lend any more cash? He could not submit to the rule of a committee, merely in order to get members of the financial establishment involved in the rescue of IOS. To the extent that it

---

*More details of this are given below, p. 486.

was required, he said, King Resources was an Establishment company. He closed his address with an assertion that indecision was inherently evil.

John King then answered questions. He assured Eli Wallitt that King Resources was quite independent of Ed Cowett. He informed Henry Buhl that King Resources had indeed made substantial profits on deals with IOS. Just how substantial, it was hard to say. Allen Cantor, a member of Beta Foundation Equipment Associates, asked for information about that controversial concern. King said that he himself had only heard of Beta one week ago. With further expressions of optimism, King and his party left the IOS Board to chew over the offer.

After James Roosevelt returned from Germany, where he was able to report that the Roosevelt charm had worked once more on the German Banking Commission, Cornfeld introduced an expert witness for his view that IOS was not in all that much need of money. This was Hugh Knowlton, from Smith, Barney & Co., who had been one of the six lead underwriters. What IOS needed was not money, Knowlton said: rather, it was credibility and reorganized management. A few million dollars, if needed, could always be raised, he thought, by pledging the stock IOS owned in its subsidiary, IOS Management. Of course, it would be necessary first to replace both Cowett and Cornfeld. With that, Mr. Knowlton departed.

The realities of the situation were now painfully clear. A surrender to Rothschilds would mean that most of those present would be purged from the positions they held. John King, who was prepared to pay $4 a share, was offering rescue, or anyway some kind of alliance, on terms to which few except Cornfeld seemed unalterably opposed. Alternatively, it was possible that IOS might survive without King. But in that case, it would be necessary for Bernie to lay down his head, in order that his colleagues should have a decent chance of preserving theirs.

It was Cornfeld's old friend, Eli Wallitt, who faced the Emperor at last. Speaking slowly and sorrowfully, he proposed that votes of confidence should be passed upon both Bernard Cornfeld and Edward Cowett. Having done that, he said, the board must decide whether to negotiate with King alone, or whether to keep looking for other help while negotiating with King. Finally, in the event that Cornfeld and Cowett should be removed, a new, small committee should be set up to run the company. Wallitt proposed a bulky portmanteau resolution covering all these points. It was late Wednesday evening.

For the moment, Cornfeld remained cool and controlled. His innate tactical sense told him that Wallitt's vast, sprawling motion could not possibly be voted as it stood, and it would have to be broken up. Indeed, the idea of removing Cornfeld was too vast to be assimilated in one gulp.

The directors decided not to vote on Eli Wallitt's resolution at all. Instead, they voted on a new motion to negotiate immediately with King. They decided that they would not take King's offer as it stood, but would try to persuade him to share his rescue with at least one American and one European partner. The immediate effect of this was to eliminate Cowett. Anxious to assure themselves that there was no unduly close connection with King, the board voted that Cowett should resign from the board, and from all his other positions, as from the time that new management should take over. The directors, all of whom were showing signs of strain, dispersed.

The evening session was not productive. Cornfeld launched a bitter tirade against King who, he said, was incapable of thinking of the operation as anything but a take-over. The man had no sense of partnership, Cornfeld complained. Allen Cantor, who was on the negotiating committee dealing with King, admitted sadly that King was steadfastly refusing to give up any more than 49 per cent to any other participants. Hammerman, the deadliest opponent of King after Cornfeld, gave the same report. King, effectively, was saying they had to go all the way with him, or not at all. And although King was willing to offer $4 apiece for IOS shares, the conviction was spreading that some more substantial participation would be required to restore confidence.

The vital step in the deposition of Cornfeld took place outside the board room itself. Before Friday's session began, Cornfeld was talking with Allen Cantor in Cantor's office at 119 Rue de Lausanne, when George von Peterffy, Richard Hammerman, and Henry Buhl came in with Eli Wallitt. The much-oppressed Emperor turned at bay, to be confronted by the man he had personally dominated during the whole of the twenty years since they had met in the Norman Thomas campaign at Brooklyn College. Cornfeld had been warned that the old bonds were snapping two days before at Bella Vista: but this time it was no windy resolution in business language that faced him. Wallitt told Cornfeld, bluntly, that he must resign from the chairmanship of the board in order for the company to survive.

Wallitt's attitude to Cornfeld, on his own admission, is one of awe and "terror." It seems remarkable that he, of all people, should be the man to face Cornfeld down at last: but the case is explained by a visit to Eli Wallitt's house. This is a spacious and elegant mansion which overlooks the Lake of Geneva and the Jet d'eau, with a distant view of the Jura. It has a wonderful floor of multicolored woods, its walls are rich with pictures. Standing on the shaded porch of his house, while his children played with a large telescope, Wallitt told us, "This is what I did it for." He was referring, at that time, to the whole history of his association with IOS—but as, curiously enough, he was just completing the purchase of the house at the time of the IOS crisis, it seems fair to apply the same words to his confrontation of Cornfeld. "If anyone tried to take this away from me," said Wallitt, "I would fight like a tiger for it." In May 1970 Wallitt believed that if Bernard Cornfeld stayed in charge of IOS, what remaining worth the company possessed would be destroyed.

Now he told Cornfeld that he must go, and the force of this, coming from Wallitt, was that all the power, all the control, all the reverence that Cornfeld had enjoyed for the last ten years was meaningless. Cornfeld, at the moment that he no longer represented wealth, became nothing.

There was a short, raw screaming match. Spouting obscenities, Cornfeld accused Wallitt of plotting against him in calculated disloyalty. No one previously had stood up to one of Cornfeld's famous rages, except those who had chosen to break with IOS. Cornfeld accused Wallitt of having been the cause of the whole crisis—it was Wallitt, he said, not the German bankers, who had sold IOS stock short.

The accusation was untrue, but it had just enough plausibility to hurt. What had happened was that Wallitt needed some cash to buy his home. He had already sold as many shares as he was entitled to. He says he got permission to sell in advance shares that would fall free at a later date. It was not a short sale, but he did sell shares, at a good time for him and a bad time for IOS. What he did not know, perhaps, was that Cornfeld had unloaded nearly half a million shares in April, and thus was in a poor position to complain. Accusations of mutual treachery mounted rapidly, until Cornfeld dashed from the room, shouting, "I made you, Wallitt," among other, less printable things.

"We said things to each other that no human beings should say," was the version Wallitt gave later.

The board meeting began at twelve-thirty on Friday and the directors had figures on the table which showed that IOS was now losing money at the rate of about a quarter of a million dollars a day.

Locked between King, who wanted a take-over, and the Rothschilds, who wanted surrender, the directors hesitated and bickered. Allen Cantor said that the Rothschild consortium required a firm answer, or they would withdraw. They regarded their offer to take up IOS shares at $1 each as speculative.

John Templeton's position was understandable in a large outside shareholder. He was in favor of the King deal. Richard Hammerman, who had to live with the City of London, thought they should negotiate with Rothschild's, not King, and try to get their price up somewhat. Martin Brooke said that the underwriters thought IOS ought to deal with Rothschild's. George Landau, who had no doubt been mulling over the cash flow that King had received from the IOS funds, argued that John King needed IOS at least as much as IOS needed King. Eli Wallitt and others wanted to enter the King deal, but to continue negotiations with Rothschild's. Barry Sterling advocated that they should do business with the first person who would put up any money.

It was, as Ossie Nedoluha observed, all internal politics. Cornfeld made a last, despairing attempt to find a deal that would reconcile all demands. He suggested that more directors should be brought in from outside, and that IOS should try once more to do a deal with King, having first got back the money King owed. At the same time, IOS should try to join the Establishment via a deal with Rothschild's—but should not surrender control of the company to anyone. John Templeton, he thought, could be temporary Chairman of the Board. Cornfeld was asked to withdraw while the board considered its position.

Sir Eric Wyndham White took over the chair, and said that he wouldn't like to see a formal vote taken against Cornfeld. It would, he thought, be more seemly just to get the feeling of the meeting. Professor von Peterffy attempted to persuade Sir Eric that any such gentle scenario "would have repercussions, with a guy like Cornfeld." Von Peterffy wanted a formal vote with sealed ballots, but Wyndham White would not go beyond a poll of the directors as they sat at the table. Malcolm Fox stood up and proposed that Bernie should be asked to resign voluntarily from the chairmanship, from all his positions in fund management, and from all his posts in subsidiaries. One by one, Wyndham White went round the table. With the exception of Allen Cantor and Wilson Wyatt, every director assented to Fox's proposal. Cantor, with tears in his eyes, was sent to convey "the feeling of the meeting" to Bernie waiting outside.

It was some minutes before Cantor came back. With him was Cornfeld, walking slowly, hands in his pockets, looking down at his feet. "If that's what you want," he told the assembled directors, almost inaudibly.

Those few muttered words counted, legally, as his resignation from the chairmanship of the board which was gathered before him. But something more was needed to convey Cornfeld's resignation from his posts throughout the other corporations of the IOS empire. Ed Coughlin had a brief, comprehensive letter of resignation typed out, and Cornfeld signed his familiar bold signature.

Silently, he took a seat as a rank-and-file member of the board, and the directors decided to call John King back in to talk to them. In the interval, while they waited for King, Cornfeld went up to Coughlin and said, "Could I have that piece of paper I just signed?" Coughlin, whose impression was that Cornfeld had been so overcome with emotion that he could scarcely have known what he was signing, thought "the guy had a right to see what he'd put his name to."

Cornfeld took the letter, and went back to his seat. And then John King came in, and began to address the IOS men on the wonders of King Resources, and the prosperity and glory that awaited the two companies once they were linked together. Almost nobody, it seemed, was looking at Cornfeld. After King had been speaking for a few minutes, Cornfeld slowly, but with deliberation, tore his letter across once, then twice. Then he crumpled it up in his hand.

The directors had not noticed Cornfeld's action. Perhaps they were spellbound by the savior. But when King withdrew, Ed Coughlin, the Secretary, said, "I must draw the attention of the board to something. Has Mr. Cornfeld resigned?"

Cornfeld now delivered a somewhat confused speech. He was bitterly certain, he said, that John King was a financial adventurer. King, he believed, would ruin IOS. As for himself, he was unwilling to resign from *all* his positions without taking legal advice. After all, simply to resign from everything might increase his legal liabilities—he didn't know. Would not the board at least let him talk to his attorneys?

His old colleagues were reluctant to remove him forcibly. His verbal resignation from the chairmanship still stood anyway: they told Cornfeld that he could delay his other resignations, if he wished, until he had taken counsel. It was an unwise concession, and it led to a prolonged and damaging series of wrangles. But even so, the imperious authority which had ruled and created IOS was at long last broken, never to be restored.

The following day, Saturday, the IOS Board unanimously voted to close a deal with John King.

The announcement that Bernard Cornfeld had been deposed, and that John King was the appointed rescuer of IOS, was received with skepticism in financial circles. "Who is going to rescue the pair of them?" asked one London banker coarsely. The point had been taken, with great clarity, that John King could not survive for long without the income he received from the IOS funds. And it was also apparent that without that income he would not have enough money to rescue IOS.

King made a brave try at dispelling this skepticism. He dealt with his difficulties by boldly denying their existence. Having spent one week examining the wreckage, he issued a statement which began with the pronouncement, "IOS Ltd. is in sound financial condition. . . .

"In addition to the company's financial strength," King continued, "the IOS sales force is the most uniquely effective sales force internationally." The facts were, of course, that the company was flat broke, and that one of the reasons for this was that its revenues were being eaten up by the sales force.

These confident noises were made on May 21. Eight days later, John King abandoned his bid for IOS, while expressing a fervent hope that someone else would rescue the company because of "the potential impact on world securities markets" if it should collapse. The immediate reason for his withdrawal was that the SEC had tossed a spanner into the works by pointing out the terms of the 1967 settlement with IOS. This provided that any company owning more than 1 per cent of IOS should be regarded as an "affiliate" of IOS, and would be prohibited from selling its own securities to Americans. In other words, if King went ahead with his takeover bid, he would become illegal in America. This price, obviously, he could not pay. But in any case

King's "rescue mission" was really a last dash for survival on his own part. The scandal of the Ohio loans shows that by early 1970, along with many of the financial wizards of the later 1960s, King was searching for money with the desperation of an elephant trying to find a water hole in the dry season.

It was a money broker named Ronald Howard, from Beverly Hills, who introduced King to his novel source of finance. Some time in March 1970, Howard asked for an interview with Keene, Wolcott, the President of John King's Colorado Corporation. Wolcott's assumption was that Howard, like everyone else in the credit squeeze, must be looking for money. "Not a penny!" he cried as Howard came into his office.

"You've got it all wrong," said Howard. "I've got fifty million to *lend*."

The reason for Howard's happy position was that through an acquaintance in Miami he had been put in touch with another money-broking firm in Ohio, called Crofter's. This was owned by three men called Sidney Griffith, Harry A. Groban, and Gerald A. Donahue. Donahue was an influential member of the Ohio Republican organization: he had been Assistant Attorney General of the State, and Tax Commissioner.

In 1967, it turned out, Ohio had passed a law which allowed the State Treasurer to invest up to $50 million of the State funds in commercial paper—short-term loans to private businesses—so long as the borrowers were rated by the National Credit Office, which is a subsidiary of Dun & Bradstreet. To qualify as commercial paper under the Credit Office rules, such loans would have to be for a period of two hundred seventy days or less. It was this time limit which got ignored in the eagerness to put Ohio's cash to work.

King Resources' loan of $3 million from the State of Ohio, which was taken on April 17, was for two years. Half of that money was immediately re-lent to King's privately owned Colorado Corporation. The loan of $5 million which King Resources took up just before John King flew to the rescue of IOS was also for two years. For this reason, they were branded as illegal when the SEC discovered them. The Commission also complained that when negotiating the loans, King Resources had not given a sufficiently complete picture of its own financial position.

King and his companies, it must be said, did not hog the new source of money for themselves. Even before the King loans were negotiated, Ronald Howard had gone to Consolidated Oil & Gas, bearing a reference from a King Resources executive. Harry Trueblood's company arranged two loans: the first, of $3 million, breached Ohio law in the same way as the King loans, because it was for two years, not two hundred seventy days. The second loan of $2 million for one year, was from the Disabled Workmen's Relief Fund, which was not subject to the same regulations. Therefore, it was controversial, rather than illegal. Consolidated paid a "finder's fee" of $50,000 to Crofter's for making the arrangements. And Crofter's got an even larger fee when they fixed a loan for Four Seasons Nursing Homes: they got $160,000 for providing $4 million out of the Ohio Treasury. Shortly afterward, Four Seasons filed a bankruptcy petition.

Actual bankruptcy was avoided by King Resources, although only narrowly. Having dropped its IOS bid, the company allowed its bills to pile up during the summer, and by early August it owed some $16 million to various trade creditors, and another $20 million in unsecured loans from banks. The creditors met several times to try and devise a plan of rescue: they were successfully persuaded to accept a version of events in which all King's troubles were due to its own attempts to rescue IOS. On August 14, at a meeting in the First National Bank of Denver, the creditors adopted a scheme which would allow King Resources to struggle on, in the hope of recovering financial stability. But John King had to resign as Chairman and President. Conceptual to the last, King bowed out with the thought that "like a human being, a corporation has a life cycle—a beginning or birth, a youth, and a maturity." Another of his Great Thoughts had been that "if you have a goal, the worst thing that can happen to you is that you might make it." If John King's aim had been, as he told the *Wall Street Journal* in May 1970, to become a billionaire, then he had been spared the worst.

• 22 •

Terminating Bernie

A great desire is manifested to "save IOS for capitalism." But the rescuers are afraid of Bernie, who isn't quite dead. An intrigue is mounted to dispose of the Emperor, who is rubbed out effectively if none too tidily.

T he only real result of the King intervention was that it ended the possibility of a rescue coming from the Rothschild group. The bankers decided that one thing they would definitely not do was get into a bidding competition with John King. Furthermore, they thought, if the directors could even consider a deal with King, they could not be very serious about wanting to change the way the business had been conducted.

This left IOS, in June, still thrashing about, searching desperately for a rescuer. And at this point it became all too clear that Bernard Cornfeld was not going to take his banishment quietly. Although his company was in a state of financial ruin, he determined to try and reconquer it. His attempts almost finished IOS off.

When John King collapsed like a leaky balloon, a period of low comedy and high intrigue set in. Immediately, titular overlordship of IOS fell into the unlikely, not to say reluctant, hands of Sir Eric Wyndham White, late Secretary General of the General Agreement on Trade and Tariffs. It was more difficult to say where actual control of the empire lay. It tended to shift from hour to hour, almost from minute to minute.

During the next twelve months of scheming and maneuvering, two essential considerations moved all the participants, both inside and outside IOS.

1. IOS Ltd.—the parent company, so recently floated, and the heart of the group—was as comprehensively impoverished and discredited as any investment company could be without actually going bankrupt. Indeed, it is probably fair to guess that only its offshore status kept it alive at all: if it had lived in some more regulated environment, IOS would have perished in a hail of lawsuits from its customers some time in 1970.

2. The stricken company still controlled one of the largest pools of fund money in the world. The IOS funds began 1970 with total assets of $2.4 billion. During May 1970, the customers were reducing that total by redeeming their shares at the rate of $3 million a day. But any international banker could work out on the back of an envelope that even a full year's redemptions at that phenomenal rate would only take $1 billion out of the funds, leaving $1.5 billion apart from shrinkage in the value of the fund investments.

Some financiers wanted to get their hands on the funds for their own profit. Some wanted to rescue the funds for the safety of capitalism. Some wanted to protect the investors who had put up the money in the first place. Other financiers were moved by various combinations of such motives. It was, however, generally agreed that even after the May crisis, the IOS funds were an interesting pile of other people's money. The key to controlling them was to gain control of IOS Ltd.

During May, the interest in rescuing IOS was almost indecent. Paul Vincent, of Banque Rothschild, to his mixed amusement and annoyance, found himself acting as a kind of informal clearinghouse for many of the transient consortia that got together to talk about IOS and then lost interest. One day, he was awakened by the first American bank at seven-thirty a.m., and he did not get away from the phone for long enough to shave until two p.m. Near the end of the month, he drew up a list of banks and other institutions that had expressed interest, which covered a large sheet of paper. The trouble was that everyone was frightened, as well as interested. On three separate occasions, Vincent got calls from senior officials of American banks, only to have another call from the same bank the next day, withdrawing the commitment.

The last real chance of an international banking consortium seems to have been at a meeting sponsored by the Banque Rothschild in Paris in early June. The banks who gathered to hear Sir Eric put the case for support could not have been mightier. They included the Bank of America, the Marine Midland Bank, Barclays Bank from Britain, and the Dresdner Bank from Germany. But, in the words of one participant, everyone was "paralytically nervous," and when news of the gathering leaked to the press, several eminent bankers tried to bolt and were calmed only with difficulty. In the end, Wyndham White was able to put his case, which revolved around the "essential soundness" of the IOS concept, but he was not able to convince them.

Sir Eric stepped into the Chairman's position, after the destruction of Cornfeld's authority in May, and he remained there because there was really no one else who could lay any useful amount of prestige on the line when dealing with potential rescuers. For a few weeks, Richard Hammerman served as President of IOS, but he made the unpopular, unforgivable mistake of trying to limit the sales bosses' incomes to a mere $100,000 a year each. He resigned on June 7. After that, Sir Eric combined the roles of Chairman and President.

Early computations by the accountants suggested that IOS Ltd. would dissipate the last of its operating cash by mid-autumn. However, a fierce program of economies extended the possible breathing space. King Resources' rescue bid had got as far as advancing $8 million of the proposed loans to IOS: this loan remained, and King Resources also repaid the King and Cowett family trust loans, some $8 million together. This scarcely compensated the Fund of Funds' customers for the money King had clawed out of their fund, but it helped IOS Ltd. to stagger on, while attempts were made to call in as many of the other loans as possible. Regular employees were dismissed steadily, at a rate which halved the staff by the end of the year. Then the sales force, which had reached its costly peak of 16,000 Associates at the New Year, was subjected to a process of "weeding out the less productive salesmen" and "attrition." By mid-summer that process was to bring it down to an official figure of 10,766: in fact, it was hard to tell how far "attrition" had gone, because many "orphan" salesmen could only be contacted through managers who had deserted or been terminated.

In this difficult moment, Sir Eric gathered around him what the IOS publicity men called "a new management," to uphold and defend the "basic soundness" of the IOS concept. If it was, by then, not easy to see what was so sound about the idea of speculative and unregulated investment funds promoted by a ferociously overpaid sales force, then it was even less easy to see any novelty in the management that succeeded Cornfeld and

Cowett. The affairs of the company were now handled by a committee of eight, including Sir Eric himself. Two were very recently promoted: a lawyer named Jay Leary, who had worked on the public offering under Cowett, and Marvin Hoffman, who had been manager of financial information since March 1969. A third member of the group was Hal Vaughan, who had been Ed Cowett's personal assistant. And the other four were Allen Cantor, Harvey Felberbaum, Richard Hammerman, and C. Henry Buhl III, who, whatever their other virtues, could hardly have been bettered as members in good standing of the Old Guard; Wyndham White himself had been on the Executive Committee in 1969. The best that these men could say about the past was that they had not known what was going on, although Hammerman, Buhl, and Wyndham White could claim to have done something toward finding out. (Lechner and von Peterffy, the ones who did most in that respect, were on the way out.)

The general attitude of the "new management" may be gauged by the reaction to a speech which Robert M. Morgenthau, formerly U.S. Attorney for the Southern District of New York, made to a Congressional committee on June 11. He said that IOS, among other things, had concealed massive loans to insiders and directors and had traded secretly in its own shares. Considering the amount of information then available, the U.S. Attorney's account was remarkably accurate. Yet Allan Conwill, IOS's New York lawyer, although he had sat in on meetings that discussed the insider loans, chose to allege that Morgenthau's remarks were those of "an ambitious but bitterly frustrated man who still grasps for publicity through sensationalism." Mr. Conwill, formerly of the SEC, now a director of the Fund of Funds, clearly did not cast himself as a new broom.

New brooms, indeed, were not welcome in IOS. Power in the company, now that Cornfeld was deposed, lay with the men who had been salesmen in the early days and were now the big shareholders. Sir Eric knew that he ruled by their sufferance. Cornfeld's old followers had acceded to the change of command because they hoped that a symbolic act would restore some value to their shares. Sir Eric's ideas of what needed to be done went a good deal beyond theirs. His strength lay in the knowledge that if he resigned, it would finish IOS off. On the other hand, if he reformed anything that was too dear to the big shareholders, they would turn back to Cornfeld.

And although he had been deposed, Cornfeld had not been banished. He had made his resignation from the chairmanship verbally, in the presence of the board, and that resignation stood. But since he had torn up, and thereby canceled, the letter which was supposed to remove him from his other posts in the company and its subsidiaries, he was still a rank-and-file member of the board. His position and residual power were ambiguous: it was all too likely that he might try to regain the leadership if the slightest opportunity should offer. And it was the shadow of Cornfeld that so frightened the eminent bankers in Paris: indeed, it was clear that, despite the fascination of the great funds, no Establishment financier was going to commit himself to IOS while Cornfeld still had anything to do with the company. Jerome Hoffman, the most eccentric offshore promoter of them all, made a ludicrous public offer to take over IOS and put the funds in the hands of Mayor Robert Wagner.* But that merely drove home the point.

Some time before the IOS shareholders' meeting scheduled for June 30, Sir Eric Wyndham White made up his mind that Cornfeld had to be finished off. And indeed, Cornfeld was duly removed from the board—effectively, if none too tidily. "It was

---

*See Chapter 18, "A Very Long Way Offshore."

not very knightly!" exclaimed Cornfeld, when he found out what had been done to him.

Wyndham White's knighthood, and the label "former British Treasury official," can give a rather misleading impression of a mandarin financial administrator. His pipe and his tweedy clothes carry a certain academic flavor. In fact, although he has worked for the Treasury and lectured at universities, Wyndham White was originally a lawyer. He spent the war practicing diplomacy and economic warfare, and he worked for a variety of international agencies before becoming Secretary General at GATT. When he assumed the chairmanship of IOS at the age of fifty-seven, he could not claim any great investment expertise, but he had a long experience of diplomacy, negotiation, and political infighting.

Although his own standards of personal integrity were plainly quite unlike those of say, Ed Cowett, Sir Eric did not show much sign of reflecting that there might be anything radically wrong with the basic idea of IOS or the whole offshore setup. Indeed, he expended much energy inquiring whether, in the name of respectability, it might be possible to set up a voluntary self-regulating body for all the offshore fund groups. His approach to the problems of IOS was that of an experienced practical diplomat: you must take things more or less as they are, patch up your troubles as best you can, and somehow keep the show on the road for the time being. If you come up against a particularly dangerous obstacle, then you may—for the sake of the cause—have to play it a bit hard yourself.

To Sir Eric and to the American ex-diplomat Harold Kaplan, who was one of his chief supporters, IOS seemed to resemble one of the international agencies in whose various causes they had both labored over the years—and which, from time to time, also had had their troubles. Wyndham White, Kaplan, and some other well-meaning men served the ailing but still greedy octopus perhaps better than it deserved.

• • •

The shareholders' meeting was held in Toronto, the company's legal home. On the morning of June 30, it was one of twenty-five business meetings scheduled in the Royal York Hotel, not counting the Latvian Song Festival. By ten-thirty a.m. there were several hundred people crowding the Ontario Room: the Cardin suits and rakish beards among them drew dour looks from the short-haired men with American flags in their lapels who were passing through to a United Auto Workers meeting next door. "Guns to the right, cameras to the left," said Harvey Felberbaum to the press as he strode through in a brown suit with a brilliant orange tie.

Apart from fifty reporters and other visitors—like Mr. S. S. Gorecki of the investigation branch of the Ontario Securities Commission—there were two hundred ninety-eight shareholders present. But the vast majority were IOS staff and Associates who had so far survived the pruning, and were fiercely loyal to the "new management." Those outside shareholders who did attend, and who tried to ask questions, got short shrift from the crowded, noisy meeting. Someone had insured that the aisle microphones were removed before the meeting began, and when one Canadian shareholder, trying to make his questions heard, asked for a microphone, Sir Eric stared coldly down at him from the platform.

"I'm not a mechanical engineer," he said. "Take the schmuck off!" bellowed an IOS Associate, enraged by the questioner.

When Dr. Peter Ackermann from Berlin tried to ask some detailed questions on behalf of two hundred German shareholders, he was all but shouted down by the claque. "Louder! Louder!"

they chorused. Sir Eric condescendingly answered what he called Ackermann's "catalogue."

Halfway through the morning, Harvey Felberbaum slipped out of the meeting for a moment, and when he came back he whispered to one of the present authors a curious piece of news. "We've just got Bernie's votes," he said. It did not make much sense at the time, except that everyone was aware that the meeting was silently dominated by the personality of the absent Cornfeld. When Sir Eric asked the candidates for the board, if present, to stand when he read their names, there was an eerie silence after the name "Bernard Cornfeld." It was as though the people in the room feared that the mere mention of his name might bring the magic leader back in spectral shape.

But however his spirit worked upon the gathering in Toronto, Bernard Cornfeld's corporeal person spent that day in his apartment on Park Avenue. For some weeks before the meeting, Cornfeld had been quietly collecting the proxy votes of a few other big shareholders, with an eye toward conducting a battle for power in Toronto. But a few days before the meeting, he abandoned that plan—because he was under the impression that he had patched up a truce with the Wyndham White management. He had even traveled across the Atlantic on the same plane as Sir Eric, and they had managed a personal chat on relatively friendly terms.

Cornfeld's name was up for re-election with the formal approval of the management. Both he and Sir Eric attended a good many meetings of IOS subsidiaries together in New York before the move to Toronto, and there was an outward show of something like amity. Cornfeld thought that if he forebore from precipitating a proxy battle, then he would be allowed to keep his seat on the board. He therefore decided not to go to the Toronto meeting, where his presence would be bound to have an unpredictable, perhaps divisive, effect. In this decision, for once, his tactical sense led him astray. For, whatever truce there may have been in New York, in Toronto Sir Eric decided that Cornfeld should be removed—and that there was a quick and effective way of doing the job.

When the counting of votes began in Toronto, around six p.m., the meeting adjourned and Sir Eric gave a press conference. It was a girl reporter who asked the question on everybody's mind. "Why is there a reluctance in this company to talk about Bernard Cornfeld?" she asked. "It's almost as if everyone hopes he'll crawl into the woodwork and disappear."

Sir Eric looked perplexed and tactful, like an undertaker coping with some sad duty. "All of us recognize," he said, "that the events of the past few months represent a considerable personal tragedy for Mr. Cornfeld. I think we respect the personal tragedy that is involved in all this for him." Nobody guessed that Sir Eric, as he spoke, already knew that management votes had been cast to throw Cornfeld off the IOS Board.

Long before, it had been provided that the Board of IOS should be elected in two groups, or "slates." This was not Sir Eric's doing: it was something cunningly devised before the public offer to keep Cornfeld, and the men who were then his friends, in power, and to insure that new investors buying shares in IOS should not actually obtain voting control of the company. The mechanism depended upon the special meaning that IOS attached to the term "preferred shares."

Normally, "preferred shares" are fixed-interest securities, carrying *lesser* voting rights than a company's common shares, or equities. In IOS, however, the preferred shares have *greater* voting rights than the common shares.

When IOS went public, it created a block of new shares to raise $52 million through the Drexel underwriting. These were *common* shares. At the same time, the existing IOS shareholders put up slices of their holdings—mostly 10 per cent—for sale in the form of common shares. The shares they kept were called "preferred shares," and the provision was that a certain number of them would be converted each year into common shares, so as to be salable. Thus Bernard Cornfeld owned, after selling 10 per cent of his holdings, 7.3 million preferred shares.

But the only *common* shares he held by the time of the Toronto meeting were the 30,000 that he had agreed to keep out of Cowett's buying spree in 1969 and 1970.*

The preferred shares held the right to elect two-thirds of the directors of IOS Ltd. The common shares had only one-third of the board on their separate slate.

In April, before the crisis, Bernard Cornfeld's name had been put on the common-stock slate. The reason then was only that his was a name that would mean something to the 25,000 common stockholders, many of them outsiders owning relatively small packets of shares. But the result, in the context of a struggle for power, was that Cornfeld's huge block of preferred shares was of no use to him for protecting his position on the board.

Cornfeld did not anticipate that any concerted move would—or even could—be made against him in the scattered ranks of the common stockholders. He had forgotten that there were in existence solid blocks of common shares much bigger than his own 30,000. These were the shares which had been stuffed into The IOS Stock Option Plan Ltd., and the ones which had been taken up by the Cowett and King trusts.

In the early hours of Tuesday, June 30, before the stockholders met at the Royal York, there was a conclave in one of the ho-

---

*See Chapter 20, "The Book of Revelations."

tel bedrooms upstairs. It was a meeting of executive directors of IOS, convened at the request of Ed Coughlin, the company Secretary. There were 830,000 common shares belonging to the stock-option plan that were registered and ready to be voted. Sir Eric and his colleagues decided to vote them against Cornfeld. Ed Coughlin, whose signature was necessary to validate the proxy documents, insisted that the directors should meet and pass a resolution giving him formal instructions—and the directors did so, there and then.

By this time, Wyndham White and his colleagues also controlled the shares from the King and Cowett trusts, for on May 29, Cowett, acting for King and for himself, had sold all 600,000 of them to a small fund run by Dean Milosis, a former Fund of Funds manager. Milosis, who paid $1.4 million for the shares at $2.35 apiece, gave the proxies to a nominee of IOS Management.

With the addition of the stock-option shares, the defeat of the unsuspecting Cornfeld was now certain. But Wyndham White and his colleagues wanted to make quite sure—and they also wanted to have Cornfeld's preferred shares working for them on the other slate.

At eight-thirty a.m. Bernard Cornfeld, in New York, received a phone call from Toronto. He was asked whether he would give the proxies on his own preferred shares to the management. And Cornfeld actually did so. A messenger was sent flying from New York to Toronto with the necessary documents, and it was their arrival that Harvey Felberbaum was reporting when he whispered: "We've just got Bernie's votes."

It was after midnight when the counting finished in Toronto, and most of the twenty people left in the room were reporters. There was astonishment when Sir Eric announced, poker-faced, that Bernard Cornfeld had not been re-elected. One person present reacted as if it were a "personal tragedy": Gladis Solomon, veteran of the innocent days in the Boulevard Flandrin. She was moved to the verge of tears.

· · ·

Redemptions, by the beginning of August, had slackened to around $2 million a day, and it was clear that the funds were not going to melt away entirely. (Almost certainly there is a "sump" of black money at the bottom of the Fund of Funds and IIT which will never be reclaimed.) But unfortunately the international bankers did not rush forward with help. Several things had happened during the time that had been required to dispose of Cornfeld, and one was that the international financial community was beginning to feel that the worst was over in the stock markets. Those who had been inspired, or partly inspired, by a feeling that IOS must be rescued for the sake of capitalism—and that had certainly been a component of the Rothschilds' approach—no longer felt the same urgency.

The point was also being grasped that huge as the IOS funds were, they might not be particularly profitable, at least to anyone who proposed to handle them along orthodox lines. This was hammered home all too clearly by the report of IOS Ltd. for the first six months of 1970. For the half-year, IOS reports a $25-million *loss*. Sales revenue had collapsed, so that even though it was being run down, the sales operation contributed vast losses. There were no performance fees, and management fees were cut by the shrinkage of the funds. Large provisions were necessary for losses expected on deals like Commonwealth United and the Canadian Channing purchase. Most of the people who had shown interest in May decided that it was just too difficult to tell how many bodies might be stuffed under the carpet at IOS. The prospect of the "first-class institutional support" that Sir Eric longed for was as far away as ever.

· · ·

Robert Vesco, the rescuer who appeared at last, certainly had his admirers. ("I want you to know," said Warren White, who had been Cornfeld's assistant, "that within a very few minutes of meeting Robert Vesco, I knew I was in the presence of one of the greatest financial geniuses of the twentieth century.") But even so, he could hardly be described as "first-class institutional support." Like C. Henry Buhl, Vesco came from Detroit, but his background was rather different. He had started work at fifteen in an automobile repair shop, and he had to study engineering at the university in the evenings. Before he was twenty, he had designed the first aluminum grille for Oldsmobile—but within a very few years he had abandoned the production side of engineering and set himself up as a kind of free-lance financial finder and adviser. He showed clearly that he was a man with an instinctive feel for financial leverage, and in 1970 he treated IOS itself as an interesting example. By this time Vesco was thirty-four, and had put together a group of small electronic and engineering concerns under the bold label of International Controls Corporation of New Jersey. The process of building International Controls was marked by aggressive take-over bids, followed on two occasions by bitter lawsuits.

Vesco's business methods, on his own admission, are uncompromising. They were minutely examined after ICC succeeded in gobbling up, against resistance, a much larger company called Electronic Specialty. Vesco began to buy Electronic Specialty shares on the quiet, but somehow the market got to know, and the price rose. At this point, a man from the *Wall Street Journal* talked to Vesco, and got the idea that ICC was *not* going to bid for control of Electronic Specialty. Publication of such a report would naturally tend to make the price fall back again: indeed, the *Wall Street Journal* did suggest that ICC was not bidding, and indeed the price did fall. Yet on the evening of the day that Vesco spoke to the *Wall Street Journal*, he informed the ICC Board that it might well be worthwhile to go ahead with a bid—which was just what ICC did two days later. After much litigation, Vesco was cleared of having attempted to mislead the market, and the court did not believe that ICC violated the securities laws. Vesco admits that he did not strive officiously to enlighten the *Wall Street Journal*'s reporter. An appeal judge ascribed the course of events to "the frailties inevitable in human communication."

Vesco was helped financially by the Bank of America and later by the Prudential Insurance Company, respectively the biggest bank and biggest insurance company in the world. Nevertheless, by the time he came to help IOS, Vesco's company was still a long way from the big league: it had total sales in 1969 of around $100 million and profits of $4.7 million. In 1968 ICC had raised a $25-million Eurodollar loan. It was what he had done with this debt that gave Vesco his admirers inside IOS.

The $25 million had been raised by issuing debentures, convertible into common shares, through Butler's Bank of the Bahamas. The loan sharply increased International Controls' indebtedness—but in rising markets that hardly mattered. In the conditions of 1970, Vesco decided that it would be advantageous to restructure this debt, so he offered to the debenture holders a higher rate of interest, plus superior conditions for conversion into common share, if they would in return wipe off 40 per cent of International Controls' indebtedness. The success of this exchange depended upon the acceptance by the largest single holder of the debenture issue: none other than "IIT, an International Investment Trust," which held $7 million worth. Vesco was negotiating in Geneva as early as November 1969.

Given the market value of the old debentures in early 1970, there was not much to choose between the two. But acceptance meant realizing a hefty loss. IIT was among the first to accept Vesco's new paper.

The success of the conversion offer in reducing International Controls' debt naturally increased his company's financial strength. And equipped with this new strength, Vesco decided to offer a $15-million loan to IOS Ltd., in exchange for warrants to buy IOS shares. Financial genius or not, by the end of July Sir Eric and his board were all too happy to accept his helping hand. There was just one snag. Vesco wanted nothing to do with Cornfeld, and Cornfeld, although riddled through and through at Toronto, was refusing to lie down. He had launched a $25-million lawsuit in New York, claiming that the "new management" had instituted a "reign of terror" in IOS: he went about the world denouncing "Sir Eric Windmill" to any financial journalist who would listen, and he threatened the hard-pressed men in 119 Rue de Lausanne with a new proxy fight, which he swore would result in his recapturing the company. More than once, he made his way into the IOS offices and subjected old comrades to withering harangues about disloyalty.

Cornfeld was now making few pretensions to financial statesmanship. This was the deal he was proposing to his old friends, the shareholders: he would give each of them a $10 bill, signed by himself. In return, they were to give him "irrevocable proxies" and an option to purchase their shares for $5 apiece by July 1971. These efforts were reinforced by appeals from big shareholders like Gladis Solomon, who tended to take the emotional position that as Bernie had created the company anyway, he was at liberty to do as he wished with it. Offensive and counteroffensive were marked more by energy than by dignity. One August morning, for instance, John Curran, still a big shareholder, was about to leave Geneva for a holiday in Spain. Bernie's man virtually stormed into his bedroom demanding proxies: Curran only got away from him just in time to get to the airport, where he was tackled again by the other side, whose envoy gave him the management pitch all the way to the passport barrier.

The project which Cornfeld devised for his comeback was a return to his old fascination with show business. It was "Cinema City": the idea was that a new town, with huge movie studios, should be conjured up in the desert somewhere between Los Angeles and Las Vegas. On Sunday, August 2, Cornfeld threw a party at the Villa Elma and tried to explain, in a brief pitch, how the IOS sales force could be remotivated by the prospect of selling plots of land and shares in the development of the Cinema City studios. Hesitantly, someone suggested that movie studios weren't doing much business in 1970. Cornfeld brushed this aside. If the studios were empty, he said, it would be easy enough to make money by showing parties of tourists around them.

"I want my company back," he said. And a few days later, he said, "I want to emphasize that this is not a proxy fight." It was not a fight, he said, because he had already won it. He claimed that he already had enough votes to control the company.

Sir Eric was now playing a dangerous three-cornered game. Vesco had money, but objected to Cornfeld. Cornfeld in his milder moments described Vesco as a "small-timer" and an "interloper." Sir Eric did not think Cornfeld could really force his way back in. (Many proxies had been promised to both sides.) But while Bernie stormed and trumpeted, the company was bleeding to death. And the worse the financial situation, the more people would be tempted to throw support to Cornfeld in a final gesture of desperation and hope. After the IOS Board formally rejected the feasibility of the Cinema City project on August 7, Sir Eric decided that he must try somehow to bring Vesco and Cornfeld together in a compromise. Summoning all his diplomatic skills, he spent the rest of the month in meetings designed to bring this about.

While this intricate battle raged, what was happening to the customers' money—to the investments of the people who had been told that IOS had beaten "the money problem of the twentieth century"? At the beginning of August, one of us ran into an acquaintance, an English veteran of the sales force, outside 119 Rue de Lausanne. The salesman explained that he had just cashed in his personal holding of the Fund of Funds. As, unlike an outside investor, he had never had to pay a sales load, and as the net asset value per share of the Fund of Funds—still inflated by the absurd Arctic gambit—stood at $18.47 per share, our friend had made some very nice gains and was looking understandably pleased. Then he frowned, unhappily.

"I wish I had been able to advise some of my old clients to sell too," he said. But there was no way to do so: they were mostly in remote parts of Southeast Asia.

It was, as it happened, really too bad about the clients. A few days later, the directors of the Fund of Funds announced that three-fifths of the supposed assets of the fund were to be removed and placed in a new corporation. This would not have an open-end structure, so there would be no more redemptions over three-fifths of what had once been the world's fastest-growing mutual fund.

It was the inevitable result of the gross speculations that had been made with the fund over the previous two or three years. The indefatigable Allan Conwill, who had been on the Fund of

Funds Board while most of the punting took place, came forward to explain the move. "Redemptions have not ceased," he said. "They will go on at a lower figure." Lower was right: Fund of Funds shares, which had been worth $18.47 the day before, were now redeemable only at $7.44. The great majority of the customers had paid more than twice that for them. Many of them, persuaded they were buying "long-term capital growth," had paid three times as much.

Meanwhile, Sir Eric's delicate negotiations had borne fruit. He had persuaded Vesco and Cornfeld, for the moment at least, that they must make some concessions to each other. Seventeen days after the collapse of the Fund of Funds, a terse press release came from 119 Rue de Lausanne:

> At a special meeting on September 3, 1970, the Board of Directors of IOS Ltd. approved a loan agreement with a subsidiary of International Controls Corp., ICC Investments Limited, providing financing of up to $15 million to IOS Ltd. The directors also elected Bernard Cornfeld to the board.

IOS had been rescued. It is time to ask whether it deserved to survive.

• 23 •

The Customers' Yachts

In which we find that the IOS sales force remained conspiratorial above all. Allen Cantor discourses upon Truth, Responsibility, and the Little People. In which we examine the actual, as against the supposed, performance of the IOS funds and figure out what happened to the customers' money.

In the summer of 1970, when a lot of people were leaving IOS, we talked to a young woman who had been on the clerical staff of the company for long enough to feel the atmosphere changing in the latter years and who was about to depart.

"You know," she said, "once it used to be Bernie's great big happy family. Then they all grew up and became millionaires, and it all turned nasty."

Again and again IOS veterans we interviewed while preparing this book would say to us, "Make sure you put in the good things as well as the problems." They wanted us to see what fun it had all been in the beginning—when it was just a crowd of bright young Americans, exploring Europe, and earning enough money, for the first time in their lives, not to have to worry about it.

If you leaf through the early editions of the *IOS Bulletin*, it is easy to see what they mean. In 1959 and 1960, the *Bulletin* was just four mimeographed sheets. Each issue listed the salesmen who had "made the bonus list" the month before. But most of the *Bulletin* was taken up with friendly gossip about the members of the family. Allen Cantor and his wife are looking after the dogs of several of their friends. John Curran has had a "small but lucky" evening in the casino at Divonne. Harvey Felberbaum has been sick, but is better now. The Gangels have a new baby. The Himeses have been visiting Jack's parents in Miami.

It was a comfort to read, if you were feeling lonely in a hotel bedroom somewhere like Djakarta or Maracaibo.

In 1960, it was news if someone spent $3000 buying a car, and became "the proud owner" of an MG, or a "new, red TR3." Ed Cowett, "peripatetic IOS attorney" bought a Sunbeam Alpine in the summer of 1960. Ten years later, Cowett went to the office in a $20,000 Maserati. MGs were secretaries' cars.

Like the cars, the *IOS Bulletin* got bigger and shinier over the years. Instead of four mimeographed pages, the March 1970 *Bulletin*—the last before the crisis—was forty glossy pages, printed in color. The artwork was sumptuous. Some of the best photographers in New York were hired to do the pictures. And the innocent, unpretentious note had vanished altogether. "IOS-ers," as they called themselves, had always believed in blowing their own trumpet. But in March 1970, with the whole edifice tottering horribly, the music of self-praise blared out *fortissimo*. The brass predominated.

"This," trumpeted Allen Cantor, "is the year of Total Financial Service, a theme which epitomizes fourteen years of historic corporate growth. . . . In that brief time, IOS has evolved into one of the world's leading financial institutions—a global force in the fields of investments, insurance, banking, and real estate."

Just what was "Total Financial Service"? When the slogan was first proposed, the same question occurred to Eric Wyndham White. "Tell me one thing, Allen," he asked Cantor, "you call your salesmen financial *advisers*. Does that mean that sometimes a salesman could advise a prospect *not* to buy?"

Cantor's answer was prompt but jesuitical. No, a salesman could never advise a client not to buy. The salesman's role was not to give advice, but to help the client to put his money in the hands of someone who could make the right decisions. It would be unreasonable, he said, to ask that every salesman should be a competent financial adviser.

In public, of course, that was exactly what they were called. But truthfully, the only Total Financial Service that the salesmen were qualified or expected to perform was to extract from the prospect the largest sum of money he could possibly be persuaded to hand over to IOS. The salesmen might take it fast or slow; in cash, or in monthly payments. They might take it in mutual-fund shares, insurance policies, or flats in southern Spain. What mattered to the sales organization, of which Cantor was the boss, was that they should continue to take it, whether the transactions were legal or illegal—"sensitive," as they preferred to call it.

That same March 1970 issue of the *IOS Bulletin* announced a forthcoming event, which became, as it happened, one of the most revealing incidents in the IOS story. It was the "Millionaires Conference" to be held between May 22 and 25 in "Hyde Park's elegant Grosvenor House, one of London's greatest hotels." A "millionaire," in this special IOS sense, meant any salesman whose personal sales volume for the previous year equaled or exceeded $1 million. There were ninety-seven millionaires listed by name as having been invited to a round of cocktail parties, dinner dances, and sessions on sales techniques. But by the time May 22 came around, the world had turned upside down. The crisis had struck IOS, the shares of the company had collapsed, and Bernard Cornfeld, who was slated to give the "keynote address" in London, had been deposed from the chairmanship of the company he created.

Cornfeld was uncertain of the reception he would receive from the master salesmen. But although there were hostile murmurs when he rose, at the end he received a rapturous, standing ovation. "In the first three weeks of this month of May," he said, "under the worst possible conditions—a falling market, a hostile press, a massive rumor campaign against us—we managed to write more than $100 million in business. . . . We are still a company that does the impossible." After the meeting, he spent an hour signing autographs.

Allen Cantor, naturally, was also present, and he made it the occasion for one of his great sales sermons. This one was upon the importance of truth and openness. The truth, he said, was the only weapon which could combat "the wave of irresponsible rumors concerning our company which have been spread by certain newspapers and individuals." With this appeal in mind, and with the intention of restoring confidence in IOS, the gathering at the Grosvenor House passed a special resolution.

"On May 22, 1970," it read, "the undersigned group, representing the leading sales associates of Investors Overseas Services [all of whom are stockholders] met in London. . . . We unanimously confirm our belief in the IOS concept of professional financial planning. We support the consolidation efforts of our Company, and will work together in the interests of our clients for the future success of our concepts and beliefs."

The resolution was an effort, on the part of the men who had each hammered home their million dollars' worth of closes, to assert that there was really nothing shadowy or dubious about

IOS—that it was really an orthodox financial concern, with everything open and aboveboard.

There was just one problem with this ringing declaration. It was signed, "The IOS Millionaires." And of the ninety-seven millionaires, true to the clandestine tradition of the sales force, fifty names were pseudonyms. For instance, the top salesman of all was listed as "Luc Sico." Some time later, when the rhetoric had echoed away, we asked Allen Cantor to tell us about the great Sico. "Luc Sico?" said the captain of the sales force, "I've never heard of him."

"Sico" along with Omar Wilde, John Fumble, and others, appeared in the list of "Asia VII." That was the code name for Italy, plus Greece and Turkey—Harvey Felberbaum's domain. Harvey Felberbaum, asked later about these performers, said, "Those? Oh, they were all phony names."

"It is essential," said Allen Cantor at the Grosvenor House, "to distinguish between what is true, and what is false." Truth, he asserted, could save IOS. Yet his appeal for truth was addressed to an audience in which the majority were invited under false identities. Like the word "millionaire," like the word "investment," "truth" had a special meaning in IOS.

The true, in the ordinary sense, is hard to tell from the false throughout the IOS story. And nowhere is it more difficult than on the question of the actual investment performance of the IOS funds—which, in the end, is the heart of the business. Many people in IOS itself accept that the investors who bought shares in IOS Ltd. were fooled, that company money was used for private advantage, that there was gross incompetence, that there were unconscionable charges, ferocious sales techniques, illegal currency transactions, and ridiculous boasting.

But somehow, the myth lives on that the actual funds—the customers' money itself—was largely insulated from all this. It is still believed that the funds did well for their investors. There are two reasons for this. One is that people tend to think that all is well unless they actually see a man putting the money in a black bag, and leaving town on the first plane. The pattern in IOS was more complex than that: it consisted of a lengthy and elaborate series of transactions, each one defended with a cunning and sophistry which might enable it, in isolation, to pass muster. It is only when something like the whole story can be assembled that the reckless and dishonest reality begins to emerge.

The other reason that people think the funds did well is that the men who ran IOS boasted, with daring persistence, that such was the case. Boasting and propaganda were what they did best. The success of their propaganda is measured by an article which appeared in the *Institutional Investor*, with whose conference in February 1970 we started our story.

In October 1970, the magazine published an article which asserted that the IOS funds had, despite the crisis, "fared remarkably well." Now, this was shortly after the Fund of Funds, the most famous IOS operation of all, had suspended redemptions upon three-fifths of the assets in the fund—thus renouncing the basic principle upon which an open-end fund is sold, which is its liquidity. At that point when three-fifths of the customers' investments became irredeemable and of dubious values, IOS was unable to give any idea when a value might be restored. The closing of redemptions was due chiefly to the grotesque Arctic adventure. Together with the decline of the remaining part of the fund, it meant that the Fund of Funds bore no resemblance to the article that the customers were persuaded to buy in the first place. The fact that immediately afterward, a sophisticated investment journal could say that the IOS funds "fared well" is a tribute to the legend that Cornfeld created.

The IOS funds were disastrous for virtually everyone except

the people who were running IOS. In order to demonstrate this some detailed arithmetic is required—which may be why Bernard Cornfeld preferred large generalities to specific figures—and some of the arithmetic is rather surprising.

Part of the reason that IOS got away with many of its extravagant claims is that the investment record of an open-end fund can be looked at in a number of different ways. It is, of course, simple enough to calculate the "net asset value per share" of a fund at any given point: it is simply a question of dividing the current value of the fund's cash and investments by the number of fund shares outstanding. The resulting figure governs the price paid by new investors coming in, and by old investors going out: it may also be compared with past net asset value figures to show whether the value of the fund is going up or going down. So far, so good. But at this point, the issue is affected by complexities such as the rate of growth of the fund, and the period of time examined.

The most obvious complexity, for an ordinary customer trying to assess IOS fund performance, is that IOS consistently falsified the records of "IIT, an International Investment Trust," which in the end was their biggest fund. IIT was launched in December 1960 at $5 per share, and in the first year of operation IIT slid down to a net asset value of $4.87 per share. Then came the collapse which we analyzed in Chapter 6, and by October 1962, IIT was down to $3.53 per share.

This early performance made it almost impossible to sell IIT, and for two or three years the maximum effort went into peddling the Fund of Funds. By early 1965, IIT had crept back to launch level of $5 per share. Then, in the middle of 1966, helped by a booming U.S. stock market, IIT got up to $7.23 per share.

At this point, the IOS men turned the early disaster into an advantage. They began to compute the new rises against the trough of 1962: they pretended systematically that IOS only began to manage IIT when it was at $3.53, and implied that someone else was responsible for it before then. The device of sawing off the embarrassing parts of the record "made it easier to sell IIT," as Ed Cowett put it, blandly.

The sophistry IOS used to conceal the first twenty-one months of IIT's life is analyzed elsewhere. It certainly made a striking difference to the "performance." Between December 1960 and December 1969, IIT shares grew in value by 77 per cent—a meager performance at best, and the 1970 crash was still to come. But between October 1962 and December 1969, IIT shares went up by 151 per cent, which was comfortable. Even on the true figures, there are difficulties about comparing the performance of IOS funds with those of regulated funds in the United States. This is because there is a basic difference in operation. American funds normally distribute to their investors the capital gains they make on the investments and the dividend income they receive. The IOS funds, however, reinvested all such gains and income that would tend to make their assets grow faster, by comparison, in periods of rising markets—although the income of IOS funds was not usually large because of the heavy charges they had to bear: for instance, IOS even used fund income to pay part of the costs of its lawsuits with the SEC.

For our comparisons between IOS funds and domestic U.S. funds, we used the analyses of investment companies prepared by Wiesenberger Financial Services. Wiesenberger's calculations of net asset value take into account both capital gains and dividends earned by the funds, but assume that, while the customer reinvests his capital-gains distributions, he takes his dividends in cash, forfeiting any further appreciation on this part of his money. So a comparison on this basis is somewhat favorable to the IOS funds.

Wiesenberger divides American funds into categories, and then gives net asset value records both for individual funds, and for the average of each category. The most suitable category for comparison with IIT and the Fund of Funds is Wiesenberger's "large growth funds," which, like the two big IOS funds, had assets of more than $300 million at the end of 1969. There were seventeen of these, including Dreyfus, Fidelity Capital, and the Enterprise Fund. It is also interesting to compare the IOS funds with Wiesenberger's category of "smaller growth funds," of which there were 107. Their investment objective is maximum capital gain, and their average net asset value per share rose slightly faster than that of the large funds between 1960 and 1969.

Wiesenberger gives figures for ten-year periods, and then breaks up each decade into subperiods of one year to ten years in length. Thus, although none of the IOS funds have run a full ten years, it is possible to make the crucial examination of fund performance through time—rather than looking only at particular moments of spectacular performance. Sharp gains can readily be made in rising markets, and the IOS funds often did so. But what matters more, especially to the "small saver" IOS claimed to be serving, is the effect on his money at the end of the day.

The life of IIT between 1960 and the end of 1969—we are not yet examining 1970—can be cut up into nine periods, ranging between one and nine years in length. In four of those periods IIT's value did better than the average of large U.S. growth funds, and in five of them it was worse. (It only exceeded the smaller-growth funds in 1969.) The four periods in which the IIT figures exceeded the large U.S. funds' average are: from the end of 1963 to the end of 1969, end 1964 to end 1969, end 1965 to end 1969, and end 1967 to end 1969. In other words, IIT had a period of sharp increases in value per share during the mid-1960s, and this appears clearly if one looks at individual years. There were three, 1965, 1966, and 1968, during which IIT's net asset value per share rose faster than the average of the large U.S. growth funds.

But over the whole *nine* years, IIT had a dismal performance. Between December 31, 1960, and December 31, 1969, the average growth of net asset value per share in the large American growth funds was 134 per cent, something like double IIT's true figure of 77 per cent. The small growth funds, with 145.5 per cent, beat IIT still more comfortably. Indeed, if adjustment is made for reinvestment of dividends, the average increase of an investment in a large U.S. growth fund would have beaten an investment in IIT by more than twice. IIT's mediocre performance was not very much better, up to 1969, than the rise of Standard and Poor's index of 500 shares, which rose 58 per cent.* IOS rewarded itself for this dismal achievement by removing $11 million from the fund in management fees.

But there are further curiosities about the IIT record—ones which Cornfeld claimed to be "impossible" when we discussed them with him. The argument begins by stating three points about the IIT investment record:

1. Between December 1960 and December 1969, IIT bought shares to a total value of nearly $2.5 billion. At December 31, 1969, the fund still held $558 million of these investments, and this market value at that date stood roughly $6 million above their purchase price.
2. During the same nine years, IIT *sold* about $1.9 billion worth of shares. The aggregate proceeds of all these sales

---

*The Dow Jones rose only 30 per cent in that period, but it is not such a good comparison because it only contains thirty industrial stocks. Both the Dow Jones and Standard and Poor's, of course, are "unmanaged," and have no reinvestment income.

came to $12 million less than the aggregate purchase price. In other words, after a vast series of share transactions, which helped increase the value of Arthur Lipper's stockbroking business to $14 million, the small $6 million of unrealized gains mentioned in paragraph (1) did not cancel out the losses made on buying and selling of shares over the whole nine years.

3. The total of nine years' income from IIT's investments came to $10 million. This was a truly pitiful performance on a fund which averaged $164 million in size during those years, and ended 1969 at $704 million. But it was just enough to cover the losses on capital and leave a minuscule $4-million profit on nine years' operation.

In other words, the worth of IIT's investments had scarcely increased at all at the end of the period 1960–1969. Yet the audited net asset value per share, which stood at $5 when the fund began, had gone up to $8.85 by 1969—the 77-per-cent rise mentioned earlier. When we asked Cornfeld how the net asset value could increase in a period when the underlying investments did not do so, he said he could not understand it. The answer, in fact, has something to do with a curious gearing effect in a fund which expands very fast during a time when stock markets decline.

The efforts of the IOS sales force did not slacken when markets fell. They had been taught to impress the prospects with the concept of "dollar-cost averaging"—which said that if it was good to buy into an up market, it was even better to buy into a down market. "For Associates," declared an IOS workshop session, "a market decline is a time for increased service calls . . . a strategic time to encourage clients to increase their investments." It was never right for an IOS salesman to say anything except *"Buy."* In the United States, it becomes difficult to sell mutual-fund shares when the markets are declining: but the men who sold IIT were often operating among unsophisticated customers who were well insulated from the condition of Wall Street.

So in 1968 and early 1969, there was a gigantic inflow of new money into IIT—about $430 million in eighteen months. The hordes of new investors mostly came in at prices of around $9 to $10 per share, which reflected the rather short-lived surge in IIT's net asset value, and took in the last fling of the stock-market boom of the 1960s. Much of this new money was not invested, but was kept in cash.

When the decline began, it was only the *invested* part of the fund which declined. In the process, gains made on share transactions in earlier years were wiped out—but the enormous sum of cash which had just been inserted into the fund retained its value, and was available as a "cushion" to spread over the whole fund. Therefore, the net asset value of the whole fund sank relatively gently from the high of $10.21 down to $8.85.

To some people, a decision not to invest cash inflow from the sales force may pass as investment management. But it might easily be argued that a mutual-fund management facing a period of decline should ease up on its sales effort. Shoveling in new money can only work to the disadvantage of the new investors who come in at peak prices: their money goes mainly to cushion the fall for the existing investors.

Admirers have claimed that the large cash proportions of IIT and other IOS funds were due to "courage and foresight" on the part of IOS investment managers. The reply to that is perhaps best made by the IOS investment chief, C. Henry Buhl III, who said to us that he had been guilty of "weakness" during this period. In particular, he said, he regretted that he had not opposed the loading down of IIT with almost $100 million of Colorado Corporation, King Resources, Commonwealth United, Four Seasons, and Giffen and other such rubbish. The figures support Mr. Buhl's self-deprecation.

During the first six months of 1969, the cash proportion of IIT rose to 32 per cent of the whole fund, which was achieved partly by leaving a lot of new money uninvested, and partly by liquidating some $90 million of existing investments. But taking the year as a whole, IIT managers actually increased their investments over-all: they bought $936 million and sold $722. This meant that, net, they put $214 million into the market. In doing so, they realized $50 million of losses, and the value of shares remaining in the portfolio fell by $38 million. So over the whole year the increase of cash in the fund came from new shareholders. They were providing, to their cost, a "cushion" which was about to be badly needed.

The record of the Fund of Funds, up to this point on the edge of crisis, is even worse than that of IIT.

The Fund of Funds was launched in autumn 1962. From December 31, 1962, to December 31, 1969, the net asset value per share of the Fund of Funds grew by 127.2 per cent, considerably worse than the average of either large or small U.S. growth funds over the same time. In each of the periods covered by Wiesenberger's figures, FOF's record is below the average of both large and small growth funds.

If the seven years are examined individually, FOF did better than the average of large funds in two separate years: 1963 and 1968. And it did better than the small funds' average in 1963, 1964, and 1969. Yet even this is an unreal comparison: in reality, the Fund of Funds only performed respectably when it was invested in public mutual funds in America. Its best years were at the start. Then came the period of speculative "proprietary funds," and the rest of the record is distorted by the Arctic revaluation. If that is removed, then the net asset value per share comes down by a disastrous 25 per cent during 1969 alone. That brings FOF's seven-year record down to 100 per cent, hopelessly inferior to the average of U.S. funds.

The Fund of Funds, unlike IIT, did not have a big flow of new money in 1969. The sales emphasis in the latter 1960s switched to IIT—largely because, on the basis of its truncated records, it could be shown as having a better growth ratel During 1969, the Fund of Funds increased its cash by liquidating some $400 million of investments, and nearly a third of the total fund was cash by the end of the year. Since, during the year there were net redemptions of $50 million, $40 million had been expended on trying to support the sagging price of IPI, the real-estate fund, and another $50 million punted into the Natural Resources Account, FOF by the year's end could hardly be called a fund with a strong liquid position.

So both IIT and FOF began 1970 in remarkably poor condition. In the early part of the year, Wall Street dipped again, instead of making the hoped-for recovery, and something like panic gripped IOS. Investment managers were dismissed abruptly, vast blocks of shares were thrown onto the market—depressing their prices even further—and IOS became, not just a victim of the market crash, but an important factor in knocking the bottom right out of things.

Now, the speculative rubbish in the IOS funds blew away—and took large segments of the customers' investments with it. IIT had to write off whole blocks of securities: $60 to $70 million was stuffed into a "special account" as there was really no other way to get rid of it. Even the remaining shares were difficult to sell when cash was needed to meet the rush of redemptions.

The fund was so comprehensively devastated that it missed the whole recovery of Wall Street at the end of 1970. Compared to other mutual funds, IIT's results were almost comically bad: even the Enterprise Fund, which dropped by 32 per cent in 1969, managed to survive 1970 with a drop of only 2.3 per cent. Quite a number of U.S. funds made small increases in 1970, and the average loss in net asset value was only about 1 per cent.* IIT dropped by a staggering 26.7 per cent during 1970.

Over ten years, after all the boasting, after all the glowing promises made to the customers, IIT managed to show an increase of just 29.8 per cent on its original value. This is so inferior to the performance of regulated U.S. funds that there is no point in comparing them. It is actually less than the increase in the Dow-Jones index, which went up by 36.2 per cent in that time. It is scarcely half the increase recorded over those ten years by Standard and Poor's 500-share index, which went up by 58.6 per cent.

So much for "the best investment advice that $2 billion can buy." You would have done twice as well leaving your money to random stock-market forces than entrusting it to IIT—and this does not take account of the sales load! You would, in fact, have done enormously better to have left your money in one of those savings-bank accounts about which Bernard Cornfeld used to sneer so eloquently.

But if you were in IIT, you were luckier than if you were in the Fund of Funds.

By August 1970, the "assets" of the Fund of Funds had been whittled away by redemptions and by falling investment value, so that the fund had fallen to $364 million from the $623 million with which it began the year. Of that $364 million, about half

---

*At the time of writing, Wiesenberger's figures for 1970 had not been published.

was accounted for by the purely notional values ascribed to the Natural Resources Account. And another $28 million was in unsalable shares of another IOS fund, Investment Properties International.

At this point, the new management of IOS acted "prudently and decisively," in the words of Henry Buhl. The natural-resources investments, the IPI shares, and $17 million in cash were simply removed from FOF, and put into a new company, Global Resources. Global Resources shares, it was announced, would be distributed eventually to FOF investors. But Global shares would not be redeemable. It was to be a closed-end company.

And what, when they appeared, would Global shares be worth? Assets with an alleged value of $217 million were shifted into Global Resources on August 7. The next day, Henry Buhl warned FOF investors that they must not "realistically anticipate short-term cash equivalents of values realistically determined by the board to be fair." Insofar as the syntax was decipherable, this seemed to mean: don't expect the company actually to be worth $217 million on the market.

The net asset value of the Fund of Funds crashed at once to $7.44. This was not only one of the fastest descents in mutual-fund history: it took the fund down to less than three-quarters of the $10 at which Cornfeld and Cowett launched it in 1962. At the end of 1970, FOF investors were being advised by executives at IOS HQ that the best thing to do if they needed to raise a little cash was to nip round to the Banque Troillet, across the Rhône. There they might be able to sell in advance their rights to Global Resources at a couple of dollars a share—to be paid if, and when, the new shares should appear.

If you were in IIT, you would mostly have done better to leave your money in a savings bank. If you were in the Fund of

Funds, you would have done better to keep your money in an old sock—or, better still, to have spent it yourself before IOS got hold of it.

The only way an investor was likely to get any benefit out of IIT or the Fund of Funds was to get out when prices were artificially high, which effectively meant taking gains at the expense of other investors. Fund of Funds investors who saw through IOS's propaganda in early 1970 could well have come away with some profit—assuming they had been in the fund long enough to beat the charges and the front-end load.

Over the IOS years, the salesmen sincerely and consistently predicted to their prospects that a lump sum put into an IOS fund would increase by three times in ten years. Even at the end of 1969, neither fund was anywhere near meeting that achievement. After the crisis of 1970 exposed the true, speculative nature of IIT and FOF, the prediction became an absurdity.

The records of some of the small funds, especially those which invested in North America, are also deplorable. Venture Fund (International) was launched in April 1969 at $10 a share, and a section was entrusted to David Meid. The share value declined from the start, standing at $9.24 at the end of 1969. Heavy with letter stock and special propositions, it went down by 17.4 per cent in 1970, ending the year at $7.63. (This was a $100-million fund.)

Regent Fund of Canada came under IOS management in 1963: during 1969, it lost 23.5 per cent and another 12.3 per cent in 1970. That left it with a feeble gain of about 50 per cent after seven years under IOS management. But its record was brilliant compared to that of the Canadian Venture Fund, which was launched at the end of 1968 and placed under Fred Alger's care. Canadian Venture declined 5.4 per cent in 1969, and then in

1970 it went right over the edge, and fell 26.6 per cent in the year.

The only relief in the IOS record is provided by the national funds. Cornfeld and Cowett never seriously got around to experimenting with new forms of investment in the national funds, except that IOS Growth Fund, which was launched late in 1969 for the German market, was given some of the Arctic action, and suffered accordingly. The main German fund, Investors Fonds, launched at 20 D-marks a share in March 1968, was at 22.24 DM two years later. By the end of 1970, however, it was down 21 per cent from that level. IOS's small Dutch fund, IVM Invest, actually grew by 11½ per cent in 1970.

Fonditalia, started in November 1967 at $10, was still fractionally ahead of the game by the end of 1970, at $10.29. Fonditalia's growth, and its forced investment in the narrow Italian market, helped hold up the Italian market for a time while others collapsed: eventually, it was the huge size of Fonditalia's holdings in Italian companies which caused the Italian government to buy out 51 per cent of the IOS Italian operation in 1970. The government realized that a collapse of confidence in Fonditalia could have dire consequences on the economy of Italy and thought the best way to avert this was to take control of the operation itself.

It was the Equity Unit Account of the Dover Plan that put up the most respectable performance: at the end of 1970 it stood 133 per cent above its 1963 launch level, a growth record which was way above the average of British unit trusts for the same period, which only rose 38 per cent* and which put the EUA right up among the leaders. Once again, however, the comparison is

*Based on figures produced by the magazine *Money Management and Unitholder*.

complex. The EUA is in some respects similar to a unit trust, but it is far from being exactly the same sort of animal. The EUA is merely a notional division of the assets of the International Life Insurance company and the calculation of its value is left to ILI. It does not for instance include all the cash held by ILI; and this exclusion would improve its performance in rising markets. It does not include any of the Dover Plan costs, or any reserve for capital-gains tax. The prices of British unit trusts, on the other hand, must be calculated in strict accordance with a formula laid down by the government.

Nevertheless on the whole the performance of the EUA was good; though it has a volatile record which deteriorated sharply at the end. For its first two and a half years it had the unique advantage of premium-free dollar investment through the original Fund of Funds, then in its best years. The EUA's most successful period, however, came when ILI, fortuitously as it turned out, had to stop investing in the dollar FOF. In 1967 and 1968 the London market rose very fast and the new Fund of Funds Sterling rose with it. Then, astutely, its managers liquidated large parts of the portfolio in the latter half of 1968, before the market broke.

After the FOF Sterling was abandoned because of its tax disadvantages, the EUA began to go the way of the other IOS funds. As markets became more difficult, the competing managers chased more and more speculative stocks. In 1969, the EUA bought large chunks of the sad Venture Fund International and the latter-day Fund of Funds. It went into "liquid real estate," with an office block in Nairobi. As a result the EUA did *worse* than the unit-trust average over the last two and three years to the end of 1970. In 1970 it fell by 15.2 per cent against the trusts' average decline of 5.7 per cent. For early investors the falls were not yet large enough to wipe out the early gains, but for later investors, coming on top of the heavy Dover Plan charges, they meant a serious fall in the value of their holdings.

After all the promises, it seems that the best account of the IOS investment operation is the one we were given by a young woman who worked for Cornfeld. "If anyone was fool enough to put their money with us," she said, "that was their problem."

There are several versions of the story of the customers' yachts. The version Cornfeld himself used to tell went like this. During the 1920s, the New York yacht harbor was a big spot on the sight-seeing programs. In the harbor were moored the yachts of all the rich bankers and brokers. "That's Mr. Morgan's yacht on the right," the guide would declaim. "The one next to it belongs to Mr. Rockefeller—the one over there is Mr. Dillon's."

One day, an innocent tourist is said to have asked, "Where are the customers' yachts?"

According to John Kenneth Galbraith, the question should be addressed to Bernie Cornfeld in the form: where are the customers' girls? However, we stuck to the original, and asked Cornfeld, in 1970, to answer this question: where were his customers' yachts?

Mr. Cornfeld considered for a moment.

"Well," he said, "somewhere up there in the Arctic . . ."

Frozen solid.

A Game of Strategic Withdrawal

Bernie sells out and Ed Cowett plays backgammon. A young man gets on a train in Bangkok.

Thereis no neat end to the story of Investors Overseas Services. As long as there is a decent amount of the customers' money lying around in Geneva, people will be interested in it—and probably wrangling over it. Although we have followed some of the subsequent intrigues, the main part of our story deals with the boom and bust of IOS, and that story ends with the crash in 1970. Many things are possible—it may even be that someone will find enough oil in the Arctic to pay back the customers of the Fund of Funds. Maybe some investment giant will arise and cause IIT and the other funds to perform genuine, as against imaginary, wonders. It does not seem especially likely, as we close our own account with a description of some of our characters as they stood in the last days of 1970 and in the first month of 1971.

There was no move to restore Ed Cowett to the IOS Board after his resignation, although he stayed on the payroll as a "consultant" until the fall of 1970. The management seemed to feel that he was the man who knew where most of the bodies were buried, and that they might need him in the event of any exhumations being required. Cowett moved into a new office just down the Rue de Lausanne, and started a new company of his own, called Emco. It was to advise private clients on taxation and investment problems. He said that he could not return permanently to America: there was too much "moral degeneracy." But he made plenty of visits: sometimes to spar with his old antagonists at the SEC, or to play in the Bob Hope golf tournament at Palm Springs.

Cowett was claiming to be "bust," but he still had the big house overlooking the lake, above the Parc des Eaux Vives, and he was still driving the blue Maserati. The Emco offices, in a converted apartment, are hardly squalid. There are long sofas, and deep armchairs, and the office equipment is all brand new. There is a telescope aimed out over the lake, and various pop-art objects, such as a huge gilded sandwich, are scattered around.

Against one wall stands a large, marble backgammon table. Bernie Cornfeld's fascination with backgammon never seemed to turn him into a very good player, but Cowett is said to be one of the best backgammon players in the world. The key to backgammon, he says, is that it is "a game of strategic withdrawal."

One bookshelf is occupied by a row of volumes, each considerably larger and fatter than a *Britannica* section, all bound in blue with silver letters tooled on the spines. The letters say, "IOS Ltd. Public Offering of Common Stock, September 1969," and underneath, in smaller letters, "Edward M. Cowett." Copies of all the letters, contracts, minutes, accounts, prospectus drafts, and Telexes connected with the public offering were bound up to make these volumes. Their bulk gives an idea of the considerable intellectual powers that were required to bring IOS to the market: certainly they represent a unique business achievement, whatever the result. At first sight, there seem to be seven of these volumes, but the seventh is only a dummy. It opens out into a backgammon set.

Cowett was still strategically withdrawing as 1971 opened. He was growing a new and rather dashing black beard, and greeting the future with confidence. "I am a natural optimist," he said. "You give me a glass and I'll never say it's half empty. To me it's always half full." One of his main preoccupations was to liquidate his obligations over certain IOS shares: he was still haunted by the 600,000 shares which he had shifted from his family trust, and the King trust, and sold to Dean Milosis's little fund, Summit Associates, in May 1970. Cowett had only persuaded Milosis to take the shares at $2.35 by promising to arrange a resale, or else buy them back, at $2.95 within a few months. By mid-summer 1970 the price of IOS shares was hopelessly below $2.95. Cowett started to repurchase them, and wrote a check for $450,000 on the International Credit Bank. Unfortunately the check bounced.

By October, Milosis and Summit Associates were getting worried. They then received a promissory note from Cowett for $1.8 million, and Cowett managed to get Robert Vesco interested in the shares. Butler's Bank of the Bahamas bought in, and an option agreement was drawn up. In early 1971, Cowett maintained that his obligations to Milosis were "in process of being honored," while Vesco himself told us that he had secured the voting rights on the shares.

The down period found Cowett more relaxed and affable than the tense days of 1969 and 1970. He was always available to advise an old colleague on a Panamanian company, to deliver a homily on the evils of speculation, or to analyze the downfall of IOS. His break with Cornfeld appeared to be absolute: quiet contempt was his most amiable mode for discussing his great collaborator. Although Cowett is secretive about the inner details of his finances, it is certainly true that his amazing manipulations with IOS shares left him with heavy obligations and no obvious profit.

But Cowett, perhaps, was one of the few men in the organization who did not "sincerely want to be rich." Obviously, he liked to have money. What he sincerely wanted was the joy and fascination of composing elegantly complicated, audaciously vast schemes and leverages, whose true beauty was known only to himself. If you ask him what he was doing it for, he says, "I just liked going into the office every day to face something completely different and new."

A good many of those who had sincerely wanted to be rich achieved their purpose. They may not have become as rich as they wanted to be, or as they thought they were. But for some of the people in IOS, all the money in the world would still not have been enough.

The one penalty of wealth was being submitted to some rather rude questions from time to time. Arthur Lipper III, for instance, the stockbroker, spent a good deal of 1970 trying to fight off the SEC. The unforgiving Commission alleged that Lipper had improperly returned parts of his brokerage commissions to IOS during 1967 and 1968. The money was paid to Investors Planning Corporation, Walter Benedick's old firm, which IOS owned in those years, before the SEC made Bernie sell it off. The sums involved only came to $1.6 million, which by this stage in the IOS story was virtually small change, but Lipper and Cowett had to appear in public hearings in New York, and at the beginning of 1971 the case was still not resolved. Lipper, no doubt, was able to comfort himself with the thought that during the years with IOS his brand-new firm had built up a net worth of $14 million.

George Landau stayed on with an office in 119 Rue de Lausanne, coming to terms with his relatively diminished wealth. Landau's shares had been worth $12 million at the offer price of IOS, and he had received $1.2 million cash for selling 10 per cent. (Theoretically, he had been worth about $28 million in the speculative heights of the pre-issue market.) In the aftermath, Landau realized he was going to have to liquidate some of the obligations to the company incurred by Ed Cowett's remarkable schemes of tax avoidance—but there was obviously going to be a million or two left. Don Q. Shaprow, his old partner, decided to retire from IOS. It took a clerk at Ferney-Voltaire a whole day to write Shaprow out of the override system.

Things really did not turn out too badly for most of the veterans. Eli Wallitt said, "I can't honestly regret those ten years. It's just that they weren't real." The solid Swiss banker's mansion that Mr. Wallitt owns, at 35 Quai de Cologny, is very real. He lives an agreeably leisured life there, occasionally slipping on a bankerly black Homburg for business trips to England or Germany.

Richard Gangel, that other old socialist, was selling a house at the end of 1970: it was in Rutland Gate, London, just by Hyde Park. Gangel was asking a million dollars for his house, the highest price ever asked for a private house in London. It was the kind of solid Victorian palace that Soames Forsyte might have lived in, except that Soames might not have bothered with a heated, indoor pool, solid gold taps throughout, and such details as a Gothic two-holer for the children. Gangel was planning to set up a company called Financial Partners International, to finance ex-IOS salesmen starting up their own businesses. For many of them, it was a much-felt need, although at the time of writing Mr. Gangel had not announced any specific ventures.

The more successful salesmen, of course, did not require it.

Werner Kunkler, for instance, had diversified sensibly into hotels and into women's hair dressing shops. However, he had an eye to the future: when we talked to him in 1970, he thought that what IOS had done was to make German savers rather frightened of the stock market. So his idea was to start up a new kind of fund which would invest entirely in businesses *not* quoted on the stock market.

The sales force as a whole was still showing some signs of life—despite wholesale terminations, which reduced its effective numbers below 10,000 by the end of 1970. Like some sprawling, primitive animal, it proved remarkably hard to kill outright. So long as there were a few customers left with enough money to pay for the front-end load, it could sell a new fund shares. In the autumn, the *IOS Bulletin* produced a special issue called *Selling Through the Apocalypse*, which sang the praises of those salesmen who were still managing reasonably good volume. Many of them, it emerged, were in France, where the name was Rothschild-Expansion, not IOS. And most of the others were finding their sales in social and economic byways: among Greek immigrants in Canada, among *gastarbeiter* in Germany, or other relatively unsophisticated communities. It was possible, one salesman remarked, to find prospects who had not heard about the troubles of IOS.

And in some places, the sales force continued to serve the real, if slightly sordid, need which made IOS rich in the first place. On November 21, 1970, for instance, a young Englishman, an Old Etonian and an IOS manager operating in Thailand, Laos, and Cambodia, caught the overnight train from Bangkok to Vientiane. As the train rolled slowly eastward, the young man ordered large quantities of drinks from the bar, consuming them more and more eagerly. It was, perhaps from nerves; for before he vomited and collapsed, he confessed to the

Sunday Times reporter who was sharing the compartment with him that he had $20,000 in his briefcase, which he was taking illegally out of Thailand. It was surprising that he should be nervous, because before becoming a "financial counselor to the middle class" he had been a mercenary soldier in the Congo under "Mad Mike" Hoare.

Some of the old sales chiefs left the company amid bitterness, such as the Canadian boss, Ira Weinstein, who departed in January 1971, and embarked on litigation with IOS immediately afterward. But that was unusual: Roy Kirkdorffer, who had been head of the British sales force, left amicably to go into the insurance-broking business in London: he seemed comfortable himself, and hoped that the Dover Plan might yet improve enough to earn a little money for the investors. Barry Sterling was also settling down in London, with a house in South Audley Street, Mayfair. Marty Seligson, the man who ran the IOS real-estate operations, had a nice piece of real estate himself: a rambling, California-style house in the hills outside Geneva. As an old developer himself, he claimed to be a little unhappy about some of the details of the house. However, it seemed to be keeping the snow out all right. As for IOS, he thought it had turned into a "real can of worms," although he was eager to defend Ed Cowett—"a much-maligned man." The shares of Investment Properties International were in pretty bad shape, he agreed. "But hell, investors have got to be able to take their lumps."

As IOS went on shedding personnel, Geneva began to grow exceptionally rich in free-lance consultants offering advice in matters of taxation, law, public relations, and investment. Ed Coughlin, as well as Ed Cowett, was among them. He had not pleased the "new management" by his reluctance to assassinate Cornfeld at Toronto.

But some old veterans continued to serve. C. Henry Buhl III hung on to his job, pointing out that it was a good thing for IOS to have some people like himself, who were *not* afraid of losing their jobs. Allen Cantor stayed: his view was that most of IOS's troubles had been got up by the press. Having addressed his salesmen on Truth, he addressed the authors on Responsibility. "How does it feel," he asked, "when you write that little word 'sell'? Do you think about the little people, the ones who get hurt in the stampede? Do you think you have a responsibility there?" What we felt responsible for, of course, was that we had *not* written that people ought to sell out of the IOS funds.

Harvey Felberbaum, who was busy turning himself into an orthodox Italian businessman, was rather franker. "You have to feel bad about putting people into some of those investments, the way they turned out. I just want to stick around long enough to see that nobody can horse around with the customers' money any more."

The miraculous institutions of the offshore world were collapsing one by one. In September, Keith Barish and Rafael Navarro of Gramco had to suspend redemptions on USIF, their "liquid real-estate" fund. "I think we've shown that this concept needs rethinking," said Robert Long, Gramco's investment chieftain. "This whole offshore business is a dead apple," Pierre Salinger told us frankly. The directors of Gramco Management met, and decided to pay themselves a suitable fee for selling off the large pile of real estate they had built up. It was hoped that by turning Gramco into an ordinary real-estate company something might be saved for the customers.

Gramco at least made some attempt to explain themselves, and Rafael Navarro sent one of the authors a velvet Christmas card. As for Jerome Hoffman, the epitome of Offshore Man, his enterprise simply melted away, to the considerable embarrassment of Reginald Maudling, Lord Brentford, and Mr. Hoffman's numerous creditors.

Not all of the customers elected to "take their lumps" quietly when it really began to sink in that large chunks of their money seemed to have vanished more or less permanently. In the nature of things offshore, it was hard to know where to sue, but people began to put lawsuits together. And in January 1971, roughly one year after the season of his greatest triumph, a group of Fund of Funds investors committed the ultimate *lèse majesté*, and filed suit against Cornfeld himself in Switzerland. At the same time, the same group filed suit against C. Henry Buhl, who was still with IOS, and Ambassador Roosevelt and Ed Cowett, who were not, but were resident in Geneva.

The circumstances must have raised a laugh at the SEC offices in Washington—after all of Cornfeld's skirmishing about keeping the identities of his customers secret. The suits against Cornfeld and his erstwhile colleagues were taken out by a group of Swiss attorneys. They were acting for a series of numbered accounts in the Fund of Funds.

The suits aimed to test, under Swiss law, firstly whether it had been legal to start putting Fund of Funds money into the Natural Resources Account, and secondly whether it was then legal to "spin off" the holdings into a separate closed-end company. These interesting points were still unresolved at the time of writing, but what was fairly clear was that it was not going to be easy to get back any substantial part of the supposed $217 million shunted into Global Resources from the Fund of Funds. On December 31, 1970—exactly one year after taking the famous fee for revaluing it—IOS admitted that a good part of the Fund of Funds Arctic holding had "little present economic value." In an "interim report" Global Resources said that many of its permits were for acreage "at water depths making development under presently available techniques impracticable."

. . .

Four days before the suit was filed, Bernard Cornfeld had severed the last of his links with Investors Overseas Services. The three months since he had been re-elected to the IOS Board had not been particularly happy ones. There was, for a start, a row over his old office with the raw-silk walls. Sir Eric Wyndham White had moved into it on assuming the chairmanship and the presidency, but a couple of days after the compromise with Vesco was fixed up, Sir Eric arrived at 119 Rue de Lausanne to find Cornfeld moving back in. There was a brief argument, which led to one of Cornfeld's famous, but now much less effective, rages. Then Cornfeld moved out again.

There had been some kind of vaguely expressed hope that Bernie might spend some time inspiring the sales force, but in fact he spent very little time in the shop, beyond going to board meetings. One reason, perhaps, was that his personal affairs required a good deal of attention.

The strict tally of Cornfeld's personal wealth had naturally been exaggerated during the boom years, when a man needed to have an alleged worth of at least $300 million in order to be considered for the title of "financial genius." Even so, while the good times lasted he was a very rich man indeed.

After he had received $8 million cash for selling a small slice of his IOS shareholding in the offer, he retained holdings in IOS worth around $90 million at the rate of $13–14 per share. He also had large load-free holdings in IIT and the Fund of Funds, and his shares in the subsidiary IOS Management were worth more than $3 million alone. He had a quarter of a million dollars in State of Israel bonds, and about half a million dollars in the Playboy enterprises, and he was about to take delivery of a BAC 1–11 airliner priced at around $4.4 million. Together with his two castles, his three town houses, and his apartments and some other investments, he was worth about $150 million around the New Year of 1970.

There were, and are, men with larger personal fortunes, although not many people have acquired so much wealth so rapidly. But in Cornfeld's case, immediate personal wealth was only the beginning. His, in any case, was more than adequate to put him on the level where, as he said himself, a few million dollars here or there really makes very little difference to standards of living. In the league he was playing, money was not about personal consumption any more, but about power and influence. And Cornfeld carried with him, concentrated upon his otherwise unremarkable person, the glamour of two and a half thousand million dollars. It was not, granted, his own money, but people did not really see the distinction. It was money controlled by IOS, and Cornfeld to an unusual degree personified the corporation that he led. Indeed, for many of his followers and admirers he was the incarnation of the idea of wealth: they would almost have weighed him in gold, as the Ismailis do with the Aga Khan.

The scale of Cornfeld's personal wealth telescoped with violent speed during the year. The shareholding which had been worth the better part of $100 million shrank to $5 or $6 million at most. And what was worst about this was that it no longer possessed the marvelous liquidity of the boom years. Cornfeld had originally created and owned, for virtually no investment, all of the shares in IOS: over the years, he had been used to selling off small parcels of this substance whenever he needed particular sums of cash, and according to his own account he sold off about $6 million worth before the public offer.

From the time of the May crisis onward, IOS shares were no longer salable in any ordinary way. Small parcels might occasionally be bought in the same spirit as a lottery ticket, but the only reason Cornfeld's holding retained real interest was that it was by far the biggest single block of shares in IOS. Therefore, anyone who wanted to gain effective control of the company must buy or in some way neutralize Cornfeld's shares. For a few months, Cornfeld remained bitterly unwilling to surrender this vestigial remnant of his once-great power.

The crisis left him, in everyday terms, still a rich man. True, by September 1970 his liabilities at the Overseas Development Bank were greater than his assets deposited with the bank—but that was a matter of how you did the sums. The only thing that put him in the red was his BAC 1–11 airliner, which had been purchased partly for tax-avoidance reasons, and partly as a piece of transport to rival Hugh Hefner's.

The airplane was bought on credit guaranteed by the Overseas Development Bank, and putting all the costs on it together, Cornfeld's liability to the bank came to some $4,470,067 on the deal. Together with guarantees he had given to various friends and business associates in bolder days, he had total liabilities at the bank of around $5.2 million. But if he could somehow dispose of these, he would have a comfortable $1.25 million at the ODB, not counting the residual value of his IOS shares, which could run to $6 or $7 million. In other words, there was every prospect that he could restore his personal finances to a distinctly cosy level: the only problems were that the market for leasable airliners was suddenly very constricted and that selling off his shares would, while restoring his finances, complete the destruction of the power and influence which he had so recently enjoyed. Plainly, it was the prospect of that loss which hurt more than the sudden diminution of a personal fortune which, on his more fantastical estimates of IOS progress, would have reached $250 million some time around 1971.

Cornfeld seemed to find it hard to believe that he had lost the ability to command the chieftains of IOS—men, who in his own eyes, were as much his own creation as the company itself. The swinging, sexually emancipated image normally obscured the authoritarian side of the Emperor's nature: now, in exile, it emerged more clearly, especially in his personal comments on unruly followers. Cowett, he declared, was "a man with a pretty strange view of stock markets." That was the man he had put in command. Henry Buhl he called a "boob"; but Cornfeld had placed Buhl in formal charge of all IOS investment policy. Melvin Lechner, Cornfeld informed us, was "a pathetic little man"—in view of the courage Lechner had displayed, the charge was unfair—but in any case, Lechner was Cornfeld's Treasurer. Other ex-colleagues were described as liars, "kickback experts," and incompetents. His anger was expressed to us, in our interviews with him, in controlled, almost philosophical, terms. But in some circumstances, the tantrums to which he had always been prone became more formidable. In October, after his clash with Wyndham White, he arrived uninvited and unexpected at a board meeting of the Overseas Development Bank. He shoved his way past the security men, and stormed and shouted at the unhappy directors for the best part of an hour. In November, his girl friend Vicki Principal went to court in London and asked successfully for an order to restrain Cornfeld from seeing her. He had, she said, attacked her more than once, kicking her and half-throttling her on one occasion. Some weeks later, there was a reconciliation—but clearly, the Emperor in exile was finding things a bit of a strain.

Some time around the end of the year, he came to terms at last with the circumstances of his diminished power, and decided that the game was up. There were still people who believed in IOS, and there was a large body of customers who had to go on believing. But Cornfeld himself decided that it was time to cash in what remained of his chips, and get out.

The deal was set up by Robert Vesco, IOS's hard-bitten young savior. Vesco had consented to Bernie's reappearance on the board only unwillingly, and had always been determined to get rid of the founder if possible. He also determined, at the end of 1970, to take the direction of IOS's affairs into his own hands—having regarded himself before then, he says, merely as a lender to the company. In December, he declared that IOS had defaulted on the loans from International Controls Corporation—partly, he said, by restoring Cornfeld to certain subsidiary posts without permission. Vesco then forced IOS to deposit $5.5 million cash at International Controls Corporation's bank, namely Butler's Bank of the Bahamas. This cash was to be deposited as security for the loans: it was actually more than Vesco's company had lent to IOS. Further, he decided to reorganize the whole capital of the company in order to break the power of the old shareholders. It was a scheme that they could not easily resist, because Vesco, if he wished to, could put the company into liquidation.

It was a case, he told us, of "getting the beast by the tail, so that we could bang its head against the wall." When it was suggested that the operation would leave nothing but a dead cat, Vesco smiled. "It could have some nice little kittens," he said.

But before the plan could go through, Cornfeld's huge holding had to be neutralized. Vesco found purchasers for Cornfeld's shares at 80¢ a share—at the time of writing, these investors still decline to reveal themselves. The price was just 20¢ a share less than Cornfeld had refused, with contempt, sixteen months earlier. But in addition, Vesco arranged to have Cornfeld's bank guarantees taken over.

Up to the last moment, Cornfeld declared that he was going to fight back—that he would retake the company, that he would give up the last of his fortune to protect the fundholders. Serious negotiations began in Geneva on Monday, January 11, 1971, and lasted into past midnight on Friday, when Cornfeld, Vesco, and some twenty lawyers and advisers decamped to London to continue the business. Just before 1 a.m. on Saturday, January 16, Cornfeld signed up at last. On Saturday afternoon, a brief statement went out from IOS headquarters in Geneva saying that Bernard Cornfeld had severed all his connections with the company. The company expressed its thanks for the many services that Cornfeld had rendered. That had been one of the conditions Cornfeld insisted upon.

Shortly afterward, Bernard Cornfeld went to London airport and boarded a plane for Acapulco.

Index

Carr, Fred, 320, 322
Casals, Pablo, 207
Casino Fund (Curaçao), 363
Cassini, Oleg, 156, 216, 221, 231–32, 348–49
Cazenove & Co. (London), 374
Cecil, Lord Eustace, 41
Chiomenti, Pasquale, 279, 280, 286, 469, 471
Chris-Craft, 332
Civil Aeronautics Board, 426
Clapp, Gloria Martica, 11, 172–74, 313
Clapp, Sam, 172, 314
Club Mediterranée, 187
Cohen, Manuel F., 164, 182
Cohen, Milton D., 183
Cohen, Seymour, 42, 44, 45
Coleman, Delbert W., 216, 317–18, 340, 465
Collier's, 196
Colombia, IOS in, 139–41, 161
Colorado Corporation, 397, 409, 423, 427–28, 457, 474, 486, 520
Color Lithography, 104
Commonwealth United Corporation, 335, 337–49 *passim*, 371, 384, 395, 429, 447, 456, 465, 470, 520
Consolidated Oil & Gas, 413–17, 477, 487
Consumentengids (Holland), 307–8
Consumers Association (Holland), 307–8
Conwill, Allan, 182, 465, 469, 493, 506
Cornfeld, Bernard, youth and upbringing, 17–22; family background, 18–20; at college and social work, 23–30, 42–46; at IPC, 42, 45–52; goes to Paris, 51–53; starts IOS in Paris, 55–61;

moves to Geneva, 63*ff.*; setting up sales organization, 64–73; IOS Ltd. (SA) formed, 83–88; IIT formed, 88–93; and IIT in 1961, 96–106 *passim*; helps Cowett, 107–9; and Fund of Funds, 112–28; forms FOF Prop., 120; and IOS investment program, 120–28 *passim*; and IOS programs in "Third World," 129–63 *passim*; visits Israel and tries to buy Tel Aviv Hilton, 155; and dispute with SEC, 164–84 *passim*; and Ramer Industries, 178–84; and relations with Swiss bankers, 185–95, 364; moves IOS to Ferney-Voltaire, 193–95, 364; and James Roosevelt, 196–214; and Shah of Iran, 202; life as head of IOS, 215–36; IOS funds sold in London, 237–42; and IOS in Germany, 257, 265, 267–77; and the Pope, 280; and Eastern Europe, 310–12; hires Meid and Carr, 320; and James Ling, 329*ff.*; and John King, 337, 387–91, 399–423, 442–46, 455–56 *passim*; and EON, 348–49; and IOS's going public, 350–51, 372–86 *passim*, 432–38; and Arctic interest, 411–31 *passim*; and "cashing in," 432–42; at *Institutional Investor* conference, 5–13, 184, 444, 449, 460, 513; after break in IOS prices, 459–67; at May 1970 Board meeting, 467–88; resignation, 483–88, 511; during Toronto meeting, 497–501; severs ties with IOS, 13, 537–42; financial assessment at end, 538–39
Cornfeld, Eugene, 20, 26

Real Estate Fund of America (REFA), 351–55

Redgrove, Clinton, 239

Reeves, Rosser, 233–34

Regency Income Corporation, 397, 413, 425

Regent Fund, 377, 524

Reich, Wilhelm, 47

Reisser, Hardy, 261

Rentsch, Adelgisa, 191

Resorts International, 315–17, 318, 325, 340, 349

Revista Económica Venezolana, 137

Rexall Drug Company, 342–45

Riklis, Meshulam, 467, 472, 473

Roberts, Richard, 33, 46, 47, 51–52

Rocky Mountain News (Denver), 395

Rolnick, Norman, 450

Roman Catholic Church, 103

Roosevelt, Franklin Delano, 198, 200

Roosevelt, James, 131, 149, 196–214 *passim*, 224, 267, 278, 304, 310–12, 364, 429, 437, 451, 454, 462, 469, 470, 478, 536

Roosevelt, Kermit, 200

Roosevelt, Theodore, 201

Rosen, Lawrence, 168–69

Rosen, Mel, 443, 453

Rosenbaum, Dr. Tibor, 144

Ross, Stamer, Wolf & Haft, 178

Rosset, Barney, 197

Roth, Archie, 21

Rothschild, Baron Alain de, 187, 300

Rothschild, Baron Edmond de, 187

Rothschild-Expansion, 300–4, 375, 533; *see also* Banque Rothschild

Rothschild, Baron Guy de, 187, 300, 464

Rothschild, Jacob, 82

Rothschild and Sons, N. M. (London), 329, 362, 373–74, 470, 472

Rothschild, Baron Yves de, 187, 300

Royal Bank of Canada, 115

Royal Resources, 394–95

Rozet, A. Bruce, 337, 338–46

Ruet, Roland, 193–94

St. John, Jill, 318

Sakellaropoulo, Michael, 211

Salinger, Pierre, 357, 535

Saller, Wolf, 269

Sanchez del Corral y del Rio, Don Antonio, 212

Sands, Sir Stafford, 315

Sassoon Banking, 361

Sayad, William, 174

Sayle, Murray, 310

Schäffer, Fritz, 267

Schatz, Dan, 168–72

Schenley Industries, 474

Schicht, Gerhard, 260

Schifreen, Edward B., 45

Schirra, Walter, 398, 425

Schleiffer, Alvin ("Bud"), 187

Schneider, Egon, 262, 273, 310

Schoch, Dr. M. Magdalena, 63

Scott, Eric, 437

Scott, William, 318

Schwabenbauer, Lothar, 261–63

Schwartz, Barry, 241, 245

Securities Act (U.S. 1933), 52, 183

Securities and Exchange Commission (SEC), 6, 10–11, 36, 52, 91, 105, 113–16, 124, 164–84 *passim*, 186, 238–40, 255, 267, 315, 318, 323, 335, 344–46, 356, 378, 385, 477, 485–87, 515, 529, 531

Security Equity Fund, 120, 313, 315

Seeburg Corporation, 317, 341

The Broadway Library of Larceny

The Library of Larceny is a collection of books about—and sometimes by—people who exploit public confidence for their own personal monetary gain. Some of them are thieves pure and simple. Some are get-along types who just happen to be standing nearby with pockets flapping when spoils are divided. And some are con artists—with equal stress on the second word of that formula—men and women who do not steal, exactly, and certainly never employ violence or strong-arm tactics, but who extract sums by means of a sort of psychic jujitsu from pigeons who are often all too willing to be plucked. These books fall into the true-crime genre, but that genre (once dominated by pipe-smoking sleuths) has lately been given over almost entirely to depressing psychopathology and gore for gore's sake. The Library of Larceny proposes instead to restore property crime to its full, glorious stature. It is, after all, a portion of the inheritance of this Land of Opportunity.

The books in the series highlight the ingenuity of their subjects, their delight in the aesthetics of their profession, their artisanal pride in a neatly turned score, and, not incidentally, their pleasure in language. For whatever reasons, swindling seems to awaken in its perpetrators a gift for vigorous, highly colored language, with accompanying deadpan humor. The metaphors so often come from the natural world—a victim is a "doe" or an "apple"; he or she is "lop-eared"; a dollar bill is a "fish" or a "bumblebee"—that it is as if we were listening to lions and tigers discussing their jobs. Add to all this an inside view of a world of poolrooms and racetracks and bars and brothels, the raffish world of professional leisure. The books will span the past century, stretching from the time after the West had been won—and the wildlife that had evolved along the way sought new outlets for its talents—right up to the present era of corporate malfeasance, by way of the hectic, wised-up city life of the cocktail age. The books, many of them long out of print, will appeal to a wide range of readers, young and old: hipsters, pirates, roués, scalawags, poets, armchair psychologists, advertising strategists, cultural theorists, promoters, touts, sibyls, and bon vivants everywhere.

Luc Sante
Series Editor

About the Series Editor

Luc Sante is a renowned writer and critic and author of the classic book on the raffish, violent, and criminal side of New York, *Low Life*. He also wrote the introduction for Anchor Book's reissue of the David Maurer classic, *The Big Con*. An authority on the history of photography, Sante is now a professor at Bard College.

About the Authors

Charles Raw was Financial Editor of the London *Sunday Times* when this book was written, having closely followed and reported on Cornfeld and the IOS for more than five years. **Bruce Page,** then Executive Features Editor at the *Sunday Times*, was co-author of two other bestselling "Insight" books, *The Philby Conspiracy* and *An American Melodrama: The Presidential Campaign of 1968*. **Godfrey Hodgson** was a Washington correspondent for the London *Observer*, where for two years he wrote the financial column "Mammon," as well as Foreign Features Editor of the *Sunday Times*. He also co-authored *American Melodrama*.

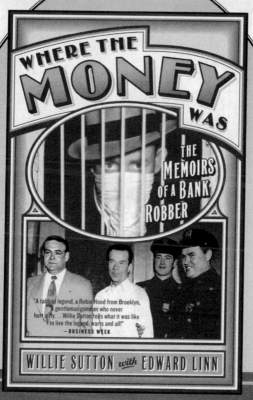

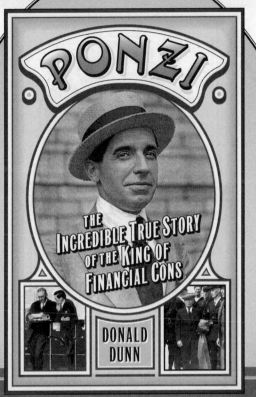